INTERNATIONAL LAW CONCERNING
CHILD CIVILIANS IN ARMED CONFLICT

International Law Concerning Child Civilians in Armed Conflict

JENNY KUPER

CLARENDON PRESS · OXFORD
1997

Oxford University Press, Great Clarendon Street, Oxford OX2 6DP

Oxford New York

Athens Auckland Bangkok Bogota Bombay
Buenos Aires Calcutta Cape Town Dar es Salaam
Delhi Florence Hong Kong Istanbul Karachi
Kuala Lumpur Madras Madrid Melbourne
Mexico City Nairobi Paris Singapore
Taipei Tokyo Toronto
and associated companies in
Berlin Ibadan

Oxford is a trade mark of Oxford University Press

Published in the United States by
Oxford University Press Inc., New York

British Library Cataloguing in Publication Data
Data available

Library of Congress Cataloging in Publication Data
Kuper, Jenny.
International law concerning child civilians in armed conflict/
Jenny Kuper.
p. cm.
Includes bibliographical references (p.).
1. Combatants and noncombatants (International law) 2. Children—
Legal status, laws, etc. I. Title.
JX5144.K87 1997 341.6'7—dc21 96-53446

ISBN 0-19-826486-0 (hc).—ISBN 0-19-826485-2 (pbk.)

Typeset by Best-set Typesetter Ltd., Hong Kong
Printed in Great Britain by
Bookcraft Ltd., Midsomer Norton, Somerset

Dedicated To
Sam Pablo, Ellie, and Joe,
and the other young ones, who
will inherit this world that we are
shaping, with our action and inaction,
our cruelty and our courage.

It's all so strange! Suddenly, it's so important, everybody asking who you are, what you do, where you come from.

So many people have been killed fighting for justice. But what justice? Do they know what they are fighting for, who they are fighting?

The weather is growing very cold now. No longer can you hear the singing of the birds, only the sound of the children crying for a lost mother or father, a brother or a sister.

We are children without a country and without hope.

—Dunja, 14, from Belgrade

'I Dream of Peace', UNICEF/HarperCollins (1994)

Preface

For a number of reasons, this book had to be converted fairly quickly from the Ph.D thesis on which it was based. Despite my efforts, it may therefore be rather doctrinal in style, and I apologise for this.

In writing on this subject I did from time to time feel constrained and frustrated by the strait-jacket of legal concepts and terminology, which seemed so remote from the devastating reality that is the experience of children in armed conflict. It was important to me constantly to bear in mind that reality, and a sense of the law as a tool in that wider context. I hope the readers of this book will find it possible to do the same.

Acknowledgements

I am grateful to many people for their advice and encouragement, and a number of organisations for their support, in the task of completing this book.

I will begin by thanking those whose generous financial assistance made this work possible. In chronological order, these were, first, the Centre for European Law at King's College London, which provided the initial grant enabling me to embark on the research. Secondly, Rädda Barnen (the Swedish Save the Children organisation) supported this work up to completion of a first draft. In particular, I am indebted to Sven Winberg of Rädda Barnen for his interest and encouragement, and to Thomas Hammarberg and Simone Ek. Finally, the most substantial financial assistance was provided by way of a grant for Research and Writing from the John D. and Catherine T. MacArthur Foundation in Chicago, and this enabled me to devote almost two years of full-time work to completing this project. I am most grateful to George Lopez of that Foundation for his encouragement and guidance.

Next, I must thank my former colleagues at the Children's Legal Centre in London, for agreeing to the sabbatical in which I began work on this book. I am also grateful to those whom I met through the Children's Legal Centre, and who initially supported my funding applications. These include: Nigel Cantwell, former Director of Programmes of Defence for Children International; David Boyd, barrister; Sir James Hennessey, former Chief Inspector of Prisons; Mark Soler, Director of the San Francisco Youth Law Centre; and Vivien Stern, former Director of the National Association for the Care and Resettlement of Offenders, London.

As regards the substance of the research, I owe thanks for his constant support to Philippe Sands, who supervised the Ph.D on which this book is based. I also greatly appreciated the interest and suggestions of Professor Christopher Greenwood of the London School of Economics (LSE) and Françoise Hampson of Essex University, who examined my Ph.D. Further, I am very grateful, for their suggestions concerning particular aspects of the research, to Jane Connors of the School of Oriental and African Studies (SOAS), London, and Angela Bedford, formerly of King's College London. In addition, Michael Meyer of the British Red Cross and Professor George Kent of the University of Hawaii made a number of useful comments in the early stages of this work.

Professor Rosalyn Higgins, then at the LSE, was very helpful in providing occasional advice on aspects of human rights law. Dr Werner Menski of

SOAS, assisted me enormously with technical advice on the form and structure of this work. Many thanks are also due to Professor Rein Mullerson of King's College London for reading and commenting on the manuscript in its final stages, and to Professor Adam Kuper for a similar undertaking. Rupert Ticehurst, Yuval Ginbar, and Lee Jackson helped greatly in checking some of the footnotes and references. Nonetheless, any inaccuracies in the text remain, of course, entirely my responsibility.

Much appreciation is due, for their diligent assistance, to the librarians at the LSE (particularly Frances Shipsey); the British Red Cross (especially Martin Folan); the Institute of Advanced Legal Studies; the London office of UNICEF; the UN Office and Information Centre in London; and the UN Library in Geneva. Thanks, too, to staff at Amnesty International in London, and the Quaker UN Office and the International Committee of the Red Cross in Geneva. For both technological and moral support, I also thank Massimo Gianuzzi, who saved the manuscript from disaster with his computer wizadry on numerous occasions.

On a more personal note, I thank my son, Sam Pablo, for his patience and his very existence, which was one of the factors that initially motivated this work. My parents, too, are present in the spirit of this book, although they were not well enough to participate in its creation and, sadly, both died before it was completed. I also acknowledge the many others who are close to me, and whose unfailing presence and warmth enabled me to complete this task.

Contents

Selected Abbreviations

General

AJIL	*American Journal of International Law*
AI	Amnesty International
BYIL	*British Year Book of International Law*
DCI	Defence for Children International
DHA	Department of Humanitarian Affairs
ETS	European Treaty Series
ECOSOC	United Nations Economic and Social Council
ICJ	International Court of Justice
ICLQ	*International and Comparative Law Quarterly*
ICRC	The International Committee of the Red Cross
ILM	International Legal Materials
ILO	International Labour Organisation
Int'l. Rev. of the Red Cross	*International Review of the Red Cross*
KDP	Kurdistan Democratic Party
NGEs	Non-governmental entities
NGOs	Non-governmental organisations
OAS	Organisation of American States
OAU	Organisation of African Unity
PUK	Patriotic Union of Kurdistan
UKTS	United Kingdom Treaty Series
UNTS	United Nations Treaty Series
UN GA	United Nations General Assembly
UN GAOR	United Nations General Assembly Official Records
UN ESCOR	United Nations Economic and Social Council Official Records
UNESCO	United Nations Educational, Scientific and Cultural Organisation
UNHCR	United Nations High Commissioner for Refugees
UNICEF	United Nations Children's Fund
WHO	World Health Organisation

Treaties and Other Legal Instruments

1868 St Petersburg Declaration	1868 St Petersburg Declaration Renouncing the Use, in Time of War, of Explosive Projectiles Under 400 grammes Weight

1899 Hague Declaration II	1899 Hague Declaration II Concerning Asphyxiating Gases
1907 Hague Convention IV	1907 Hague Convention IV Respecting the Laws and Customs of War on Land
1923 Hague Draft Rules	1923 Hague Rules of Aerial Warfare
1924 Declaration	1924 Declaration of the Rights of the Child
1925 Geneva Protocol	1925 Geneva Protocol for the Prohibition of the Use in War of Asphyxiating, Poisonous or Other Gases, and of Bacteriological Methods of Warfare
1949 GC IV	1949 Geneva Convention IV Relative to the Protection of Civilian Persons in Time of War
1959 Declaration	1959 Declaration of the Rights of the Child
1977 GP I	1977 Geneva Protocol I Additional to the Geneva Conventions of 12 August 1949, and Relating to the Protection of Victims of International Armed Conflicts
1977 GP II	1977 Geneva Protocol II Additional to the Geneva Conventions of 12 August 1949, and Relating to the Protection of Victims of Non-International Armed Conflicts
1980 Inhumane Weapons Convention	1980 Convention on Prohibitions or Restrictions on the Use of Certain Conventional Weapons Which May be Deemed to be Excessively Injurious or to Have Indiscriminate Effects
1989 CRC	1989 Convention on the Rights of the Child
1993 Chemical Weapons Convention	1993 Convention on the Prohibition of the Development, Production, Stockpiling and Use of Chemical Weapons and on their Destruction
ACHPR	1981 African Charter on Human and People's Rights
ACHR	1969 American Convention on Human Rights
ACRWC	1990 African Charter on the Rights and Welfare of the Child
ADRDM	1948 American Declaration of the Rights and Duties of Man
CEDAW	1979 Convention on the Elimination of All Forms of Discrimination Against Women
ECHR	1950 European Convention on Human Rights
ESC	1961 European Social Charter
GCs	Geneva Conventions of 12 August 1949

GPs	1977 Geneva Protocols Additional to the Geneva Conventions of 12 August 1949
ICCPR	1966 International Covenant on Civil and Political Rights
ICESCR	1966 International Covenant on Economic, Social and Cultural Rights
Protocol of San Salvador	1988 Additional Protocol to the American Convention on Human Rights in the Area of Economic, Social and Cultural Rights
UN Charter	Charter of the United Nations
UDHR	Universal Declaration of Human Rights

Table of Treaties and Other
Selected Legal Instruments and Documents

Table of Cases

1

Introduction

1.1 AIMS AND SCOPE

Lawyers and other professionals concerned with human rights, and particularly with children's rights, may be congratulating themselves on international legal developments primarily in the years since World War II. However, the millions of people worldwide who are suffering from abuses of those rights, many in countries which officially support the post-War international legislation, could be forgiven for wondering (if news of these developments has reached them) whether indeed there is any cause for celebration. Nowhere is the contrast between lofty ideals, as enshrined in various instruments of international law, and reality more stark than in relation to child civilians embroiled in situations of armed conflict.

The United Nations Children's Fund (hereafter UNICEF) has estimated that child victims of armed conflict '[d]uring the last decade ... have included: 2 million killed; 4–5 million disabled; 12 million left homeless; more than 1 million orphaned or separated from their parents; some 10 million psychologically traumatized'.[1] Although it is difficult to judge the accuracy of such statistics, it is beyond doubt that each year many thousands of children are killed or injured as a direct result of armed conflict.[2]

Moreover, the harm suffered by children as a result of armed conflict is not limited to death and injury. It can also include illness; long-term disability; deprivation due to family impoverishment; separation from families; missed schooling; displacement from home; torture; arrest and detention; sexual and physical abuse; abduction; recruitment into armed forces; and distortion of values by exposure to violence.[3] Many of these are not the immediate effects of combat, but are delayed.

[1] UNICEF, *The State of the World's Children 1996* (Oxford, 1995), 13. For earlier estimates, see UNICEF, *Children and Development in the 1990s: A UNICEF Sourcebook* (New York, 1990), 193, and UNICEF, *The State of the World's Children 1995* (Oxford, 1994), 4.

[2] As regards children killed in armed conflict, see E. M. Ressler, J. M. Tortorici, and A. Marcelino, *Children in War: a Guide to the Provision of Services* (New York, 1993), 66. These writers point out that children's deaths in this context can be caused by intentional killing, when they are purposefully targeted; non-discriminatory killing, when they are among targeted victims, but not singled out; negligent killing, by neglecting to provide essential life-support services; consequential killing, when children die as a secondary consequence of the action taken; and inadvertent killing, or accidental deaths.

[3] These are the factors identified by Ressler, Tortorici, and Marcelino, *ibid.* 37–47. For the perspectives of children interviewed regarding their own experiences of armed conflict see, for example, R. Rosenblatt, *Children of War* (New York, 1983).

The fact that so many children are affected by armed conflict, and in so many ways, imparts a degree of urgency to this and other research which aspires to contribute to efforts to ameliorate their suffering.

This book will examine international law concerning child civilians in armed conflict,[4] and it has three main aims. These are: to describe the provisions of the relevant law and its various implementation mechanisms; to assess its impact, particularly in relation to a series of recent conflicts involving Iraq; and to make proposals regarding ways in which this body of law could more effectively be implemented in practical terms.[5] The focus is therefore on summarising and evaluating the pertinent law, and on making suggestions, from that basis, regarding possible strategies for strengthening its impact.

Although certain of the issues addressed in this research have been discussed by other authors, the three central tasks attempted here, with the specific emphasis on child civilians, have not been tackled together in a systematic and comprehensive fashion.[6] It is hoped that this book will therefore add constructively to the body of existing work.

The book has eight chapters, the first of which is this introductory chapter describing its purpose, framework, terminology, and certain significant questions and concepts, such as the notion of 'children's rights'.

Chapters 2 to 4 summarise international human rights and humanitarian law relating to child civilians in armed conflict. The emphasis here is prima-

---

[4] The information in this book is generally current to mid-May 1996. The main exception to this is information gathered from United Nations (hereafter UN) documents, some of which reach the London depositary libraries many months after their publication.

[5] The emphasis of this book is on legal measures which relate to the protection of children from the more immediate impact of armed conflict. It will not, therefore, deal in any depth with the issue of child refugees, or the long-term rehabilitation and recovery of children generally in the aftermath of armed conflicts. Nor will it examine the many non-legal strategies that are being pursued, or that could and should be pursued, to improve the situation of children in armed conflict. These include, e.g., the development of adequate medical and psychological facilities for treating such children.

[6] Certain authors, as described in n. 8 below, have to some extent summarised and analysed the relevant law, and their work is pertinent to the first task tackled in this book. In relation to the study of the Iraqi conflicts, the literature has not addressed in any depth questions concerning the impact of the applicable international law as regards child civilians involved in those conflicts. Again, regarding the third and concluding section, little has been written which attempts exclusively to propose strategies for enhancing the effectiveness of international law concerning child civilians. However, a number of authors have addressed issues relating to the treatment of children in armed conflict generally. Perhaps the most pertinent work in this context is the summary of a 1994 conference: G. H. Aldrich and Th. van Baarda, *Conference on the Rights of Children in Armed Conflict* (The Hague, 1994). Other relevant publications include, e.g.: G. Kent, *War and Children's Survival: Occasional Paper No 2* (Hawaii, 1990); Ressler, Tortorici, and Marcelino (1993), and G. S. Goodwin-Gill, and I. Cohn, *Child Soldiers* (Oxford, 1994). Once more, though, the focus of these works is not primarily on the enforcement of international law in relation to child civilians, in that, e.g., they may deal equally with non-legal strategies and/or with child soldiers. There are also international lawyers who are working on issues concerning the implementation of human rights or humanitarian law in general, and these are cited in the text where relevant.

rily on treaty law, although a number of authoritative legal instruments, such as resolutions of the UN General Assembly, are discussed. Case law is not, in general, included.[7]

The law set out in Chapters 2 to 4 will, for two reasons, be examined in some detail. First, it has not been described in depth anywhere in the literature.[8] Secondly, an overview of this body of law is essential background information in attempting to assess its impact in relation to the Iraqi conflicts (Chapter 7); to make recommendations which address its weaknesses (Chapter 8); and to encourage its wider use by children's advocates, among others.

Chapter 2 accordingly summarises human rights law relating to the treatment of child civilians. It discusses relevant principles, both as established in general global and regional human rights instruments and as set out in international human rights law exclusively concerning children. Chapter 3 focuses on the laws of armed conflict concerning the protection of civilians generally, applicable to both adults and children. The provisions of international humanitarian law which directly concern the treatment of child civilians are then discussed in Chapter 4.

A broad consideration of the pertinent law, as set out in Chapters 2 to 4, is required, since it would be simplistic and inaccurate to describe the international treaties which refer specifically to child civilians in armed

---

[7] In any event, as one writer has pointed out, international decisions are rare in respect of any of the humanitarian law treaties, with war-crimes cases being the exception rather than the rule: C. Greenwood, 'Customary Law Status of the 1977 Geneva Protocols', in A. J. M. Delissen and G. J. Tanja (eds.), *Humanitarian Law of Armed Conflict* (Dordrecht, 1991), 99. This may, of course, be changing, as the Yugoslav and Rwandan International Criminal Tribunals gather momentum, and the establishment of an international criminal court becomes more probable (see sect. 6.2.1 below).

[8] However, brief descriptions of this law can be found in various publications. See in particular: D. Plattner, *Protection of Children in International Humanitarian Law: Extract of the International Review of the Red Cross* (Geneva, May–June 1984), and S. Singer, *The Protection of Children During Armed Conflict Situations: Extract of the International Review of the Red Cross* (Geneva, May–June 1986). See also D. Plattner, 'Protection of Children in International Humanitarian Law', in M. Kahnert, D. Pitt, and I. Taipale (eds.), *Children and War: Proceedings of Symposium at Siuntio Baths, Finland* (Helsinki, 1983), 198–213; J. Kuper, 'Briefing: International Law and Children in Armed Conflict' 92 *Childright* 9 (1992); F. Krill, 'The Protection of Children in Armed Conflicts', in M. Freeman and P. Veerman (eds.), *The Ideologies of Children's Rights* (Dordrecht, 1992), 347–56; R. C. Hingorani, 'Protection of Children During Armed Conflicts', in F. Kalshoven (ed.), *Assisting the Victims of Armed Conflict and Other Disasters* (Dordrecht, 1989), 133–8; G. Van Bueren, 'Special Features of the Assistance and Protection of Children as Victims of Armed Conflict', *ibid.* 127–31, and G. Van Bueren, 'The International Legal Protection of Children in Armed Conflicts' 43 *ICLQ*, 809 (1994). Some of the applicable international legal materials are collected in G. Van Bueren, *International Documents on Children* (Dordrecht, 1993). Another publication by the same author presents a summary of the rules regarding children in armed conflict, but with its more general focus it does not, e.g., draw out the human rights and customary law principles particularly relevant to child civilians: G. Van Bueren, *The International Law on the Rights of the Child* (Dordrecht, 1995), 328–55. Other materials which touch, to a lesser extent, on the applicable law are mentioned where pertinent in the text of this book.

conflict as the only, or even the primary, source of international law relevant to such children.[9] While these directly relevant treaties are an essential element of international law regarding the protection of child civilians, and will be discussed in Chapter 4 at some length, they are nonetheless only part of the applicable law. It is therefore necessary also to consider pertinent international law which applies universally to wide sections of the community, and which incorporates children, as members of the community, within its scope. It is for this reason that general human rights and humanitarian law are discussed in Chapters 2 and 3.

There is, of course, no question that the killing and injuring of civilians (children or not) is unlawful in international human rights and humanitarian law, except in certain limited circumstances. Is it, then, purely of academic interest to demonstrate the extent of the illegality? Does it matter that there are numerous prohibitions on this, in treaty and in custom? According to one authority, in relation to a similar question regarding the customary nature of the Geneva Conventions of 12 August 1949 (hereafter the GCs), 'consensus that the Geneva Conventions are declaratory of customary international law would strengthen the moral claim of the international community for their observance by emphasizing their humanitarian underpinnings and deep roots in tradition and community values'.[10] In the same way, repeated prohibitions (explicit or implicit) on the unlawful killing and injuring of child civilians, as expressed in both international treaty and customary law, must surely enhance the protection to which such children are, at least in theory, entitled.

After discussing, in Chapters 2 to 4, the pertinent law and issues such as the above, Chapter 5 looks briefly at the possible customary nature of certain legal norms relevant to the treatment of child civilians in situations of armed conflict. It emphasises the importance of establishing the existence of customary norms in this context, and argues that there is evidence of, at least, the evolving customary status of some of the applicable principles.

Chapter 6 then provides an overview of the many bodies that have a role in monitoring, implementing, and/or enforcing international law concerning child civilians in armed conflict. These include, in particular, the UN Committee on the Rights of the Child, established under the 1989 Convention on the Rights of the Child (hereafter the 1989 CRC).[11] Also considered in this chapter are the principal organs of the UN; agencies operating under the auspices of the UN, such as UNICEF and the United Nations High Commissioner for Refugees (hereafter UNHCR); the International Com-

---

[9] A similar point is made in relation to child soldiers by Goodwin-Gill and Cohn (1994), 149.

[10] T. Meron, 'The Geneva Conventions as Customary Law', 81 *AJIL* 350 (1987) and T. Meron, *Human Rights and Humanitarian Norms as Customary Law* (Oxford, 1989), 8.

[11] The 1989 CRC. 28 ILM 1448 (1989).

mittee of the Red Cross (hereafter ICRC); and non-governmental organisations (hereafter NGOs) such as Amnesty International (hereafter AI).

Following this, Chapter 7 aims to evaluate the impact of the applicable law with regard to three conflicts involving Iraq between 1987 and 1991.[12] These conflicts are: (1) the use of chemical weapons against the Iraqi Kurds in 1987 and 1988; (2) the 1990 occupation of Kuwait by Iraq and the 1991 Gulf War which this precipitated; (3) the Kurdish (and Shia) uprisings of 1991 and their aftermath. This cluster of conflicts was selected by way of example since it arguably incorporates the three main categories of conflict identified in international humanitarian law: international armed conflict, non-international armed conflict, and internal disturbance (as discussed in Chapter 3). Further, the 1991 Gulf War was the first major international armed conflict in the 'post-Cold War' era, and state practice in this conflict remains of some relevance to the issues being examined here.

Chapter 7 accordingly describes each of the three conflicts under consideration. With reference to the applicable human rights and humanitarian law, this chapter then employs certain indicators, such as UN decisions and debates, to assess the effectiveness of this body of law in terms of the extent to which it seems to have been observed in these conflicts. In assessing effectiveness, the issues addressed include the following: when child civilians were, or seemed likely to be, killed, injured, or otherwise seriously harmed, did the international community in its reaction comply with the relevant law to any extent, even if it was not explicitly invoked? Alternatively, was it explicitly invoked without being acted upon? Or was it fully implemented, by being both invoked and acted upon? If so, did these interventions seem to have, even to a limited extent, the effect of preventing or ameliorating the existing or probable future harm to the child civilians concerned?[13]

In the light of the Iraqi study, the concluding chapter, Chapter 8, summarises the main findings of the research, analyses certain core issues, and makes a number of recommendations regarding strategies which could possibly strengthen the impact of the body of law concerning child civilians in situations of armed conflict.

---

[12] The 1980–8 Iran–Iraq war is not discussed here, primarily because it seemed unlikely that a detailed analysis of that conflict would uncover information substantially different from that revealed in relation to the more recent conflicts, as regards the impact of international law concerning child civilians. Indeed, for similar reasons (as well as practicalities of time and space), this book does not examine in detail other recent conflicts, such as those in the former Yugoslavia; Rwanda; Chechnya; Somalia; Afghanistan; the Sudan; and many others.

[13] One writer argues that international law is primarily a *process* for resolving problems, rather than simply a set of rules. See discussion in R. Higgins, *Problems and Process: International Law and How We Use It* (Oxford, 1994), 1–16. This approach provides a useful perspective in examining, e.g., state practice in the Iraqi conflicts, and in addressing questions in Ch. 8 regarding the development of the law concerning child civilians.

Thus, in examining the relevant international law and its implementation, and in making recommendations regarding possible reforms of these, this book should have a practical, as well as academic, application. Among other things, it is hoped that is will be of use to international lawyers, NGOs, and others wishing to challenge violations of international law affecting child civilians. In addition, the aim is to present an overview of this complex subject and to indicate issues, beyond the scope of the present work, for future in-depth study.

1.2 WHY *CHILD* CIVILIANS?

A question which must be addressed at the outset is: what purpose is served by singling out *child* civilians? Surely their situation is no different from that of all other civilians? This question can be answered in a number of ways.

One answer is that children are not in fact in a different position from any other civilian in armed conflict. They suffer similar hardships and violations, and do not normally exist independently of others in the civilian population. They are entitled to protection under the terms of international human rights law, and, as members of the civilian population, under the laws of armed conflict. It could therefore be argued that there is little to gain by looking separately at the situation of civilians who happen to be children.

An alternative answer to the question 'Why *child* civilians?' is that children are in a special position, in that they are generally more vulnerable than adults and therefore entitled to certain distinct rights, as is widely recognised in both national and international law. This applies particularly in situations such as armed conflict, where children are politically powerless and where they are normally denied any other participatory role (with the limited exception of child soldiers).

Moreover, on a purely pragmatic level there are a number of arguments for emphasising the specific requirements of child civilians. First, their vulnerability means that no nation wants to be seen, in an international forum, to be killing or injuring children (again, with the possible exception of child soldiers). Accordingly, the fact that children are being killed or injured can serve to mobilise public opinion and international pressure in a particular situation, to the benefit of the civilian population as a whole.[14] In any event, children almost inevitably form a substantial proportion of any civilian population, since they are estimated to constitute nearly 30 per cent

---

[14] Goodwin-Gill and Cohn ((1994), 149) make a similar point regarding child soldiers. In the same vein, another writer argues that the concept of children as a zone of peace (discussed below, in Chs. 4 and 8), 'may be the idea which will eventually cut across the bombast and calculations of the arms manufacturers and the warmakers': V. Vittachi, *Between the Guns: Children as a Zone of Peace* (London, 1993), 136. UNICEF also maintains that 'insisting on the rights of children is one of the best ways of reasserting core humanitarian values': UNICEF (1995), 40.

of the world's population.[15] Secondly, there is in existence international law specifically concerned with child civilians in armed conflict, and this, along with all other related law, should be used or at least referred to in appropriate situations if it is not to be meaningless. In addition, a number of international organisations exist which, either in whole or in part, are specifically concerned with children, and a focus on child civilians allows their resources to be tapped.

The two arguments set out above are not mutually exclusive. In reality child civilians form part of the broader civilian population, but they do also require particular attention. This is recognised in the relevant law, which makes provision for all civilians, and for children as a discrete group with requirements additional to those of other civilians. This book reflects that reality.

1.3 TERMINOLOGY

The focus of this book is on *child civilians*, as distinguished from child soldiers,[16] and it does not therefore generally discuss the issue of child soldiers.[17]

Accordingly, it is pertinent here to note only that international law does allow for children, regardless of the age of majority in their particular country, to serve as combatants from the age of 15. This is expressed, for example, in Article 77(2) of the 1977 Geneva Protocol I Additional to the Geneva Conventions of 12 August 1949, and Relating to the Protection of Victims of International Armed Conflicts (1977 GP I).[18] Similar provision is

---

[15] See estimate in UN Doc. A/CONF.151/26/Rev.1 (Vol. 1) (1993), 'Report of the United Nations Conference on Environment and Development', 380, para. 25.1. Further, according to the 'Report of the Fourth World Conference on Women' (UN Doc. A/CONF.177/20 (17 Oct. 1995), para. 40), 'Half of the world's population is under the age of 25, and most of the world's youth—more than 85 per cent—live in developing countries.'

[16] Graca Machel, appointed to prepare the UN study on children in armed conflict (see sect. 6.1.1.2 below) apparently prefers not to use the term 'child soldier', on the basis that 'a true soldier has a sense of right and wrong as well as a sense of honour. The 12 year old who has been trained for only 3 weeks, the child who was taught to shoot not at targets but at live persons, is not a soldier': T. A. El-Haj, 'The Impact of Armed Conflict on Children', 122 *Childright* 12 (Dec. 1995). This is a valid point, but nonetheless this book uses the phrase 'child soldier' as a term of convenience, which is, at this time, in common usage.

[17] The only exception to this is the description in Ch. 4 of the drafting of Art. 38 of the 1989 CRC, which incorporates child soldiers. For further information on international law and policy concerning child soldiers, see generally Goodwin-Gill and Cohn (1994); H. Mann, 'International Law and the Child Soldier' (1987); 36 *ICLQ* 32 (1987); M. T. Dutli, *Enfants-Combattants Prisonniers: Extract from the International Review of the Red Cross* (Geneva, Sept.–Oct. 1990); D. Woods, *Child Soldiers* (Quaker UN Office, Geneva 1993), and C. Hamilton, 'Children in Armed Conflict—New Moves for an Old Problem' 7.1 *Tolley's Journal of Child Law* 38 (1995).

[18] 1977 GP I. 1125 UNTS 3 (1979); 16 ILM 1391 (1977). Art. 77(2) states that '[p]arties to the conflict shall take all feasible measures in order that children who have not attained the age of fifteen years do not take a direct part in hostilities'.

made in Article 38(2) of the 1989 CRC and in Article 4(3)(c) of the 1977
Geneva Protocol II Additional to the Geneva Conventions of 12 August
1949, and Relating to the Protection of Victims of Non-International
Armed Conflicts (1977 GP II).[19]

Of course, despite international norms, many child soldiers are below the
age of 15, and the distinction between a child civilian and a child soldier is
not always clear. Nor do child soldiers necessarily choose this role voluntar-
ily: many are coerced (as happened in recent conflicts in, *inter alia*, El
Salvador, Ethiopia, Mozambique, and Peru).[20]

Child combatants participate in armed conflicts either directly, as
fighters, or indirectly, when they may be involved in sabotage, the transmis-
sion of military information, or the transport of arms, ammunition, and
other military equipment. The term 'child civilians' in this research refers to
children who are simply present in the conflict, and do not actively participate in it, either directly or indirectly. Again, there are inevitably situations
in which the distinction will be blurred.

Nor is the definition of '*child*' in international law a simple matter. As
regards the beginning of childhood, international legal protection normally
starts at birth although states can, in their domestic legislation, extend this
protection to date from conception. States which prohibit abortion obviously favour the latter approach.

The 1989 CRC adopts a flexible definition, stating in Article 1 that, for
the purposes of this Convention, 'a child means every human being below
the age of 18 years unless, under the law applicable to the child, majority is
attained earlier'. This effectively begs the question of the beginning of
childhood, and in fact the 1989 CRC leaves this unresolved.

Thus the Preamble to the 1989 CRC contains a provision citing the
1959 Declaration of the Rights of the Child (hereafter the 1959 Declaration)[21] to the effect that children need special safeguards 'before as well as
after birth'. However, the legal effect of this provision is tempered by a
statement that was included in the *travaux préparatoires* as a compromise between those states opposed to abortion and those in favour.[22] By
making it clear that the Preamble does not grant the foetus an
absolute right to life, this statement essentially retains the *status quo*,
leaving the issue of the beginning of childhood to individual state discre-

---

[19] 1977 GP II. 1125 UNTS 609 (1979); 16 ILM 1442.

[20] Goodwin-Gill and Cohn (1994), 24–8. See also generally Woods (1993).

[21] The 1959 Declaration. UN GA Res. 1386(XIV), UN GAOR, Fourteenth Sess. Supp. No.
16 (A/4354) (1960).

[22] The statement in the *travaux* reads: 'In adopting this preambular paragraph, the Working
Group does not intend to prejudice the interpretation of article 1 or any other provision of
the Convention by State Parties.' See UN Doc. E/CN.4/1989/48 (2 Mar. 1989), 'Report
of the Working Group on the Question of a Draft Convention on the Rights of the Child',
para. 43.

tion.[23] The controversial nature of the definition of the beginning of childhood has been reflected in the declarations and reservations made by certain governments on signing or ratifying the 1989 CRC.[24]

As regards the end of childhood, this is not usually defined in international global or regional human rights instruments (although there are exceptions[25]). This means that states effectively define in their own national legislation the age at which their citizens reach adulthood, and there is, inevitably, diversity between states in this regard. Nonetheless, as one writer observes, acceptance of 18 as the age of 'civil majority . . . represents a continuing trend in the legal definition of "child" '.[26] That trend is becoming more pronounced, so that arguably the age of 18 is now increasingly accepted as the norm for defining the end of childhood.

In any event, regardless of the age of majority in different countries, many international treaties establish age limits for undertaking or ceasing certain activities relating to children. This will be seen, for example, in provisions of humanitarian law discussed in Chapter 4, where various age limits are specified below which children are entitled to different types of protection, as in the 1949 Geneva Convention IV Relative to the Protection of Civilian Persons in Time of War (1949 GC IV).[27]

Bearing these complexities in mind, the term 'child' will be used in this research to apply generally to those aged under 18, in accordance with Article 1 of the 1989 CRC.

In the context of contemporary international law, the crucial question is whether the imprecision regarding the definition of 'child' is a major impediment to the operation of the pertinent law. The answer to this question must be that it is not, given that precise age limits are sometimes specified in the legislation, and, more importantly, that certain guiding principles are

[23] As one writer puts it, the 1989 CRC recognises in the Preamble the right of the foetus to protection, but its right to life *per se* is not recognised: P. Alston, 'The Legal Framework of the Convention on the Rights of the Child' *91/2 Bulletin of Human Rights: The Rights of the Child* 3 (1992). Another writer emphasises that the 1989 CRC 'deals only with the rights of the born child': A. Lopatka, 'Importance of the Convention on the Rights of the Child', *ibid.* 64.

[24] See, e.g., declarations/reservations made by France, the Holy See, and the United Kingdom: UN Doc. CRC/C/2/Rev.4 (1995), 17, 19, and 31.

[25] As regards exceptions, see, *inter alia*, the Hague Convention on Civil Aspects of International Child Abduction 1980 (19 ILM 1501 (1980)) and the European Convention on the Recognition and Enforcement of Decisions Concerning Custody of Children and on Restoration of Custody of Children 1980 (ETS 105). These treaties both define a child as being under 16.

[26] A. M. Pappas, 'Introduction', in A. M. Pappas (ed.), *Law and the Status of the Child* (New York, 1983), XL. Freeman confirms that 'most developed countries currently draw the line at 18' between childhood and adulthood, but he emphasises that this is arbitrary: M. Freeman, 'The Limits of Children's Rights', in Freeman and Veerman (eds.) (1992), 34–5. See also Van Bueren (1995), 38.

[27] 1949 GC IV. 75 UNTS 287 (1950); UKTS 39 (1958), Cmnd. 550.

established, namely: that childhood begins at birth if not before, and that there is the developing norm of 18 as the age of majority.

As regards the use of other key terms in this research, a further concept requiring some clarification is that of *special treatment* for child civilians in situations of armed conflict. As is mentioned in section 1.5 below, the provision to children of special treatment does not always denote more beneficial treatment, and indeed in some circumstances such treatment is arguably less beneficial. However, when the phrase 'special treatment' is used here in relation to child civilians it has a positive construction, meaning the entitlement of such children to additional assistance and protection.

The terms *'laws of armed conflict'* or *'humanitarian law'*, are preferred here to 'laws of war'.[28] As one writer comments, the term 'war' is still in everyday use, but has been disappearing from legal language over the past few decades 'for "war" has gradually been outlawed, even though resort to force, be it called "war" or not, continues to exist. Thus it is at present more correct to use the term "armed conflict" as its very vagueness may be considered an advantage. Recently coined, it covers any occurrence, whatever its legal character, where two or more parties oppose each other in arms.' Nonetheless this writer notes that 'it will be appropriate, indeed necessary, to use at times one or the other term'.[29]

1.4 RELEVANCE OF TWO CONCEPTS: CHILDHOOD AND CHILDREN'S RIGHTS

Having clarified certain key terms employed in this research, it remains to consider the relevance of two significant concepts: 'children's rights' and 'childhood'.

---

[28] 'Humanitarian law' has been defined as 'international rules, established by treaties or custom, which are specifically intended to solve humanitarian problems directly arising from international or non-international armed conflicts and which, for humanitarian reasons, limit the right of Parties to a conflict to use the methods and means of warfare of their choice or protect persons and property that are, or may be, affected by conflict': ICRC, *Commentary on the Additional Protocols of 8 June 1977 to the Geneva Conventions of 12 August 1949* (Geneva, 1987), XXVII. Apparently, the ICRC now prefers the term 'humanitarian law of armed conflict' to 'law of armed conflict': J. G. Gardam, *Non-Combatant Immunity as a Norm of International Humanitarian Law* (Dordrecht, 1993), 2.

[29] S. Nahlik, *A Brief Outline of International Humanitarian Law: Extract from the International Review of the Red Cross* (Geneva, July–Aug. 1984), 7. As regards this terminology, see also A. Roberts and R. Guelff (eds.), *Documents on the Laws of War* (Oxford, 1989), 1, and H. McCoubrey, 'Jurisprudential Aspects of the Modern Law of Armed Conflicts', in M. Meyer (ed.), *Armed Conflict and the New Law* (London, 1989), 38. The UN Charter (UKTS 67 [1946], Cmnd. 7015), in Art. 2(4), outlawed the use of force except in certain limited circumstances, most notably in self-defence (Art. 51). Hence the use of the term 'war' has become contentious. See, e.g., discussion in C. Greenwood, 'The Concept of War in Modern International Law' 36 *ICLQ*, 283 (1987), and O. Schachter, 'The Right of States to Use Armed Force', 82 *Michigan Law Review* 1620 (April/May 1984).

1.4.1 'Children's Rights'

Although the term 'children's rights' is used in this book, too great a reliance on this term can reduce the concept to a cliché. Where possible, therefore, other more precise language will be employed to describe the particular entitlements of children in various situations.

In any event, it is not the intention here either to defend or attack on a philosophical level the concept of children's rights, since the topic of this research, with its pragmatic emphasis, does not require this.

Nonetheless, some of the debates regarding children's rights will be briefly referred to below, in order to place this concept in the context of international law concerning child civilians in armed conflict. Reference will not be made to the continuing philosophical deliberations on the notion of 'rights' generally, as many writers have tackled this subject.[30]

Indeed, an increasing number of writers are also, in the aftermath of the adoption of the 1989 CRC, exploring certain philosophical debates specifically regarding children's rights.[31] One of these, in considering the history of the children's rights movement, notes that 'the pioneers' in campaigning on behalf of children can be traced as far back as the middle of the last century.[32] Since that time the emphasis has 'shifted from protection to autonomy, from nurturance to self-determination, from welfare to justice',[33] and the concept of children's rights has been fiercely debated by proponents and opponents. There are those who defend this concept to the

---

[30] See, *inter alia*, W. Hohfeld, *Fundamental Legal Conceptions as Applied in Judicial Reasoning* (New Haven, Conn., 1919); M. Cranston, *What Are Human Rights?* (New York, 1973); R. Dworkin, *Taking Rights Seriously* (London, 1978); K. Vasak (ed.), *The International Dimensions of Human Rights* (Westport, Conn., 1982), and R. Lillich, *International Human Rights. Problems of Law, Policy and Practice* (Boston, Mass., 1991). For a discussion of certain of these concepts in relation to children, see, e.g., C. P. Cohen, 'The Relevance of Theories of Natural Law and Legal Positivism', in Freeman and Veerman (eds.) (1992), 53–70; and T. D. Campbell, 'The Rights of the Minor: As Person, as Child, as Juvenile, as Future Adult' and O. O'Neill, 'Children's Rights and Children's Lives', in P. Alston, S. Parker, and J. Seymour (eds.), *Children, Rights and the Law* (Oxford, 1992), 1–23 and 24–42 respectively. As regards comparative approaches to human rights, see, *inter alia*, A. A. An-Na'im (ed.), *Human Rights in Cross-Cultural Perspectives* (Philadelphia, Penn., 1992); J. Shestak, 'The Jurisprudence of Human Rights', in T. Meron (ed.), *Human Rights in International Law: Legal and Policy Issues* (Oxford, 1984), 76–83 and 99–104; and R. P. Anand, 'Attitude of the Asian-African States Toward Certain Problems of International Law' 15 *ICLQ* 55 (1966).

[31] See, e.g., P. Veerman, *The Rights of the Child and the Changing Image of Childhood* (Dordrecht, 1992); Alston, Parker and Seymour (1992); Freeman and Veerman (eds.) (1992), and, to some extent, P. Alston (ed.), *The Best Interests of the Child* (Oxford, 1994). For an earlier work, see C. Wringe, *Children's Rights: A Philosophical Study* (London, 1985).

[32] Veerman names a Swedish woman, Ellen Key, born in 1848, as one of the earliest writers on this issue: Veerman (1992), 75–83. Also mentioned by Veerman in this context are Eglantyne Jebb (87–91) and Janusz Korcazk (93–105), before Veerman goes on to discuss the 'modern pioneers' (113–27).

[33] M. Freeman, 'Introduction: Rights, Ideology and Children', in Freeman and Veerman (eds.) (1992), 3.

hilt,[34] while others question some of its most fundamental precepts.[35] It has been analysed and sub-divided into categories.[36]

Controversy has raged between those labelled the 'child savers' (emphasising the child's need for nuture and protection and calling for society to provide services for the child), and the 'kiddy libbers' (advocating self-determination for children over various aspects of their lives).[37]

It is not necessary here to enter into this debate. A pragmatic assessment of the situation of child civilians in armed conflict dictates that the emphasis must generally be on 'child saving', to use the above terminology. However, this can be seen positively as the child's entitlement to special treatment in situations of extreme danger.[38] The concept of children having this right in situations of armed conflict may smack of paternalism to those within the 'children's rights movement' who prefer to see children first and foremost as autonomous beings entitled to self-determination. Nonetheless, in situations of armed conflict the reality is that the primary need of most children, particularly young children, is for some form of protection from the conflict and its consequences.

In any event, the entitlement of children to protection and their entitlement to self-determination are not mutually exclusive. As one writer puts it, 'taking children's rights more seriously' has certain consequences, including

---

[34] These include particularly the central figures in the so-called 'children's liberation movement', John Holt and Richard Farson. See, e.g., J. Holt, 'Why not a Bill of Rights for Children?', in B. Gross and R. Gross (eds.), *The Children's Rights Movement* (New York, 1977), 319–25; J. Holt, *Escape From Childhood* (New York, 1974), and R. Farson, *Birthrights: A Bill of Rights for Children* (New York, 1974). Interestingly, Veerman criticises the 'kiddie libbers' for denying children the right to be children! See Veerman (1992), 397.

[35] These include, among others, Prof. Dr L. Apostel, 'Children's Rights and Needs or/and Human Rights and Needs', in E. Verhellen and F. Spiesschaert (eds.), *Ombudswork for Children* (Leuven, Belgium, 1989), 47–87. Certain recent critics of the concept of children's rights and of the 1989 CRC are discussed in M. F. Lücker Babel, 'Rights of the Child: Ideologies and Realities' 10.1/2 *International Children's Rights Monitor* 18 (1993).

[36] See, e.g., the categories devised by M. Wald, 'Children's Rights: A Framework for Analysis', 12 *University of California Davis Law Review* 255 (1979). See, too, the categories suggested, with reference to Wald's work, by M. Freeman, *The Rights and Wrongs of Children* (London, 1983), 40–52. Both John Holt and Richard Farson also categorised the rights they considered fundamental for children. See Holt (1974) and Farson (1974).

[37] See, e.g., R. Mnookin, 'Children's Rights: Beyond Child Savers and Kiddie Libbers. Address to the American Psychological Association' (1977), as cited in A. Skolnik, 'Children in Their Own Right: The View From Developmental Psychology', in Verhellen and Spiesschaert (eds.) (1989), 89. See also F. Olsen, 'Children's Rights: Some Feminist Approaches to the United Nations Convention on the Rights of the Child', in Alston, Parker and Seymour (eds.) (1992), 213, and D. Archard, *Children: Rights and Childhood* (London, 1993), 45–57.

[38] This approach is reflected in the language of Art. 77(1) of 1977 GP 1 (discussed in Ch. 4 below) which sets out the guiding principle regarding children in armed conflict that they 'shall be the object of special respect and shall be protected against any form of indecent assault'.

that it 'demands of us that we adopt policies, practices, structures and laws which both protect children and their rights. Hence the *via media* of "liberal paternalism".'[39]

1.4.2 'Childhood'

In addition to debates regarding the philosophical basis for notions of children's rights, and controversy concerning the age limits which define 'child' in international law, there is also a wider controversy concerning the history of the concept of childhood.[40] Is this concept timeless? Did it have its origins as late as the seventeenth or eighteenth century?[41] Or can it be traced to the thirteenth century?[42] Some writers argue that childhood is, ultimately, a relative concept, which changes 'according to historical time, geographical environment, local culture, and social-economic conditions'.[43] This latter approach, in acknowledging the danger of a Eurocentric perspective, has much to recommend it.

Certain recent works on this subject conclude that the image of childhood has changed during our century, and particularly in recent decades, so that 'a more profound respect for children seems to be manifesting itself'.[44] This book reveals evidence which both supports and contradicts that conclusion, as will be seen.

[39] M. Freeman, 'Taking Children's Rights More Seriously', in Alston, Parker and Seymour (eds.) (1992), 69. Another writer emphasises the link between the concepts of 'rights' and 'protection' as expressed in the 1989 CRC, stating that this Convention highlights two complementary aspects: 'the child as the holder of fundamental rights and freedoms, and the child as the recipient of special protection': M. Santos Pais, 'The United Nations Convention on the Rights of the Child', 91/2 *Bulletin of Human Rights*, 75 (1992).

[40] One writer usefully describes the age-limit debate as being about the 'boundaries' of childhood, and also examines other aspects of the concept of childhood: Archard (1993), 23–7.

[41] See particularly: P. Aries, *Centuries of Childhood* (New York, 1962), and L. de Mause, 'The Evolution of Childhood', in L. de Mause (ed.), *The History of Childhood* (New York, 1974), 1–52. These two writers, although differing from each other in their approach and certain of their conclusions, argued that the modern concept of childhood only began to emerge in about the 17th or 18th century. See also D. K. Weisberg, 'Evolution of the Concept of the Rights of the Child in the Western World', 21 *Review of the International Commission of Jurists* 43 (Dec. 1978).

[42] V. Fox, 'Historical Perspectives on Children's Rights', in Verhellen and Spiesschaert (eds.) (1989), 297–311.

[43] L. Dasberg, 'What is a Child and What are its Rights', in Verhellen and Spiesschaert (eds.) (1989), 35. Veerman, too, emphasises the relativity of the concept of childhood: Veerman (1992), 398. See also B. Franklin, *The Rights of Children* (Oxford, 1986), 7–12. This author examines the definition of 'child' and concludes, *inter alia*, that 'childhood is not a single universal experience of any fixed duration', and that the existing division between childhood and adulthood 'is arbitrary and incoherent'.

[44] E. Verhellen, 'Changes in the Images of the Child', in Freeman and Veerman (eds.) (1992), 90–1. See also Veerman (1992), 396–8.

1.4.3 The Significance of the Concepts of 'Childhood' and 'Children's Rights' in Relation to this Research

What, then, is the significance of the two concepts 'childhood' and 'children's rights', in the context of this research concerning child civilians in armed conflict?

'Childhood' (meaning that period of time in which a person is legally considered a child) is, despite its complexity, an important concept in the relevant law. This is because it determines the period in which the child possesses those rights which are linked to his or her status as a minor.[45] During that time, the child therefore enjoys certain entitlements additional to those shared in principle by all individuals. Indeed, the enjoyment by children of additional rights during childhood is a central feature of international law regarding the treatment of child civilians in armed conflict.

Concerning the concept of 'children's rights', in a *legal* context it is clear that inasmuch as the notion of human rights has validity, so too does the notion of children's rights, which arguably now forms an established part of both conventional and customary law, including that applicable to child civilians in armed conflict (as described in Chapters 2 to 5 below).[46] Certainly the international community has spent considerable time and money in devising laws which make unique provision for children, and most countries possess legislation exclusively concerning them. Regardless of the moral, philosophical, or political bases of this body of law, it exists, and it exists for a purpose: namely, to provide specifically for children as having a status and entitlements which differ from those of adults, both in times of peace and of conflict. Whether it succeeds in this purpose is clearly a different issue, and one which this book aims, in part, to address.

1.5 THE STATUS OF CHILDREN GENERALLY

The granting to children of a special status and additional entitlements in situations of armed conflict is, of course, linked to their status and entitlements in law and society generally. It is therefore worth considering briefly here the question of the extent to which children are commonly recognised as a discrete group with identifiable rights and needs. This book argues, among other things, that the recognition of children as such a group

[45] As discussed in sect. 1.3 above, the current definition of 'child' in international law is not precise, but it is sufficiently clear to serve its purpose.

[46] As Freeman writes, 'The case that children have rights has to a large extent been won: the burden now shifts to monitoring how well governments honour the pledges in their national laws and carry out their international obligations': Freeman, in Freeman and Veerman (eds.) (1992), 39.

is now increasingly accepted as a principle which underlies much of the relevant international human rights and humanitarian law.

In writing about Article 38 of the 1989 CRC (concerning children in armed conflict), the Quaker UN Office made the point that:

It has long been recognized that members of certain groups may be vulnerable to violations of their human rights and fundamental freedoms.[47] Children are considered as such a group and may be entitled to special measures. Such special treatment is not considered to be discriminatory because its purpose is to ensure equality.[48]

Arguments for the special treatment of children usually rely on two main factors: first (as in the above quotation), the particular vulnerability of children, and secondly, the fact that they are the new generation, and to be cherished in that they represent the future.[49]

In international law the idea that special treatment should be granted to the child is found, for example, in the guiding norm that 'mankind owes to the child the best it has to give' (first set out in the 1924 Declaration of the Rights of the Child (hereafter the 1924 Declaration));[50] in the almost universal international support for the 1989 CRC; and in the existence of over eighty international instruments which are to some extent concerned with the entitlements of children as distinct from those of adults.[51]

[47] The issue of children's vulnerability was usefully analysed in a draft document prepared for submission to the UN Committee on the Rights of the Child. This stated bluntly that '[c]hildren are vulnerable', and categorised this vulnerability in two ways. First, as an 'inherent vulnerability' based on their physical weakness and lack of knowledge and experience; and secondly, as 'structural vulnerability', based on their lack of political and economic power and of civil rights in society: Children's Rights Development Unit, *Civil and Political Liberties: Consultation Document* (London, May 1993), 3.

[48] Quaker UN Office, *The Rights of the Child* (Geneva, 1988), 1. In a similar vein, it is stated elsewhere that in general '[c]hildren . . . share common minority status in the eyes of the law and are treated as a distinct social group in a wide range of social and governmental matters': E. Ressler, N. Boothby, and D. Steinbock, *Unaccompanied Children* (New York, 1988), 259. See also M. G. Flekkøy, 'Attitudes to Children—Their Consequences for Work for Children', in Freeman and Veerman (eds.) (1992), 144; Goodwin-Gill and Cohn (1994), 121, and L. Muthoga, 'Violations Committed Against Children' in OMCT/SOS Torture, *Africa: A New Lease on Life* (Geneva, 1993), 105–6.

[49] The latter approach is exemplified in the following extract from the UNHCR Policy on Refugee Children: 'Children, including refugee children, are the future. They need special protection and care to realize their potential': UNHCR, *Refugee Children: Guidelines on Protection and Care* (Geneva, 1994), 166.

[50] The 1924 Declaration. League of Nations Official Journal, Special Supp. No. 23 (Geneva, 1924), 181. This Declaration was recently reaffirmed in the Preamble to the 1989 CRC.

[51] See S. Detrick (ed.), *The United Nations Convention on the Rights of the Child: A Guide to the Travaux Préparatoires* (Dordrecht, 1992), 20. In addition to the 1924 Declaration, its successor the 1959 Declaration, and the 1989 CRC, such international legal instruments include the human rights and humanitarian law instruments discussed in Chs. 2–4 below. See also W. Bennett, 'A Critique of the Emerging Convention on the Rights of the Child', 20.1 *Cornell International Law Journal* 1 (1987). He sets out, *inter alia*, a useful categorisation of: 'multilateral instruments dealing in part with children's rights'; 'treaties not specifically directed at children but affecting them'; and 'human rights treaties'.

Further, although the focus of this book is on international law, it is pertinent to mention here that states generally, in their domestic law, also make express legal provision for children.[52] For example, research published in 1983 by the UN Institute for Training and Research, which involved participation from representatives of forty-seven countries, contained detailed information concerning the legal status of children in thirteen countries from diverse parts of the world.[53] This research indicated that all thirteen countries possessed legislation making special provision for children as regards, among other things, family relations; the protection of children's health and welfare; education; child labour; economic rights; and judicial procedures. Moreover, debates in the UN during the final stages of drafting the 1989 CRC confirmed that many states make particular provision for children, and demonstrated widespread support for this practice.[54]

The granting of a distinct legal status to children therefore seems to some extent to be a cross-cultural phenomenon.[55] Such a status is a feature of the legal systems of many Western countries rooted in the Judeo-Christian tradition, and can also be found in other traditions.

In African customary law, for example, there is some evidence that children enjoy special entitlements, although the diversity of African cultures and traditions makes it difficult to generalise. One writer asserts that:

infancy is a concept that has universal legal validity among all African societies, though the age at which it terminates naturally varies from one community to another. Particular ages entitle the individual to particular types of social participation in the various affairs of life, and legal capacity or incapacity accompanies certain ages.[56]

In Zaïre, under traditional customary law children were entitled to special protection, although childhood was not defined strictly by age. Childhood

---

[52] In addition to examples cited here in the text, further information regarding the domestic practice of states can be found, *inter alia*, in an 'Information Sheet' on age limits for acquiring various legal rights in Western European countries (43 *Childright* 11 (Jan. 1988)). See also K. Tomasevski, *Children in Adult Prisons* (London, 1986), 50–62 and 80–102, for a summary of 'minimum-age legislation' enacted by different countries, particularly as regards the imprisonment of children with adults.

[53] Pappas (ed.) (1983). The 13 states were: Australia, China, Colombia, Congo (now Zaïre), Cuba, Czechoslovakia, Egypt, Greece, Israel, Kenya, Norway, England, and the USA.

[54] E.g., see comments by, *inter alia*, representatives of countries as diverse as Senegal, Brazil, Belgium, Morocco, Sri Lanka, Poland, Tunisia, and Uruguay, quoted in the Rädda Barnen report, *United Nations Draft Convention on the Rights of the Child: Commission on Human Rights, Debate of 8 March 1989* (Stockholm, 1989), 7–11, 11–13, 26–8, 36–9, 45–8, 57–9, 60–1, and 64–6 respectively. This report was one of those prepared by Rädda Barnen, the Swedish Save the Children organisation, in order to supplement the UN summary records with a full account of key debates on the drafting of Art. 38.

[55] For discussion of the legal status of children in a cross-cultural context, see generally Alston (ed.) (1994).

[56] T. O. Elias, *The Nature of African Customary Law* (Manchester, 1956), 102–3.

began at birth and continued until the child attained a degree of economic independence and fully participated in the work of adults, which was normally between the ages of 17 and 20.[57] Further, Sesotho customary practice (prevalent in parts of Southern Africa) dictated that every child had the right to claim maintenance in the form of food, clothing, shelter, and necessary medical expenses.[58]

Cross-cultural recognition of the special status of children can also be found, for example, in Islam. According to one writer, the

importance of children as a class unto themselves is derived from Quranic provisions as well as the Muslim tradition of holding the family as the focal unit within the community. Although 'childhood' is not explicitly defined, the predominant view is that social responsibilities attach to individuals upon puberty, which is often held to be the age of fifteen. The protections due to children, therefore, should apply at least up to that age.[59]

Islamic law explicitly grants children a number of entitlements, incorporating, *inter alia*, rights to maintenance (with special provision for illegitimate children); to establish parentage; and to upbringing (including, for younger children, custody and 'fosterage', and, when older, care and guardianship).[60]

However, while it is possible to identify certain cross-cultural practices that grant children special status, these practices are not necessarily coterminus with the granting to children of additional rights and/or protection. In some cases the opposite applies, for example as regards female (and arguably male) circumcision, and child marriage.[61]

---

[57] J. F. Tchibinda and N. Mayetela, 'The Rights of the Child in the People's Republic of the Congo', in Pappas (ed.) (1983), 183.

[58] A. N. R. Ramolefe, 'Sestho Marriage, Guardianship and the Customary-Law Heir', in M. Gluckman (ed.), *Ideas and Procedures in African Customary Law* (London, 1969), 198. See also, in relation to other parts of Africa, A. N. Allott, 'Legal Personality in African Law', *ibid.* 184, and H. Mursal, 'Report on the Situation in Somalia', in Aldrich and van Baarda (1994), 27.

[59] M. Elahi, 'The Rights of the Child Under Islamic Law: Prohibition of the Child Soldier', 19.2 *Columbia Human Rights Law Review* 270 (Spring, 1988). See also A. A. Siddiqui, 'Children's Rights Within the Moslem Family', 11.2/3 *International Children's Rights Monitor* 4 (1994). He confirms that puberty (assumed to be set at a younger age for girls) is the deciding factor. See also F. Krill, 'The UN Convention on the Rights of the Child and His Protection in Armed Conflicts' 3 *Mennesker og Rettigheter* 42 (1986).

[60] J. Nasir, *The Islamic Law of Personal Status* (2nd edn., London, 1990), 193–200, 245, and 156. See also D. Pearl, *A Textbook on Muslim Personal Law* (2nd edn., London, 1987), 85–98 and 138–87. One writer, however, argues that 'Islamic laws have very little to say about children' apart from certain general principles, and that it tends to regard them mainly as 'future adults': Siddiqui (1994), 4.

[61] See, e.g., J. Ngandjui, 'Do Traditions Clash With Children's Rights?' 10.4 *International Children's Rights Monitor* 6 (1993), and A. Belembaogo, 'The Best Interests of the Child—The Case of Burkina Faso', in Alston (ed.) (1994), 202–26. In fact, the impetus behind Art. 24(3) of the 1989 CRC, urging governments to abolish 'traditional practices prejudicial to the health of the child', arose partly from a desire to prohibit female circumcision. See discussion of the drafting of Art. 24(3) in D. Johnson, 'Cultural and Regional Pluralism in the Drafting of the UN Convention on the Rights of the Child', in Freeman and Veerman (eds.) (1992), 109–10.

Indeed, one author asserts that the concept of human rights is itself 'particular and modern', and therefore argues against surveying world religions and cultures to establish a human rights consensus.[62] If this argument is accepted, a consensus on that basis regarding the rights of children seems even more dubious.

Accordingly, while there is evidence of a degree of cross-cultural consensus that children have an identifiable and separate status in society,[63] this consensus may be open to challenge, and in any event the special status of children does not uniformly entitle them to more beneficial treatment. In relation to child civilians in armed conflict therefore, it seems unwise to base arguments for their entitlement to additional protection and assistance on cross-cultural norms rooted in tradition.

Nonetheless, it is submitted here that some cross-cultural evidence does seem to reveal an acceptance of children as a distinct social group, and more recent international legal initiatives acknowledge the entitlement of this social group (which clearly incorporates children in armed conflict) to special treatment, including certain additional rights, and a greater degree of protection than the adult population generally.

1.6 SUMMARY OF INTRODUCTION

In summary, in addition to outlining the aims and structure of this book and the terminology used, this Chapter argues that there are valid reasons for considering, as a separate category, international law concerning *child* civilians in armed conflict. Further, it indicates that the concept of children's entitlement to special treatment in situations of armed conflict may in some ways be antithetical to the more radical notions of children's rights, and possibly to certain cross-cultural norms, while nonetheless deriving from them some basic principles. In particular, such principles include at least a consensus that children are a discrete category within the population and entitled to separate consideration as such.

---

[62] R. E. Howard, 'Dignity, Community and Human Rights', in An-Na'im (ed.) (1992), 81 and 99. Nonetheless, she accepts that human rights are now 'in principle universally applicable, although not universal in origin': *ibid.* 82.

[63] One writer asserts categorically that '[a]ll cultures appear to know that children are importantly different from adults': Archard (1993), 28. A similar sentiment is expressed by Vittachi (1993), 9–10.

2

International Human Rights Treaty Law and Related Instruments Relevant to Child Civilians in Armed Conflict

This Chapter aims to summarise principles of international human rights law which form an integral part of the legal regime applicable to child civilians in situations of armed conflict. It shows that all the major international human rights instruments make provision, to a greater or lesser extent, for the special treatment of children, in the sense of granting them additional protection and assistance. They also affirm the right not to be arbitrarily deprived of life. Further, the human rights instruments specifically concerning children emphasise that the entitlement of children to special treatment must be particularly observed when children are experiencing extreme difficulty or danger, as in situations of armed conflict.

The Chapter begins by considering the applicability, to children and to situations of armed conflict, of provisions of human rights law. It then discusses the measures in general human rights law, both global and regional, that are particularly relevant as regards child civilians in armed conflict.[1] This is followed by a description of pertinent human rights law exclusively concerning children. The customary nature of certain fundamental human rights principles is discussed later, in Chapter 5.

2.1 RELEVANT PRINCIPLES IN GENERAL HUMAN RIGHTS LAW

As regards human rights in armed conflict generally, it is clear that, as one writer puts it, 'human rights and dignity are frequently among the first casualties of war', and that some of the most blatant violations arise from 'extreme denials of human rights experienced by civilian victims of armed conflict'.[2] Many of these victims are, of course, child civilians, and many of

---

[1] It is useful to consider regional as well as global treaties since, as expressed by Van Boven, '[t]he view now prevails, after many years of experience with the coexistence of global and regional instruments, that they are complementary and that they mutually reinforce each other': T. Van Boven, 'The International System of Human Rights: An Overview', in UN, *Manual on Human Rights Reporting* (New York, 1991), 7.

[2] R. Bilder, 'Rethinking International Human Rights: Some Basic Questions' II *Human Rights Journal* 576 (1969).

the violations experienced by such children are in breach of principles in both human rights and humanitarian law.

As international human rights instruments do not refer specifically to child civilians in situations of armed conflict, the pertinent measures must be gleaned from provisions which fall into one of two categories: first, those dealing with the special status and treatment of children, and, secondly, those particularly relevant to armed conflict, in this context primarily in relation to the right to life. The question to be addressed here is: do the global and/or regional human rights instruments normally provide for the special treatment of children, and for protection from arbitrary deprivation of the right to life? This Chapter finds that in general these instruments do so provide, and that the pertinent provisions form part of the legal regime governing the treatment of child civilians in armed conflict.

International human rights law prohibiting the use of torture and inhuman and degrading treatment also constitutes a significant element in the legal protection of child civilians in situations of armed conflict. However, the scope of this book must necessarily be limited, and therefore it does not deal with this aspect of the law. Nonetheless, it is relevant to the subject under consideration to note that the prohibition on torture and other maltreatment appears as a guiding principle in all the instruments described in this Chapter which deal with civil and political rights.[3] The arguments set out here in relation to the right to life therefore arguably apply equally to this principle, so that, under human rights law, child civilians in situations of armed conflict should be entitled also to protection from torture and analogous treatment.

The provisions of human rights and humanitarian law fall broadly into two strands: those which establish a negative obligation, that is, an obligation not to harm a person or persons (which can be described as a duty to respect), and those establishing a positive obligation to assist and care for a person or persons (which can be described as a duty to assist and/or protect). As regards human rights law, children are generally included within the scope of both negative and positive obligations, and, in both categories, are additionally entitled to special treatment by virtue of specific child-oriented provisions. The distinction between negative and positive obligations is particularly significant in relation to humanitarian law, as will be discussed in that context (see section 4.3 below).

[3] The prohibition on torture can accordingly be found in the two main global human rights instruments dealing with civil and political rights, discussed in sect. 2.1.2 below, namely the 1966 International Covenant on Civil and Political Rights (hereafter the ICCPR) (UN GA Res. 2200 (XXI), UN Doc. A/6316 (1966); 999 UNTS 171 (1976)) and the Universal Declaration of Human Rights (hereafter the UDHR) (UN GA Res. 217A (III), UN Doc. A/811, adopted on 10 Dec. 1948). It is also found in the relevant regional instruments, outlined in sect. 2.1.3.

2.1.1 Applicability of General Human Rights Instruments to Children, and to Situations of Armed Conflict

The starting point in considering the relevant human rights instruments, both global and regional, is that their provisions as a whole generally apply to children. This is apparent from the terminology used in these instruments,[4] and, as one author puts it, from the 'self-evident fact that children are human beings'.[5]

When such instruments do specifically refer to children, there is no standard terminology. Thus, for example, children may be described as minors, juveniles, and/or youth, and these expressions can have different meanings according to the particular instrument.

Not only can human rights treaties be construed as generally applying to children, but fundamental human rights provisions normally continue to apply in situations of armed conflict. This is either by virtue of the customary nature of certain of these, (as outlined in Chapter 5), and/or because the parties to the conflict have ratified one or more of the relevant human rights treaties. The fundamental and non-derogable human rights provisions would thus apply in both international and non-international armed conflicts,[6] and regardless of whether the parties to the conflict have ratified the pertinent humanitarian law treaties.

This is significant, since in certain conflict situations the provisions of human rights law may provide the only, or primary, available legal safeguard for child civilians. Such situations include, in particular, internal disturbances falling below the level of an 'armed conflict' and therefore largely unregulated by international humanitarian law.[7] Moreover, the applicability of international human rights treaties is important in that certain of these establish individual complaints mechanisms, currently lacking in international humanitarian law, which can be invoked in relation

---

[4] International human rights instruments use terms such as 'everyone' and 'all human beings' to describe those to whom they apply. They can thereby be interpreted as generally incorporating children, although some writers do not take this view. See further sect. 2.1.2.1 below.

[5] M. de Langen, 'The Meaning of Human Rights for Children', in Freeman and Veerman (eds.) (1992), 257. A similar point is made by Campbell, in Alston, Parker and Seymour (eds.) (1992), 17, and A. Lopatka, 'The Rights of the Child are Universal', in Freeman and Veerman (eds.) (1992), 48. Nonetheless, not all human rights are equally exercisable by all children, as this depends, *inter alia*, on the evolving capacities of children as they mature. See, e.g., M. G. Flekkøy, 'Children as Holders of Rights and Obligations', in D. Gomien (ed.), *Broadening the Frontiers of Human Rights: Essays in Honour of Asbjørn Eide* (Oxford, 1993), 97–120. See also E. Verhellen, 'Children's Rights in Europe', 1.3/4 *International Journal of Children's Rights* 359 (1993).

[6] The classification of different types of armed conflict is discussed later, in sect. 3.1.2.

[7] In contrast to internal disturbances, international armed conflicts and, to much lesser extent, non-international armed conflicts are generally regulated at least by humanitarian law measures in the widely ratified 1949 GCs (see sect. 3.1.2 below).

to violations committed in the course of armed conflicts (see, for example, the discussion in section 6.1.3.3 below on the Human Rights Committee).

Accordingly, in conflict situations, fundamental human rights provisions can coexist with rules of humanitarian law, and can also fill the void in circumstances where humanitarian law does not apply.[8] This is the case despite the fact that most international human rights treaties do, in periods of national crisis, allow for derogation from certain of their provisions,[9] although other provisions normally remain non-derogable at all times.[10]

Where permitted by the particular treaty, derogation is nonetheless only allowed in general to the extent that it is absolutely necessary in the circumstances, and it must not be inconsistent with the state's other international legal obligations, or involve discrimination. Moreover, to derogate properly from its human rights obligations, a state must normally take formal action indicating its intention to derogate and giving the reasons for

---

[8] For further discussion on the relationship between human rights law and the laws of armed conflict, see generally Meron (1989); T. Meron, *Human Rights in Internal Strife: Their International Protection* (Cambridge, 1987), 3–70; Y. Dinstein, 'Human Rights in Armed Conflict', in Meron (ed.) (1984), 345–68; F. Hampson, 'Human Rights and Humanitarian Law in Internal Conflicts', in Meyer (ed.) (1989), 55–80; F. Hampson, 'Using International Human Rights Machinery to Enforce the International Law of Armed Conflicts' XXXI *Revue de Droit Militaire et de Droit de la Guerre* 117 (1992); E. R. Cohen, *Human Rights in the Israeli-Occupied Territories 1967–1982* (Manchester, 1985), particularly 1–13, 65–71, and 188–283; P. H. Koojmans, 'In the Shadowland Between Civil War and Civil Strife: Some Reflections on the Standard-Setting Process', in Delissen and Tanja (eds.) (1991), 225–47; R. Quentin-Baxter, 'Human Rights and Humanitarian Law—Confluence or Conflict' 9 *Australian Year Book of International Law* 94 (1985); D. Schindler, 'The International Committee of the Red Cross and Human Rights' 19 *Int'l. Rev. of the Red Cross* 3 (Jan./ Feb. 1979), and D. D. Nsereko, 'Arbitrary Deprivations of Life: Controls on Permissible Deprivations', in B. G. Ramcharan (ed.), *The Right to Life in International Law* (Dordrecht, 1985), 268–83. For a recent case using human rights machinery to address the killing and injuring of civilians, including children, in an internal disturbance, see App. No 21895/93 to the European Commission of Human Rights, *Ramazan Cagirge* v. *Turkey*, 82–1 *European Commission on Human Rights. Decisions and Reports* (Strasbourg 1995), 20–4.

[9] The subject of this book does not require a detailed examination of the issue of derogability from human rights provisions. For a discussion of this issue, see, e.g., R. Higgins, 'Derogations Under Human Rights Treaties' 48 *BYIL* 281 (1976–7). See also generally J. Oraa, *Human Rights in States of Emergency in International Law* (Oxford, 1992). On derogation from human rights law in internal conflicts, see Hampson, in Meyer (ed.) (1989), 56–65.

[10] To take as an example the ICCPR, with the exception of certain Arts. specified in Art. 4(2), Art. 4(1) does allow for derogation 'in time of public emergency which threatens the life of the nation and the existence of which is officially proclaimed'. For discussion of the ICCPR derogation provisions, see T. Buergenthal, 'To Respect and to Ensure: State Obligations and Permissible Derogations', in L. Henkin (ed.), *The International Bill of Rights: The Covenant on Civil and Political Rights* (New York, 1981), 32–71. As Buergenthal points out, 'war' is the most dramatic example of a public emergency: *ibid.* 79. However, certain human rights instruments, including the 1989 CRC, do not explicitly allow for derogation.

this.[11] Many hurdles must therefore be cleared before a state can legitimately derogate from these obligations.

Even when a state can legitimately derogate, it is arguable that the two particular entitlements under consideration here (the special treatment of children and the right to life) are both largely non-derogable.

Certainly the right to life (or, to be more precise, the right not to be arbitrarily deprived of life[12]) is generally non-derogable in human rights law, or derogable only in extreme and narrowly-defined circumstances.[13]

By contrast, the entitlement of children to special treatment is not normally specified in human rights treaties as non-derogable, although there are exceptions.[14] In any event, derogation from the principle of the special treatment of children would run counter to other international legal obligations of the majority of states and is not therefore generally permissible. Such international obligations include, for example, the obligation of governments to grant special treatment to children in accordance with the overall intention and detailed provisions of the 1989 CRC, as well as in accordance with measures in other widely-ratified treaties such as the 1949 GC IV; the 1977 GPs; the ICCPR; and the 1966 International Covenant on Economic, Social, and Cultural Rights (the ICESCR),[15] as discussed in this Chapter and Chapters 4 and 5 below.

On the basis of the arguments outlined above, it is submitted here that the provisions in human rights law granting children special assistance and protection, and the right to life, are generally non-derogable even in treaties that permit derogation, and accordingly states parties to the relevant treaties should be obliged to observe these two principles in times of peace and in situations of conflict.

[11] E.g. Art. 4 ICCPR only allows states to derogate 'to the extent strictly required by the exigencies of the situation, provided that such measures are not inconsistent with their other obligations under international law and do not involve discrimination' (Art. 4(1)). The derogating state must also inform the other States Parties to this Convention, through the UN Secretary General, of the obligations derogated from, and provide an explanation (Art. 4(3)). The Human Rights Committee's General Comment 5(13) on Art. 4 emphasises the importance of proper derogation: UN Doc. CCPR/C/21/Rev.1 (19 May 1989), 4.

[12] Not all deprivations of the right to life constitute an infringement of international law, but only those which are 'arbitrary', as is discussed later in sect. 2.1.2.2 below.

[13] E.g., derogation is allowed only in relation to deaths resulting from 'lawful acts of war' under Art. 15(2) of the 1950 European Convention on Human Rights (hereafter the ECHR) UKTS 71 (1953), Cmnd. 8969; 213 UNTS 221 (1955); ETS 5. Ramcharan emphasises that even in armed conflict the right to life should be respected in relation to the 'civilian population, particularly to women and children': B. G. Ramcharan, 'The Concept and Dimensions of the Right to Life', in Ramcharan (ed.) 1985, 12.

[14] As regards exceptions, see, e.g., the 1969 American Convention on Human Rights (hereafter the ACHR), 9 ILM 673 (1970); 65 *AJIL* 679 (1971). Under Art. 27(2), this Convention forbids suspension of, *inter alia*, Art. 19 (Rights of the Child), even '[i]n time of war . . . or other emergency'.

[15] ICESCR. UN GA Res. 2200 (XXI), UN Doc. A/6316 (1966); 993 UNTS 3 (1976).

Nonetheless, one important limitation remains as regards the application of human rights treaties to situations of armed conflict. That is, such treaties normally apply only between states, and accordingly their provisions would largely not pertain to the actions of non-governmental entities (hereafter NGEs), such as dissident forces.[16]

However, as regards the responsibilities of states, it is argued above that relevant principles of human rights law would generally apply to children (even if not specifically referring to them) and in situations of armed conflict. The question to be considered now is: do the main human rights treaties in fact make provision for the special treatment of children and/or the right to life? This question is considered in sections 2.1.2 and 2.1.3 below.

2.1.2 General International Human Rights Instruments of Global Application

In relation to international human rights instruments of global application, consideration must particularly be given to the three most influential and widely supported of these, namely, the Universal Declaration of Human Rights (hereafter the UDHR);[17] the ICESCR; and the ICCPR.[18]

2.1.2.1 Global Human Rights Instruments and the Special Treatment of Children

Looking first at the question of the extent to which the special treatment of children is affirmed in global human rights instruments,[19] the discussion in this section will show that the UDHR, the ICCPR, and the ICESCR do all, in varying degrees, validate this principle

The wide acceptance of this principle in human rights law is also emphasised by its recognition, to a greater or lesser extent, in other global human

---

[16] One writer argues, however, that human rights law does apply to certain categories of armed opposition groups. See generally N. Rodley, 'Can Armed Opposition Groups Violate Human Rights?', in K. Mahoney and P. Mahoney (eds.), *Human Rights in the Twenty-First Century* (Dordrecht, 1993), 297–318. In any event, NGEs could be subject to principles of international humanitarian law in circumstances outlined in sect. 3.1.2 below.

[17] For commentary on the UDHR generally, see A. Eide, G. Alfredsson, G. Malander, L. A. Rehof, A. Rosas, and T. Swinehart, *The Universal Declaration of Human Rights: A Commentary* (Drammen, Norway, 1992). On Art. 25 (concerning children), see 385–403.

[18] For further information on the ICESCR, see, e.g., P. Alston, 'The International Covenant on Economic, Social and Cultural Rights', in UN (1991), 39–77. On the ICCPR, see generally F. Pocar, 'The International Covenant on Civil and Political Rights', in *ibid.* 79–125; Henkin (ed.) (1981) and M. Bossuyt, *Guide to the 'Travaux Préparatoires' of the International Covenant on Civil and Political Rights* (Dordrecht, 1987).

[19] These instruments will be considered here in chronological order. Relevant provisions in the Charter of the UN, which pre-dates the UDHR, are outlined later, in sect. 6.1.2. For a useful summary of the main international human rights instruments, see, e.g., UN, *United Nations Action in the Field of Human Rights* (New York, 1994), 40–62.

rights instruments.[20] For example, the 1948 Convention on the Prevention and Punishment of the Crime of Genocide (the Genocide Convention)[21] specifically takes account of the treatment of children. Thus the prohibition against genocide, widely accepted as a principle of customary law,[22] is articulated in this Convention to include certain 'acts committed with intent to destroy, in whole or in part, a national, ethnical, racial or religious group'. Among the prohibited acts are the imposition of 'measures intended to prevent births within the group' and '[f]orcibly transferring children of the group to another group' (Article II(d) and (e)). These two provisions acknowledge the fundamental importance of children to the survival of any group. The Genocide Convention also confirms that genocide is a crime, whether committed in war or peace (Article I).[23]

Further, the 1979 Convention on the Elimination of All Forms Of Discrimination Against Women (CEDAW),[24] although primarily concerned with the issue of sex discrimination, does, in certain Articles, make separate provision for children.[25] Similarly, the 1990 International Convention on the Protection of the Rights of all Migrant Workers and their Families applies, as is evident from its title, to migrant workers *and their families*.[26] Again, this treaty includes measures granting children distinct entitlements.[27]

[20] In addition to the instruments described in this sect. which specifically mention children, there are a number of international human rights treaties which apply broadly to children as to all human beings. These include, e.g., the 1984 Convention Against Torture and Other Cruel, Inhuman or Degrading Treatment or Punishment (UN GA Res. 39/46, 10 Dec. 1984; UN GAOR 39th Sess. Supp. No 51 (A/39/51), 197); the 1951 Convention Relating to the Status of Refugees (189 UNTS 150 (1954); UKTS 39 (1954), Cmnd. 9171); the 1967 Protocol Relating to the Status of Refugees (606 UNTS 267 (1967)), and the 1966 International Convention on the Elimination of All Forms of Racial Discrimination (660 UNTS 195 (1969); 5 ILM 352 (1966)). See also the instruments mentioned in Y. Kubota, 'The Protection of Children's Rights and the United Nations' 58 *Nordic Journal of International Law* 9–10 (1989).

[21] 1948 Genocide Convention. Annex to UN GA Res. 260 A(III) (9 Dec. 1948); 78 UNTS 277 (1951).

[22] See, e.g., the International Court of Justice (hereafter ICJ) case: *Reservations to the Convention on Genocide* [1951] ICJ Rep. 15 (Advisory Opinion of 28 May), at 23. Further, the *Barcelona Traction case* referred, *inter alia*, to the prohibition on genocide as an obligation *erga omnes* (see reference to this concept in sect. 5.1.1 below): *Barcelona Traction, Light and Power Co. Ltd (Belgium* v. *Spain)* [1970] ICJ Rep. 3, 32 (Judgment of 5 Feb.).

[23] One authority emphasises that the Genocide Convention can 'quite legitimately be viewed as part of the laws of war, and also of the human rights stream of law': A. Roberts, 'The Protection of Civilians in War' 5.4 *Interights Bulletin* 59 (1990).

[24] 1979 CEDAW. Annex to UN GA Res. 34/180 (18 Dec. 1979); UN GAOR 34th Sess. Supp. No 46 (A/34/46) (1979), 193; 19 ILM 33 (1980).

[25] See particularly reference to children in Arts. 5(b) (concerning 'family education' as regards maternity and child-rearing) and 16(1)(d) (regarding the elimination of discrimination in marriage and family relations).

[26] 1990 International Convention on the Protection of the Rights of all Migrant Workers and their Families. UN GA Res. 45/158 (18 Dec. 1990); 30 ILM 1521 (1991). At the time of writing, this treaty was not yet in force.

[27] While aiming generally to grant migrant workers and their families a wide range of human rights, this Convention specifically refers to children in, e.g., Arts. 29 (the right to name, birth registration, and nationality) and 30 (access to education).

Turning now to the key global human rights instruments, the UDHR, the ICCPR, and the ICESCR, only the central provisions relating to the principle of children's entitlement to special treatment are considered below. These three instruments also contain more detailed provisions, not discussed here, concerning specific areas of children's lives, such as education, health, or family contact.[28]

To start with the UDHR, this early resolution of the UN General Assembly established a series of basic human rights principles intended to serve, according to its Preamble, as 'a common standard of achievement for all peoples and all nations'.[29] The UDHR applies to 'all human beings' (Article 1), and therefore includes children within the scope of its provisions.[30] In addition, this instrument makes specific reference to the treatment of children in Article 25(2), which articulates the significant principle that '[m]otherhood and childhood are entitled to special care and protection'.

Further, it proclaims the right to education, which should 'promote understanding, tolerance and friendship . . . and . . . the activities of the United Nations for the maintenance of peace' (Article 26(2)).

The UDHR is considered by some writers to represent customary law. One authority observes that 'some of its provisions either constitute general principles of law (see the Statute of the International Court of Justice, Article 38(1)(c)), or represent elementary considerations of humanity'.[31] This instrument is therefore of some significance, despite the fact that it is simply a UN resolution, and not a treaty. As a number of writers have pointed out, 'soft law' (that is, non-treaty law which is not, *per se*, legally binding) can be extremely influential in shaping international standards.[32] This applies particularly to UN resolutions which are unanimously adopted

---

[28] These more detailed provisions can be found in Van Bueren (1993), 51–6.

[29] Thus, in addition to the Arts. cited here in the text, the UDHR also sets out fundamental rights, such as the right to liberty and security of the person (Art. 3), to protection from torture (Art. 5), and to freedom of expression (Art. 19).

[30] See Ressler, Boothby, and Steinbock ((1988), 233) for comment on this point.

[31] I. Brownlie, *Basic Documents in International Law* (4th edn., Oxford, 1995), 255. Also, see the Proclamation of Tehran, which confirmed that the UDHR, *inter alia*, imposed 'an obligation for the members of the international community': UN Doc. A/CONF.32/41, 'Final Act of the International Conference on Human Rights, Tehran, 22 April–13 May 1968', 4, para. 2. The topic of this research does not require additional discussion of this Proclamation, other than to note that it did make the link between armed conflict and gross denials of human rights (*ibid.*, para. 10). It also affirmed the importance of the protection of the family and the child (*ibid.*, para. 16). For further information on this Proclamation, see, e.g., T. Van Boven, 'Prevention of Human Rights Violations', in OMCT/SOS Torture, *Manila 91: International Symposium: Democracy, Development, Human Rights* (Geneva, 1992), 184–5.

[32] These writers include: R. Higgins, *The Development of International Law Through the Political Organs of the United Nations* (London, 1963), 1–10 and generally; I. Brownlie, *Principles of Public International Law* (4th edn., Oxford, 1990), 14 and 699; O. Schachter, 'The Twilight Existence of Nonbinding International Agreements', 71 *AJIL* 296 (1977); N. Rodley, 'Soft Law, Tough Standards', 7.3 *Interights Bulletin* 43 (1993); B. Cheng, 'United Nations

by the General Assembly, as was the case with the UDHR,[33] as well as with the 1924 and the 1959 Declarations discussed in section 2.2.1 below.

The ICESCR and the ICCPR are the two other key international human rights instruments of general application. The former sets out a series of economic, social, and cultural rights (such as the right to work (Articles 6 and 7) and education (Article 13)), which States Parties undertake to implement progressively, while the latter establishes binding civil and political rights (such as the right to protection from torture and slavery (Articles 7 and 8) and to due process (Article 14)). Again, their provisions apply broadly to all human beings including children,[34] and these treaties also contain some Articles exclusively concerning children.[35]

These two treaties are particularly significant in international law as they establish basic human rights standards, and also as they are quite widely ratified. The Covenant most pertinent to the subject of this research, the ICCPR, had, by 31 December 1995, been ratified by 132 states; the ICESCR by 133.[36] Further, under the 1966 Optional Protocol to the ICCPR[37] (ratified, at the same date, by eighty-seven states[38]), individuals can petition the

Resolutions on Outer Space: "Instant" International Customary Law?' 5 *Indian Journal of International Law* 23; (1965), and D. W. Bowett, *The Law of International Institutions* (London, 1982), 45–7. One authority, in discussing 'the binding quality of resolutions', concludes that 'there is no easy answer to the question: what is the role of resolutions of international organisations in the process of creating norms in the international system', and argues that the answer lies, *inter alia*, in the subject matter of the resolutions, the majorities supporting these, and state practice in relation to them: Higgins (1994), 24–8.

[33] The UDHR was adopted on a vote of 48 in favour and none against (1948 UN GAOR, 3rd Sess, Part I (Meetings 21 Sept.–12 Dec.), 71; *Yearbook of the United Nations*, 1948–9, 535). However, there were 8 abstentions, and this makes less clear the extent of state support for the UDHR on its adoption. (On a similar point, see Gardam (1993), 47–8).

[34] One writer states categorically that the term 'everyone' in the ICCPR 'is applicable to men and women and to children of both sexes': F. Volio, 'Legal Personality, Privacy and the Family', in Henkin (ed.), (1981), 186. For a contrary view, see C. P. Cohen, 'The Human Rights of Children', 12 *Capital University Law Review* 380 (1983). In any event, the 1989 CRC now explicitly reaffirms, in relation to children, many of the rights expressed in these Covenants. It is submitted here that children *are* generally included in the provisions of the two Covenants (and see further discussion on this point in the text of this sect.), although certain of the rights conferred may not be fully exercisable by younger children.

[35] It seems that those within the UN involved in drafting the Covenants largely accepted that their provisions did incorporate children. Indeed, a number of delegates opposed, on that ground, the inclusion in the ICCPR of a separate Art. specifically on the rights of the child. Delegates arguing in favour of a separate Art. did so on the basis that, *inter alia*, children's requirements are in some respects different from those of adults. They did not argue that the Covenant excluded children. See, e.g., UN GAOR, 18th Sess., Annexes, 1963, Agenda Item 48, 19; and UN ECSOR, 36th Sess., Supp. No 8, Commission on Human Rights, *Report of the Nineteenth Sess.*, 80. See also Bossuyt (1987), 455–69.

[36] See UN Doc. ST/HR/4/Rev.13 (1995), 10.

[37] The Optional Protocol to the 1966 ICCPR. Annex to UN GA Res. 2200 (XXI), 999 UNTS 302 (1976); UKTS 6 (1977), Cmnd. 6702. This Protocol, and the UDHR, the ICCPR, and the ICESCR constitute the four parts of the 'International Bill of Rights', and together define the concept of human rights, as invoked in the UN Charter. See generally Van Boven (1991), 3–10.

[38] See UN Doc. ST/HR/4/Rev.13 (1995), 10.

influential Human Rights Committee, established by the ICCPR, alleging violations of their rights by states which are party to this Protocol. Accordingly, not only are the civil and political rights set out in the ICCPR, including those particularly concerning children, applicable in many countries engaged in armed conflict, but violations of those rights can sometimes be subject to censure under the Optional Protocol, as discussed in section 6.1.3.3 below.

As regards the ICCPR, this instrument contains a number of Articles dealing with children, most notably Article 24(1). This rather vague but significant Article affirms that:

Every child shall have, without any discrimination as to race, colour, sex, language, religion, national or social origin, property or birth, the right to such measures of protection as are required by his status as a minor, on the part of his family, society and the State.[39]

On Article 24, the Human Rights Committee in 1989 published one of its authoritative General Comments, which serve as guidelines to States Parties to the ICCPR regarding their reporting obligations. This General Comment confirmed that, under Article 24, states must adopt 'special measures to protect children in addition to the measures that States are required to take under Article 2 to ensure that everyone enjoys the rights provided for in the Covenant'. Further, 'reports submitted by States parties often seem to underestimate this obligation and they supply inadequate information on the way in which children are afforded enjoyment of their right to special protection' (a right later described as belonging 'to every minor child because of his status as a minor'). This General Comment also emphasised that States Parties were obliged 'to include in their reports information on measures adopted to ensure that children do not take a direct part in armed conflicts'.[40]

Concerning the ICESCR, the key provision of relevance here is Article 10(3). This begins by stating: 'Special measures of protection and assistance should be taken on behalf of all children and young persons without any discrimination for reasons of parentage or other conditions'. It then articulates a number of measures to prohibit 'economic and social exploitation' of children.[41] Commenting on Article 10, one authority states that, while 'all of the rights in the Covenant apply to children', reports must give particularly

---

[39] Art. 24 also specifies that children should be entitled to both name and nationality (Art. 24(2) and (3)).

[40] UN Doc. CCPR/C/21/Rev.1, 21 and 22. Further, this General Comment states that 'as individuals, children benefit from all of the civil rights enunciated in the Covenant', and not just under Art. 24: *ibid.* 21.

[41] The Committee on Economic, Social, and Cultural Rights, which monitors the ICESCR, has issued guidelines to assist States Parties to this Covenant with their reporting obligations. Those on Art. 10 request detailed information, in state reports, on children. See Alston, in UN (1991), 58, para. 6.

full information on them 'because the Covenant requires special protection for children ... and ... they are often far more vulnerable than other groups'.[42]

Accordingly, the three most widely accepted general human rights instruments of global application, the UDHR, the ICCPR, and the ICESCR, all make specific provision for children, acknowledging to a greater or lesser extent their entitlement to special treatment (as, arguably, do the other global instruments, such as the Genocide Convention and CEDAW, briefly referred to above). As already discussed in section 2.1.1, this principle would generally apply in situations of armed conflict.

The notion that children should benefit from additional entitlements in international human rights law was supported by Mr Lasso, the UN High Commissioner for Human Rights, in addressing the UN Committee on the Rights of the Child in 1994. He stated that 'only one person should be regarded as privileged and that was the child'. He affirmed his intention to adopt that stance in his task of overseeing human rights under the UN mandate, and went on to describe children as 'the most important part of mankind'.[43]

What does the above discussion mean in practice, as regards child civilians in armed conflict? It implies that child civilians are to be granted additional 'measures of protection', in accordance with principles in human rights instruments such as the UDHR, the ICESCR, and, particularly, Article 24 of the ICCPR. At the least this means they should not be arbitrarily killed or otherwise unlawfully harmed. A more positive construction would entitle child civilians to special protection and assistance generally. Accordingly, where, for example, a State Party to the ICCPR unlawfully kills, injures, or otherwise maltreats child civilians, it is in breach of its obligations under human rights law, and diplomatic and other political pressure could be brought to bear on that state, in the UN or other fora, to cease and to remedy the unlawful activity. Pressure could also be exerted through the reporting procedure under the ICCPR. Further, where the offending state has ratified the Optional Protocol of the ICCPR, a case could be brought by the child, or on the child's behalf, to the Human Rights Committee, as described in section 6.1.3.3 below. The effectiveness of such measures in influencing state practice is a separate question, as discussed in Chapters 6, 7, and 8 below.

2.1.2.2 Global International Human Rights Instruments in Relation to Armed Conflict and the Right to Life

Having established in section 2.1.2.1 above that global human rights instruments do generally express the principle that children are entitled to

---

[42] *Ibid.*, 59.
[43] UN Doc. CRC/C/SR.152 (12 Apr. 1994), 4.

special treatment, in situations of armed conflict as well as in times of peace, the question now to be considered is to what extent do such instruments also enshrine the right to life?[44]

This right, although not absolute, is, of course, fundamental.[45] It is repeatedly asserted in international human rights instruments, and, as already discussed, is largely non-derogable, so that the right to life, too, applies generally in situations of armed conflict as in times of peace.[46] Again, it applies to children as it does to adults.

The right to life is set out in Article 3 of the UDHR, which states simply that '[e]veryone has the right to life, liberty and security of person'. It is also enshrined in Article 6(1) of the ICCPR, which reaffirms the right to life, and states that this right 'shall be protected by law. No one shall be arbitrarily deprived of his life.' Article 6(5) of the ICCPR specifically prohibits the imposition of the death penalty on those who commit crimes while under the age of 18, and on pregnant women.[47] An analogous prohibition exists in international humanitarian law, as discussed in Chapter 4.

In the ICCPR the right to life is listed in Article 4 as being among those (also including genocide) from which no derogation is permitted even 'in time of public emergency which threatens the life of the nation'.[48] In its General Comment on Article 6 of the ICCPR, the Human Rights Committee 'considers that States have the supreme duty to prevent war, acts of genocide and other acts of mass violence causing arbitrary loss of life'. The Committee emphasises that the 'protection against arbitrary dep-

---

[44] For further discussion on the right to life generally, see Ramcharan (ed.) (1985).

[45] The Human Rights Committee's General Comment on Art. 6 of the ICCPR asserts that the rights to life 'is the supreme right from which no derogation is permitted even in time of public emergency which threatens the life of the nation': UN, Doc. CCPR/C/21/Rev.1, 5–6. Other writers concur. See, e.g., in relation to the ICCPR, Volio, in Henkin (ed.) (1981), 183, and Y. Dinstein, 'The Right to Life, Physical Integrity, and Liberty', *ibid.* 114. Further, see generally Ramcharan (ed.) (1985); T. Meron, *Human Rights Law-Making in the United Nations* (Oxford, 1986), 186, and Higgins (1976–7), 282. The latter argues here that '[t]here certainly exists a consensus that certain rights—the right to life, to freedom from slavery or torture—are so fundamental that no derogation may be made.'

[46] However, for opposing arguments, as presented to the ICJ, concerning the right to life in relation to the use of nuclear weapons, see *Legality of the Use by a State of Nuclear Weapons in Armed Conflict (Request for Advisory Opinion Submitted by the World Health Organisation) and Legality of the Threat or Use of Nuclear Weapons (Request for Advisory Opinion Submitted by the General Assembly of the United Nations)*; ICJ Verbatim Record CR–95/32 (14 Nov. 1995), 68–70 and ICJ Verbatim Record CR–95/34 (15 Nov. 1995), 51–2 and 83–4.

[47] In addition, Art. 6 deals with other state obligations regarding the death sentence and genocide. Although widely ratified, these provisions of the ICCPR are not unequivocally accepted. For example, while the US has (as at 8 June 1992) become party to the ICCPR, it has entered a reservation which in effect allows it to continue to execute people who committed offences when under 18: UN Doc. ST/LEG/SER.E/13, 'Multilateral Treaties Deposited with the Secretary General: Status as at 31 December 1994', 118 and 125 (para. 2).

[48] The ICCPR also contains two further relevant provisions: Art. 20(1), stating that '[a]ny propaganda for war should be prohibited by law', and Art. 20(2) which prohibits '[a]ny advocacy of national, racial or religious hatred that constitutes incitement to . . . violence'.

rivation of life which is explicitly required by . . . article 6(1) is of paramount importance'.[49]

The ICCPR has now been strengthened by a Second Optional Protocol pertaining to the right to life.[50] This aims to prohibit use of the death penalty, requiring States Parties to abolish capital punishment within their jurisdictions (Article 1). It allows no reservations, except for those made when a state becomes party to this Protocol, and which permit execution in time of war for 'a most serious crime of a military nature' (Article 2(1)).

As for the ICESCR, this treaty, dealing with economic and social rights, does not explicitly refer to the right to life. Nonetheless it can be seen as implicitly confirming this right, among others, by Article 5(2) to the effect that:

No restriction upon or derogation from any of the fundamental human rights recognized or existing in any country in virtue of law, conventions, regulations or custom shall be admitted in the pretext that the present Covenant does not recognize such rights or that it recognizes them to a lesser extent.[51]

However, while the right to life is central to human rights protection, it is, as already mentioned, not an absolute right. International law currently allows a number of exceptions, including the possibility of capital punishment, and of certain civilian, and obviously combatant, deaths in armed conflict. This limitation on the right to life is clearly expressed in a UN study which emphasised that, despite its non-derogable status, the text of Article 6 of the ICCPR,

corroborated by its legislative history, demonstrates that Article 6 . . . would not guarantee the right to life as an absolute right without exceptions . . . To the extent that in present international law 'lawful acts of war' are recognised, such lawful acts are deemed not to be prohibited by Article 6 . . . if they do not violate internationally recognised laws and customs of war.[52]

Accordingly, in the context of armed conflict the right to life remains enshrined in the duty to ensure that civilians are not 'arbitrarily' deprived of

---

[49] UN Doc. CCPR/C/21/Rev.1, 5, paras. 2 and 3.

[50] Second Optional Protocol to the International Covenant on Civil and Political Rights, Aiming at the Abolition of the Death Penalty, UN GA Res. 44/128 (15 Dec. 1989). See also UN GA Res. 44/159, 'Principles on the Effective Prevention and Investigation of Extra-Legal, Arbitrary and Summary Executions' (24 May 1989), and Y. Terlingen, 'Principles for the Effective Prevention and Investigation of Extra-Legal, Arbitrary and Summary Executions', 5.1 *Interights Bulletin* 15–16 (1990).

[51] The ICCPR expresses a similar caveat in its Art. 5(2).

[52] Report of the Secretary-General on Respect for Human Rights in Armed Conflicts, UN Doc. A/8052, 104 (1970). See also Dinstein, in Henkin (ed.) (1981), 116; Ramcharan, in Ramcharan (ed.) (1985), 19; C. K. Boyle, 'The Concept of Arbitrary Deprivation of Life', *ibid.* 221–45; Meron, *Human Rights in Internal Strife* (1987), 23., and Hampson (1992), 130–4. The latter examines the meaning of the prohibition against 'arbitrary deprivation of life', observing that there is a two-fold test: (1) was the use of force legitimate (that is, directed against a legitimate target)? and (2) was it proportionate?: *ibid.* 130.

their lives, and that civilian deaths are therefore limited only to those which are an unavoidable consequence of legitimate military activity. This concept relates to the body of humanitarian law discussed in Chapters 3 and 4.

In summary, it is evident that the major global human rights instruments establish two largely non-derogable principles of fundamental importance to the protection of child civilians: their entitlement to special treatment, owing to their status as minors, and their right not to be arbitrarily deprived of life, as 'persons' under human rights law. These key principles arguably apply to child civilians in many conflict situations, including internal disturbances falling below the level of an armed conflict, as stated in section 2.1.1 above.

2.1.3 General Regional Human Rights Instruments

Turning now to the regional human rights instruments, the central question here, as with the global instruments, is: do they contain measures relevant to child civilians in armed conflict, in terms of providing for, first, the special status and treatment of children, and, secondly, the right to life? If indeed the regional instruments do so provide, this surely lends these two principles additional weight as expressing core rights of children in situations of armed conflict. In this case, many states would be doubly obliged to observe these rights, and their obligations could be enforced through regional, as well as global, human rights mechanisms, where applicable.

The regional instruments referred to below all set out, in terms broadly similar to the global instruments, certain civil and political, and/or economic, social, and cultural rights which the participating states undertake to observe in relation to the inhabitants of that region. All these instruments apply generally to children in the same way as do the global human rights instruments described above, referring, for example, to 'all persons' and 'everyone'.[53]

The pertinent provisions of each treaty will be only briefly summarised below, since the main arguments have already been presented in relation to the global human rights treaties.

Starting with the oldest regional organisation, the relevant law includes, within the Organisation of American States (hereafter OAS):[54] the 1948

---

[53] See, e.g., Art. 1 of the ECHR, and Art. 2 of the ACHR.

[54] For a general description of the working of this regional human rights system see, e.g., T. Buergenthal, R. Norris, and D. Shelton, *Protecting Human Rights in the Americas* (3rd edn., Kehl, 1990). See also C. M. Cerna, 'Promotion and Protection of Human Rights by the Inter-American System', 5.1 *Interights Bulletin* 3 (1990); T. Buergenthal, 'The Inter-American Court, Human Rights and the OAS' 7 *Human Rights Law Journal* 157 (1986), and R. Norris, 'Observations *In Loco*: Practice and Procedure of the Inter-American Commission of Human Rights', 15 *Texas International Law Journal* 46 (1980).

American Declaration of the Rights and Duties of Man (hereafter the ADRDM),[55] which, according to its Preamble, articulates certain 'essential human rights' and duties applicable to those in the Americas; the 1969 ACHR, dealing largely with civil and political rights; and the 1988 Additional Protocol to the American Convention on Human Rights in the Area of Economic, Social and Cultural Rights (known as the 'Protocol of San Salvador').[56]

Within the Council of Europe, the pertinent instruments are: the 1950 ECHR and its eleven substantive Protocols, covering civil and political rights,[57] and the 1961 European Social Charter (hereafter the ESC),[58] which focuses on economic and social rights. The 1975 Final Act of the Conference on Security and Co-Operation in Europe will not be considered here, although it does include, *inter alia*, a section on human rights.[59]

In the context of the Organisation of African Unity (hereafter the OAU),[60] there is the 1981 African Charter on Human and People's Rights (hereafter the ACHPR), also known as the 'Banjul Charter'.[61] This incorporates in one treaty civil, political, economic, social, and cultural rights, and is the most recent of the major regional human rights treaties. The OAU has also adopted the 1990 African Charter on the Rights and Welfare of the Child (hereafter the ACRWC),[62] discussed in section 2.2.3.2 below.

Other regional human rights treaties are, at the time of writing, either in draft form (see, for example, the Draft Pacific Charter of Human

---

[55] The 1948 ADRDM. OAS Off. Rec. OEA/Ser.L./V/II.23, doc. 21, rev. 6; 43 *AJIL* Supp. 133 (1949).

[56] The 1988 'Protocol of San Salvador'. OEA/Ser. P, AG Doc. 2325/8/rev 1, 17 Nov. 1988. At the time of writing, this Protocol was not yet in force.

[57] For a detailed analysis of the ECHR see particularly P. Van Dijk and G. J. H. Van Hoof, *Theory and Practice of the European Convention on Human Rights* (Deventer, 1984).

[58] The 1961 ESC. UKTS 38 [1965], Cmnd. 2643.

[59] The 1975 Final Act of the Conference on Security and Co-Operation in Europe. 14 ILM 1292 (1975). The human rights section here does not specifically refer to children, although it does contain some measures particularly applicable to them, concerning family contacts and family reunification: *ibid.*, Principle 7, Basket III, 'Co-operation in Humanitarian and Other Fields', para. 1(a) and (b).

[60] For a general assessment of the OAU and human rights, see O. Ojo and A. Sesay, 'The OAU and Human Rights: Prospects for the 1980s and Beyond' 8.1 *Human Rights Quarterly* 89 (Feb. 1986). On the monitoring of human rights standards in Africa and recent developments under the ACHPR, see H. Ben Salem, 'The African System for the Protection of Human and Peoples' Rights', 8.3 *Interights Bulletin* 55 (1994), and E. Ankumah, 'Towards an Effective Implementation of the African Charter', *ibid.* 59.

[61] The ACHPR. OAU.CAB/LEG/67/3/Rev.5; (1982), 21 ILM 59. Further information on this treaty, and other human rights documents pertaining to Africa, can be found in G. Hamalengwa, C. Flinterman, and E. V. O. Dankwa, *The International Law of Human Rights in Africa: Basic Documents and Annotated Bibliography* (Dordrecht, 1988). See also E. Kodjo, 'The African Charter on Human and People's Rights' 11 *Human Rights Law Journal* 271 (1990).

[62] The ACRWC. OAU.CAB/LEG/153/Rev.2; 'African Legal Materials' 3 *African Journal of International and Comparative Law* 173 (1991).

Rights[63]), or adopted but not yet in force (the Arab Charter on Human Rights[64]). These will not be discussed here.

2.1.3.1 Regional Human Rights Treaties and the Special Treatment of Children Generally

In relation to the principle of children's entitlement to special treatment, the first issue to be addressed in the regional context is, again, whether or not this can be considered non-derogable. The regional human rights instruments referred to above largely allow for derogation in a similar manner to the global instruments. Thus, among other things, they forbid derogation where this is inconsistent with other international legal
• obligations.[65] Such obligations include the duty to provide children with special treatment, in accordance with principles expressed in the almost universally ratified 1989 CRC, as well as other widely supported treaties (as discussed in section 2.1.1 above). Accordingly, the argument in relation to the global instruments, that provision for the special treatment of children is generally non-derogable even in conflict situations, applies equally in the regional context.

In examining the regional instruments, as with the global instruments, only the key measures establishing the entitlement of children to special treatment will be mentioned, although these instruments, too, contain more detailed Articles concerning particular aspects of children's lives.[66]

Here, once more, the question is: do some or all of the pertinent instruments make provision for the special treatment of children? Again, the answer is in the affirmative.

Accordingly, within the OAS, the ADRDM emphasises the special position of the child. It states in Article 7 that 'all children have the right to special protection, care and aid'. The ACHR contains a number of provisions which deal with the special treatment of children. Of particular interest here is Article 19, entitled 'Rights of the Child', asserting that: 'Every minor child has the right to the measures of protection required by his condition as a minor on the part of his family, society, and the State.' As already mentioned in section 2.1.1, this right is listed, in Article 27 as one

---

[63] The Law Association for Asia and the Pacific, *The Draft Pacific Charter of Human Rights* (Kensington, NSW, 1989). This contains an Art. (18A) specifically providing for children.

[64] The Arab Charter on Human Rights was adopted by the League of Arab States on 15 Sept. 1994 but has thus far only been signed by Iraq. It can be obtained, in Arabic, from the Arab League, Takrir Square, Cairo, Egypt. An English translation of this Charter was, at the time of writing, not available. For an earlier version of a regional treaty for the Arab World, see International Institute of Higher Studies in Criminal Sciences, *The Draft Charter on Human and People's Rights in the Arab World* (Syracuse, NY, 1987) (and see Art. 15, concerning children).

[65] See, e.g., Art. 27 of the ACHR, and Art. 15 of the ECHR.

[66] For more detailed provisions concerning children in the regional instruments, see Van Bueren (1993), 69–84.

which is non-derogable. Finally, the 'Protocol of San Salvador' sets out, in Article 16, its guiding principle concerning children under the heading 'Rights of Children'. In terms similar to Article 19 of the ACHR, the key passage here states that '[e]very child, whatever his parentage, has the right to the protection that his status as a minor requires from his family, society and the State'.

Turning now to the European system, the relevant treaties both, to some extent, make particular provision for children. The ECHR is surprisingly weak in this regard, and contains no pivotal Article regarding the treatment of children generally, although certain Articles do explicitly refer to them. These include Article 5(1)(d) (permitting deprivation of a minor's liberty in certain circumstances), and Article 6(1) (making provision for the exclusion of press and public from a trial 'where the interests of juveniles' require).[67] In contrast, the ESC articulates numerous measures on the protection of children in the context of economic and social rights. Of special interest here is Article 7, entitled 'The right of children and young persons to protection', which sets out a list of ten provisions concerning employment, particularly in relation to working conditions and minimum ages.

Within the OAU, the ACHPR, in relation to children, asserts in Article 18(3) that '[t]he State shall . . . ensure the protection of the rights of the woman and the child as stipulated in international declarations and conventions'.[68] Otherwise this Charter does not include Articles regarding the specific rights of children. It generally accords with African customary law in focusing primarily on entitlements and obligations of the family as a whole, rather than on the situation of individuals.[69]

The regional human rights treaties set out above therefore do all acknowledge, to a greater or lesser extent, the special status of children. In relation to child civilians in situations of armed conflict, this means that, where such children are unlawfully harmed in breach of the provisions of one of these treaties, the responsible government could, *inter alia*, be subject to political and other pressure in a regional context. Further, a child, or someone acting on the child's behalf, could invoke the regional human rights implementation mechanisms (if applicable), possibly on the grounds

---

[67] See also Art. 8 of the ECHR regarding respect for, among other things, 'family life'. Further, Art. 2 of Protocol 1 (ETS 9 (20 Mar. 1952)) and Art. 5 of Protocol 7 (ETS 117 (22 Nov. 1984)) to this Convention expressly refer to children. These measures concern, respectively, their education, and the responsibility of states to safeguard their interests while ensuring equality of rights between spouses.

[68] Under the terms of Art. 18(3), the ACHPR clearly includes within its ambit the 1924 and the 1959 Declarations, discussed in sect. 2.2.1 below. The 1989 CRC would not fall within Art. 18(3) as it was not even in final draft form when the ACHPR was adopted, but, in any event, African states generally are now party to the 1989 CRC.

[69] See, e.g., on the entitlements of the family (Arts. 18(1) and (2)).

of violation of the child's right to special treatment, and/or of other rights, such as the right to life (discussed below).[70]

2.1.3.2 Regional Human Rights Treaties in Relation to Armed Conflict and the Right to Life

Regarding the right to life, as in the global human rights treaties already discussed, the largely non-derogable right to life appears within the first provisions of the treaties governing civil and political rights in all three regions described above.

In the American system, the right to life is set out in Article 1 of the ADRDM and, in greater detail, in Article 4 of the ACHR.[71] Article 27 of the ACHR, like the analogous provision of the ICCPR, allows for limited derogation of certain rights 'in time of war, public danger, or other emergency' as long as specified conditions are complied with. Article 27 does not, however, permit 'any suspension of', *inter alia*, Article 4.

The European system is of interest in that, while the ECHR affirms the right to life in Article 2(1), it specifically allows derogation from that Article 'in respect of deaths resulting from lawful acts of war' (Article 15(2)).[72] The emphasis here must be on the concept of '*lawful* acts of war', and therefore in any armed conflict it would in principle ultimately be for the European Court or Commission, or other appropriate forum, to determine the legality of the act causing death. The ECHR also has an additional Protocol (Protocol 6[73]), abolishing the death penalty (Article 1) except 'in respect of acts committed in time of war or of imminent threat of war', when it can nonetheless only be carried out subject to certain conditions (Article 2).

Under the African system, the right to life is set out in Article 4 of the ACHPR, which emphasises that '[n]o one may be arbitrarily deprived of this right'.[74] No explicit provision is made for derogation from this or indeed from any other Article in the ACHPR.

---

[70] E.g., within Europe children have invoked the ECHR in a number of cases, brought either by children themselves or on their behalf, alleging human rights violations. For a summary of these, see in particular: Council of Europe, *The Protection of Minors Under the European Convention on Human Rights: Analysis of Case Law* (Strasbourg, 20 June 1990). See also the recent case of *Ramazan Cagirge* v. *Turkey*, n. 8 above.

[71] The ADRDM states simply that: 'Every human being has the right to life, liberty and the security of his person.' The ACHR, on the other hand, starts by stating: 'Every person has the right to have his life respected. This right shall be protected by law, and, in general, from the moment of conception. No one shall be arbitrarily deprived of his life' (Art. 4(1)). It then goes on to make more detailed provision as regards the imposition of the death penalty.

[72] For a discussion of the right to life under the ECHR, see Van Dijk and Van Hoof (1984), 184–91. See also n. 13 above.

[73] ETS 114 (28 Apr. 1983).

[74] Also relevant in the context of armed conflict is Art. 23(1) of the ACHPR which declares: 'All people shall have the right to national and international peace and security.'

As would be expected, given its fundamental nature, the right to life is therefore found in all the regional human rights instruments outlined above. Accordingly in this context, too, child civilians in armed conflict are to be protected from arbitrary deprivation of their right to life, and action could be taken against an offending state, as outlined above in section 2.1.3.1.

2.1.4 Recent Initiatives

In discussing general human rights principles pertinent to children in armed conflict, it is worth briefly mentioning five recent international initiatives: the 1992 Conference on Environment and Development, held in Rio de Janeiro, (the Rio Conference); the 1993 World Conference on Human Rights, held in Vienna (the Vienna Conference); the 1994 International Conference on Population and Development, held in Cairo (the Cairo Conference); the 1995 World Summit for Social Development, held in Copenhagen (the Copenhagen Summit); and the 1995 Fourth World Conference on Women, held in Beijing (the Beijing Conference). Although none of these conferences were particularly concerned with children in armed conflict, or indeed specifically with children, they all reflected a growing practice for such international conferences to consider children as a discrete group with particular entitlements.

Accordingly, the report adopted by consensus at the Rio Conference[75] included a chapter entitled 'Children and Youth in Sustainable Development' which, among other things, urged countries to 'combat human rights abuses against young people'.[76] Further, the Vienna Declaration and Programme of Action, set out in the report of the 1993 Vienna Conference,[77] specifically addressed the situation of children in armed conflict. In particular, the section concerning the rights of children called for 'national plans of action' to combat emergencies resulting from, *inter alia*, armed conflicts, and for the implementation of 'humanitarian norms' and other measures to 'facilitate assistance to children in war zones'. It also supported proposals for a UN study 'into means of improving the protection of children in armed conflicts'.[78]

---

[75] UN Doc. A/CONF.151/26/Rev.1 (Vol. 1) (1993).

[76] Ch. 25, para. 25.8, 381. Although it did not explicitly refer to children in armed conflict, the report on the Rio Conference referred to the 'destructive' effect of armed conflict generally (Principles 24 and 25, p. 7). Moreover, para. 25.14(b) supported wide ratification of the 1989 CRC, and para. 25.13(a) endorsed the goals of the 1990 World Summit for Children, discussed in sect. 2.2.4 below.

[77] UN Doc. A/CONF.157/24 (Pt. I) (13 Oct. 1993), 'Report of the World Conference on Human Rights'.

[78] Vienna Declaration, sect. II(B)(4), 38 and 39, paras. 47 and 50. Other relevant principles regarding children can be found in sect. I, 26, para. 21, (which, *inter alia*, welcomed both the 1989 CRC and the 1990 World Summit), and generally in sect. II(B)(4) entitled 'The Rights of the Child', 38–9.

As regards the Programme of Action of the 1994 Cairo Conference,[79] this encompassed many principles concerning children. It emphasised, *inter alia*, that '[a]ll states and families should give the highest possible priority to children' (Principle 11 in Chapter II), and paid particular attention to the need generally to empower and educate the girl child.[80] Further, this document contained a section on 'children and youth' in the context of population growth and structure,[81] and one on 'child survival and health'.[82] The Declaration and Programme of Action of the Copenhagen Summit, too, repeatedly referred to the situation and needs of children.[83] In addition, it called for particular efforts to be made for the protection of children by, among other things, '[i]mproving the situation and protecting the rights of children in especially difficult circumstances including in areas of armed conflict'.[84]

Finally, the Declaration and Platform for Action of the 1995 Beijing Conference made numerous references to the specific situation of children.[85] One section of this document is devoted entirely to the issue of women and armed conflict,[86] emphasising, *inter alia*, the particular vulnerability of women and girls to sexual abuse and the need for measures to address this.[87]

The explicit inclusion of children in these five reports indicates that children increasingly feature as a distinct group on the agendas of major international conferences which have a human rights component. Indeed, it now appears unthinkable for the final reports of such conferences *not* to refer separately, and at some length, to children. Again, this indicates an increasing trend within the international community to acknowledge that

---

[79] UN Doc. ST/ESA/Ser.A/149: 'Population and Development (Vol. 1): Programme of Action Adopted at the International Conference on Population and Development, Cairo, 3–15 Sept. 1994'.

[80] See, e.g., Ch. IV, 'Gender Equality, Equity and Empowerment of Women' (particularly paras. 4.1 and 4.9), and Sect. B focusing entirely on the girl child (paras. 4.15–4.23). Ch. IV also contains a sect. entitled 'Male responsibilities and participation', which calls, *inter alia*, for '[s]pecial emphasis' to be placed on preventing violence against children and women (para. 4.27).

[81] This sect., *inter alia*, in Ch. VI (para. 6.7) again expressed support for the 1990 World Summit and the 1989 CRC.

[82] See Ch. VII, 'Health, Morbidity and Mortality', paras. 8.12–8.18.

[83] UN Doc. A/CONF.166/9 (19 Apr. 1995), 'Report of the World Summit for Social Development'. For references to children, see, e.g., in the Declaration, paras. 10 (in support of the 1990 World Summit), 16, and 26(j). In the Programme of Action, see, e.g., paras. 15(g), 34(h), 36(a)(f), 37(a)(c)(e), 39(a), 64(c), and 79(a)(c)(h)(k).

[84] *Ibid.*, Programme of Action, para. 39(e).

[85] UN Doc. A/CONF.177/20 (1995). See, e.g., in Annex I, the Beijing Declaration, paras. 6, 9, 10, 23, 27, 31, 32, 33 (on humanitarian law), and 34. In Annex II, the Platform for Action, see, *inter alia*, paras. 2, 8, 10, 20, 34, 37, 38, 39, and 40. Annex II also contains a sect. devoted to women and armed conflict (see immediately below) and one on the girl child (112–21).

[86] *Ibid.*, Sect. E, 59–65.

[87] See, e.g., paras. 132, 135, 144(b), and 145.

children, including children affected by armed conflict, should benefit from entitlements which are both separate from and additional to those enjoyed by the population generally.

2.1.5 Summary: General Global and Regional Human Rights Instruments and Initiatives

In summary, this section (2.1) of Chapter 2 has looked at both global and, to a lesser extent, regional human rights instruments, and related international initiatives, in order to assess whether these enshrine certain principles central to the protection of child civilians. These are: (1) that children are generally entitled to the protection granted in international human rights law to all human beings; (2) that, in addition, children are entitled to special treatment and have a distinct status in international human rights law; (3) that all people, including children, have a right to life, at least in that they must not be arbitrarily deprived of life; and (4) that these principles generally apply both in times of peace and in situations of armed conflict. The Chapter has found that the relevant international human rights instruments do incorporate these principles, to a greater or lesser extent.

Obviously these principles cannot be said to infer into the pertinent treaties an explicit prohibition on the arbitrary killing or injuring of child civilians in situations of armed conflict. However, it is arguable that these concepts, taken together, imply the following: that no one should be deprived of fundamental human rights, including (with very limited exceptions) the right to life, even in armed conflict. Further, this protection should apply particularly to children, precisely because of their status as children, which entitles them generally to special care and assistance.

As mentioned above, a state in breach of its global and/or regional obligations to respect these principles could, on that basis, be subject to diplomatic or other political pressure. It could also, among other things, be held accountable through various reporting mechanisms, under regional complaints procedures, or, where party to it, under the Optional Protocol to the ICCPR. Accordingly, for example, Kurdish children arbitrarily killed or injured in the 1987–8 chemical-weapon attacks by the Iraqi government could have been, and were to a limited extent, the subject of concern voiced by the Human Rights Committee, and of international political and diplomatic pressure and protests, on human rights grounds, against Iraq (which is, *inter alia*, party to the ICCPR[88]), as discussed in Chapter 7. Had Iraq been party to the Optional Protocol to the ICCPR

---

[88] UN Doc. ST/HR/4/Rev.13, 4.

(which it is not[89]), cases against Iraq could also have been brought before the Human Rights Committee by or on behalf of individual children.

The former course of action, diplomatic or other pressure, depends largely on political will. The latter, use of individual complaints mechanisms, depends on many factors. These include the victims' awareness of the applicable international legal remedies (if indeed there are any in the particular case) and the availability of adequate evidence. Since all these ingredients tend to be in short supply, the pertinent procedures have not generally been much invoked in relation to children in conflict situations. It is to be hoped that greater use will increasingly be made of such procedures, and indeed this book aims in part to assist and encourage this.

Violations of fundamental human rights in armed conflict can, of course, be addressed in other fora, such as war crimes tribunals. These are referred to below in Chapter 6, and the final Chapter puts forward proposals regarding ways in which, as regards child civilians, greater use could be made of a range of monitoring and enforcement mechanisms.

2.2 INTERNATIONAL LEGAL INSTRUMENTS AND INITIATIVES EXCLUSIVELY CONCERNING CHILDREN

Legal principles relevant to the protection of child civilians and articulated in general international human rights instruments were described in section 2.1 above. The focus will now be narrowed as this section of Chapter 2 examines such law drafted exclusively for the benefit of children.

The three main global legal instruments which delineate the general rights of children are the 1924 and the 1959 Declarations and the 1989 CRC. Only the last is an international treaty, the others being Declarations of, respectively, the Assembly of the League of Nations and its successor, the UN General Assembly. All three are considered below.

Subsequently this section outlines other international legal instruments relevant to children, including the one existing regional treaty: the ACRWC. It concludes with reference to a pertinent recent international initiative: the 1990 World Summit for Children.

The legal instruments and initiatives discussed in this section all acknowledge that children have special entitlements, based on their particular needs and vulnerabilities. In general they also include measures which relate specifically to the situation of children in armed conflict, and thus add further to the applicable body of law.

[89] UN Doc. ST/HR/4/Rev. 13, 4.

2.2.1 The 1924 Declaration of the Rights of the Child and the 1959 Declaration of the Rights of the Child

As regards the 1924 and the 1959 Declarations, the intention here is to look at those aspects most pertinent to the subject of this book, rather than to examine these instruments and their history in any detail.[90]

The 1924 Declaration (also known as the 'Declaration of Geneva'), was drafted largely by Eglantyne Jebb, founder, in 1920, of the Save the Children International Union. She was motivated to set up the Union by her alarm at the 'catastrophic situation of children' after World War I, and the Union was initially to serve as an emergency relief agency to assist child victims of armed conflict.[91] She promoted the idea of a 'Charter' for children which would pave the way for improved conditions.[92]

The resulting 1924 Declaration was adopted unanimously by the Assembly of the League of Nations on 26 September 1924.[93] Although the initial impetus arose from concern for children in armed conflict, this Declaration was intended to apply equally in times of peace.

Its Preamble articulates the now familiar assertion that 'mankind owes to the child the best it has to give'.[94] It then sets out five simple provisions which deal in broad terms with key social, emotional, and economic requirements of children.[95] The principle in this Declaration which is most relevant to the protection of child civilians is the third, stating that '[t]he child must be the first to receive relief in times of distress'.[96] The third principle was undoubtedly intended to apply to situations of armed conflict,

---

[90] A detailed examination is not central to this research, and has, in any event, already been undertaken elsewhere. See in particular Veerman (1992), 155–80. See also UN (1994) paras. 1919–22, and Van Bueren (1995), 6–12.

[91] See E. Chanlett and G. M. Morier, 'Declaration of the Rights of the Child' XXII(22) *International Child Welfare Review* 4 (1968). These writers point out that the 1924 Declaration went further than Pt. XIII of the Treaty of Versailles, which, in its Preamble, mentioned the protection of the young: *ibid.*

[92] *Ibid.*

[93] League of Nations Official Journal, Special Supp. No 23 (Geneva, 1924), 181.

[94] One writer points out that the phrase 'the best it has to *give*' (emphasis added) represents a traditional view which focuses on children's vulnerability and need for protection, rather than their rights as active participants in events: Lücker-Babel (1993), 20 (see discussion in sect. 1.4.1 above).

[95] The principles set out in this Declaration are: (1) the child must be given the means requisite for its normal development, both materially and spiritually; (2) the child that is hungry must be fed; the child that is sick must be nursed; the child that is backward must be helped; the delinquent child must be reclaimed; and the orphan and the waif must be sheltered and succoured; (3) (in text); (4) the child must be put in a position to earn a livelihood, and must be protected against every form of exploitation; (5) the child must be brought up in the consciousness that its talents must be devoted to the service of its fellow-men.

[96] According to Edward Fuller, editor of 'The World's Children', this principle is particularly important, as 'it is the only one which, in so many words, insists that the child shall be *first*': E. Fuller, 'Great Britain and the Declaration of Geneva III' in V.5 *The World's Children*, at 75, as cited in Veerman (1992), 158.

although Eglantyne Jebb made it clear that this principle applied not only to 'acts of war', but that children should always have priority.[97]

The 1924 Declaration is significant for a number of reasons. It was the first global human rights instrument exclusively concerning the general entitlements of children.[98] Further, it provided for children to be granted priority in receiving assistance particularly in 'times of distress'. Such times would clearly include situations of conflict.

As regards the second Declaration of the Rights of the Child, the 1959 Declaration, this developed from discussion, as early as 1946, within the UN after the dissolution of the League of Nations.[99] The intention initially was to have the 1924 Declaration confirmed by the UN. In undertaking this initiative, the Temporary Social Commission of the Economic and Social Council was motivated partly by the suffering of children in armed conflict, as it wrote that '[t]he welfare of children must be the first concern of every nation, particularly having regard to the ravages of two world wars'.[100]

The long process which led to the adoption of the 1959 Declaration commenced formally in the spring of 1948, when a 'Children's Charter' appeared for the first time on the agenda of the Social Commission.[101] It ended on 20 November 1959 with the unanimous adoption by the UN General Assembly of the second Declaration of the Rights of the Child.

In presenting this Declaration to the UN General Assembly, Mr Cancino, Rapporteur of the Third Committee,[102] stated that the Declaration's 'point of departure is the undisputed principle that the child is weak and therefore requires special care and safeguards'. He added that '[c]hildhood is the only privileged class which transcends societies and epochs.'[103]

The 1959 Declaration consists of a Preamble and ten principles. The Preamble reaffirms that 'mankind owes to the child the best it has to give', and states that 'the child by reason of his physical and mental immaturity, needs special safeguards and care, including appropriate legal protection'. It refers, among others, to the 1924 Declaration and the UDHR as recognising the need for such safeguards.

---

[97] E. Jebb, *Save the Child!*, 41, as cited in Veerman, *ibid.*

[98] It was, however, preceded by other international instruments concerning children in specific circumstances. These include, e.g., the International Labour Organisation (ILO) Convention Concerning the Night Work of Young Persons Employed in Industry (1919) (ILO Convention No. 6, revised in 1948 as ILO Convention No 90; 38 UNTS 93 (1949)).

[99] See Veerman (1992), 159–60.

[100] UN, 'Report of the Temporary Social Commission', 29 Apr.–14 May 1946. Cited in Veerman (1992), 159.

[101] Veerman (1992), 161. For an account of the history of the 1959 Declaration, see also Chanlett and Morier (1968), 4–5.

[102] The Third Committee of the UN General Assembly, one of its six main committees, deals with social, humanitarian, and cultural matters.

[103] UN GAOR, 14th Sess., 15 Sept.–13 Dec. 1959, 3rd. Committee, Agenda Item 4, 592.

The 1959 Declaration adds to the principles enunciated in the 1924 Declaration by, for example, incorporating measures regarding children's entitlement to a name and nationality (Principle 3), to leisure (Principles 4 and 7), and to have their best interests considered a priority (Principles 2 and 7).[104]

One of the principles in this Declaration most relevant to the protection of child civilians in armed conflict is Principle 2, which states:

The child shall enjoy special protection, and shall be given opportunities and facilities, by law and other means, to enable him to develop . . . in a healthy and normal manner and in conditions of freedom and dignity. In the enactment of laws for this purpose, the best interests of the child shall be the paramount consideration.

Also particularly pertinent is Principle 8: 'The child shall in all circumstances be among the first to receive protection and relief.' The phrase 'among the first' differs from the wording in Principle 3 of the 1924 Declaration.[105] The revised wording reflects the reality that situations might arise where, for example, elderly or disabled adults required more immediate assistance than older children. Principle 8 also affirms that it applies 'in all circumstances', and not just 'in times of distress' as does the analogous Principle 3 of the 1924 Declaration.

Further, the 1959 Declaration emphasises that children should 'be brought up in a spirit of understanding, tolerance, friendship among peoples, peace and universal brotherhood' (Principle 10). It therefore recognises the importance of raising children in ways that can minimise the likelihood of their resolving conflicts by violent means.

In summary, some conclusions can be reached regarding principles relevant to child civilians in armed conflict, as set out in the 1924 and 1925 Declarations. These Declarations, while somewhat vague and aspirational, nonetheless carry weight as early manifestations of an international consensus that children have special needs and entitlements. Although non-binding 'soft law', they possess a certain legal force,[106] particularly given their unanimous adoption and reaffirmation in recent instruments such as the 1989 CRC.

Specifically, these two Declarations originated in a concern for child civilians, bearing in mind that the impetus behind them was, to a greater or lesser extent, a desire to ameliorate the suffering of children caught up in

---

[104] For a comparison of the two Declarations, see Chanlett and Morier (1968), 8.

[105] On Principle 8, Mr Cancino said: 'it is the child who guards our future . . . and this future must be protected. Hence his privileged position among those who in the event of danger should receive protection and relief': UN GAOR, 14th Sess., Third Committee (1959), 592. When Principle 8 was discussed in the Third Committee prior to its adoption by the GA, there was dissension regarding the amendment substituting the phrase 'among the first' for 'the first'. In the event, the amendment was adopted by 36 votes to 8, with 1 abstention: *ibid.* 82.

[106] See discussion of 'soft law' in relation to the UDHR (sect. 2.1.2.1. above).

armed conflict. Further, they contributed to international standards for the protection of child civilians by providing evidence of an emerging recognition within the international community that children should 'in all circumstances be among the first to receive protection and relief'.[107] This principle emphasises children's entitlement to priority in receiving protection and assistance, including in situations of armed conflict.

More generally, these Declarations affirm that children should receive special treatment, by reason of their status as minors. This is stated explicitly in both Declarations, in the key phrase that 'mankind owes to the child the best it has to give'. It is also implicit simply in the fact that these Declarations specifically concerning children were felt to be necessary, and were unanimously adopted by the international community as represented by the League of Nations and the UN.[108]

Accordingly, in a situation where a state unlawfully kills, injures, or otherwise harms child civilians in any category of conflict, these two important precepts—the entitlement of children to special treatment generally and to priority in receiving assistance and protection—arguably form part of the applicable international law in a very broad sense, as accepted international standards. Therefore, if, for example, the unlawful acts were to be the subject of a complaint under the Optional Protocol to the ICCPR, these two principles could be included in the legal argument against the offending state, particularly if it had originally voted for the 1924 Declaration and/or the 1959 Declaration. Together with other legal principles, they could also be invoked in political fora, in support of measures censuring the offending state.

2.2.2 The 1989 Convention on the Rights of the Child

The 1924 and the 1959 Declarations paved the way for the negotiation of the 1989 CRC. This Convention, a multilateral treaty setting out rights to which children are in principle entitled, is a major development in international law regarding children. However, Article 38, the specific Article in the 1989 CRC which focuses on children in situations of armed conflict, is far from satisfactory, as is discussed in section 4.2.5 below. Nonetheless, the Convention as a whole and particularly aspects of its implementation and monitoring procedures have the potential to strengthen the observance of international legal principles regarding child civilians. The 1989 CRC therefore merits careful consideration here.

---

[107] This is the wording of Principle 8 of the 1959 Declaration, based on Principle 3 of the 1924 Declaration.

[108] As one writer puts it, the 'essential theme underlying . . . these non-binding declarations was that children need special protection and priority care': Detrick (ed.) (1992), 19.

Despite its flaws,[109] this Convention offers new possibilities for tackling problems concerning the entitlements of children in all spheres, as it covers civil, political, economic, social, and cultural rights, and incorporates both human rights and elements of humanitarian law.[110] Moreover, it does not merely codify existing rights, but is in some respects innovative.[111] The simple fact that there now exists an international treaty which specifically addresses the rights of children and creates, within the UN, a supervisory Committee on the Rights of the Child, is significant.[112] At the very least, these developments indicate a formal acknowledgement in international law of many entitlements peculiar to children.

Since the 1989 CRC is a relatively recent treaty, its potential has not been fully explored. However, it has already generated certain initiatives within the UN regarding, among other things, children in armed conflict, as discussed in section 6.1.1 below.

The speed with which the 1989 CRC entered into force, coupled with its level of support, makes it unique among international treaties. It was adopted by the UN General Assembly without a vote on 20 November 1989.[113] On its adoption, the then UN Secretary-General Perez de Cuellar commented: '[f]irst, it addresses the needs of those who are humanity's most vulnerable as well as its most cherished resource. It is axiomatic that they should be afforded special protection.'[114]

---

[109] The Chairman of the Working Group on the Question of a Convention on the Rights of the Child (the Working Group), which drafted the 1989 CRC, acknowledged, e.g., when presenting it to the UN Commission on Human Rights, that 'sometimes it reflects rather a realistic common denominator than the most ambitious goals': Rädda Barnen, *Commission on Human Rights, Debate of 8 March 1989* (Stockholm, 1989), 3. Speaking in the same debate on behalf of 35 NGOs, the representative of Defence for Children International (hereafter DCI) referred to 'great misgivings about several issues', including the article dealing with children in armed conflict: *ibid.* 86 and 87.

[110] The fact that it is primarily a human rights instrument, but incorporates provisions concerning humanitarian law, is an unusual feature of the 1989 CRC as compared with other global international treaties. See, e.g., comment on this point in Veerman (1992), 205.

[111] Detrick lists a number of Arts. in the 1989 CRC which make 'notable improvements and innovations'. These include certain Arts. of particular relevance here, such as Arts. 3, 12, 37, and 39, discussed later in this sect.: Detrick (ed.) (1992), 28–9. See also Veerman (1992), 182–5.

[112] One writer observed that '[t]he concept that children can and should have rights is often seen as such an alien and radical notion that endorsement of the concept by the international community, in the form of a legally binding multilateral treaty, can provide a much needed legitimization of the concept': S. Fox, 'The Convention on the Rights of the Child: Risks and Potential', in Verhellen and Spiesschaert (eds.) (1989), 409.

[113] The adoption of the 1989 CRC was timed to mark a decade since the UN declared 1979 the International Year of the Child, which itself marked two decades since the adoption of the 1959 Declaration. More recently, the UN declared 1994 the International Year of the Family, thus again calling attention to issues involving children. See UN GA Res. 44/82(1989), para. 1.

[114] UN GA, Provisional Verbatim Record of the 61st Meeting, UN, Doc. A/44/PV.61, 28 Nov. 1989, 8.

On 26 January 1990 the UN in New York hosted a ceremony at which sixty-one states signed the 1989 CRC. Less than a year after its adoption by the General Assembly, on 2 September 1990, this Convention entered into force, having been ratified by the requisite twenty States Parties (as specified in Article 49(1)).[115] A few months later, on 27 February 1991, the members of the Committee on the Rights of the Child were elected.[116] Within a short period the 1989 CRC had accumulated a remarkable number of States Parties. As at 1 March 1996, 187 states had become party to this Convention,[117] making it, at that time, by far the most widely ratified of all the international human rights treaties.

The structure and relevant substantive Articles of the 1989 CRC are outlined below in this section,[118] with the exception of Article 38 of the 1989 CRC, which focuses on children in armed conflict and is discussed in Chapter 4. This Convention's implementation and monitoring procedures, specified in its Parts II and III, are considered in Chapter 6.

Only those substantive Articles most pertinent to international law concerning child civilians in armed conflict will be summarised here, largely in the order in which they appear in the Convention.

However, since the 1989 CRC contains no general derogation provision, it is arguable that, with the possible exception of those Articles with limitations clauses,[119] the remainder are at all times in force. As one writer points out, '[v]iolence or conflict is one dimension of the context in which a state must comply with its Convention obligations'.[120] She emphasises that 'in a given country struggling with conflict all children are "children in

---

[115] UNICEF described the initial signing of the Convention by 61 states as an 'unprecedented first day response', and its entry into force as the 'speediest entry into force of any human rights treaty': UNICEF, *Convention on the Rights of the Child: Information Kit* (Geneva, 1990).

[116] The first 10 members elected to the Committee on the Rights of the Child were: Mrs Santos Pais (Portugal); Mr Hammarberg (Sweden); Mr Kolosov (USSR); Mrs Belembaogo (Burkina Faso); Mrs Badran (Egypt); Mr Mombershora (Zimbabwe); Ms Mason (Barbados); Mrs Borges de Omena (Brazil); Mgr Gastelumendi (Peru); and Mrs Corpuz-Eufemio (Philippines): UN GA, Doc. A/47/14, 'Report of the Committee on the Rights of the Child' (1 June 1992).

[117] See UN Doc. CRC/C/53 (11 Mar. 1996).

[118] The history of the drafting of this Convention is not described in this research, other than to note here that one of the reasons put forward in support of the initial draft was the desire to create a binding legal instrument to safeguard children 'suffering through wars and other forms of aggression': UN ESCOR Supps. 2–6 (1978). Report on the 27th Sess., 20 Mar.–5 Apr. 1978, 75. For accounts of the drafting history, see, e.g., Veerman (1992), 181–4 and Detrick (ed.) (1992), 1–2, and 20–7.

[119] These include Arts. on family reunification (Art. 10(2)); freedom of expression (Art. 13(2)); freedom of thought, conscience, and religion (Art. 14(3)), and freedom of association (Art. 15(2)).

[120] I. Cohn, *Comments to the UN Committee on the Rights of the Child, 5 October 1992: Children and Armed Conflict* (Geneva, 1992), 4. A similar point is made by T. Hammarberg, 'Keynote Speech: Children as a Zone of Peace: What Needs to be Done', in Aldrich and van Baarda (1994), 11–12.

war"', and hence even in these situations states should respect, for example, 'the due process rights, the rights of the detained, the right to privacy, education, health, social services, a name and a nationality' of all children.[121] She accordingly argues that, depending on the applicable legal norms in a particular state, children in conflict situations may be entitled, in many aspects of their lives, to higher levels of protection than adults.[122]

To start with the Preamble to the 1989 CRC, this refers, *inter alia*, to the UN Charter, the UDHR, the ICCPR, and the ICESCR, as well as the 1924 and the 1959 Declarations. It reiterates in particular the sentiment expressed in the Preamble to the 1959 Declaration that 'the child . . . needs special safeguards and care, including appropriate legal protection', and it mentions children worldwide living 'in exceptionally difficult circumstances' (obviously including armed conflict) who 'need special consideration'.

The substantive Articles in the 1989 CRC fall into three main categories: first, the provision to children of adequate nutrition, shelter, family contact, education, health care, and recreation; secondly, protection from abuse and exploitation, which incorporates the important principle of prevention; and finally, the participation of children in decisions made about themselves, and in social, economic, religious, and political life.[123] Part 1 of the 1989 CRC contains forty-one provisions, most of which specify particular entitlements of children within those three categories.

The first four Articles set out in Part I of this Convention establish basic principles to be applied in respect of all children. These include: the definition of the term 'child' (Article 1, discussed in section 1.3 above); a non-discrimination clause (Article 2);[124] the principle that 'in all actions concerning children . . . the best interests of the child shall be a primary consideration' (Article 3);[125] and an obligation for States Parties to 'undertake all appropriate legislative, administrative, and other measures for the

---

[121] Indeed, in situations of armed conflict many of those legal entitlements assume a particular importance. These include Art. 8, concerning children's right to preserve their identity (including name and nationality); Art. 23, on the provision of special care for disabled children; Art. 24, specifying the entitlement of children to 'the highest attainable standard of health'; and Art. 28, providing for the education of children.

[122] Cohn (1992), 4.

[123] The substantive rights can also be categorised in other ways. See, e.g., J. Martenson, 'Preface', in Detrick (ed.) (1992), p. ix, and V. Muntarbhorn, 'The Convention on the Rights of the Child: Reaching the Unreached?' 91/2 *Bulletin of Human Rights* 66–7 (1992).

[124] This states generally that all rights in the Convention apply to all children without exception, and that governments party to the Convention must take steps to ensure this. The prohibition on discrimination can be particularly important for children in situations of armed conflict, where they may find themselves disadvantaged, e.g., as refugees, as enemy aliens, or as members of a persecuted religious or political group.

[125] For discussion of this concept in a cross-cultural context, see generally Alston (ed.) (1994).

implementation of the rights recognized in the present Convention', with a proviso concerning available resources in relation to economic, social, and cultural rights (Article 4).

Article 6 enshrines the right to life, asserting that 'States Parties recognize that every child has the inherent right to life' and that they 'shall ensure to the maximum extent possible the survival and development of the child' (Article 6(1)). It therefore reaffirms the centrality of this fundamental principle as regards children, both in times of peace and of armed conflict. However, the drafting of Article 6(1) has been criticised, in that, *inter alia*, it does not specify that this right should be protected by law.[126]

Article 6(2) also obliges States Parties to ensure 'to the maximum extent possible the survival and development of the child'. Related to the concept of survival and development is Article 24(c), under which States Parties must, in safeguarding the health of children, take 'appropriate measures', *inter alia*, to provide children with 'nutritious food and clean drinking water'. This Article could be applicable to children deprived of necessities in armed conflict situations (and see section 5.2.4 below).

One of the cornerstones of the 1989 CRC is Article 12, which specifies that children of sufficient capacity should be entitled to express their views in matters affecting them and to have these taken into account. Although in situations of armed conflict the available choices for children may be extremely limited, nonetheless the government responsible (which is likely to be party to this Convention, given its extensive ratification) should endeavour to ensure that Article 12 is respected and applied as fully as possible in these situations.

It is widely accepted that certain Articles of the 1989 CRC constitute guiding principles, or core rights, which underpin the other Articles. There is some controversy as to which Articles fall into this category, but there is consensus that these at least include Article 12.[127] In addition, Article 3, although open to a range of subjective interpretations, should arguably be included, as it is a fundamental principle of this Convention.

The 1989 CRC also contains a number of Articles concerning children's entitlements in relation to their families, some of which could apply to children in situations of armed conflict. Thus, Article 9 prohibits the separation of a child from his or her parents, unless this is in the child's best interests.[128] Article 10 provides, with certain limitations, for family reunification when, for example, a child and his or her parents are in

---

[126] See discussion in D. Hodgson, 'The Child's Right to Life, Survival and Development' 2.4 *The International Journal of Children's Rights* 391–2 (1994). He emphasises that e.g., Art. 6(1) of the ICCPR, does provide for the right to life to be 'protected by law': *ibid.*

[127] See, e.g., Veerman (1992), 189.

[128] This Art. includes a proviso that, when such separation results from government action, such as detention, exile, or death of a child or its parents, the child or other family members must normally be informed of the whereabouts of the absent person(s).

different states. Other provisions pertinent in this context include Article 20, establishing a duty for the state to provide 'special protection and assistance' to a child 'temporarily or permanently deprived of his of her family environment'. These three Articles emphasise the importance to children of maintaining family contact and continuity. This principle is fundamental to the well-being of children in armed conflict and is acknowledged in the 1949 GCs and the 1977 GPs, as discussed in Chapter 4.

Further, this Convention addresses the problem of trafficking in children (including unlawful adoption), and their illicit transfer and non-return (Articles 11, 21, and 35), which again, are hazards sometimes faced by child civilians in situations of armed conflict or their aftermath. In these circumstances, for example, unaccompanied children are particularly at risk, and desperate parents may agree to the adoption of children whom they feel unable to sustain or protect.

In addition, the 1989 CRC addresses another major issue for children, and especially girl children, in situations of armed conflict, and that is their entitlement to protection from all forms of physical or mental violence, including sexual abuse and exploitation (Articles 19 and 34). Sexual abuse of young girls was rife, for example, in the recent conflicts in both the former Yugoslavia[129] and Rwanda,[130] and indeed is commonplace in many situations of armed conflict.

Article 22 makes provision for refugee children, granting them, among other things 'appropriate protection and humanitarian assistance'. It is estimated that half of the world's refugees are children,[131] and many of these children become refugees by reason of conflicts in their country of origin.

Article 29 approaches the issue of children in armed conflict from a different perspective: that of educating children concerning peaceful means of resolving conflict. They should accordingly be educated in a spirit of 'understanding, peace, tolerance and friendship among all peoples', and with respect for the principles of the UN Charter.[132]

---

[129] See, e.g., UN Security Council Doc. S/1994/674, 'Letter Dated 24 May 1994 from the Secretary-General to the President of the Security Council' (27 May 1994), 56–60. This points out that the ages of women raped in the former Yugoslavia ranged from 5 to 81 (para. 236) and that 'young women and virgins are targeted for rape' (para. 250(a)). Similar information is contained in a report by Mr Mazowiecki, the Special Rapporteur on former Yugoslavia: UN Doc. E/CN.4/1994/110 (21 Feb. 1994), para. 226.

[130] In the 1994 conflict in Rwanda, rape was widespread. After visiting Rwanda at the beginning of 1995, Dr C. Bonnet was quoted as saying that 'virtually every woman or girl past puberty who was spared from massacre by the militias had been raped': *Guardian*, 11 Feb. 1995. See also J. Eriksson, *The International Reponse to Conflict and Genocide: Lessons from the Rwanda Experience. Synthesis Report. Joint Evaluation of Emergency Assistance to Rwanda* (Copenhagen, 1996), 37.

[131] UNHCR (1994), 163. As mentioned in Ch. 1, n. 5, this research does not deal in any detail with the issue of child refugees.

[132] See also the Declaration on the Promotion among Youth of the Ideals of Peace, Mutual Respect and Understanding Between Peoples. UN Doc. GA Res. 2037(XX) (7 Dec. 1965).

Also relevant is Article 37, dealing with torture and deprivation of liberty. This prohibits, among other things, the 'torture or other cruel, inhuman or degrading treatment or punishment' of children. During the course of armed conflicts, and/or in their aftermath, many child civilians experience treatment falling within the terms of Article 37. This aspect of the legislation is not explored in this book (see section 2.1. above), although it, like the right to life, is one of the fundamental precepts of the pertinent human rights law.

As already mentioned in this section, the Article which directly deals with the rights of children in situations of armed conflict is Article 38, which is cited in full and discussed in section 4.2.5 below.

Finally, the 1989 CRC contains two further substantive Articles which pertain particularly to the situation of child civilians. One of these, Article 39, obliges states to 'promote physical and psychological recovery and social reintegration of a child victim' of, *inter alia*, armed conflict. Such treatment must take place in an environment that promotes the dignity, self-respect, and health of the child. This provision breaks new ground, since no previous international legislation articulated the entitlement of the child to rehabilitative care. It is increasingly recognised that such care can be crucial for the recovery of children from the many traumas they suffer in situations of armed conflict.[133]

Article 41 then enshrines the important principle that wherever national and international law concerning the rights of the child sets higher standards than those expressed in the 1989 CRC, the higher standard shall apply. Article 41 is significant in relation to legal provisions concerning children in armed conflict, in that it could be invoked to raise the unsatisfactory standard set in Article 38 (as discussed in section 4.2.5 generally).

The Articles highlighted here thus all form part of the legal regime applicable to child civilians. Of these, Articles 1 to 4, 12, and 41 express general underlying principles of the 1989 CRC applicable to all children and States Parties at all times. The other Articles cited have a particular relevance for children in situations of armed conflict, among others, and certain of these Articles are arguably central. The latter category includes Article 6 (right to life); Article 37 (prohibition of torture); and Article 38 (rights of children in armed conflict).

In articulating this fairly comprehensive set of human rights and humanitarian law principles, the 1989 CRC clearly constitutes an important element of the international law relevant to child civilians in situations of armed conflict. It consolidates the human rights provisions discussed earlier in this Chapter, including the key principles that children in armed conflict

---

[133] See generally, e.g., Ressler, Tortorici, and Marcelino (1993). Although Art. 39 does specifically refer to children in armed conflict and is a significant provision, this Art. is not considered in depth in this book for the reasons specified in Ch. 1, n. 5.

are entitled to special treatment and to protection from arbitrary deprivation of the right to life.

2.2.3 Additional International Instruments Exclusively Concerning Children

In addition to the three main legal instruments of global application which
specifically concern children, described in sections 2.2.1 and 2.2.2 above,
there are many others which provide for children in particular contexts
(such as children in employment, the adoption or foster-care of children,
aspects of child health, or children in penal custody). Further, there is the
one existing regional treaty, the ACRWC, concerning children.

Apart from the ACRWC, these instruments are of limited relevance in
relation to international law concerning children in armed conflict. They
serve here largely to illustrate the extent to which the specific and separate
needs and entitlements of children, as a vulnerable group within the population, are recognised by international law in many different spheres. Accordingly, these diverse instruments are not discussed in any detail,[134] and
only a few feature below, by way of example.

2.2.3.1 Miscellaneous International Legal Instruments

Among the most obvious and significant international legal instruments
regarding children in specific circumstances are certain conventions of the
ILO which establish restrictions on the employment of children. They deal
with issues such as the age of employment (for example, the Minimum Age
for Admission to Employment Convention 1973[135]); working hours and
conditions for children (for example, the Night Work of Young Persons
(Industry) Convention 1919 (revised in 1948)[136]), and the protection of
children from dangerous work and substances (for example, Medical
Examination of Young Persons (Industry) Convention 1946[137]).

In addition, there are other international instruments, broadly concerned
with human rights, that provide specifically for children. They include, for
example, the UN Standard Minimum Rules for the Administration of Juvenile Justice (1985);[138] the Declaration on Social and Legal Principles Relating to the Protection and Welfare of Children, with Special Reference to
Foster Placement and Adoption Nationally and Internationally (1986);[139]

---

[134] For further information, see, e.g., documents in Van Bueren (1993), 85–326, and certain
instruments described by Veerman (1992), 309–93.
[135] ILO Convention No 138. 1015 UNTS 297 (1976).
[136] Cited in n. 98 above.
[137] ILO Convention No 77. 78 UNTS 197 (1951).
[138] UN GA Res. 40/33 (29 Nov. 1985), also called 'The Beijing Rules'.
[139] UN GA Res. 41/85 (3 Dec. 1986).

the UN Rules for the Protection of Juveniles Deprived of Their Liberty (1990);[140] and the UN Guidelines for the Prevention of Juvenile Delinquency (The Riyadh Guidelines) (1990).[141] The titles of these instruments are self-explanatory.[142] They do not establish binding rules, but rather embody principles of good practice regarding the treatment of children in particular circumstances, and are authoritative as such.

As well as the type of specialised legal instrument mentioned immediately above, there is a plethora of national, regional, ideological, and sectarian declarations, focusing on children. These have been described elsewhere.[143]

2.2.3.2 *The African Charter on the Rights and Welfare of the Child 1990 (the ACRWC)*[144]

After the above overview of miscellaneous international legal instruments regarding children in specific circumstances (section 2.2.3.1 above), the ACRWC now merits attention as the first potentially binding regional convention which concerns children exclusively.[145] At the time of writing, it was open for ratification by member states of the OAU, but not yet in force.

This Charter was preceded by the non-binding and less comprehensive Declaration of the Rights and Welfare of the African Child,[146] adopted at an OAU meeting in July 1979, the International Year of the Child.

To a large extent the ACRWC is similar to the 1989 CRC, but it is in some respects specifically oriented to the African context.[147] The Preamble,

[140] UN GA Res. 45/113 (14 Dec. 1990).

[141] UN GA Res. 45/112 (14 Dec. 1990).

[142] The first two documents cited here appear in the Preamble to the 1989 CRC, and the latter two do not, presumably as they were only adopted in 1990.

[143] Veerman (1992), Chs. 11, 12, and 13 (231–393).

[144] Other regional treaties concerning children's rights were, at the time of writing, in draft form. In particular some progress was being made in this regard in Europe. For a discussion of these developments, see, e.g., P. Boucaud, *The Council of Europe and Child Welfare: The Need for a European Convention on Children's Rights* (Strasbourg, 1989); Verhellen (1993), and P. Veerman, 'Proposals From Strasbourg and Brussels' 11.1 *International Children's Rights Monitor* 19 (1994). Indeed, at the end of 1995 the Council of Europe adopted a 'Draft Convention on the Exercise of Children's Rights' concerning the rights of children in family proceedings, to be opened for signature in 1996. See 'Draft European Convention on the Exercise of Children's Rights', 121 *Childright* 9 (Nov. 1995).

[145] Existing non-binding regional statements of principle regarding children include: the Charter of the Rights of the Arab Child of the League of Arab States (n.d.), the Declaration of the Rights of the Child in Israel (1989), and the Declaration of the Rights of Mozambican Children (1979). These are described in Veerman (1992), 260–3, 263–7, and 267–70 respectively.

[146] Declaration of the Rights and Welfare of the African Child. OAU Doc. AHG/ST.4 Rev.1; Van Bueren (1993), 31–2.

[147] One writer points out that certain provisions in the ACRWC, based on the 1989 CRC, in fact run counter to African traditions and customary law, e.g. in relation to marriage and legitimacy: B. Thompson, 'Africa's Charter on Children's Rights. A Normative Break with Cultural Traditionalism' 41 *ICLQ* 432 (1992).

for example, asserts 'that the situation of most African children remains critical' owing to certain 'unique factors', specifically including armed conflicts. It adds here that 'the child, by reason of his physical and mental immaturity, needs special safeguards and care'.

The substantive Articles in the ACRWC which particularly express an African perspective include those that prohibit 'harmful social and cultural practices' (Article 21, intended to apply, *inter alia*, to female circumcision); that focus on the needs of children living under regimes practising racial and other forms of discrimination (Article 26), and that stress the responsibilities of the *child* 'towards his family and society' (Article 31).

The ACRWC is of interest in relation to children in armed conflict, in that its Article 22, concerning such children, is stronger than Article 38, the analogous Article in the 1989 CRC. In particular, Article 22(2) affirms that States Parties must ensure that 'no child shall take a direct part in hostilities and refrain in particular, from recruiting any child'. Therefore, in an African context this forbids the direct participation in armed conflicts of children under 18 (the age of majority as loosely defined in both the ACRWC and the 1989 CRC), whereas Article 38(2) of the 1989 CRC sets the applicable age at 15. Further, in Article 22(3) the ACRWC, unlike the 1989 CRC, explicitly extends to situations of 'internal armed conflicts, tension and strife' the duty of States Parties to protect civilians generally and children in particular, 'in accordance with their obligations under international humanitarian law'. Accordingly, its application is not strictly limited to high-intensity situations of armed conflict as defined in the 1949 GCs and the 1977 GPs (see section 3.1.2 below).

Moreover, again in contrast to the 1989 CRC, this treaty contains provision for the submission, to the Committee established thereunder, of communications 'from any person, group or non-governmental organisation' relating to matters covered by the ACRWC (Article 44(1)).

The ACRWC is therefore a good example of the difference in emphasis between a global and a regional treaty concerning children. It illustrates the potential of the latter to address issues of particular regional concern, and to raise international standards, including standards in the area under discussion here, regarding children in armed conflict.

2.2.4 The 1990 World Summit for Children

In the context of considering international human rights law exclusively concerning children, it is appropriate finally to mention one recent international initiative of political significance. The 1990 World Summit for

Children (hereafter the 1990 World Summit) was held at the UN on 30 September 1990, at the instigation of UNICEF.[148]

This Summit gathered together representatives of 159 nations, including an unprecedented seventy-one heads of state.[149] It was addressed briefly by each head of state,[150] and the meeting culminated in the representatives signing the 'World Declaration on the Survival, Protection and Development of Children; and Plan of Action for Implementing the World Declaration on the Survival, Protection and Development of Children in the 1990s'.[151]

This Declaration articulated various goals which pertain directly or indirectly to the protection of children in armed conflict. It set out a ten-point programme 'to protect the rights of children and to improve their lives' (paragraph 20). One element of this programme expressed a commitment to 'work carefully to protect children from the scourge of war and to take measures to prevent further armed conflicts' (paragraph 20(8)). It added that '[t]he essential needs of children and families must be protected even in times of war', and specifically asked 'that periods of tranquillity and special relief corridors be observed for the benefit of children, where war and violence are still taking place'. This last concept is important in relation to the protection of children in armed conflict, as discussed in sections 4.2.1.2 and 8.3.1 below.

In order to achieve its goals, the Declaration called for support from children themselves, as well as the UN and other international and regional organisations and NGOs (paragraphs 22 and 23). The 'Plan of Action' to implement this Declaration again contained provisions regarding, *inter alia*, the importance of providing special protection for children in armed conflict,[152] and emphasising the need for effective implementation (paragraph 33).

---

[148] For a fuller description of the Summit and its Declaration and Plan of Action, see Veerman (1992), 209–16 and UNICEF, *The State of the World's Children 1992* (Oxford, 1991), 1–11.

[149] In his 1990 report on the work of the UN, the then Secretary-General commented that the Summit was 'remarkable for being the first summit of leaders from the North, the South, the East and the West and thus facilitating dialogue on a universal scale': J. P. de Cuellar, *Report of the Secretary-General on the Work of the Organisation* (Geneva, 1990), 36.

[150] In her speech, the then Prime Minister of the UK, Margaret Thatcher, referred to the killing of Kurdish children by the Iraqi government as an example of violence committed against children. This is of interest in relation to Ch. 7 below, particularly given the rather muted response of the UK government at the time of the chemical weapon attacks.

[151] See Annex, UN GA Doc. A/45/625 (18 Oct. 1990). The UN welcomed this initiative, as in UN GA Res. 45/217 (21 Dec. 1990), 'World Summit for Children'.

[152] See, e.g., the Introduction, which set out as one of its major goals the 'protection of children in especially difficult circumstances, particularly in situation of armed conflicts' (para. 5(g)). See also para. 15.

It is of some significance to the issues under consideration here that a World Summit of this magnitude was held to make a commitment in relation to the status and treatment of children.[153] It is obviously not a coincidence that this took place soon after the adoption of the 1989 CRC. Time will tell to what extent this initiative bears fruit.[154]

In any event, as regards child civilians in armed conflict, the concepts of 'periods of tranquillity' and 'special relief corridors', reaffirmed in the Declaration, are useful. Moreover, breach of commitments made by governments that attended the World Summit could, in principle, be cited in censuring such governments in political fora if they unlawfully kill, injure, or otherwise harm child civilians in situations of armed conflict.

2.3 SUMMARY: RELEVANT HUMAN RIGHTS INSTRUMENTS AND INITIATIVES

In summary, this Chapter has illustrated that there is a mass of human rights law, both treaty and 'soft law', general and child-specific, which recognises the distinct status and particular requirements of children. This weighty body of law and related policy has emerged from global and regional fora, some of which are primarily law-making, others primarily political. Its fundamental principles apply broadly to children in all contexts, including child civilians in situations of armed conflict, and enshrine the concept that they must not arbitrarily be deprived of life. Further, this body of law establishes at the very least that children, owing to their particular vulnerability and their significance as the future generation, are entitled to special treatment generally, and, in situations of danger, to priority in the receipt of assistance and protection.

---

[153] Further, as one writer has noted, it is also significant that this Summit went ahead, despite the fact that it was held on the eve of the 1991 Gulf War: Veerman (1992), 209.

[154] In any event, the World Summit has given rise to national action programmes for children in a number of countries. At the beginning of 1995 UNICEF stated that this Summit had led to 'concrete action on a significant scale in more than 100 countries, which together account for more than 90% of the developing world's children': UK Committee for UNICEF, *News in Brief* (London, Feb. 1995), 2–3.

3

Treaty Law of Armed Conflict and Related Instruments: The Protection of Civilians, and Use of Chemical Weapons

The objective of the preceding chapter was to demonstrate that human rights principles form a significant part of the body of international law broadly applicable to child civilians in situations of armed conflict. This Chapter now outlines provisions in international humanitarian law concerning the treatment of civilians of all ages, and not those which explicitly refer to child civilians. It is important to summarise these general provisions of international humanitarian law since child civilians are entitled to protection under this body of law both as members of the civilian population as a whole (discussed here), and as a specific particularly vulnerable group within the civilian population (discussed in Chapter 4).

This book is concerned with *jus in bello* (the rules which apply in situations of armed conflict), and not *jus ad bellum* (the rules governing the resort to armed force). There is a massive body of law on both these aspects of armed conflict, and a substantial literature.[1] Accordingly, only the most pertinent of the main treaties are to be examined in this Chapter and in Chapter 4, as well as a small number of other instruments, such as UN resolutions. The selected provisions are, nonetheless, numerous. It appears that those drafting this body of law, especially in the aftermath of World War II, were acutely aware of the need to provide civilians, and sometimes explicitly child civilians, with protection from the horrors and dangers of armed conflict.

The modern laws of armed conflict developed from what were originally three separate trends in international law. Two of these were initially con-

---

[1] For further reading, see, among others, Roberts and Guelff (eds.) (1989); L. Oppenheim, (H. Lauterpacht (ed.)), *International Law: A Treatise. Vol. II: Disputes, War and Neutrality* (7th edn., London, 1952); J. Pictet, *Development and Principles of International Humanitarian Law* (Dordrecht, 1985); F. Kalshoven, *Constraints on the Waging of War* (Geneva, 1987); I. D. De Lupis, *The Law of War* (Cambridge, 1987); D. Schindler and J. Toman, *The Laws of Armed Conflict* (3rd edn., Dordrecht, 1988); H. McCoubrey, *International Humanitarian Law* (Aldershot, 1990); L. C. Green, *The Contemporary Law of Armed Conflict* (Manchester, 1993); G. Best, *Humanity in Warfare* (London, 1980); and G. Best, *War and Law Since 1945* (Oxford, 1994). For a text focusing largely on *jus ad bellum*, see, e.g., I. Brownlie, *International Law and the Use of Force by States* (Oxford, 1963).

solidated in the 1860s: the law of Geneva, concerned largely with the protection of victims of armed conflict who were in enemy hands (such as interned civilians), and the law of The Hague, relating to the conduct of armed conflict itself, and limitations on the means and methods employed. During the 1960s and the 1970s, the New York trend emerged, focusing on the entitlement to fundamental human rights in situations of armed conflict.[2] In more recent years there has been a tendency for these approaches to merge, as evidenced in the 1977 GPs. To the extent that it is necessary to distinguish them, these three trends are all relevant to the protection of child civilians in armed conflict.

The discussion below will incorporate consideration of the rules applicable (or not applicable) in internal disturbances such as riots, although these, strictly speaking, fall below the level of 'armed conflict' and therefore generally outside the remit of international humanitarian law. The inclusion here of internal disturbances is necessary because of the prevalence of such disturbances in the world today; the significance of this category of conflict in relation to the Iraqi study (Chapter 7); and the fact that conflicts of this nature frequently affect large numbers of children. Further, the categorisation of particular conflicts can be imprecise and contentious (as discussed in section 3.1.2 below) so that some may classify as an internal disturbance what others may see as a non-international armed conflict.

3.1 TREATY LAW OF ARMED CONFLICT AND RELATED INSTRUMENTS REGARDING THE CIVILIAN POPULATION IN GENERAL

There are three ways in which civilians can become victims of an armed conflict. First, their person and/or property can be harmed as a direct or indirect result of the actual conduct of hostilities. Secondly, they may fall under the control of an occupying force through belligerent occupation of the territory they inhabit. Finally, they may become enemy civilians living in the territory of a party to the conflict.[3]

---

[2] For further information on these three trends, see Kalshoven (1987), 7–23. See also, e.g., McCoubrey, in Meyer (ed.) (1989), 45–9. Green (1993), 320 emphasises that both Geneva and Hague law have a similar aim: to minimise the horrors of armed conflict by balancing military necessity with humanitarian considerations. Another writer observes, in discussing the 'paradox of humanitarianism in armed conflict', that it is '*prima facie* curious to find a structure of legal norms which is designed to regulate the conduct of a state of international relations which is in essence a descent into extra-legal violence'. McCoubrey (1990), 2.

[3] As outlined, e.g., in Y. Van Dongen, *The Protection of Civilian Populations In Time of Armed Conflict* (Amsterdam, 1991), 3.

Measures to safeguard civilians in all these categories are incorporated in the various laws of armed conflict. Indeed, the protection of civilians, including child civilians, is one of the principles which lie at the heart of this body of law.[4]

According to one authority, notions that non-combatants are to be treated humanely and respected 'are not characteristic of western civilisations alone; they are also found in the basic philosophies and religions of Islam, India and the Far East'.[5] However, this principle has not necessarily been honoured in all times and cultures.[6]

The need to enhance the protection of civilians has become more pressing in recent decades. This is partly due to changes in the nature of armed conflict. The majority of these are now non-international armed conflicts, in which it can be difficult to distinguish combatants from civilians.[7] It is also due to changes in the conduct of armed conflict, for example, in terms of weapon development. The resulting increase in losses among civilians is evidenced by statistics estimating that in World War I about 5 per cent of those killed were civilians; in World War II, about 48 per cent; and in some non-international armed conflicts, such as in Lebanon, the civilian casualties apparently reached the staggering figure of 90 per cent, many of them children.[8] These figures are particularly disheartening, considering

---

[4] As one writer emphasises, 'Non-combatant immunity is regarded as one of the cornerstones of the humanitarian law of armed conflict': Gardam (1993), 2. See also, e.g., J. Pictet, *Humanitarian Law and the Protection of War Victims* (Leiden, 1973), 28–34.

[5] J. Pictet (ed.), *Commentary on Geneva Convention IV Relative to the Protection of Civilian Persons in Time of War* (Geneva, 1958), 201. See also, e.g., a series of articles on humanitarian law in the Asian context, summarised in M. Sornarajah, 'An Overview of the Asian Approaches to International Humanitarian Law' 9 *Australian Year Book of International Law* 238 (1985). As regards Africa, see E. Bello, *African Customary Humanitarian Law* (Geneva, 1980). For reference to the protection of child civilians in Islam and in customary African law, see sect. 4.1 below.

[6] See, e.g., comment on this point in McCoubrey (1990), 6–11.

[7] According to one writer, 9 out of 10 armed conflicts in 1988–9 were internal conflicts: C. Ahlström, *Casualties of Conflict* (Uppsala, 1991), 1. See also Gardam (1993), 1, and ICRC, 'Report on the Protection of War Victims', 296 *Int'l. Rev. of the Red Cross* 403 (1.2(b)) (Sept.–Oct. 1993).

[8] See UNICEF, UN Doc.E/ICEF/1986/CRP.2, 'Children in Situations of Armed Conflict', 3, and Singer (1986), 11. Slightly different percentages are quoted by Ahlström (1991), 7, 8, and 19 respectively. However, see B. Abramson, *Children and War: A Background Paper with Recommendations for the Committee on the Rights of the Child and its Working Group on Children in Armed Conflict* (Geneva, 1992), 20, who describes as largely a myth statistics that indicate escalating numbers of civilian deaths. He argues that civilians have been the primary victims of armed conflict in many periods of history. In any event, one authority points out that the 1991 Gulf War ran counter to the trend that an increasing proportion of casualties of armed conflict are civilians: F. Hampson, 'Means and Methods of Warfare in the Conflict in the Gulf', in P. Rowe (ed.), *The Gulf War 1990–1991 in International and English Law* (London, 1993), 100. See also B. Jongman and J. van der Dennen, *The Great 'War Figures Hoax': An Investigation in Polemomythology* (Groningen, 1987), cited in Van Dongen (1991), 224. These writers argue that statistics regarding casualties of armed conflict should be regarded with caution.

that in the so-called 'post-war' period (since 1945) there have been an estimated 105 major armed conflicts, largely within the less industrialised countries.[9]

Given the significance of this problem, it is not surprising that, in addition to the literature on the laws of armed conflict generally (cited in Note 1 above), a number of writers have comprehensively described those provisions of international humanitarian law which aim to regulate the treatment of civilians.[10] Since the focus of this research is largely on international treaty law and related instruments concerning *child* civilians in armed conflict, this Chapter, as background to the chapter on child civilians which follows, will do no more than touch briefly, in chronological order, on the most relevant provisions concerning civilians generally.

3.1.1 The Early Instruments: Pre-World War II

Although there were pertinent initiatives prior to 1868,[11] the key provisions to be considered here start with the 1868 St Petersburg Declaration Renouncing the Use, in Time of War, of Explosive Projectiles under 400 Grammes Weight (hereafter the 1868 St Petersburg Declaration).[12] This brief declaration, in attempting to limit the use of certain types of weapons 'in times of war, between civilised nations' expresses the concept that there are limits at which 'the necessities of war ought to yield to the requirements of humanity', and asserts that 'the only legitimate object which States should endeavour to accomplish during war is to weaken the military force of the enemy'. Thus it embodies what one writer describes as the two basic principles regarding the use of weapons in armed conflict: that they should

---

[9] See Ahlström ((1990), 5, who employs the criteria used by K. Lindgren (cited by Ahlström as *Wars in the World* (Stockholm, 1990)) to define a major armed conflict. In relation to the Iraqi study in Ch. 7, under these criteria both Iranian and Iraqi Kurdish areas were involved in such conflicts even in 1988–9: *ibid.* 59. For information on current conflicts in 1993, see, e.g., C. McCrystal, 'The World At War', *Independent on Sunday*, 14 Mar. 1993, and H. Pick, 'Death and Suffering Behind the Curtain of Indifference', *Guardian*, 31 Dec. 1993.

[10] See in particular Van Dongen (1991), which summarises and provides a historical analysis of the law regulating the treatment of civilians in armed conflict. Also most relevant is Gardam (1993), which contains a comprehensive examination of the principle of non-combatant immunity. See also, e.g., Roberts (1990), and relevant sections in De Lupis (1987); Schindler and Toman (1988); Oppenheim (1952); McCoubrey (1990), and Pictet (1958).

[11] For a chronology of relevant developments prior to the St Petersburg Declaration, including the 'Leiber Code' (F. Leiber, 'Instruments for the Government of Armies of the United States in the Field', General Orders No 100, 1863) see, e.g., Van Dongen (1991), 11–21 and Gardam (1993), 12–17.

[12] 1868 St Petersburg Declaration. 18 Martens NRG, 1ère sér. (1860–73), 474–5; 1 *AJIL* Supp. 95–6 (Eng.) (1907).

not cause unnecessary suffering to combatants and that they should not be used when they indiscriminately affect both combatants and non-combatants.[13]

The 1907 Hague Convention IV Respecting the Laws and Customs of War on Land (hereafter the 1907 Hague Convention IV)[14] is also significant in the context of civilian protection. The well-known 'Martens Clause' originated in this Convention. This clause emphasises that, in cases where no express treaty provision is made, both civilians and combatants 'remain under the protection and the rule of the principles of the law of nations, as they result from the usages established among civilized peoples; of the laws of humanity; and dictates of the public conscience'.[15]

The regulations annexed to 1907 Hague Convention IV contain a number of provisions concerning civilian protection, including the fundamental principle in Article 22 that '[t]he right of belligerents to adopt means of injuring the enemy is not unlimited.' This treaty makes no direct reference to children as a category separate from adult civilians, but Article 46 calls for '[f]amily honour and rights, [and] the lives of persons' to be respected. Article 25, although very limited in its scope, prohibits attack on or bombardment of undefended localities. This indicates that, at an early stage in the development of international treaty law regarding armed conflict, the concept of zones for civilian protection already had some currency. This concept is pertinent to the subject of this research, as discussed in Chapters 4 and 8.

Also of some relevance here are the 1923 Hague Rules of Aerial Warfare (the 1923 Hague Draft Rules).[16] The authority of these rules is questionable, since they were never adopted in legally binding form. However, when drafted, they were considered largely to represent customary law, and they affirm the well-established prohibition on direct attacks against civilians.[17]

[13] See W. D. Fenrick, 'New Developments in the Law Concerning the Use of Conventional Weapons in Armed Conflict' 19 *The Canadian Yearbook of International Law* 231 (1981).

[14] 1907 Hague Convention IV. 3 Martens NRG, 3ème sér. (1862–1910), 461–503; UKTS 9 [1910], Cmnd. 5030.

[15] Thus this clause provides for the continued relevance of customary law when treaty law is not applicable. See Green (1993), 32. The 1994 Draft Declaration on the Rights of Children in Armed Conflict (Declaration of Amsterdam), discussed in sect. 4.4.2 below, affirms the continuing importance of the Martens Clause: Aldrich and van Baarda (1994), 133. The Martens Clause has been restated, in a modified form, in a number of subsequent treaties, including Art. 1(2) of 1977 GP I and the Preamble to 1977 GP II.

[16] 1923 Hague Draft Rules, UK Misc. 14 [1924], Cmnd. 2201; 17 *AJIL* (1923), Supp. 245–60.

[17] As expressed by one authority: '[t]he immunity of non-combatants from direct attack is one of the fundamental rules of the international law of war': Oppenheim (1952), 523. The emphasis here is on *direct* attack. See W. O'Brien, 'Biological/Chemical Warfare and the International Law of War', 51.1 *The Georgetown Law Journal* 39–42 (1962). See also L. Doswald-Beck, 'The Value of the 1977 Geneva Protocols for the Protection of Civilians', in Meyer (ed.) (1989), 152–158.

Of particular interest is Article 22, forbidding '[a]erial bombardment for the purpose of terrorizing the civilian population, of destroying or damaging private property not of military character, or of injuring non-combatants'.[18]

3.1.2 Post World War II: The 1949 GC IV and the 1977 GPs

The pivotal, and most widely known, of the international instruments enshrining principles for the humane treatment of civilians are the 1949 GC IV[19] and the two 1977 GPs.[20]

The 1949 GCs have been widely accepted by the international community. As at 3 October 1995, 186 states were party to these treaties.[21] The GPs have not been accepted to the same extent. By the same date, 140 states were party to 1977 GP 1 and 131 to 1977 GP II.[22] In any event, a number of measures concerning civilian protection in the 1949 GCs and the 1977 GPs arguably form part of customary law (see Chapter 5 below), and are therefore in principle binding on states, whether or not they are party to these treaties.

However, despite their wide ratification, and the customary nature of some of their provisions, many conflicts escape regulation under the terms of these treaties. One reason for this is that there can be a subjective element in defining whether a particular conflict falls into one of five categories:[23] traditional international armed conflicts; conflicts categorised as international armed conflicts by virtue of Article 1(4) of 1977 GP I, in which the dissident forces have made a declaration of intention to apply the 1949

---

[18] Although these rules contain other provisions regarding the treatment of civilians, the prohibition on bombing the civilian population for the 'mere purpose of terrorization' is described by one authority as their only provision which still carries much weight. See H. Lauterpacht, 'The Problem of the Revision of the Law of War' 29 *BYIL* 368 (1952). See also Gardam (1993), 20–25.

[19] The three other 1949 GCs concern: wounded and sick combatants on land (1949 GC I); wounded, sick, and shipwrecked combatants at sea (1949 GC II); and prisoners of war (1949 GC III). The GCs are linked by common Arts., including Art. 3 (Common Art. 3), discussed in sect. 3.1.2.2 below. One group of these Common Arts. primarily concerns the application of the 1949 GCs and the role of the Protecting Powers, and another deals with breaches of humanitarian law. For more information on the GCs generally, see the references cited in n. 1 above.

[20] For a more detailed discussion of provision for civilian protection in the 1977 GPs, see Doswald-Beck, in Meyer (ed.) (1989). For information regarding the drafting history of the 1977 GPs, see H. S. Levie (ed.), *Protection of War Victims: Protocol I to the 1949 Geneva Conventions* (New York, 1979–1981)), and H. S. Levie (ed.), *The Law of Non-International Armed Conflict: Protocol II to the 1949 Geneva Conventions* (Dordrecht, 1987).

[21] ICRC, 'Geneva Conventions of 12 August 1949 and Additional Protocols of 8 June 1977—Signatures, Ratifications, Accessions and Successions—Addendum' (Geneva, 3 Oct. 1995).

[22] *Ibid.*

[23] See discussion in H. A. Wilson, *International Law and the Use of Force by National Liberation Movements* (Oxford, 1988), 183.

GCs and the 1977 GPs;[24] non-international armed conflicts fulfilling the criteria set out in 1977 GP II (Article 1(1));[25] non-international armed conflicts subject only to Common Article 3; or internal disturbances falling below the level of an armed conflict.[26] The first four types of conflict are regulated to a greater or lesser extent under the 1949 GCs and the 1977 GPs. The final category, internal disturbances, falls outside the scope of those treaties and is governed primarily by national law and fundamental principles of international law.[27] There is currently no authority empowered to pronounce definitively on the categorisation of particular conflicts, and thereby to determine the applicable body of law.

States may on occasion use this subjective element to their advantage. For example, in the prelude to the 1991 Gulf War Iraq denied that its occupation of Kuwait amounted to an international armed conflict, on the grounds that it considered Kuwait to be a province of Iraq (see section 7.2.4.2).

An additional difficulty with the scope of this body of law is that, with certain exceptions, it applies only to government forces.[28] The forces of NGEs would therefore not generally be bound.

The problem of lacunae in this body of law has serious implications in relation to the legal protection of child civilians in armed conflict situations, as illustrated in the Iraqi study below. It is also an issue that has been addressed by a number of writers, especially in relation to the inadequate

---

[24] By Art. 1(4) of 1977 GP I, the category of international armed conflicts described in Common Art. 2 of the GCs is expanded to include those in which 'peoples are fighting against colonial domination and alien occupation and against racist regimes in the exercise of their right to self-determination'. By Art. 96(3) of 1977 GP I, the authority representing such 'peoples' can make a unilateral declaration undertaking to apply the 1949 GCs and the 1977 GPs.

[25] According to the criteria in Art. 1(1), the conflict must reach a level of intensity where, among other things, the armed opposition operates under responsible command, controls territory, and is capable of implementing the provisions of 1977 GP II.

[26] It is not necessary to describe further here the somewhat complex guidelines regarding the scope of these terms, as set out largely in these three treaties. For information on this, see the texts cited in n. 1 above. One author describes the distinction between categories of armed conflict as 'fundamental—though truly artificial': R. Abi-Saab, 'Humanitarian Law and Internal Conflicts: The Evolution of Legal Concern', in Delissen and Tanja (eds.) (1991), 209. Indeed, various writers have argued for the removal of these distinctions, and the application of one body of law to all armed conflict situations. See, e.g., Gardam (1993), 182.

[27] However, see discussion in sect. 3.1.2.2 below, regarding Common Art. 3, which some writers claim should apply in principle even to internal disturbances. In any event, non-derogable human rights law would apply in all five categories of conflict (sect. 2.1.1 above). See also R. Brett, *Discussion Paper on Ways of Improving the Implementation of Human Rights and Humanitarian Law* (Quaker UN Office, Geneva, Jan. 1994), 2.

[28] The exceptions, under which NGEs could be bound, include Common Art. 3 (which states, without further elaboration, that it applies to 'each Party to the conflict'), and, where applicable, the provision made in Arts. 1(4) and 96(3) of 1977 GP I, see n. 24 above.

regulation of internal disturbances.[29] Efforts in the international community are under way to draw up guidelines applicable to such disturbances.[30]

One means of circumventing these uncertainties is through the conclusion, in the course of an armed conflict, of special agreements between the belligerents.[31] These agreements regarding the conduct of the conflict can significantly improve and, in any event, may not detract from the protection offered to civilian populations, including children, under international humanitarian law.

Having touched on the scope of the 1949 GCs and the 1977 GPs, and some of their limitations, the main provisions regulating the treatment of civilians as set out in 1949 GC IV and 1977 GP I concerning international armed conflict will now be outlined below. Common Article 3 and 1977 GP II, both applicable to non-international armed conflicts, will then be looked at.

3.1.2.1 The Treatment of Civilians in International Armed Conflict: 1949 GC IV and 1977 GP I

1949 GC IV, finalised in the aftermath of World War II, was the first international treaty concerning the laws of armed conflict that exclusively addressed the treatment of civilians. This Convention is not primarily designed to shield civilians from fighting as such, and focuses largely on regulating the treatment of those who are detained and/or who are in occupied territory.[32] The substantive Articles are subdivided into three parts, each dealing with separate aspects of this problem.[33]

At the core of the 1949 GCs lies the precept that protected persons (in this case civilians, as defined in Article 4 of 1949 GC IV) are to be respected

---

[29] See, *inter alia*, Hampson, in Meyer (ed.) (1989), 67; Goodwin-Gill and Cohn (1994), 56–69, and T. Meron, 'On the Inadequate Reach of Human Rights Law and the Need for A New Instrument', 77 *AJIL* 589 (1983).

[30] See, e.g., Institute for Human Rights, Åbo Akademi University, *Declaration of Minimum Humanitarian Standards* (Turku/Åbo, 1991). This document has been endorsed by the UN Sub-Commission on the Prevention of Discrimination and Protection of Minorities. See UN Doc. E/CN.4/1995/L.33 (1995). See also ICRC, 'New Draft Declaration of Minimum Humanitarian Standards', 282 *Int'l. Rev. of the Red Cross* 328 (May–June 1991); H. Gasser, 'A Measure of Humanity in Internal Disturbances and Tensions: Proposal for a Code of Conduct', 28 *Int'l Rev. of the Red Cross* 38–58 (1988), and T. Meron, 'Towards a Humanitarian Declaration on Internal Strife', 78 *AJIL* 859 (1984).

[31] The 1949 GCs make provision for such agreements, e.g., in Art. 7 of 1949 GC 1V, and in Common Art. 3. This concept is referred to further in n. 29, Ch. 8 below.

[32] However, Pt. II of 1949 GC IV applies more generally to the whole civilian population of the countries in conflict (see Art. 13). Van Dongen (1991), 122, observes that this Convention aims primarily to protect civilians against arbitrary action by the enemy, rather than against the dangers of military operations themselves. See also Kalshoven (1987), 42, and Gardam (1993), 25.

[33] Pt. I sets out 'General Provisions'; Pt. II deals with 'General Protection of Populations Against Certain Consequences of War', and Pt. III concerns the 'Status and Treatment of Protected Persons'.

and protected in all circumstances, and treated humanely.[34] States Parties must, under Article 1, undertake to 'respect and ensure respect for' the provisions of these Conventions, clearly including the duty to safeguard civilians.

The key Article in 1949 GC IV concerning the treatment of civilians is Article 27. This expresses the fundamental principle of respect, protection, and humane treatment for the protected persons.[35] Article 27 defines this principle widely, to include, *inter alia*, respect for 'their persons, their honour, their family rights' and protection from acts or threats of violence, insults, and public curiosity. It specifically prohibits 'any attack on the honour' of women, such as rape or enforced prostitution, thereby acknowledging the particular danger faced by women, including young girls, in this regard.

Under Section I, Part III of 1949 GC IV, Article 27 applies to civilians in the territories of parties to the conflict and to those in occupied territories. This Article is described by one authority as the '*leitmotiv* of the four Geneva Conventions', and 'the basis on which the Convention (IV) rests'.[36]

In addition to the guiding principles in Article 27, 1949 GC IV goes on, *inter alia*, more explicitly to prohibit the maltreatment of civilians, including their 'physical or moral coercion' (Article 31); any measures which could cause 'the physical suffering or extermination of protected persons in their hands' (Article 32), and collective penalties, intimidation, and reprisals against civilians (Article 33). It establishes rules for the benefit of civilians in occupied territories, including, among others, that the Occupying Power must ensure provision of food and medical supplies (Article 55).[37]

In a similar vein, 1977 GP I, the other treaty under consideration here which applies to situations of international armed conflict, contains a number of provisions expanding on the civilian protection measures in 1949 GC IV.[38] Unlike 1949 GC IV, this treaty contains various measures designed to safeguard civilians who happen to be in the theatre of military operations.

Included among its 'Basic Rules' is the familiar admonition that the 'right of Parties to the conflict to choose methods or means of warfare is not unlimited', and the prohibition on weapons that cause unnecessary suffering (Article 35(1) and (2)).

[34] See, e.g., Kalshoven (1987), 42.

[35] Some writers note that Art. 27 does not specifically refer to the right to life, but that this must be implied: Van Dongen (1991), 134, and Green (1993), 224–5.

[36] Pictet (1958), 201.

[37] For a discussion of the rules regarding the general rights and duties of Occupying Powers, see Green (1993), 246–57.

[38] Regarding the principle of non-combatant immunity generally in 1977 GP I, see Gardam (1993), 109–123.

The relevant substantive provisions in 1977 GP I are dealt with in Part IV, concerning the civilian population, under three main headings. First, Section I concerns the protection of civilians (broadly defined in Article 50) against the effect of hostilities. Here, the key Article 48 states that 'the Parties to the conflict shall at all times distinguish between the civilian population and combatants and between civilian objects and military objectives and accordingly shall direct their operations only against military objectives'.[39]

In this context, 1977 GP I sets out, in Article 51, various specific rules for the protection of the civilian population against dangers arising from military operations, including a prohibition on direct attacks on civilians and the civilian population (Article 51(2)).[40] Of central importance here is Article 51(5)(b) which articulates the proportionality principle in prohibiting attacks, even on military objectives, which might be expected to cause incidental harm to civilians that 'would be excessive in relation to the concrete and direct military advantage anticipated'.

Section I of Part IV also prohibits starvation of civilians as a method of warfare (Article 54(1)). Further, it provides for the establishment of two kinds of zones for the purpose of sheltering civilians. These zones, discussed below (section 4.2.1.2, in relation to Articles 14 and 15 of 1949 GC IV), are non-defended localities (Article 59) and demilitarised zones (Article 60).

Section II then sets out measures for relief of the civilian population. These include an obligation that, in occupied territory, an Occupying Power must ensure the provision to the civilian population of certain necessities such as bedding and shelter (Article 69). These necessities are additional to the essential supplies, such as food and medicine, specified in 1949 GC IV.[41] Further, this section allows for relief actions in the event that the obligation to supply necessities is not met (Article 70).

Finally, Section III in Part IV stipulates conditions for the treatment of persons in the power of a party to the conflict. The central provisions in this section are the 'Fundamental Guarantees' in Article 75, which articulate minimum standards for humane treatment (including a prohibition on, *inter alia*, violence to life) and measures regarding, for example, fair trial and internment. These guarantees apply to civilians who have fallen into enemy hands and who do not benefit from other provisions offering more

---

[39] Military objectives are lawful objects of attack, defined in 1977 GP I as 'those objects which . . . make an effective contribution to military action and whose total or partial destruction, capture or neutralisation, in the circumstances ruling at the time, offers a definite military advantage' (see 1977 GP I, Art. 52(2)).

[40] Art. 51 of this Protocol and Art. 13 of 1977 GP II are the first treaty provisions to enshrine the principle that civilians, unless or until they participate in hostilities, are entitled to protection against the dangers of military operations.

[41] See, e.g., Arts. 23 (sect. 4.2.1.4 below) and 55 (referred to above, in this section) of 1949 GC IV.

favourable treatment under the 1949 GCs or 1977 GP I. There is controversy regarding whether they apply to a state's own nationals (see further
section 4.2.1 below).

3.1.2.2 The Treatment of Civilians in Non-International Armed Conflict: Common Article 3 and 1977 GP II

As regards non-international armed conflicts, both Common Article 3 and
1977 GP II, like 1949 GC IV and 1977 GP I above, set out measures
providing for the protection of civilians.

Common Article 3 calls for humane treatment of 'persons taking
no active part in the hostilities', where the conflict takes place in the territory of one State Party. It prohibits 'at any time and in any place
whatsoever . . . a) violence to life and person . . . b) taking of hostages . . . c)
outrages upon personal dignity . . . d) the passing of sentences and the
carrying out of executions without previous judgment pronounced by a
regularly constituted court'.[42]

Article 3 applies in 'armed conflict not of an international character'
which, as indicated in section 3.1.2 above, is a term open to subjective
interpretation. The protection offered by Common Article 3 may therefore
be forfeited if, for example, a State Party regards a particular conflict in its
territory as an internal disturbance which falls below the level at which it
could be classified as an 'armed conflict'.[43]

Indeed, the government delegates involved in finalising the GCs at the
1949 Diplomatic Conference attempted to define more clearly the meaning
of the phrase 'armed conflict not of an international character', but consensus was not reached, and ultimately this phrase remained undefined.[44]

In any event, some writers support a wide application of Article 3, possibly extending both to internal disturbances and, at the other end of the
spectrum, to situations of international armed conflict.[45] This argument has

[42] Art. 3 has been described as containing minimum standards 'that no respectable government could disregard for any length of time without losing its aureole of respectability':
Kalshoven (1987), 60. See also Green (1993), 328.

[43] The reluctance of governments to agree that an internal disturbance has reached the level
of an 'armed conflict' stems largely from their unwillingness to grant additional legal protection to their opponents. See, e.g., Roberts and Guelff (eds.) (1989), 447.

[44] Pictet (ed.) (1958), 35. See also Van Dongen (1991), 124, and discussion in G. I. A. D.
Draper, 'Humanitarian Law and International Armed Conflicts', 13 *Georgia Journal of International and Comparative Law* 263–72 (1983).

[45] See in particular Pictet (1958), 36 and 38. See also Y. Khushalani, *The Dignity and
Honour of Women as Basic and Fundamental Human Rights* (The Hague, 1982), 41, and
Hampson, in Meyer (ed.) (1989), 67. The latter argues for a wide application of Art. 3 'on
humanitarian grounds if no other'. Indeed, the International Criminal Tribunal for the former
Yugoslavia has stated, as regards Common Art. 3, that it applies to international and non-
international armed conflicts, as 'the character of the conflict is irrelevant'. See *International
Criminal Tribunal for the Former Yugoslavia: Decision in Prosecutor v. Duško Tadić* 35 ILM
64 (1996).

some merit, given the customary status of most, if not all, of the standards outlined in Article 3 (see section 5.2.3).

Turning now to a consideration of 1977 GP II, this treaty offers more stringent measures of protection for civilians than does Common Article 3, but applies to potentially fewer situations.[46] This is because 1977 GP II contains a more exacting set of requirements which must be met before it can apply, and it therefore comes into play in particularly high intensity non-international armed conflicts (see section 3.1.2 above).[47] At the time of writing, it had apparently only been applied twice: in El Salvador and in the Philippines.[48]

Provisions in Part II of this Protocol, under the heading of 'Humane Treatment', reaffirm the general principle that '[a]ll persons who do not take a direct part or who have ceased to take part in hostilities . . . are entitled to respect for their person, honour and convictions and religious practices. They shall in all circumstances be treated humanely, without any adverse distinction' (Article 4(1)).[49] In addition, 1977 GP II sets out further safeguards for those who are 'deprived of their liberty for reasons related to the armed conflict', such as interned civilians. These include measures concerning the health and safety of such persons, as well as, for example, entitlements to practise their religion (Article 5).

Part IV of 1977 GP II, dealing specifically with the civilian population, provides, *inter alia*, that civilians, unless and until they participate directly in hostilities, 'shall enjoy general protection against the dangers arising from military operations' (see Article 13(1) and (3)).[50] Attacks on civilians, and actual or threatened violence in order to terrorise them, are forbidden (Article 13(2)), as is the starvation of civilians (Article 14).[51]

Concerning the relationship between Common Article 3 and 1977 GP II, one writer argues that:

Nothing in Common Article 3 requires that the dissident armed forces satisfy organisational requirements or hold territory. Nor is there any minimum threshold of violence to trigger its application. It would appear that in some situations both

---

[46] For a more detailed discussion of non-combatant immunity as set out in 1977 GP II, see Gardam (1993), 124–31.

[47] Meron argues that it would have been preferable for Protocol II to apply a lower threshold of applicability, as under Common Art. 3. Meron (1983), 599.

[48] R. Brett, *Recruitment of Children: The International Legal Standards and How They Could be Improved* (Quaker UN Office, Geneva, 1994), 3.

[49] Art. 4 as a whole is entitled '[f]undamental guarantees', and, in Art. 4(2), lists prohibitions on, *inter alia*: 'a) violence to life, health and physical or mental well-being . . . ; b) collective punishments; c) taking of hostages; d) acts of terrorism; e) outrages upon personal dignity'.

[50] This corresponds, in abbreviated form, to Art. 51 of 1977 GP I (sect. 3.1.2.1 above).

[51] See also Arts. 17 (placing restrictions on the forced movement of civilians) and 18 (regarding the provision of relief).

Article 3 and Protocol II will be applicable whereas in others, if the conditions of Protocol II are not satisfied, Article 3 alone will be applicable as it applies to *all* armed conflicts not of an international character.[52]

In either case, civilians are accorded a measure of protection in non-international armed conflict, although the law here is less comprehensive and detailed than that pertaining to civilians in international armed conflict.

3.1.3 Other Instruments Applicable to Civilians Generally

Finally, as regards treaties which set out the laws of armed conflict in relation to civilians generally, there is the 1980 Convention on Prohibitions or Restrictions on the Use of Certain Conventional Weapons Which May be Deemed to be Excessively Injurious or to Have Indiscriminate Effects (hereafter 1980 Inhumane Weapons Convention).[53] This is unlike previous agreements on specific conventional weapons as it focuses to a large extent on civilian protection. Thus the Preamble reaffirms the principle of the protection of civilians from the effects of hostilities, and this principle is explicitly incorporated in a number of the substantive provisions.[54]

These provisions are contained in four annexed Protocols which aim to restrict the use of specific categories of weapons. Protocol 1 concerns fragments not detectable by X-rays; Protocol II concerns mines, booby traps, and other devices; Protocol III concerns incendiary weapons; and Protocol IV concerns blinding laser weapons. Protocol II particularly articulates measures for safeguarding child civilians, as discusssed in section 4.2.4 below.

The 1980 Inhumane Weapons Convention has been criticised on a number of grounds. These include its lack of verification procedures and inadequate enforcement mechanisms. An additional problem is the low level of state ratification of this Convention.[55] Two recent international conferences, one in 1995 and one in 1996, to review the 1980 Inhumane Weapons Convention, have failed significantly to strengthen it in another important respect, regarding the use of land-mines (see again section 4.2.4).

---

[52] Hampson, in Meyer (ed.) (1989), 67.

[53] 1980 Inhumane Weapons Convention. UN GA Doc. A/CONF. 95/15, 27 Oct. 1980, and Corr. 1, 2, 3, 4, and 5; 1342 UNTS 137 (1983).

[54] See, e.g., Art. 3(2) of Protocol II to this Convention, and Art. 2(1) of Protocol III, which prohibit the use of the specified weapons 'against the civilian population as such' or individual civilians.

[55] As at Jan. 1996, only 57 states had become party to it. See ICRC, *Convention on Prohibitions or Restrictions on the Use of Certain Weapons Which May be Deemed to be Excessively Injurious or to have Indiscriminate Effects* (Geneva, 12 Jan. 1996).

In addition to the 1980 Inhumane Weapons Convention, there are other international instruments, not summarised above, which set out guidelines concerning the treatment of civilians in armed conflict. These largely correspond to principles in the international humanitarian treaties already outlined, and are, for the sake of completeness, simply mentioned here. They include, for example, UN resolutions[56] such as UN General Assembly Resolution 2444 (XXIII), entitled 'Respect for Human Rights in Armed Conflict' (19 December 1968),[57] and UN General Assembly Resolution 2675 (XXV), 'Basic Principles for the Protection of Civilian Populations in Armed Conflicts' (9 December 1970).[58] The latter is one of a series of five 1970 UN General Assembly resolutions concerning humanitarian law generally.[59]

Other initiatives of interest in the context of civilian protection include the 1971 Zagreb Resolution of the Institute of International Law on Conditions of Application of Humanitarian Rules of Armed Conflict to Hostilities in which United Nations Forces May be Engaged (1971 Zagreb Resolution).[60] This confirms the duty of UN forces to apply the humanitarian rules of the law of armed conflict, including rules concerning the protection of civilians. Further, there are the 1978 Red Cross Fundamental Rules of International Humanitarian Law Applicable in Armed Conflicts (1978 Red Cross Fundamental Rules).[61] These rules summarise key principles of international humanitarian law, including: that the lives of civilians must be respected; that they must be treated humanely; and that they are to be distinguished from combatants and not attacked (see rules 1, 3, and 7).

---

[56] Reference is made here only to resolutions which exemplify those concerning civilians in armed conflict generally. Other UN resolutions, which incorporate sections regarding civilians, but which, for instance, deal more specifically with children, are included below in Ch. 4. For a chronological citation of UN resolutions on humanitarian law from 1962–1971 see Khushalani (1982), 92–100.

[57] UN GA Res. 2444(XXIII), UN GAOR 23rd Sess., Supp. No. 18. (A/7218) (1969), 50–1. This resolution was reaffirmed by UN GA Res. 2597(XXIV) (16 Dec. 1969). For discussion of these resolutions and related initiatives, see, e.g., Gardam (1993), 85–6 and 171.

[58] UN GA Res. 2675 (XXV), UN GAOR 25th Sess., Supp. No. 28 (A/8028) (1971), 76.

[59] The others, all dated 9 Dec. 1970, are UN GA Res. 2673(XXV); 2674(XXV); 2676(XXV); and 2677(XXV). During that period, the UN Secretary General also produced three reports on Respect for Human Rights in Armed Conflicts: UN Doc. A/7720 (1969); UN Doc. A/8052 (1970); and UN Doc. A/8370 (1971). This flurry of activity preceded the 1974–7 Diplomatic Conferences responsible for drafting the 1977 GPs (see further sect. 4.1. below).

[60] 1971 Zagreb Resolution. 54.II Annuaire de L'Institut de Droit International 465 (1971); 66 *AJIL* 465 (1972).

[61] 1978 Red Cross Fundamental Rules. ICRC and League of Red Cross Societies, *Fundamental Rules of International Humanitarian Law Applicable in Armed Conflicts* (Geneva, 1979).

3.2 TREATY LAW AND RELATED INSTRUMENTS REGARDING THE USE OF CHEMICAL WEAPONS

Finally, in the context of humanitarian law generally concerning civilian protection, this section will briefly consider provisions, pertinent to the Iraqi study (Chapter 7), regarding the use of chemical weapons. These provisions do not specifically refer to children, but they are outlined here to indicate the extent of the illegality of Iraq's use of chemical weapons against Kurdish civilians, including large numbers of children.

Chemical warfare is defined by one authority as 'the use of chemical agents as a means of injuring the enemy . . . in an armed conflict. Such agents are chemical substances, whether gaseous, liquid, or solid which might be employed because of their direct toxic effects on men, animals or plants'.[62]

Despite controversy regarding the precise legal status of a ban on the use of chemical weapons,[63] there has for many years been consensus that the first use of lethal chemical weapons is prohibited under international law.[64]

A number of international legal instruments, dating from the 1868 St Petersburg Declaration, contain principles pertinent to the prohibition on the use of chemical weapons.[65] These include the 1899 Hague Declaration II Concerning Asphyxiating Gases (1899 Hague Declaration II),[66] the regulations attached to 1907 Hague Convention IV,[67] and the 1923 Hague Rules of Aerial Warfare.[68]

---

[62] R. Bernhardt (ed.), *Encyclopedia of Public International Law. Vol. 3: Use of Force: War and Neutrality, Peace Treaties* (Amsterdam, 1982), 83. See also the more technical definition in Art. II(1)(a)(b)(c) of the 1993 Convention on the Prohibition of the Development, Production, Stockpiling and Use of Chemical Weapons and on their Destruction (the 1993 Chemical Weapons Convention). 32 ILM 800 (1993).

[63] See, e.g., O'Brien (1962), 55.

[64] See, among others, O'Brien (1962), 56; Roberts and Guelff (eds.) (1989), 139, and H. McCoubrey, 'The Regulation of Biological and Chemical Weapons', in H. Fox and M. Meyer (eds.), *Armed Conflict and the New Law: Vol. II—Effecting Compliance* (London, 1993), 123.

[65] As already mentioned in sect. 3.1.1 above, this Declaration articulated the concept of unnecessary suffering. This notion was preceded by early prohibitions on the use of poison and poisoned weapons. See, e.g., Roberts and Guelff (eds.) (1989), 29; O'Brien (1962), 21, and McCoubrey, in Fox and Meyer (eds.) (1993), 124.

[66] 1899 Hague Declaration II. 26 Martens NRG, 2ème sér (1899), 998–1002; UKTS 32 [1907], Cmnd. 3751. This prohibits 'the use of projectiles the sole object of which is the diffusion of asphyxiating or deleterious gases.' Thus it is limited in applying to *projectiles* whose *sole* object is the diffusion of certain gases.

[67] See the general limitation in Art. 22 (sect. 3.1.1 above) regarding the means of warfare. More specifically, see Art. 23(a) prohibiting the use of 'poison or poisoned weapons' and Art. 23(e) forbidding the use of 'arms, projectiles, or material calculated to cause unnecessary suffering'. See also O'Brien (1962), 21.

[68] Although of questionable authority, these rules articulate principles, e.g., in Art. 22, which are arguably relevant as regards the prohibition on the use of chemical weapons, particularly when these are directed against the civilian population by means of aerial bombardment (as in the Iraqi conflicts, Ch. 7).

The pivotal 1949 GCs and the 1977 GPs do not make specific reference to chemical weapons.[69] Nonetheless, Article 3 of the 1949 GCs may be interpreted as limiting the use of such weapons against non-combatants primarily in non-international armed conflict. As already discussed (section 3.1.2.2 above), Article 3 lists as one of the prohibited acts in relation to non-combatants: 'violence to life and person'. Such violence would almost inevitably result from a chemical weapon attack. Article 4(2)(a) of 1977 GP II (again, in section 3.1.2.2) can be interpreted in a similar vein.[70]

Indeed, it is arguable that, even in internal disturbances, the use of chemical weapons against the civilian population would be prohibited under the terms of the (customary) principles enunciated in Common Article 3, and, in any event, under human rights law.[71]

In relation to international armed conflicts, both 1949 GC IV and 1977 GP I contain a number of general provisions which aim to protect the civilian population by limiting the conduct of armed conflict in terms that would arguably preclude resort to chemical weapons (see section 3.1.2.1 above).[72] Further, 1977 GP I prohibits the use of methods of warfare which 'cause superfluous injury or unnecessary suffering' (Article 35(2)), and it emphasises that civilians must not be the object of 'indiscriminate attacks'.[73]

However, prior to the adoption of the 1993 Chemical Weapon Convention, the most significant treaty as regards the prohibition on the use of chemical weapons was arguably the 1925 Geneva Protocol for the Prohibition of the Use in War of Asphyxiating, Poisonous, or Other Gases, and of Bacteriological Methods of Warfare (the 1925 Geneva Protocol).[74] This Protocol is quite widely ratified, although many states have done so on a

---

[69] 1977 GP I was apparently 'negotiated on the basis that it did not intend to broach problems relating to atomic, bacteriological and chemical warfare': Fenrick (1981), 233.

[70] See also the *Tadić* case, in which the Yugoslav Tribunal stated, in relation to the use of chemical weapons against the Iraqi Kurds, that there was clearly a consensus in the international community that such use was prohibited in internal armed conflicts: 35 ILM 69 (1996).

[71] See, e.g., UN. Doc. E/CN.4/Sub.2/1990/37, 'Human Rights and Scientific and Technological Developments, Respect for the Right to Life: Elimination of Chemical Weapons', 12. This states that '[i]n situations of internal conflicts . . . basic and universally accepted human rights, such as the right to life, to physical integrity and to freedom from inhuman treatment could be invoked to justify prohibition on the use of chemical weapons.' This document also refers, *inter alia*, to children's particular vulnerability to chemical weapons (*ibid.* 10).

[72] See, e.g., Art. 27 of 1949 GC IV, regarding the humane treatment of protected persons, and, in 1977 GP I, Art. 35(1), which reiterates the basic rule limiting the right of the parties to the conflict to choose methods or means of warfare.

[73] This Protocol defines indiscriminate attacks, *inter alia*, as those which, under Art. 51(5)(b), breach the proportionality principle. A chemical weapon attack involving civilians is certainly likely to do so. See also Art. 51(4)(b) and (c).

[74] The 1925 Geneva Protocol. XCIV LNTS (1929), 65–74; 26 Martens NRG, 3ème sér. (1932–3), 643–50.

'first use' basis only.[75] Given its wide ratification, one authority states 'the majority view is that . . . the prohibitions embodied in the Protocol should be viewed as having become a part of customary international law'.[76] However, controversy concerning interpretation of the 1925 Protocol, and the character of the reservations made, has cast doubt on its customary law status.[77]

The 1925 Protocol is succinct, declaring, *inter alia*, that the 'use in war of asphyxiating, poisonous or other gases . . . has been justly condemned by the general opinion of the civilised world', and that the prohibition on the use of these gases shall bind 'alike the conscience and the practice of nations'. The parties to the Protocol must accept this prohibition and agree between themselves to observe it.

The final legal instrument to be mentioned in this brief overview of the law regarding chemical weapons is the 1993 Chemical Weapons Convention.[78] Although not in force at the time of writing, this is potentially of great importance in that its purpose is not only to limit the manufacture and possession of chemical weapons, but also to prohibit their use 'under any circumstances' (see Article 1(1)).[79]

States Parties to this Convention are obliged, *inter alia*, to destroy chemical weapon stocks (Article 1(2)), and to control the manufacture of chemicals in their territories (Article VI(2)), and this Convention provides for different levels of response to the breach of its provisions (Article XII). Chemical agents are listed in three Schedules according to their potential for legitimate use. The 1993 Chemical Weapons Convention also provides for compliance to be monitored by the International Organisation for the Prohibition of Chemical Weapons, whose powers include the ability to institute on-site challenge inspections at short notice (Article IX(8)–(25)).

[75] In relation to the Iraqi study in Ch. 7, it is of interest that the parties include Iraq, with a 'first use' reservation (Roberts and Guelff (eds.) (1989), 142). Such reservations mean that states will be bound by the terms of the Protocol only in relation to others so bound, and they will cease to respect it if it is breached by an adversary.

[76] *Ibid*. 138–9.

[77] Nonetheless, no doubts are expressed regarding the customary nature of the 'first use' prohibition. See, e.g., R. R. Baxter, and T. Buergenthal, 'Legal Aspects of the Geneva Protocol of 1925', 64 *AJIL* 853 (1970), and UN Doc. E/CN.4/Sub.2/1990/37, 12.

[78] For detailed commentary, see W. Krutsch and R. Trapp, *A Commentary on the Chemical Weapons Convention* (Dordrecht, 1994). The 1993 Chemical Weapon Convention was preceded by the 1972 Convention on the Prohibition of Development, Production, and Stockpiling of Bacteriological (Biological) and Toxin Weapons and on their Destruction: 1015 UNTS 164 (1976); XI.2 ILM 309 (1972). The 1972 treaty was originally intended to incorporate chemical weapons, but ultimately did not do so: Schindler and Toman (1988), 137.

[79] Earlier UN initiatives on restricting the use of chemical weapons include, e.g., UN GA Res. 2603 A(XXIV) of 16 Dec. 1969, 'Question of Chemical and Bacteriological (Biological) Weapons'. For more recent initiatives, see, among others, UN GA Res. 43/74 of 7 Dec. 1988 and UN GA Res. 44/115 A of 15 Dec. 1989, both entitled 'Chemical and Bacteriological (Biological) Weapons', and UN Doc. A/44/561, 'Report of the Secretary-General on Chemical and Bacteriological (Biological) Weapons' (4 Oct. 1989).

The adoption of the 1993 Chemical Weapons Convention therefore seems to complete the proscription of the manufacture, possession, and use of chemical weapons. However, its impact in practice remains to be seen.[80]

3.3 SUMMARY OF PRINCIPLES CONCERNING CIVILIANS GENERALLY IN INTERNATIONAL HUMANITARIAN LAW

This overview indicates that there is a considerable body of existing international humanitarian law concerning the treatment of civilians, including children, in international and non-international armed conflicts, and that certain principles arguably apply even in internal disturbances. The protection of civilians appears as a fundamental precept of the relevant law, and one which has been restated in increasing detail in treaties and other legal instruments from the mid-1860s to the present day.

Accordingly, civilians are to be protected not only from direct attack, but also from indiscriminate attack, and, as far as possible, from the indirect effects of attack. In this context, at the very least the 'first use' of chemical weapons is also prohibited. Further, provision must be made for the physical and mental well-being of civilians, and they are to be treated humanely and protected from violations when in the hands of the enemy.

The applicable law incorporates negative obligations, or the duty of respect, as explicitly expressed, for example, in the pivotal Article 27 of 1949 GC IV. Other negative obligations in that Convention include, among others, prohibitions on the maltreatment of civilians (Article 31) and on measures which would cause their physical suffering (Article 32). The pertinent law also encompasses positive obligations, or obligations to assist and care for civilians. These include, for example, rules regarding the establishment of zones for civilian protection (as in Articles 59 and 60 of 1977 GP I), and for the provision of certain necessities (as in Articles 69 and 70 of 1977 GP I).

Inasmuch as armed conflict is to be accepted as a necessary evil, the thrust of these rules is that it is an evil from which both adult and child civilians should, whenever possible, be spared. In practice the reality does not begin to conform to this aspiration, as is clearly illustrated in the Iraqi study in Chapter 7.

---

[80] A comment also made by McCoubrey, in Fox and Meyer (eds.) (1993), 128.

4

Treaty Law of Armed Conflict and Related Instruments Specifically Regarding Child Civilians

The previous chapter outlined the main principles of international humanitarian law regarding civilians generally. This Chapter will now focus on provisions in this body of law regarding the subject matter at the heart of this research: the protection of child civilians in situations of armed conflict.

As one writer emphasises, '[t]here can be no doubt that in time of war children are in even greater need of protection and assistance than in peace-time'.[1]

This Chapter looks first, in some detail, at measures in international humanitarian treaty law which specifically concern child civilians. It considers those applicable to all child civilians in both international and in non-international armed conflicts, and also describes certain measures which, in international armed conflict, provide only for children in particular categories (such as those in occupied territories, or enemy aliens).

Chapters 3 and 4 together accordingly illustrate that children can be entitled to three levels of protection under international humanitarian law: first, as members of the civilian population generally; secondly, as children, owing to their particular vulnerability; and finally, as members of a specific category of child civilian (such as an enemy alien) if they qualify as such.

Following the discussion of pertinent treaty law, this Chapter briefly analyses such law in terms of whether it expresses the negative duty not to harm or the positive obligation to assist. It then concludes by considering certain non-treaty initiatives relating to international humanitarian law and the treatment of children.

4.1 BACKGROUND

As with civilians generally, the entitlement of children to protection in armed conflict has traditionally been honoured in many cultures, although

---

[1] Krill, in Freeman and Veerman (eds.) (1992), 347. See also Mann (1987), 48.

there have been exceptions.[2] One writer, for example, refers to a consensus among Islamic jurists that those 'who did not take part in fighting, such as women, children, monks . . . were excluded from molestation'.[3] Another writer confirms that 'Mohammad . . . forbade killing or molesting of, *inter alia*, women, infants and minors'.[4] Similarly, children were excused from participating in *jihad* (defined as 'a form of religious propaganda that can be carried on by persuasion or by the sword'[5]) until they were mature.[6]

In much of West Africa, too, 'fighting was subject to a genuine code of conduct. For instance, it was forbidden to kill women, children or old people'.[7] In countries such as Senegal, Ghana, Togo, and Upper Volta, 'as fighting was always outside the village, the combatants, in this way, protected the village and the children and old people, or they removed the children and old people to a safe place so that they would not be harmed during the fighting'.[8] According to this writer, the rules regulating the conduct of armed conflict in West Africa can be seen as 'nothing more than the expression of the same humanitarian principles which inspired the authors of the Geneva Conventions'.[9] However, another writer points out that there were no universal humanitarian laws applying to the many different peoples of Africa, and the conduct of armed conflict therefore varied considerably.[10]

Further, in India there is some evidence of respect for the principle that children should be shielded from the effects of armed conflict. Thus, one writer confirms that Hindu traditions customarily prohibited the killing of 'youngsters' and infants.[11] Moreover, to the extent that it can be viewed as an expression of Indian customary practice, the epic Mahabharata poem states: 'You shall kill neither the aged nor the young nor yet the women'.[12]

---

[2] On exceptions, which are not discussed further here, see, e.g., Grotius, 'De Jure Belli ac Pacis Libri Tres' (1625) (English trans. by F. Kelsey) in J. Scott, (ed.), *The Classics of International Law* (New York, 1964), Ch. IV, B. III, 648. Writing in the 17th century, Grotius maintained that in a 'public war' every enemy, including women and children, could be subject to violence and was spared only as an act of mercy.

[3] Khadduri, *War and Peace in the Law of Islam* (New York, 1979), 103–4.

[4] Elahi (Spring 1988), 274.

[5] Khadduri (1979), 56.

[6] *Ibid.* 84. See also Elahi (1988), 274. She specifies 15 as the age at which children could participate in *jihad*.

[7] Y. Diallo, *African Traditions and Humanitarian Law: Similarities and Differences* (Geneva, 1976), 16.

[8] *Ibid.* 9. See also E. M. Ressler, *Evacuation of Children from Conflict Areas* (Geneva, 1992), 15.

[9] Diallo (1976), 15–16.

[10] Bello (1980), 3. He states that '[s]ome tribes took pride in according respect and human rights to women, children and old persons: others were ready to kill everyone who might be considered a potential enemy': *ibid.* 28, and see also 54.

[11] See L. R. Penna, 'Traditional Asian Approaches: An Indian View' 9 *Australian Year Book of International Law* 189–90 (1985).

[12] Quoted in ICRC, 'The ICRC and Disarmament' 18 *Int'l. Rev. of the Red Cross* 91 (Mar.–Apr. 1978).

In the international context, an attempt was made in 1939 to incorporate into international law a Convention for the Protection of Children in the Event of International Conflict or Civil War. A draft was prepared by the ICRC and the International Union for Child Welfare, but the outbreak of World War II put an end to this work. After the war the principles in the draft Convention were incorporated into 1949 GC IV, and the separate Convention, providing specifically for children in armed conflict, was abandoned.[13]

Prior to the 1949 GCs, therefore, international humanitarian law made no specific mention of child civilians as a particularly vulnerable group requiring special consideration. 1949 GC IV remedies this omission and contains numerous provisions dealing with children, as does 1977 GP I and, to a lesser extent, 1977 GP II.

Indeed, the 1974-7 Geneva Diplomatic Conferences, which finalised the drafting of the 1977 GPs, were convened largely as a result of rising international concern at flaws in certain aspects of 1949 GC IV.[14] Such flaws included inadequacies in relation to the legal protection of children and other vulnerable civilians in armed conflict. These inadequacies were becoming increasingly evident, partly due to changes in the nature and conduct of armed conflicts in the period after World War II, as described in section 3.1 above.

According to UNICEF, the major armed conflicts since World War II have caused an estimated 20 million deaths.[15] Of these, the majority have been women and children[16] (and see sections 1.1 and 3.1 above). Further, the suffering of children and other vulnerable civilians in situations of armed conflict has largely been accepted as an inevitable side-effect of these. As one writer comments, on the rules governing military activity: 'These rules assume the silence and suffering of women and children and this suffering has been endless. One looks in vain at the numerous war

[13] See Pictet (1958), 186. See also Singer (1986), 8; van Bueren (1995), 329 and Hingorani in Kalshoven (ed.) (1989), 135.

[14] For a summary of some of the discussions, during the 1974-7 Geneva Diplomatic Conferences, on children in armed conflict, see Mann (1987), 38–50. Regarding these conferences more generally, see, e.g., Gardam (1993), 84–6, and F. Kalshoven, 'Reaffirmation and Development of International Humanitarian Law Applicable in Armed Conflicts: The Diplomatic Conference, Geneva 1974–77. Part I: Combatants and Civilians' 8 *Netherlands Yearbook of International Law* 107 (1977).

[15] UNICEF statistics cited in Ressler, Tortorici, and Marcelino (1993), 21. These authors refer to a UNICEF estimate of 150 'large armed conflicts' since World War II, (*ibid.*), but see Ahlström (sect. 3.1) who estimates 105 major armed conflicts in this period.

[16] Ressler, Tortorici, and Marcelino (1993), 21. One writer points out that, statistically, far fewer children are killed in armed conflict than are killed by 'structural violence', defined as malnutrition and disease largely attributable to the social structures in which they live: Kent (1990), 11–14. This does not, of course, diminish the significance of the deaths of children in armed conflict, nor of efforts to limit such deaths.

memorials listing the military dead of these conflicts, for any recognition of the thousands of women and children victims of these battles.'[17] This point cannot be over-emphasised.

In the recent conflict in the former Yugoslavia, for example, it was estimated that, by the end of 1993, 281,000 children were living in besieged enclaves and war zones; 620,000 were refugees or displaced; over 15,000 children had been killed; and over 35,000 wounded in the fighting.[18] Similarly, estimates concerning the 1994 conflict in Rwanda indicated that by the end of that year over one-third of the 800,000 people killed were children, and that 120,000 children were separated from their families by the crisis.[19] Such statistics are a hopelessly inadequate tool to assist in comprehending the suffering of children in these conflicts, (and their accuracy may be dubious (see Note 8, Chapter 3)), but they give some idea of its scale.

As regards child civilians, the most pertinent provisions of 1949 GC IV and the 1977 GPs, and certain related developments in international law, will now be examined below.

4.2 RELEVANT TREATY PROVISIONS REGARDING THE PROTECTION OF CHILD CIVILIANS

The pertinent measures in international humanitarian treaty law are considered here in five categories. First, there are those that deal with the general protection of all child civilians in international armed conflict, under 1949 GC IV and 1977 GP I. Secondly, there are those which offer additional protection to specific categories of child civilians, again in international armed conflict, namely: children in occupied territory as residents or internees; children who are orphaned or separated from their parents; non-repatriated aliens; and the sick and wounded. The third section looks at 1977 GP II provisions applicable to child civilians in noninternational armed conflict, while the fourth looks briefly at Protocol II of the 1980 Inhumane Weapons Convention. Article 38 of the 1989 CRC is then discussed.

The provisions to be considered here are numerous. In relation to 1949 GC IV and the 1977 GPs, the former contains seventeen substantive Articles providing specifically for the protection of children in armed conflict,[20]

[17] J. Gardam, 'The Law of Armed Conflict: A Feminist Perspective', in Mahoney and Mahoney (eds.) (1993), 420.
[18] UK Committee for UNICEF, 'Former Yugoslavia', *News In Brief* 3 (Dec. 1993).
[19] R. Block, 'Saving Rwanda's Lost Children', *Independent on Sunday*, 18 Dec. 1994.
[20] These are found in Pt. II (General Protection of Populations Against Certain Consequences of War) Arts. 14, 17, 23, 24, 25, and 26; and in Pt. III (Status and Treatment of Protected Persons), Sect. II (Aliens in the Territory of a Party to the Conflict), Art. 38, and Sect. III (Occupied Territories), Arts. 49, 50, 51, 68, 76, 81, 82, 89, 94, and 132.

while 1977 GP I contains seven such Articles,[21] and 1977 GP II only two.[22] The discussion here will not generally include provisions which only, for example, refer to 'expectant mothers', or which forbid discrimination on the grounds, among others, of age.[23]

Surprisingly, the underlying principle of children's entitlement to special treatment is not expressly stated anywhere in 1949 GC IV, despite the fact that this Convention contains many Articles providing for the special treatment of child civilians in particular circumstances. Article 16, by which 1949 GC IV explicitly grants 'particular protection and respect' to civilians who are wounded and sick, infirm, and expectant mothers, does not specifically include children. Instead, international humanitarian treaty law first expresses the broad principle of children's entitlement to special treatment, in international armed conflicts, in Article 77(1) of 1977 GP I. In relation to non-international armed conflicts this principle is articulated, although less strongly, in Article 4(3) of 1977 GP II.[24]

Indeed, in relation to children, the 1977 GPs were apparently intended to address three lacunae in the 1949 GCs. One of these was precisely that 'as a particularly vulnerable category of person they had a right to special protection, but this principle was not explicitly stated in any article'.[25]

Concerning terminology, neither 1949 GC 1V nor the 1977 GPs generally define childhood. Rather, they adopt six different age categories for specifying particular entitlements of children in armed conflict. As will be seen, these categories are: new born babies, children under 7 years of age, those under 12 years of age, those under 15, those between 15 and 18, and those under 18.

---

[21] These are found in Pt. II (Wounded, Sick and Shipwrecked), Art. 8(a); and in Pt. IV (Civilian Population), Sect. II (Relief in Favour of the Civilian Population), Art. 70, and Sect. III (Treatment of Persons in the Power of a Party to the Conflict), Ch. I (Field of Application and Protection of Persons and Objects), Arts. 74 and 75(5), and Ch. II (Measures in Favour of Women and Children), Arts. 76, 77, and 78.

[22] These are found in Pt. II (Humane Treatment), Arts. 4(3) and 6(4).

[23] For examples of Arts. referring to age as one criterion, see, in 1949 GC IV, Art. 119 (age to be taken into account in the punishment of internees) and Art. 85 (age to be a consideration in the provision of sleeping quarters for internees).

[24] On this point, see, e.g., Plattner (1984), 3.

[25] Singer (1986), 11. The other two lacunae were (a) the use of children in military operations, and (b) the considerations that should be taken into account as to 'their immaturity if they committed offences during conflict': *ibid*. As already mentioned in sect. 1.3 above, the two 1977 GPs therefore also, for the first time in international humanitarian law, prohibit the use of child soldiers under the age of 15. Although child soldiers are not generally discussed in this book, it should be noted that if children under 15 are, despite the prohibition, actively involved in hostilities, they are entitled to special protection as children if they 'fall into the power of an adverse party'. (Art. 77(2) and (3) of 1977 GP 1, and Art. 4(3)(c) and (d) of 1977 GP II).

4.2.1 Provisions Concerning the Treatment of All Child Civilians in International Armed Conflict: 1949 GC IV and 1977 GP I

To begin with provisions regarding the treatment of child civilians in international armed conflict generally, the measures cited below from 1949 GC IV are found in Part II, concerning the protection of civilians from certain of the consequences of armed conflict. The provisions cited from 1977 GP I are set out in its Part IV, dealing with the civilian population, and particularly in Section III of Part IV, concerning the treatment of civilians 'in the power of a party to the conflict'.[26] There is controversy as to the exact scope of Section III, especially about whether it applies to the nationals of a party to the conflict.[27] The ICRC Commentary on the 1977 GPs maintains that 'it must be conceded that the provisions of this Section do so apply, except where the article itself indicates otherwise'.[28]

In the discussion below, the relevant Articles are loosely grouped according to subject matter. However, the categories do inevitably overlap to some extent,[29] and these provisions have been differently categorised by other writers.[30]

4.2.1.1 The Special Treatment of Children

The pivotal Article 77(1) (referred to in section 4.2 above) is found in Section III, Part IV, of 1977 GP I. Article 77(1) applies widely to all children in the territories of the parties to the conflict,[31] and articulates the fundamental precept that children 'shall be the object of special respect and shall be protected against any form of indecent assault'. The prohibition on indecent assault incorporates the rape and other sexual abuse of children, which, as indicated in section 2.2.2 above, so frequently affects girls, particularly, in situations of armed conflict (as was seen in the recent conflicts in the former Yugoslavia and in Rwanda).

Article 77(1) also specifies that the parties must provide children 'with the care and aid they require, whether because of their age or for any other

---

[26] According to Art. 72 of Sect. III, the provisions of Sect. III are additional to the humanitarian provisions of 1949 GC IV, 'as well as to other applicable rules of international law relating to the protection of fundamental human rights during international armed conflicts'.

[27] On this point, see also sect. 3.1.2.1 above.

[28] ICRC (1987), 837.

[29] E.g., certain principles relating to the importance of the family are included here in the category of measures concerning evacuation, as in Art. 78(1) of 1977 GP I (the necessity for obtaining parental consent).

[30] See Krill, in Freeman and Veerman (eds.) (1992), 348–350, and Plattner (1983), 199–211.

[31] One writer points out that the phrase 'parties to the conflict' used in Art. 77(1) indicates that this provision 'may apply to non-State entities': Cohn (1991).

reason'. This important injunction was intended to prevent injury to children and to provide for their normal development as far as is possible in armed conflict situations.[32]

Article 77 is significant in extending, to *all* children in the power of parties to the conflict, the general principle of their entitlement to special treatment. Previously some provisions under 1949 GC IV only applied to children who fell within a particular category of protected person, such as children in occupied territory.

The ICRC Commentary on this Article observes that the word 'children' is not defined here, but asserts '[t]here is no doubt that all human beings under fifteen should, within the meaning of the Fourth Convention and this Protocol, be considered and treated as children'.[33] However, as already discussed in section 1.3 above, the age of 18 years should now arguably be accepted as the appropriate international standard.

4.2.1.2 Zones

Another significant concept, articulated in both 1949 GC IV and 1977 GP I, is that of zones for the protection of the civilian population, sometimes explicitly including child civilians (as discussed further in section 8.3.1 below).[34]

Indeed, the general provisions in 1949 GC IV concerning children start in Part II with Article 14, which allows for, but does not make obligatory, the establishment of hospital and safety zones and localities.[35] The purpose of these is to protect from the effects of armed conflict children under 15, expectant mothers, and mothers of children under 7, among others. These zones and localities may accommodate any civilian in the specified categories, regardless of whether they are, for example, enemy aliens. They can be established in peace time by parties to 1949 GC IV. Alternatively, in times of armed conflict the belligerents may conclude agreements with each other

---

[32] M. Bothe, K. Partsch, and W. Solf, *New Rules for Victims of Armed Conflicts* (The Hague, 1982), 476. These authors also point out that the phrase 'or for any other reason' was intended to incorporate children with physical or mental disabilities. ICRC (1987), 900.

[33] ICRC (1987), 899.

[34] As already mentioned in sect. 3.1.1, this concept appears in international law before the 1949 GCs, as in Art. 25 of the Regulations to 1907 Hague Convention IV. See also the 1938 Draft Convention for the Protection of Civilian Populations Against New Engines of War, adopted by the International Law Association (*Report of the Fortieth Conference: Amsterdam* (Suffolk, 1939)). This includes provision for safety zones for the protection of 4 categories of civilians, one of which is '[p]ersons under the age of 15 years'. See generally Arts. 10–21. For further information on zones see, e.g., Green (1993), 95–8.

[35] According to Pictet, the term 'locality' is used to describe a specific place of limited area, usually containing buildings. 'Zone' describes a relatively large area of land, which may contain one or two localities: Pictet (1958), 120. He emphasises that those entitled to shelter are 'persons who are taking no part in the hostilities and whose weakness makes them incapable of contributing to the war potential of their country: they thus appear to be particularly deserving of protection': *ibid.* 125.

to recognise such zones either in their own territory or in occupied areas.[36] They can call on the good offices of the ICRC or the Protecting Power for this purpose.[37]

One authority points out that although Article 14 has never been implemented, hospital and safety zones could prove particularly appropriate in the context of a 'guerilla', or non-international armed conflict, where it may be difficult to distinguish combatants and civilians.[38] Given that such zones are only open to certain fairly clearly identifiable categories of individuals unlikely to be combatants, the opposing party in such a conflict might be more willing to sanction their establishment.[39]

In addition to the measures in Article 14, Article 15 of 1949 GC IV provides for neutralised zones. These differ from hospital and safety zones in that they are open, among others, to all civilians not directly engaged in hostilities, rather than to any particular category of civilians. Thus no specific mention is made of child civilians, although they would clearly be entitled to shelter. Neutralised zones are, on the initiative of a party to the conflict, and by mutual agreement set up in the combat arena and are established during hostilities. There have been a number of conflicts in which zones of this nature were set up, although Article 15 was not necessarily invoked.[40]

In addition to the measures in Articles 14 and 15 of 1949 GC IV, 1977 GP I establishes two further categories of protected areas: non-defended

---

[36] 1949 GC IV contains, in Annex 1, a model 'Draft Agreement Relating to Hospital and Safety Zones and Localities'. This specifies, e.g., the categories of civilians entitled to shelter (Art. 1), the conditions for the existence of the zones (Art. 4), and the obligations of those in control (Art. 5).

[37] The Protecting Power is 'a state which is mandated by one of the parties to an armed conflict to safeguard its interests in humanitarian matters *vis-à-vis* the other party to the same conflict' (as defined in H. Gasser, 'Ensuring Respect for the Geneva Conventions and Protocols: The Role of Third States and the UN', in Fox and Meyer (eds.) (1993), 26). This role can be assumed by the ICRC or a similar organisation when no Protecting Power has been accepted or nominated: Green (1993), 234–5. For discussion of the concept and role of the Protecting Power generally, see, e.g., *ibid*. 234–41. See also Best (1994), 371, and A. Cassese, *International Law in a Divided World* (Oxford, 1986), 4.

[38] Y. Sandoz, 'Localitiés et Zones Sous Protection Spéciale', in Institut Henry-Dunant, *Quatre Études du Droit International Humanitaire* (Geneva, 1985), 46. Sandoz also points out that particular types of zones, such as these, should be preserved as a legal concept even if they have not been used in practice, since it is not possible to predict future conflicts and humanitarian needs: *ibid*. Apparently the ICRC did attempt, unsuccessfully, to establish safety zones in World War II: Van Dongen (1991), 89.

[39] Strictly speaking, the provisions of Art. 14 do, of course, apply only to international armed conflicts under 1949 GC IV. However, the concept can be extended, by analogy, to non-international armed conflicts.

[40] Sandoz cites examples of such zones, largely set up by the ICRC in response to particular events. All these zones were temporary, in the region of combat, and for the benefit of non-combatants in general. The concept of neutralised zones predated the 1949 GCs (e.g., those established in Madrid, Shanghai, and Jerusalem), while others were established after 1949 (as in Dacca, Nicosia, and Saigon): Sandoz (1985), 42.

localities (Article 59) and demilitarised zones (Article 60). Again, these do not specifically make provision for children, but clearly incorporate them. They are briefly described here since the concept of zones as a whole is particularly relevant as regards international law for the protection of child civilians.

The 1977 GP I zones can be distinguished from the zones specified in 1949 GC IV in that they aim to remove from the combat arena certain existing localities and all their inhabitants, rather than to create a refuge which will attract certain categories of people. The goal remains the same: the protection of those not actively involved in combat.[41] One authority suggests that respect for non-defended and demilitarised zones is arguably a precept of customary law.[42]

Non-defended localities must fulfil certain conditions. Such conditions include, for example, that all combatants must have been evacuated (Article 59(2)(a)), and that no acts of hostility shall be committed by those in the locality (Article 59(2)(c)). If, after negotiation between the belligerents, the localities are accepted as non-defended, they are, by their very nature, protected. The only question that can be contested is whether they fulfil the necessary conditions to qualify as non-defended.

Demilitarised zones, on the other hand, are similar to neutralised zones in that they are established for the safety of the civilian population as a whole, but here shelter is provided not only in an improvised manner and in the combat arena, but in an organised way and in designated places.[43] Again, certain conditions must be fulfilled.[44] These zones could previously have been used for military purposes, but one condition for their establishment is that 'any activity linked to the military effort must have ceased' (Article 60(3)(d)). Such zones are established by agreement, which can be concluded even in times of peace.

The establishment of any of these types of zones in an armed conflict clearly has considerable potential to ameliorate the suffering of the child civilians involved. But the under-use, in practice, of the relevant provisions indicates that these concepts are problematic. In establishing such zones questions have to be resolved, such as who is to be responsible for their control, and for ensuring, for example, that they do not shelter combatants and/or house weapons? Further, it is psychologically difficult to prepare, in times of peace, for the establishment of zones in a hypothetical period of armed conflict. In addition, the placement of a zone depends, particularly in a small country, on the character and place of a future attack, which may be

---

[41]   *Ibid.*, 41. For clarification of the differences between the various types of zones, see Bothe, Partsch and Solf (1982), 375–80.

[42]   Meron (1989), 64. See sect. 5.2.3 below.

[43]   Sandoz (1985), 42.

[44]   As with non-defended localities, these include a stipulation regarding the evacuation of combatants (Art. 60(3)(a)), and a prohibition on acts of hostility (Art. 60(3)(c)).

difficult to predict.[45] Another problem with such zones is that their establishment can obscure the duty of the belligerents to take further precautions
for the protection of civilian populations outside the zones (and see section
8.3.1).[46]

Also relevant to the concept of zones is the related practice of establishing humanitarian 'zones of peace', in which hostilities are temporarily
halted, or passage is permitted to areas in the combat arena, to facilitate the
provision of humanitarian relief.[47] Indeed, this concept was to some extent
implemented during the 1991 Gulf War, particularly for the benefit of
children (see Chapter 7). Such humanitarian cease-fires are not undertaken
according to specific provisions of international humanitarian law, but are
simply negotiated independently by groups involved with humanitarian
issues.[48] A number of initiatives of this kind have been organised, for
example, by UNICEF, such as the 'days of tranquillity' in El Salvador, the
Lebanon, and the Sudan. In these cases, agreement was reached that hostilities should cease for periods of a few days in order to immunise children
against preventable childhood diseases, and/or to provide them with food
and other necessities.[49]

Finally, in addition to the various types of zones specified in 1949 GC IV
and 1977 GP I, and humanitarian 'zones of peace', the UN Security Council
is empowered, under Chapter VII of the Charter of the UN, to establish
areas protected from hostilities. Again, such areas can contribute substantially to the protection of child civilians. The creation of the 'safe havens' in
the aftermath of the 1991 Gulf War (see Chapter 7) is an example. However, 'safe havens' can also, on occasion, fail dramatically to protect those
seeking shelter, as illustrated by the recent conflict in the former Yugoslavia. This issue is considered further in Chapters 7 and 8.

4.2.1.3 *Removal and/or Evacuation of Child Civilians*

To turn now to the concept of removing or evacuating child civilians from
the combat arena, here the intention is to safeguard children by taking them

[45] These considerations are identified by Sandoz (1985), 47.

[46] See also comment on this point by Doswald-Beck, in Meyer (ed.) (1989), 146, and Van
Dongen (1991), 77 (in relation to discussions at the 1938 meeting of the International Law
Association, n. 34 above).

[47] UNICEF describes the 'zone of peace concept' as 'safeguarding children from direct
combat and terrorism in areas of armed conflict, ensuring that they are not separated
from their families, and that children's services and facilities are protected from disruption
or occupation by parties to a conflict': UNICEF, *Children and Development in the 1990s*
(1990), 197.

[48] Such groups could be an NGO, a humanitarian organisation, or the belligerents themselves. Ressler, Tortorici, and Marcelino, 29.

[49] *Ibid.*, 92–4. For discussion of the concept of children as a zone of peace and
UNICEF initiatives in this context (including, as well as those cited here, initiatives in
Uganda, Iraq, and the former Yugoslavia), see Vittachi (1993) generally. See also UNICEF
(1995), 34–6.

elsewhere, rather than by creating zones, immune from hostilities, in which they can shelter.

Article 17 of 1949 GC IV therefore provides for the removal from besieged or encircled areas of, among others, 'children and maternity cases'.[50] 1949 GC IV does not here specify an upper age limit for assessing children's eligibility for evacuation, and this is subject to agreement by the belligerents. According to Pictet, writing in the late 1950s, 'the upper age limit of 15 years of age . . . seems reasonable and would appear to merit adoption in the present instance'.[51] Again, the age of 18 should now be preferred to that of 15.

In relation to the evacuation of children, 1977 GP I articulates a series of provisions that are largely considered to have superseded those in Article 24 of 1949 GC IV.[52] The latter broadly encouraged the evacuation of children who were orphaned or separated from their parents. Thus it stated that the belligerents 'shall facilitate the reception of such children in a neutral country for the duration of the conflict', subject only to the consent of the Protecting Power (if any) and to certain safeguards concerning maintenance, religion, and education.

In contrast, the 1977 GP I measures aimed to take into account the experiences of children who participated in mass evacuations, both in World War II and in the conflicts thereafter, sometimes with tragic consequences. For example, many such children had great difficulty in returning to their families and/or country of origin, and indeed large numbers never did return.[53] As one writer points out, most evacuations are organised on the assumption that they will last for only a short period. However, the duration is often extended owing to unforeseen events.[54] Article 78 of 1977 GP I, on the evacuation of children, must be seen in this context.

Thus Article 78(1) of 1977 GP I allows for evacuation only in specified circumstances. Under this Article, a party to the conflict must not evacuate

[50] This was a new concept in the laws of armed conflict, as previously civilians could be besieged indefinitely: Pictet (1958), 138.

[51] *Ibid.*, 139.

[52] For those states party to both 1949 GC IV and 1977 GP I, the binding principles regarding evacuation of foreign unaccompanied children are now contained in the latter. States not party to 1977 GP I should still arguably accept the standards established by its Art. 78 as more authoritative. See Boothby, Ressler and Steinbock (1988), 252.

[53] Sometimes mass evacuations have taken the form of large-scale inter-country adoption (such as the Vietnam war 'Operation Babylift'), which can also be fraught with difficulty. Major conflicts which have resulted in substantial evacuations of children include the Spanish Civil War, World War II, and the Greek Civil War. For descriptions of such evacuations, see generally *ibid.*, 10–133, and Ressler (1992), 4–16. The conflict in the former Yugoslavia, again, witnessed large-scale evacuations of children, some of whom had subsequently not been traced. See, e.g., David, P. 'Tracing Work is a Delicate Affair', 11.2/3 *International Children's Rights Monitor* 9 (1994), and *Guardian*, 2 Dec. 1993.

[54] Ressler (1992), 22.

unaccompanied children 'other than its own nationals, to a foreign country except for a temporary evacuation where compelling reasons of the health or medical treatment of the children, or except in occupied territory, their safety, so require.' The written consent of parents or guardians (or, in their absence, such consent of those 'primarily responsible' for the child's care) must be given,[55] and arrangements must be made for the supervision of the evacuation by the Protecting Power in agreement with the parties concerned. All 'feasible precautions' must be taken to avoid endangering the evacuation.

Article 78(1) therefore indicates a significant change in emphasis from the analogous provisions in Article 24 of 1949 GC IV. The former draws a firm distinction, in relation to the evacuation of children, between conduct permissible by the state of which the children are nationals, and conduct permissible by a foreign state. It allows the principles of 1949 GC IV to apply to children who are the nationals of the party organising the evacuation, but it greatly restricts the authority of an Occupying Power to evacuate children from occupied territories, and also limits the evacuation of alien children who are in the territory of a party to the conflict.

In relation to occupied territories, Article 78(1) allows only temporary evacuation of such children, and only for reasons related to health, not safety, as it was feared that Occupying Powers could abuse their discretion in this regard. However, under 1949 GC IV (Article 49), the legislation still permits the evacuation of family groups from occupied territories for reasons of safety.[56]

Article 78 also articulates other safeguards concerning the evacuation of children. Thus, according to Article 78(2), each child's education, including religious and moral education, should be provided 'with the greatest possible continuity' while s/he is away. The emphasis on 'greatest possible continuity' was intended to exclude propaganda that would alienate children from their culture of origin.[57]

Article 78(3) then sets out requirements for facilitating the return of children to their families and countries. These include arrangements for each child to have an identifying card, sent to the Central Tracing Agency of the ICRC,[58] containing information on the child's names, sex, age, nationality, native language, address, blood group, parents' names,

---

[55] This provision was specifically designed to avoid consent being given by those with only temporary responsibility, such as teachers: Ressler, Boothby, and Steinbock (1980), 249.

[56] See Bothe, Partsch and Solf (1982), 481–4. For a summary of the application of these complex provisions to different categories of children, see ICRC (1987), 912. See also sect. 4.2.2.1.1 below.

[57] Bothe, Partsch, and Solf (1982), 484.

[58] The creation of such an agency is provided for in Art. 140 of 1949 GC IV. In practice, the work of the Central Tracing Agency is conducted from Geneva by the ICRC. See Kalshoven (1987), 53.

and other pertinent information, as long as such information 'involves no risk of harm to the child'. The aim of the caveat concerning harm was to ensure that information prejudicial to the child's safety could be withheld.[59]

UNHCR and UNICEF published, in 1992, two Joint Statements on the Evacuation of Children from former Yugoslavia,[60] which emphasise and expand upon many of the principles in Article 78 of 1977 GP I. These documents confirm, for example, the importance of family unity, and of protecting and assisting children in place, if possible.[61]

4.2.1.4 Consignments

Another measure applicable to children in international armed conflict generally is found in Article 23 of 1949 GC IV. This Article is significant in relation to the Iraqi study, as discussed in Chapters 7 and 8 below. It provides for the free passage, between parties to this Convention, 'of all consignments of medical and hospital stores and objects necessary for religious worship intended only for civilians'. Further, free passage must be permitted of 'essential foodstuffs, clothing and tonics intended for children under fifteen, expectant mothers and maternity cases'.[62]

A distinction is therefore drawn between consignments such as medical supplies on the one hand, and essential foodstuffs, clothing, and tonics, on the other. The reason for this distinction was that the first category was deemed not to be such that it could reinforce the war economy and was therefore allowed passage to the civilian population generally. However, the latter category qualifies for free passage only when destined for the vulnerable category of civilians specified.[63]

Regarding 'essential' foodstuffs, one authority defines these as 'basic foodstuffs, necessary to the health and normal physical and mental development of the persons for whom they are intended'.[64]

Article 23 also imposes certain conditions on the supply of necessities to civilians, including a proviso against this in circumstances where it may aid the military efforts of the enemy. Further, the distribution of the consignments may be made subject to supervision by the Protecting Power, if there is one.

---

[59] Bothe, Partsch, and Solf (1982), 484. Such information could include, e.g., reference to the child's religion in conflicts where religion is at issue.

[60] Set out in Ressler (1992), 25–32.

[61] *Ibid.*, 29.

[62] The duty in Art. 23 is expressed as mandatory: that each party '*shall* allow the free passage'. This sort of positive duty, as opposed simply to a duty, e.g., to take 'feasible measures', is also found in other Arts. of 1949 GC IV (such as Art. 26 (sect. 4.2.1.5 below) and 50 (sect. 4.2.2.1.2 below)). See also sect. 4.2.5.3.3 below, concerning debates during the drafting of Art. 38 of the 1989 CRC.

[63] Pictet (1958), 179. As he points out, the distinction is based on military considerations.

[64] *Ibid.*

This Article as a whole again takes into account the experience of World War II, in which blockades sometimes extended to food and essential relief supplies for the civilian population.[65] It is significant that, in the 1991 Gulf War and its aftermath, the entitlement to necessities of particularly vulnerable groups of civilians, including child civilians, was to some extent respected, as discussed in Chapter 7.

In 1977 GP I, relevant measures concerning the provision of relief for the civilian population are found in Article 70(1). This Article is concerned only with the provision of relief to the civilian population of territory under the control of a party to the conflict, other than occupied territory.[66] It specifies that in the distribution of humanitarian relief consignments 'priority should be given to those persons, such as children, expectant mothers, maternity cases and nursing mothers who, under the Fourth Convention or under this Protocol, are to be accorded privileged treatment or special protection'. This Article therefore provides that children, among others, are to be given priority in receiving a wide range of essential supplies, including, for example, clothing, bedding, and means of shelter. It augments Article 23 of 1949 GC IV, which grants such entitlement only in relation to a limited category of essentials.

Specifically as regards the provision of food, Article 54(1) of 1977 GP I (mentioned in section 3.1.2.1 above), strengthens Article 23 of 1949 GC IV by imposing an absolute ban on starvation of the civilian population as a method of warfare.

4.2.1.5 *The Importance of the Family: Family News; Family Reunification; Arrest, Detention or Internment*

The provisions of 1949 GC IV concerning the treatment of all child civilians also include measures for the communication of family news, and for family reunification. These are among many Articles in both 1949 GC IV and the 1977 GPs that acknowledge the tremendous significance of the family as a bulwark for children against the traumas of armed conflict.[67]

As regards family news, Article 25 of 1949 GC IV provides that persons in the territory of a party to the conflict, or in occupied territory, should be able to give strictly personal news to family members and to receive such news in return. Prompt communication must be facilitated. This Article also

---

[65] Van Dongen (1991), 93.

[66] Provision for meeting the 'basic needs' of inhabitants of occupied territory generally is already made in Art. 69 of 1977 GP I, which augments Art. 55 of 1949 GC IV (mentioned in sect. 3.1.2.1 above).

[67] Many writers have emphasised the importance of family unity for children in armed conflict. See, e.g., Ressler, Boothby, and Steinbock (1988), 134; Hingorani in Kalshoven (ed.) (1989), 133, and Ressler, Tortorici, and Marcelino (1993), 11, 141, and 171, among others. This concept also features prominently in guidelines issued by UNHCR regarding the treatment of refugee children: UNHCR (1994), 23 and 43.

makes provision for alternative methods of exchanging news in the event of disruption to ordinary postal services, and it limits the restrictions which can be placed on correspondence.[68]

Concerning family reunification, 1949 GC IV specifies in Article 26 that the parties to the conflict 'shall' (thereby imposing a mandatory obligation) facilitate enquiries between dispersed family members, with the object of their resuming contact, and, if possible, of meeting.[69] The parties must also encourage the family reunification work of 'acceptable' organisations that conform with their security requirements.

Article 74 of 1977 GP I, also concerning family reunification, is more strongly worded than Article 26 of 1949 GC IV. It states that both the parties to the conflict *and* the parties to 1977 GP I 'shall facilitate in every possible way the reunion of families dispersed as a result of armed conflicts'. Accordingly Article 74 both expands the category of parties responsible for this task and changes, to a more positive role, the duty of the parties. Further, again with a proviso regarding security, Article 74 specifies that the parties must encourage the family reunification work of humanitarian organisations in accordance with the 1949 GCs and the 1977 GPs, thereby apparently removing the discretion to assess the organisations' acceptability.

In acknowledging the importance of family continuity and stability, 1977 GP I also contains a number of measures regarding those who are arrested, detained, or interned. Thus, Article 75(5) provides that detained or interned families should, whenever possible, be accommodated in the same place as family units.[70] Again, in relation to pregnant women and women with dependent children who are arrested, detained, or interned for reasons connected with the armed conflict, Article 76(2) specifies that their cases must be considered 'with the utmost priority'. Finally, Article 77(4) provides for children arrested, detained, or interned for reasons related to the conflict to be accommodated separately from adults, except when families are accommodated together. The age below which an unaccompanied child is to be separately accommodated is not specified

---

[68] Pictet notes that 1949 GC IV is silent on payment for the correspondence, and concludes that the cost must be borne by the sender, as a non-interned civilian: Pictet (1958), 195. This could, in some circumstances, be one of many obstacles faced by child civilians in attempting to communicate with absent family members.

[69] Pictet comments that this Art. is intended to 'safeguard the family unit', and that accordingly it relates, among others, to measures regarding identity discs in Art. 24(3): *ibid.*, 196.

[70] Art. 75(5) thereby extends the entitlement to family accommodation to all those in the power of a party to the conflict. Previously this entitlement only applied to those interned in occupied territory, under Art. 82 of 1949 GC IV (see sect. 4.2.2.1.3 below).

here. This is left to national law, tradition, and the decision of the parties to the conflict.[71]

4.2.1.6 The Death Penalty

Finally, as regards provision for all children in situations of international armed conflict, Article 77(5) of 1977 GP I deals with the death penalty. It proscribes the carrying out of the death penalty on persons who were below the age of 18 years at the time at which they committed an offence 'related to the armed conflict'. 1977 GP I thereby strengthens 1949 GC IV by extending the exemption from the death penalty to *all* such children, including a party's own nationals.[72] Under Article 68 of 1949 GC IV (discussed below, section 4.2.2.1.2, in relation to occupied territory), this exemption previously applied only to protected persons in occupied territory who were under 18 at the time of the offence.[73]

The protection of children is also taken into account in Article 76(3) of 1977 GP I, which specifies that the death sentence should, whenever possible, not be pronounced on pregnant women or mothers of dependent infants, for offences related to the armed conflict. It goes on to prohibit the carrying out of the death penalty on such women.

4.2.2 Provisions Concerning the Protection of Specific Categories of Child Civilians in International Armed Conflict: 1949 GC IV and 1977 GP I

The above section (section 4.2.1) considered measures in international armed conflict regarding child civilians generally as set out in 1949 GC IV and 1977 GP I. This section now considers measures specifically applicable, in such conflicts, to children in four categories: those in occupied territories; children who are orphaned or separated from their families; those who are enemy aliens; and children included in the definition of the 'wounded and sick' in 1977 GP I. Except when otherwise specified in the legislation, these measures are largely additional to the more general provisions outlined in section 4.2.1 above. Accordingly, for example, children in occupied territories are still entitled to special treatment as children (Article 77(1) of 1977 GP I), and to receive shelter in hospital and safety zones (Article 14 of 1949 GC IV).

---

[71] Bothe, Partsch, and Solf (1982), 478.
[72] States Parties to the ICCPR are bound by a similar prohibition under Art. 6(5). See Sect. 2.1.2.2 above.
[73] In this context, it is worth noting that, in addition to reaffirming existing rights for protected persons, certain sections of Art. 77 of 1977 GP I impose new legal obligations as regards a party's own nationals, and in relation to others who are not protected persons. These new obligations are found primarily in Arts. 77(2) (child soldiers); 77(4) (internment); and 77(5) (the death penalty): Bothe, Partsch, and Solf (1982), 476.

4.2.2.1 Children In Occupied Territories—1949 GC IV and 1977 GP I[74]

International law regarding occupied territories can be interpreted as aiming to preserve as far as possible the *status quo* until peace is restored. In any event, the provisions concerning children in occupied territories are largely designed to minimise disruption of their lives during the conflict, and hence to ensure the maximum continuity in crucial areas such as family life, schooling, and place of residence. In situations of prolonged belligerent occupation the applicable legal regime becomes more complex, but this issue will not be examined here,[75] other than to emphasise that in such situations human rights law, including measures specifically concerning children, can become increasingly pertinent as hostilities cease and the situation stabilises.[76]

As already mentioned (section 4.2.1), Part IV of 1977 GP I contains various Articles concerning child civilians generally, which include and apply to children in occupied territories.[77] These are Articles 74 (reunion of

---

[74] Children in occupied territory can be particularly vulnerable to abuse, as has been well documented in relation to the Israeli occupation of the Palestinian territories. See, e.g., information on children killed in the Intifada (the uprisings in the West Bank and Gaza Strip which began in Dec. 1987): B'Tselem, *The Killing of Palestinian Children and the Open-Fire Regulations* (N.p. June 1993); B'Tselem, *Khan Yunis December 1992: Case Study No 2* (Jerusalem, 1993); and B'Tselem, *Violations of Human Rights in the Occupied Territories 1992/1993* (Jerusalem, n.d), 22–6 and 49–65. Also particularly pertinent to children in the occupied territories are the issues of school closure (see n. 80 below), and family reunification (see, e.g., B'Tselem, *Annual Report 1989: Violations of Human Rights in the Occupied Territories* (Jerusalem, 1989), 101–4; B'Tselem, *Violations of Human Rights in the Occupied Territories 1990/1991* (Jerusalem, n.d.), 147–55; and B'Tselem, *Renewal of Deportation of Women and Children from the Occupied Territories on Account of 'Illegal Residency'* (Jerusalem, n.d.)). For general information on violations of international law affecting civilians in that situation, see, e.g., Al-Haq, *Punishing a Nation: Human Rights Violations During the Palestinian Uprising, December 1987– December 1988* (West Bank, 1988), and the B'Tselem annual reports on *Violations of Human Rights in The Occupied Territories* (1989, 1990/1991, and 1992/1993), as above.

[75] This issue will not be discussed primarily because the relevant law and the problem of its implementation have been analysed elsewhere, most notably in relation to the Israeli occupation of the Palestinian territories. See, e.g., Cohen (1985); Y. Dinstein, 'The International Law of Belligerent Occupation and Human Rights' 8 *Israel Yearbook on Human Rights* 104 (1978), and E. Playfair (ed.), *International Law and the Administration of the Occupied Territories: Two Decades of Israeli Occupation of the West Bank and Gaza Strip* (Oxford, 1992).

[76] Such measures could include principles expressed in the UDHR, as well as the ICCPR and the ICESCR. See, e.g., Cohen (1985) generally. Thus, according to this writer, 'there are situations . . . in which the law of human rights can serve to limit the more brutal requirements of military necessity contained in the law of armed conflicts. Such a situation is that of prolonged belligerent occupation after the cessation of general hostilities' (p. xvi). See also *ibid.*, pp. xvii, 9, 190, 284, and 289; E. Playfair, 'Introduction', in Playfair (ed.) (1992), 21, and A. Roberts, 'Prolonged Military Occupation: The Israeli-Occupied Territories 1967–1988', in *ibid.*, 77–8.

[77] Despite the generally inclusive nature of the provisions of 1977 GP I, certain Arts., such as Art. 78(1) regarding evacuation (sect. 4.2.1.3 above), do specifically make additional provision for children in occupied territory.

dispersed families), 75 (fundamental guarantees), 76 (custody of pregnant women and mothers of young children), 77 (protection of children), and 78 (evacuation of children). These Articles will not be repeated here, although it is important to emphasise their relevance to children in occupied territories.

1949 GC IV, on the other hand, contains separate measures exclusively for the protection of children in occupied territories, and these are set out below in the order in which they appear in this Convention.

4.2.2.1.1 Evacuation: 1949 GC IV

Although generally prohibiting 'individual or mass forcible transfers' and deportations from occupied territory, Article 49 of 1949 GC IV makes allowance for the evacuation of the civilian population in certain circumstances, such as situations in which the security of the population is in danger (and see section 4.2.1.3 above). This Article specifies that in this eventuality members of the same family are not to be separated.[78]

According to Pictet, commenting on Article 49 in 1958, in the light of the experience of World War II, '[t]he thought of the physical and mental suffering endured by these 'displaced persons', among whom there were a great many women, children, old people and sick, can only lead to thankfulness for the prohibition embodied in this paragraph, which is intended to forbid such hateful practices for all time'.[79] In view of subsequent events, such as the conflict in the former Yugoslavia which witnessed numerous forcible transfers of civilians, Pictet's optimism seems sadly misplaced.

4.2.2.1.2 Miscellaneous Provisions Regarding the Treatment of Child Civilians in Occupied Territory: 1949 GC IV

Regarding the treatment of child civilians while in occupied territory, Article 50 of 1949 GC IV states that '[t]he Occupying Power shall . . . facilitate the proper working of all institutions devoted to the care and education of children'.[80] No age limit is specified.[81]

---

[78] The analogous Art. of 1977 GPI, Art. 78, also emphasises family continuity, as mentioned in sect. 4.2.1.3 above. Pictet notes that Art. 49 is an appropriate addition to other Arts. in 1949 GC IV, such as Arts. 25, 26, 27, and 82, dealing generally with respect for family rights: Pictet (1958), 281.

[79] *Ibid.* 278.

[80] This requirement to provide educational institutions for children in occupied territories has become particularly contentious in the course of the Israeli occupation of the West Bank and Gaza Strip, where the Israeli authorities have repeatedly resorted to school closures, sometimes for protracted periods. See, *inter alia*, Al-Haq (1988), 295–316, and B'Tselem, *Closure of Schools and Other Setbacks to the Education System in the Occupied Territories* (Jerusalem, 1990).

[81] Interestingly, although Pictet again sees 15 as a reasonable age limit here, he points out that there must be flexibility depending on the young person concerned and the legislation in the particular country: Pictet (1958).

If local institutions are inadequate, Article 50 specifies that suitable alternative arrangements must be made, particularly for children orphaned or separated from their parents because of the armed conflict and who cannot be adequately cared for by a close relative or friend. Article 50 accordingly makes provision for orphaned children or those separated from their parents who are in occupied territory, while Article 24 provides for such children in other circumstances (see sections 4.2.1.3 above and 4.2.2.2 below).

Under Article 50, Occupying Powers are also forbidden to change the 'personal status' of children, nor must they enlist the children in organisations subordinate to them.[82] This latter measure was apparently intended to prevent any renewal of the compulsory mass enrolments of World War II, when many children were automatically made members of organisations devoted primarily to political ends.[83]

Further, Article 50 specifies that Occupying Powers must facilitate the identification of children and the registration of their parentage by, among other things, establishing for this purpose a special section of the Information Bureau to be set up under Article 136. According to Article 136, each party to a conflict must establish its own official Information Bureau 'responsible for receiving and transmitting information in respect of the protected persons who are in its power'.

Finally, Occupying Powers must, within the terms of this Article, maintain pre-existing preferential measures as regards food, medical care, and protection against the effects of armed conflict 'in favour of children under fifteen years, expectant mothers, and mothers of children under seven years'.

Pictet's Commentary on Article 50 of 1949 GC IV notes that children 'were the innocent victims of events which afflicted them all the more cruelly because they were young and weak; they suffered hardships in violation of one of the most sacred of human laws—the law that children must be protected, since they represent humanity's future'.[84]

Article 51 of 1949 GC IV limits the types of work which the Occupying Power can compel protected persons to undertake, and includes a caveat against such compulsory labour for protected persons under the age of 18.

As regards the imposition by the Occupying Power of the death penalty, according to Article 68 this should only occur where the protected person has committed certain serious offences, such as espionage. In any event, the death sentence may only be pronounced against a protected person who

---

[82] Pressure or propaganda to secure voluntary enlistment of civilians generally is also prohibited by Art. 51.

[83] Plattner (1983), 207.

[84] Pictet (1958), 284.

was over 18 years of age at the time of the offence.[85] Since Article 68 states that the death sentence should not even be 'pronounced' on children under 18 at the time of the offence, as opposed to 'executed', it sets a higher standard than 1977 GP I (Article 77(5)).

One consequence of this discrepancy is that, in international armed conflicts where both 1949 GC IV and 1977 GP I apply, the pronouncement of the death sentence continues to be prohibited as regards the relevant protected persons in occupied territories (under Article 68, 1949 GC IV), but otherwise only its execution is prohibited under 1977 GP I.[86]

4.2.2.1.3 Treatment of Children who are Detained or Interned in Occupied Territory: 1949 GC IV

According to Article 76 of 1949 GC IV, when protected persons are accused of offences and detained in occupied territory, conditions of detention should be such that '[p]roper regard shall be paid to the special treatment due to minors'.[87]

In relation to those who are interned in occupied territory, 1949 GC IV makes detailed provision, including several Articles focusing on children. In Article 81, it calls on the Detaining Power to support those dependent on the internees, if such dependents have no alternative means of support. Article 82 states that the Detaining Power should accommodate family members, particularly parents and children, in the same place of internment. Temporary separations are permitted for specified reasons, such as those necessitated by employment or health. Further, internees can request that 'their children who are left at liberty without parental care' are interned with them.[88] The phrase 'without parental care' means that a parent in internment would not, under this Article, have the right to demand the interment with him or her of children being cared for by the other parent.[89]

The nutritional and educational requirements of child internees are

---

[85] According to Pictet, this prohibition is based on the notion that a person under 18 is 'not fully capable of sound judgment, does not always realize the significance of his actions, and often acts under the influence of others' if not constrained: *ibid*. 347. This sentiment is clearly not in accord with current notions of the capacity of, particularly, older children (see discussion in sect. 1.4 above).

[86] Bothe, Partsch, and Solf (1982), 478. The term 'pronounced' was altered to 'executed' in the drafting of 1977 GP I, as the representative of the Japanese government argued that the law of his country could only accept the latter. See 'Diplomatic Conference on the Reaffirmation and Development of International Law Applicable in Armed Conflicts. Geneva 1974–1977', CDDH/III/SR 59, paras. 17, 54, and 55.

[87] This provision was apparently intended to refer specifically to the guarantees regarding the treatment of minors set out in Art. 50: Pictet (1958), 342.

[88] The experiences of internees in World War II emphasised that internment was less difficult to bear when the internees could be grouped together as families. Children were able to benefit from the presence of their parents, and were able, e.g., to attend school in the camps: *ibid*. 379.

[89] *Ibid.*, 381.

emphasised in Article 89. In particular, '[e]xpectant and nursing mothers, and children under fifteen years of age' must be given additional food, 'in proportion to their physiological needs'.[90] Moreover, Article 94 specifies that the Detaining Power must encourage intellectual and recreational pursuits among internees, and particularly among children. Schooling and special playgrounds should be provided.

Finally as regards child internees in occupied territory, Article 132 of 1949 GC IV requires the Detaining Power to arrange the release, repatriation, or return of 'in particular children, pregnant women and mothers with infants and young children'. This provision aimed to address the problem that in World War II some states tended automatically to intern enemy nationals. This was expensive for the Detaining Powers and caused needless suffering to many internees, such as women, children, and elderly people, who did not pose a threat to public safety.[91]

4.2.2.2 Children Orphaned or Separated From Their Parents: 1949 GC IV

In addition to children in occupied territory, another category of children specifically provided for under 1949 GC IV are 'children under fifteen, who are orphaned or are separated from their families as a result of the war' (Article 24). This Article sets out a number of safeguards for such children. Again, these provisions were in response to the mass migrations, bombing raids, and deportations of World War II, in which many children, without means of identification, were separated from their families.[92] Under Article 24, measures must be taken by the parties to the conflict to ensure that the specified category of children are not left to fend for themselves, and that their education and the exercise of their religion are facilitated.

Further, the belligerents are encouraged to make arrangements for the reception of such children in a neutral country for the duration of the conflict, and to ensure that all children under 12 are identified by identity discs or by other means. However, as mentioned above, the measures in Article 24 regarding evacuation have now been largely superseded by Article 78 of 1977 GP I (see section 4.2.1.3 above).

As regards children orphaned or separated from their parents in occupied territory, see Article 50 of 1949 GC IV (section 4.2.2.1.2 above).

4.2.2.3 Alien Children: 1949 GC IV

A third category of children, in international armed conflict, specifically provided for in humanitarian law are those who are enemy aliens in the territory of a party to the conflict.

---

[90] Pictet argues that in the case of children, 'deficiency diseases would be particularly deplorable, as they would affect future generations': *ibid.*, 392.

[91] *Ibid.*, 510.

[92] *Ibid.*, 185, and see sect. 4.2.1.3 above.

Article 38 of 1949 GC IV provides that in general the situation of enemy aliens should still be regulated by provisions concerning aliens in time of peace. In any event, under this Article they are entitled to certain rights, including that '[c]hildren under fifteen years, pregnant women and mothers of children under seven years shall benefit by any preferential treatment' enjoyed by the nationals of the state concerned (Article 38(5)). Such preferential treatment can include, for example, supplemetary rationing cards, facilities for medical treatment, and admission to hospital and safety zones.[93] The intention here is to ensure, as far as possible, equality of treatment between children (and other vulnerable civilians) who are enemy aliens and those who are not.

4.2.2.4 *Protection of the Wounded, Sick, and Shipwrecked: 1977 GP I*

Finally, a fourth category of children explicitly singled out in international humanitarian law is that specified under the 1977 GP I definition of 'wounded' and 'sick' persons. The definition includes 'new-born babies' as well as 'maternity cases' and 'other persons who may be in need of immediate medical assistance or care, such as the infirm or expectant mothers, and who refrain from any act of hostility' (Article 8(a)).[94]

Under Article 10 of this Protocol, the 'wounded, sick and shipwrecked' should be respected and protected. Further, in all circumstances they must be treated humanely and must, as far as possible, receive the medical care and attention they require.

The inclusion of new-born babies in the category of 'wounded and sick' emphasises the extreme vulnerability of the new-born and their entitlement to particular care. Babies do, of course, also qualify for protection as child civilians under all the other general provisions discussed in section 4.2.1 above, and to additional measures, if applicable, for example as inhabitants of occupied territory.

4.2.3 Provisions Concerning the Treatment of Child Civilians in Non-international Armed Conflict: 1977 GP II

Sections 4.2.1 and 4.2.2 above described measures in international humanitarian law regarding child civilians in international armed conflict, as set out in 1949 GC IV and 1977 GP I. The rules concerning child civilians in non-international armed conflict will now be considered. The relevant provisions of 1977 GP II are largely contained in one fairly concise Article, Article 4(3).

---

[93] *Ibid.*, 248.

[94] Although this definition includes babies, it is not necessary to describe in detail here the provisions, in Pt. II of 1977 GP I, designed generally for the protection of the wounded, sick, and shipwrecked. For information on this, see the texts cited in Ch. 3, n. 1 above.

This Article begins by stating simply that children 'shall be provided with the care and aid they require', no mention being made of the need for special respect and protection from indecent assault, as in Article 77(1) of 1977 GP I. Nonetheless, this statement is significant in acknowledging, *inter alia*, the child's entitlement to the provision of necessities in situations of non-international armed conflict.

Article 4(3) then elaborates on this principle, listing various entitlements and prohibitions pertaining to children. These are: (a) a right to education, including religious and moral education, in accordance with the views of their parents or other responsible adult; (b) a proviso for appropriate steps to be taken to facilitate family reunion; (c) a prohibition on recruitment and participation in hostilities of child soldiers under the age of 15; (d) a provision that child soldiers who are under the age of 15 (in contravention of Article 4(3)(c)) should nonetheless not forfeit 'the special protection provided by this Article' if captured; and (e) an entitlement to temporary evacuation, in the care of a responsible adult, from the area in which hostilities are occurring to a 'safer area within the country'.[95] Such evacuation is subject to certain conditions. It should only be undertaken, if possible, with parental consent or the consent of persons primarily responsible for the child's care. Further, the child should be accompanied by someone responsible for his or her safety and well-being.

This Article can be seen as a summary of some of the core provisions regarding children in international armed conflict, as set out in 1949 GC IV and 1977 GP I. Its brevity reflects the difficulties faced by those drafting the 1977 GPs in achieving a consensus on detailed measures to be observed by states in non-international armed conflicts.

In relation to Article 4(3), the ICRC Commentary asserts: 'children are particularly vulnerable; they require privileged treatment in comparison with the rest of the civilian population. This is why they enjoy specific legal protection'.[96]

1977 GP II (Article 6(4)) also reiterates the prohibition in 1949 GC IV and 1977 GP I on the death penalty in relation to those aged under 18 at the time of committing an offence related to the armed conflict. The two 1977 GPs therefore both explicitly allow children from the age of 15 to risk death by participating as combatants in hostilities, while forbidding their execution for certain offences committed while under 18.

Like Article 68 of 1949 GC IV, Article 6(4) of 1977 GP II sets a higher standard than 1977 GP I (Article 77(5)) in stating that the death sentence

---

[95] The proviso regarding removal to a safer area within the same country assumes that in non-international armed conflicts there is normally such an area. This may, of course, not be the case.

[96] ICRC (1987), 1377.

should not be 'pronounced' on children under 18 at the time of the offence, as opposed to 'executed'.

The provisions of 1977 GP II, summarised here, therefore largely include the key principles concerning the protection of children in armed conflict, but without the detail contained in the legislation regulating international armed conflicts.

4.2.4 1980 Inhumane Weapons Convention

In addition to the 1949 GCs and the 1977 GPs, Protocol II of the 1980 Inhumane Weapons Convention (see section 3.1.3 above) merits consideration here, in the context of treaty provisions specifically referring to the treatment of children. This Protocol forbids the indiscriminate use of mines, booby-traps, and 'other devices'. It emphasises that these must not be used against the civilian population or individual civilians (Article 3(2)). Certain types of booby traps are explicitly prohibited, including booby traps associated with 'children's toys or other portable objects or products specially designed for the feeding, health, hygiene, clothing or education of children' (Article 6(b)(v)).

Nonetheless, anti-personnel landmines, some of which resemble children's toys, have caused and continue to cause death and serious injury to children in a number of countries.[97] According to one estimate, these 'cruel weapons . . . kill as many as 25 people a day—most of them civilians, many of them children'.[98] Further, this source quotes an ICRC estimate that about 800 people are killed by landmines every month, of whom 30 to 40 per cent are children under 15. It emphasises that although such mines are

designed to maim rather than to kill . . . children are more likely than adults to be killed outright. . . . Children are also at risk because of their innate curiosity and love of play. In countries like Iraq and Afghanistan, landmines are such familiar objects that children make a hobby of collecting different models. . . . Everyday tasks such as herding livestock and fetching water also take them into remote mined areas, where they may perish in excruciating pain before aid arrives. Those who do survive are maimed for life.[99]

[97] See, e.g., B. Abramson, 'Children's Rights in the Age of Landmines: Part One', 11.2/3 *International Children's Rights Monitor* 35 (1994); ICRC, *A Perverse Use of Technology* (Geneva, 1992); UNICEF, *Anti-Personnel Land Mines: A Scourge on Children* (New York, 1994); and UNICEF/UK, 'Landmines—A Scourge on Children', *Children First!* 9 (Winter 1994).

[98] UK Committee for UNICEF, 'Landmines to Top Agenda at Conference on Inhumane Weapons', *News in Brief* 1 (Sept. 1995).

[99] *Ibid.*, 2. See also UNICEF, *Anti-Personnel Land Mines.* (1994); UNICEF (1995), 26–9, and AI (UK), 'Landmines: The Blind Sentinels', *Working Group for Children Newsletter* 1 (Spring 1996).

Indeed, some refugees, including children, were injured by mines when fleeing Iraq in the aftermath of the 1991 Gulf War (see section 7.2.3.2 below).

The 1995 Review Conference on the 1980 Inhumane Weapons Convention (mentioned in section 3.1.3) failed to agree a total ban on the production, use, and export of landmines, despite pressure from the ICRC, among others.[100] At the Final Review Conference in 1996, once again, agreement was not reached on this point, leading to strong condemnation from many quarters, including the UN Secretary General, Mr Boutros-Ghali. He pointed out that, by the time the next Review Conference on this Convention takes place, in the year 2001, an estimated 'additional 50,000 human beings will have been killed, and a further 80,000 injured, by landmines'.[101]

4.2.5 Article 38 of the 1989 CRC

Article 38, which is the focal provision in the 1989 CRC regarding the protection of children in armed conflict, is the final measure to be discussed here in the context of international humanitarian treaty law specifically concerning child civilians.[102] Many other provisions of the 1989 CRC may, however, continue to apply in situations of armed conflict, as discussed in section 2.2.2 above.

Since Article 38 is a relatively recent measure in international law, and state compliance with it is subject to monitoring by the Committee on the Rights of the Child, it is significant in the context of this research. Exceptionally, therefore, the drafting history of this Article is outlined below.[103]

---

[100] UNICEF and the ICRC, in conjunction with a number of other organisations and some governments, campaigned for this conference to declare a total ban on land mines. See also Aldrich and van Baarda (1994), 130–1, and B. Abramson, 'Children's Rights in the Age of Landmines: Part Two', 11.4/12.1 *International Children's Rights Monitor* 28 (1994– 5).

[101] See the UK Working Group on Landmines, *Report on the Review Conference of the 1980 UN Inhumane Weapons Convention—final session held in Geneva from 22 April to 3 May 1996* (London, 1996), 1. Some concessions were, however, agreed at this conference, such as an extension of the applicability of this Convention to non-international armed conflicts. Further, Canada was planning to host a meeting of 'pro-ban countries' in Sept. 1996. See *ibid.* 3 and generally.

[102] As already mentioned (sect. 2.2.2), Art. 39, concerning rehabilitation, is not considered at length in this book, although it also specifically refers to children in armed conflict.

[103] For further information on the various versions of Art. 38 (originally Art. 20) considered during the drafting process, and of the discussions of the Working Group, see Detrick (ed.) (1992), 502–17 and Krill, in Freeman and Veerman (eds.) (1992), 350–2. See also, e.g., DCI, *Memorandum: Art. 38 of the Draft Convention on the Rights of the Child and the Participation of Children in Armed Conflicts* (Geneva, Mar. 1989); Krill (1986), and Quaker UN Office, *The Rights of the Child* (Geneva, 1988).

Article 38 has been described as 'the most publicised of all aspects of the text', and as the Article which 'has come to symbolize the whole Convention for many'.[104] This Article certainly proved controversial, particularly in relation to child soldiers, but also as regards child civilians.

Article 38 reads as follows:

1. States Parties undertake to respect and to ensure respect for rules of international humanitarian law applicable to them in armed conflicts which are relevant to the child.

2. States Parties shall take all feasible measures to ensure that persons who have not attained the age of 15 years do not take a direct part in hostilities.

3. States Parties shall refrain from recruiting any person who has not attained the age of 15 years into their armed forces. In recruiting among those persons who have attained the age of 15 years but who have not attained the age of 18 years, States Parties shall endeavour to give priority to those who are oldest.

4. In accordance with their obligations under international humanitarian law to protect the civilian population in armed conflicts, States Parties shall take all feasible measures to ensure protection and care of children who are affected by an armed conflict.

4.2.5.1 Scope of Article 38

Article 38 does not distinguish between international and non-international armed conflicts, except inasmuch as it incorporates these categories by referring, in subsections (1) and (4), to existing rules of international humanitarian law. It therefore appears to apply to any armed conflict. However, by using the term 'armed conflict' and referring to existing international humanitarian law, Article 38 does not appear to extend to internal disturbances.

Further, the 1989 CRC as a whole applies only to States Parties, and therefore NGEs that are engaged in armed conflict are not generally bound by its provisions. However, when NGEs are subject to other treaty obligations, as when they have made an undertaking under Article 96(3) of 1977 GP I (discussed in section 3.1.2), the 1989 CRC clearly does not negate that obligation.[105]

---

[104] See Rädda Barnen, *No Child Soldiers* (Stockholm, Sept. 1989), 1. Other writers and participants in the drafting process have expressed similar sentiments. Thus, e.g., in the Working Group debate at the end of 1988, Art. 38 was described by the Australian representative as 'critical to my government's decision or ability even to become a party to this Convention': Rädda Barnen, *United Nations Draft Convention on the Rights of the Child: Debate on Children in Armed Conflicts, Geneva, December 8, 1988* (Stockholm, 1989), 12. See also Detrick (ed.) (1992), 26 and C. P. Cohen, 'United Nations Convention on the Rights of the Child: Introductory Note'. 28 ILM 1450 and 1452 (1989).

[105] In any event, under Art. 41 of the 1989 CRC, the higher standard must always apply.

4.2.5.2 Background to Article 38

The original Polish draft Convention on the Rights of the Child submitted to the UN Commission on Human Rights in 1978 did not include an Article on children in armed conflict.[106] In 1985, such an Article was proposed to the Working Group.[107] A version of the text proposed in 1985 was, after a lengthy debate, adopted as Article 20 in 1986.[108]

Interestingly, in the same year a draft Article submitted by Iran, in the throes of the Iran/Iraq war, was considered by the Working Group. This invoked international customary and 'Geneva law', and referred to the use of chemical and bacteriological weapons. It specifically prohibited 'military attack and bombardment of . . . the civilian population, inflicting incalculable suffering, especially on children who are the most vulnerable members of the population'.[109] Also in 1986, the NGOs involved in the Working Group submitted a text which included provision for humanitarian law to apply to children in internal disturbances. However, no government was prepared to sponsor this text, and accordingly it was not discussed.[110]

Article 38 gave rise to a number of contentious points. Of these, the most relevant to the subject of this book was the discussion, in relation to Article 38(4), of the level of protection to be accorded to child civilians. There was also intense debate in the Working Group on the standards to be applied in relation to child soldiers (Article 38(2)). Although child soldiers are not generally discussed here, the debate on this issue, too, will exceptionally be outlined below in order to place the controversy surrounding the drafting of Article 38 more fully in context.

The drafting of the 1989 CRC was largely completed between 1979 and 1987 in the week-long annual meetings of the Working Group. In 1988, in order to complete the drafting by the end of 1989 (the tenth anniversary of

---

[106] This convention was in the form of a draft resolution (UN Doc. E/CN.4/L.1366/Rev.1) sponsored by Austria, Bulgaria, Colombia, Jordan, Poland, Senegal, and the Syrian Arab Republic: UN ESCOR (1978), Supp. No 4, UN Doc. E/1978/34.

[107] See UN Doc. E/CN.4/1986/39, 26–30. The Art. was proposed by delegates from the Netherlands, Sweden, and Finland, supported by Peru, Belgium, and Senegal. It was apparently introduced at the instigation of various NGOs: Krill (1986), 40. See also Krill, in Freeman and Veerman (eds.) (1992), 351.

[108] See UN Doc. E/CN.4/1986/39, Annex I, 12. This read: '1. The States Parties to the present Convention undertake to respect and to ensure respect for rules of international humanitarian law applicable to them in armed conflicts which are relevant to the child.
2. States Parties to the present Convention shall take all feasible measures to ensure that no child takes a direct part in hostilities and they shall refrain in particular from recruiting any child who has not attained the age of 15 years into their armed forces.
3. In accordance with their obligations under international humanitarian law to protect the civilian population in armed conflicts, States Parties to this Convention shall take all feasible measures to ensure protection and care of children who are affected by an armed conflict.'

[109] See UN Doc. E/CN.4/1986/39, 26–30. It can be assumed that this was in response to Iraqi chemical weapon attacks in the Iran/Iraq war.

[110] Krill (1986), 41.

the International Year of the Child), the Working Group met for two fortnightly sessions: the First Reading of the draft Convention at the beginning of the year, and the Second Reading, which agreed the final text, at the end. Much of the discussion which follows will focus on the debates and decisions of the Second Reading.

4.2.5.3 Key Issues in the Drafting Process

There were three main issues which were contentious in the drafting of Article 38, concerning: the relevant applicable rules of international humanitarian law (Article 38(1)), and the appropriate standards in relation to child soldiers (Article 38(2)) and child civilians (Article 38(4)).

4.2.5.3.1 Relevant Rules of International Humanitarian Law (Article 38(1))

It is of interest that, in addition to the problems with Article 38(2) and (4), the contentious issues in the drafting of Article 38 originally included an objection by some participants to the wording of paragraph (1), to the effect that States Parties 'undertake to respect . . . rules of humanitarian law applicable to them'. The Working Group considered the qualifying phrase 'applicable to them' potentially ambiguous. Does it mean, for example, that the relevant rules depend on ratification by particular countries of conventions such as the 1949 GCs and 1977 GPs, or does it refer to the customary law obligations of all states? This issue was debated in the Working Group in 1986,[111] but the phrase was ultimately incorporated and some ambiguity therefore remains.[112]

Moreover, Article 38(1) confronts the problem, which this book aims to address, as to the precise content of the rules of international humanitarian law which are 'relevant to the child'. Given the complexity of this body of law and the fact that it is scattered throughout various treaties that are not universally ratified, there may well be uncertainty about the detailed rules that apply to particular states party to the 1989 CRC. State reports to the Committee on the Rights of the Child regarding their compliance with Article 38(1), and the Committee's task in evaluating these, may therefore be problematic.[113] This issue, and the need for a General Comment on Article 38, have been raised before the Committee, as discussed in section 6.1.1.2 below.

---

[111] See UN Doc. E/CN.4/1986/39, 28.

[112] Thus, according to one writer, the rules by which a country is bound under Art. 38(1) depend on the treaties which that state has signed, and on its understanding of customary law: Abramson, *Children and War* (1992), 21.

[113] Nonetheless, all countries reporting to the Committee would by definition be bound by the underlying ethos of the 1989 CRC to grant children a degree of special treatment generally. Further, given its wide ratification, they are also likely at least to be bound by 1949 GC IV, as well as by pertinent customary norms. The Committee can therefore assume a fairly high level of state obligation as regards children in armed conflict.

4.2.5.3.2 *Child Soldiers (Article 38(2))*

In relation to Article 38(2), which deals with the participation of children in hostilities, there were three main points at issue.

One concern expressed initially by some participants in the Working Group was the use of the word 'feasible' to describe measures States Parties should take to prevent involvement of children in hostilities.[114] The word 'feasible' in the context of international humanitarian law has been described as meaning that which is practicable or practically possible, taking into account all the circumstances at the time, including those relevant to the success of military operations.[115] Certain participants felt that the duty imposed on states in Article 38(2) should be the more stringent standard implied by the word 'necessary'.[116] However, this argument was not accepted and the word 'feasible' remained in the text.

Another point at issue regarding Article 38(2) concerned the type of participation prohibited: that is, whether it should include only direct participation in hostilities (as set out in 1977 GP I), or direct and indirect participation (as found in 1977 GP II).[117]

In the Working Group discussion at the beginning of 1988, a number of delegates were opposed to a formulation which prohibited only 'direct' participation.[118] One argument against this formulation was that it implicitly condoned indirect participation even in non-international armed conflicts, thus undermining the standard established in 1977 GP II.[119]

The final and most contentious issue regarding Article 38(2) related to the appropriate age limit above which children could legitimately participate in hostilities. The first draft of Article 38, adopted at the 1986 meeting of the Working Group, called on States Parties to 'take all feasible measures to ensure that no child takes a direct part in hostilities'.[120] However, members of the Working Group were concerned about the possible consequences of the use of the word 'child' without further definition. They argued that the rather flexible 1989 CRC definition of 'child' could mean that it would be compatible with the 1989 CRC for children even under 15, the age specified in the 1977 GPs, to take part in hostilities, if they had achieved majority under national law.[121]

---

[114] See UN Doc. E/CN.4/1988/28, 19–20.

[115] Bothe, Partsch, and Solf (1982), 372–3.

[116] UN Doc. E/CN.4/1988/28, 19–20.

[117] Art. 77(2) of 1977 GP I prohibits direct participation of persons under 15, while Art. 4(3)(c) of 1977 GP II states that children under 15 should not be 'allowed to take part in hostilities'. The latter, more general, formulation can be interpreted as including direct and indirect participation.

[118] See summary of discussion in UN Doc. E/CN.4/1988/28, 19–20.

[119] *Ibid.* See also DCI (1989), 3.

[120] See n. 108 above.

[121] As already mentioned (sect. 1.3), by Art. 1 of the 1989 CRC 'child' includes all persons under 18 unless they achieve majority earlier by national law.

At the Second Reading of the draft Convention, efforts were made to amend this provision, among others. A drafting group (comprising eleven states, UNHCR, and, unusually, the ICRC and two NGOs) had considered possible amendments.[122] These included one from Sweden which aimed to raise existing standards so that States Parties would be obliged to take all 'necessary' measures to ensure that persons under 18 did not take part in hostilities either directly or indirectly, and it also prohibited absolutely any participation of those under 15.[123]

The drafting group had been unable to reach a consensus, and its report to the Working Group accordingly contained two versions of what is now Article 38(2).[124] The first version of Article 38(2) attempted to raise existing standards on the age of child participants and the manner of participation, in accordance with the Swedish amendment. The second and shorter version merely sought that States Parties should take 'all feasible measures to ensure that persons who have not attained the age of 15 years do not take a direct part in hostilities'.

The Working Group had a fairly heated discussion on these alternative versions of Article 38(2). The delegates of twenty-five countries and the ICRC supported the first and more stringent version of Article 38(2), but the United States and the USSR expressed a preference for the second. Only the US delegate stated that he was not willing to accept a consensus in favour of the first version. He was opposed to amendments which elevated norms of international legal protection above those specified in the 1949 GCs and 1977 GPs, and argued, *inter alia*, that the Working Group was not the proper forum in which to tamper with standards set by the governments which met in the 1977 Diplomatic Conference.[125]

The Working Group operated on the basis of consensus, which effectively amounted to giving each representative a veto. Confronted by this impasse, the Chairman decided, to the consternation of many delegates (see section 4.2.5.4 below), that the second, weaker, version should be put forward. This version was ultimately incorporated into the 1989 CRC. Accordingly, Article 38(2) sets the age limit at 15 years, and prohibits only direct participation.

---

[122] The drafting group consisted of representatives of Angola, Australia, Austria, France, India, Italy, Mozambique, the Netherlands, Norway, Sweden, the USA, UNHCR, ICRC, Friends World Committee for Consultation, and Rädda Barnen. See UN Doc. E/CN.4/1989/WG.1/WP.65, cited in UN Doc. E/CN.4/1989/48, 111.

[123] See UN Doc. E/CN.4/1988/WG.1/WP.19.

[124] These are set out in UN Doc. E/CN.4/1989/WG.1/WP.65. For summary of the discussion, see UN Doc. E/CN.4/1989/48, 110–16.

[125] See Rädda Barnen, *Debate of December 8, 1988* (1989), 4. This argument was rebutted by a number of delegates including the Australian representative, who contended that the Working Group had the task of developing international law, not of maintaining a status achieved 15 years ago: *ibid.*, 12. See also UN Doc. E/CN.4/1989/48, 110–16.

4.2.5.3.3 Child Civilians (Article 38(4))

Article 38(4) deals with the subject at the heart of this research: the treatment to be accorded to child civilians in situations of armed conflict.

On this issue there was disagreement within the Working Group on the level of obligation to be imposed on States Parties regarding the protection of child civilians. Once more, the argument focused on whether states should be required to take 'feasible' measures, or whether there should be a more exacting standard. Again, many participants in the drafting group felt 'feasible' set too low a standard, and they proposed the word 'necessary' as an alternative.[126] Thus, in the latter formulation, Article 38(4) would have read: 'States Parties shall take all *necessary* measures to ensure protection and care of children who are affected by an armed conflict'.

At the Second Reading, consensus could not be reached on this point, with the US representative in particular expressing a strong preference for the word 'feasible'. He argued that it would be impossible to fulfil a duty to take all 'necessary' steps to protect child civilians, as armed conflicts inevitably have harmful consequences for civilians and it would be impossible to ensure their protection. He posited that a duty to take all 'necessary' steps to protect such children might even undermine the state's inherent right to self-defence, as set out in the UN Charter.[127]

The ICRC representative, among others, argued against the US position, stating that 'this wording presents the greatest danger to the weakening of international humanitarian law were the word "feasible" to be kept'. She pointed out that 'as the guardians and promoters of humanitarian law' the ICRC wished to emphasise 'a fundamental aspect of that law which stipulates that the parties to the conflict shall at all times draw the distinction between the civilian population and combatants', and that the former should never be the object of attack. She stressed that this 'right to care and assistance is an absolute'. The ICRC representative also cited a number of Articles in 1949 GC IV, which she observed had been ratified at that time by 165 states, and by all the states present in the Working Group. These Articles all used stronger wording than the word 'feasible'.[128]

The ICRC contribution was followed by that of the Swedish Red Cross, which presented to the Working Group a 'universal youth statement' initiated by the Swedish Red Cross Youth and apparently supported

---

[126] See summary of this discussion in UN Doc. E/CN.4/1989/48, 110–16.

[127] See Rädda Barnen, *Debate of December 8, 1988*, (1989), 6.

[128] *Ibid.*, 7. The 1949 GC IV Arts. cited included Arts. 20(1), 23(1), 50(2), and 68(4). See also Krill, in Freeman and Veerman (eds.) (1992), 353–4.

by groups representing millions of young people worldwide. This statement, *inter alia*, criticised the proposed text of Article 38(4) for not containing an 'explicit recognition . . . of the absolute ban against targeting civilians'.[129]

As the discussion continued on Article 38(4), representatives of some twenty countries, and the ICRC, argued in favour of the higher standard required by the word 'necessary'. According to the UN record of that debate, '[t]his group of participants took this position because they felt that the word "necessary" more accurately reflected the absolute nature of protection which international instruments accorded civilians in times of armed conflict'.[130]

In an attempt to achieve a compromise, various participants proposed additional alternative wordings to either 'feasible' or 'necessary', but these too met with disagreement.[131] Given the lack of consensus, the Chairman therefore once more put forward the weaker version, which allowed only for 'feasible' measures.[132]

4.2.5.4 Final Outcome of Debates Concerning Article 38(2) and (4)

At the Second Reading, immediately following the Working Group's adoption of the weaker version of Article 38(2), a number of the participants protested, many of them stating that they could not join in the consensus on this paragraph.[133] After adoption of the final paragraph, Article 38(4), the Swedish representative asked, exceptionally, for a transcript of the meeting 'since we adopted an article . . . on the basis of a debate which I do not think is reflected in that decision'.[134]

Article 38 was also discussed in the Commission on Human Rights in March 1989, and a number of governments and other bodies expressed grave concern at the inadequacies of paragraphs (2) and (4). The ICRC and Rädda Barnen went so far as to urge the Commission to improve these

---

[129] Rädda Barnen, *Debate of December 8, 1988*, 9. The statement, based on a letter sent by the Swedish organisation, was said to have received a 'positive response' from 654 organisations. Apparently the membership of 337 of these amounted to a total of more than 100 million young people, from over 118 countries (letter circulated by Swedish Red Cross, Box 27316, S–102 54 Stockholm).

[130] See UN Doc. E/CN.4/1989/48, 110–16, at para. 618 (which also lists the 20 countries).

[131] The UK representative proposed the word 'practicable', and this was supported by the USSR, USA, and India. However, the Australian observer found this unacceptable and proposed 'possible', but this was opposed by the USA: *ibid.*, para. 619.

[132] Rädda Barnen, *Debate of December 8, 1988*, (1989), 26. See also UN Doc. E/CN.4/1989/48, 110–16 at para. 620.

[133] These included Austria, Finland, Italy, Norway, Sweden, and Venezuela: Rädda Barnen, *Debate of December 8, 1988*, (1989), 31–3, and UN Doc. E/CN.4/1989/48, 110–16, at para. 612.

[134] Rädda Barnen, *Debate of December 8, 1988*, (1989), 33, and UN Doc. E/CN.4/1989/48, 110–16, at para. 622.

paragraphs before the Convention went any further, and put forward proposed amendments which were not accepted.[135]

Concern about the standards set in Article 38 was voiced subsequently, when the 1989 CRC was discussed by the Third Committee of the UN General Assembly in November 1989. In this forum, the Polish representative acknowledged, as regards the protection of children in armed conflict, that he hoped the standards in the 1977 GPs would be invoked with reference to Article 41 of the 1989 CRC, as the 1977 GPs contain the higher standard.[136]

Prior to the final adoption of the 1989 CRC by the UN General Assembly, Rädda Barnen circulated a document arguing, *inter alia*, that, as regards the standard implied by 'feasible measures' in Article 38(4), '[t]he least that has to be done is to make clear for the *travaux préparatoires* that this formulation is not intended to lower the standards of international humanitarian law with regard to the protection of children'.[137]

In the event, the lower standards discussed in the Working Group in relation to Article 38(2) and (4) have nonetheless found their way into the final version of the 1989 CRC.[138] However, as regards Article 38(2) in particular, the controversy has by no means abated, and it has generated pressure within the UN for the adoption of a Protocol to this Convention (mentioned in section 6.1.1.2 below).

Further, of the 187 countries which had signed, ratified, or acceded to the 1989 CRC as at 1 March 1996, a number had entered specific declarations or reservations concerning Article 38. These generally objected to the age of 15 as establishing too low a threshold for participation in armed conflict, and expressed the intention to apply a higher standard.[139]

---

[135] See generally Rädda Barnen, *United Nations Draft Convention on the Rights of the Child: Commission on Human Rights, Debate of 8 March 1989* (Stockholm, 1989). Rädda Barnen suggested that Art. 38(2) should be amended so that States Parties would be obliged to take 'all feasible measures to ensure that no child takes a direct part in hostilities': *ibid.*, 72–3. The ICRC argued that only the 1st para. of Art. 38 should be retained: *ibid.* 92. Government representatives who criticised Art. 38 included those from Sweden, Belgium, Australia, Italy, Austria, Switzerland, Portugal, and the Netherlands. See generally *ibid.* See also Krill, in Freeman and Veerman (eds.) (1992), 354.

[136] See UN Doc. A/C.3/44/SR.38 (10 Nov. 1989), para. 4.

[137] Rädda Barnen, *No Child Soldiers* (1989), 4.

[138] A number of writers have criticised the standards set by Art. 38. See, e.g., Krill, in Freeman and Veerman (eds.) (1992), 354; Mann (1987), 56; and H. J. Heintz, 'The UN Convention and the Network of the International Human Rights Protection by the UN', in Freeman and Veerman (eds.) (1992), 75.

[139] As at 30 June 1995, the countries which had made reservations or declarations to Art. 38 were Argentina, Austria, Colombia, Germany, Netherlands, Poland, Spain and Uruguay. See UN Doc. CRC/C/2/Rev.4 (1995), 12 (Argentina and Austria), 15, 19, 27, 28, 29, and 32 respectively. Of these, all except Poland objected to the age limit of 15. See also D. O'Donnell, 'The Reservation Generation', 9.1 *International Children's Rights Monitor* 13 (1992), and J. Kuper, 'Reservations, Declarations and Objections to the 1989 Convention on the Rights of the Child', to be published in J. P. Gardner (ed.), *Human Rights as General Norms and a State's Right to Opt Out: Reservations and Objections to Human Rights Conventions* (London, 1997).

The above examination of the drafting history of Article 38 of the 1989 CRC reveals the contentious process that contributed to its inadequacies. In the end, the lowest common denominator prevailed in certain crucial respects. The drafting history of Article 38 is both a tribute to the work and ideals of a number of governments and NGOs, and a sad testament to their ultimate failure.

4.3 THE DUTY TO RESPECT AND THE DUTY TO PROTECT

The provisions of international humanitarian treaty law specifically concerning child civilians, summarised in this Chapter, (like those concerning civilians generally (Chapter 3)), incorporate both the duty to respect (that is, the negative duty not to harm) and the duty to protect (that is, the positive obligation to assist).

These two aspects of the legislation are clearly evidenced in, particularly, 1949 GC IV and the 1977 GPs.

Accordingly, the duty to respect child civilians can be found most notably in Article 77(1) of 1977 GP I articulating the fundamental principle of their entitlement to 'special respect'. Other provisions also express the duty to respect, such as those limiting resort to the death penalty (Articles 68 of 1949 GC IV; 77(5) of 1977 GP I; and 6(4) of 1977 GP II).

In general, however, most of the measures specifically concerning child civilians articulate the duty to protect, or actively to assist them. Thus Article 77(1) of 1977 GP I also expresses this principle, in specifying that the belligerents must protect them from indecent assault and 'provide them with the care and aid they require'.

In addition, the duty to protect child civilians can be found, among others, in the provisions applicable to international armed conflicts concerning hospital and safety zones (Article 14 of 1949 GC IV); removal and/ or evacuation (as in Articles 17 and 24 of 1949 GC IV, and Article 78 of 1977 GP I); relief consignments (Article 23 of 1949 GC IV and Article 70(1) of 1977 GP I), and the treatment of child civilians in occupied territory (as in Articles 50, 51, 76, 89, and 132 of 1949 GC IV). Similarly, the emphasis of the provisions concerning non-international armed conflict is on the duty to protect (see generally Article 4 of 1977 GP II).

International humanitarian law therefore differentiates child civilians from civilians generally, and it also goes further. It is significant that this body of law recognises the particular vulnerability of child civilians in situations of armed conflict by focusing predominantly on measures concerning the duty to protect, or positively to assist, them, rather than on measures simply to respect them.

4.4 OTHER INTERNATIONAL INITIATIVES REGARDING THE PROTECTION OF CHILD CIVILIANS

This Chapter has considered conventional measures in international humanitarian law specifically concerned with children in armed conflict. Certain other related initiatives will now be described below.

4.4.1 UN General Assembly Resolution 3318 (XXIX)

UN General Assembly Resolution 3318 (XXIX),[140] entitled 'Declaration on the Protection of Women and Children in Emergency and Armed Conflict' and adopted in December 1974, was preceded by numerous discussions under the ægis of the UN Economic and Social Council (hereafter ECOSOC), largely in the Commission on the Status of Women.[141] Although not innovative, this Declaration served to underscore the plight of women and children in armed conflict, and probably exerted some influence on the outcome of the 1974–7 Geneva Diplomatic Conferences.

It has a lengthy Preamble which, *inter alia*, expresses concern at the suffering of civilian women and children in situations of armed conflict. It also invokes provisions of international humanitarian law relevant to the protection of women and children, and affirms the General Assembly's awareness 'of its responsibility for the destiny of the rising generation' and of 'the need to provide special protection of women and children belonging to the civilian population'.

The six substantive provisions of this Declaration are all germane to the subject under consideration here. The first two provisos, of particular relevance in relation to the Iraqi study (Chapter 7), are set out fully below, while the others will be summarised.

First, '[a]ttacks and bombings on the civilian population, inflicting incalculable suffering, especially on women and children, who are the most vulnerable members of the population, shall be prohibited, and such acts shall be condemned.'

Secondly, use 'of chemical and bacteriological weapons in the course of

---

[140] UN GA Res. 3318 (XXIX) (14 Dec. 1974), UN GAOR, 29th Sess. Supp. No. 31 (A/9631) (1975), 146. Certain recent UN resolutions, such as UN GA Res. 48/157 and Commission on Human Rights Res. 1994/94, concerning children in armed conflict, are discussed in sect. 6.1.1.2 below, in connection with the Committee on the Rights of the Child.

[141] For chronology of resolutions on this issue in the Commission on the Status of Women and in ECOSOC generally, see Khushalani (1982), 109–11. See also her discussion of the two reports prepared by the UN Secretary General at that time on 'Protection of Women and Children in Emergency or Wartime, Fighting for Peace, Self-Determination, National Liberation and Independence' (one in 1972 (UN Doc. E/CN.6/561) and one in 1973 (UN Doc. E/CN.6/586)), cited in Khushalani (1982), 111–13.

military operations constitutes one of the most flagrant violations of the Geneva Protocol of 1925, the Geneva Conventions of 1949 and the principles of international humanitarian law, and inflicts heavy losses on civilian populations, including defenceless women and children, and shall be severely condemned'. This second paragraph is of singular interest here in that this UN General Assembly Declaration, specifically concerned with the protection of children and women in armed conflict, cites the use of chemical weapons (as deployed against the Iraqi Kurds) as a particularly flagrant violation.

The Declaration proceeds to call on states to abide by pertinent international legal instruments, and exhorts states involved in armed conflicts 'to spare women and children from the ravages of war', and to prohibit, *inter alia*, torture and violence particularly in relation to them. It asserts that cruel and inhuman treatment of women and children by belligerents should be considered criminal and, finally, that belligerents must provide civilian women and children with shelter, food, medical aid, and 'their inalienable rights'.[142]

4.4.2 1994 'Draft-Declaration on the Rights of Children in Armed Conflict' (Declaration of Amsterdam)

One final document is worthy of mention in the context of the development of international law regarding the protection of child civilians. This is the 1994 Draft Declaration of Amsterdam.[143] Although neither treaty law nor, at the time of writing, a UN document, the Amsterdam Declaration is of interest for two main reasons. First, it is a recent initiative which sets out fairly comprehensive legal and policy guidelines concerning the treatment of children in armed conflict. Secondly, the aim of those who drafted this Declaration was that it ultimately be adopted as 'an official United Nations document'.[144] However, since it has not, at the time of writing, been formally adopted by the UN, this document will be described fairly briefly here.

---

[142] In support of these rights, the Declaration invokes the UDHR, the ICCPR, the ICESCR, and the Declaration of the Rights of the Child 'or other instruments of international law'.

[143] Declaration of Amsterdam, in Aldrich and van Baarda (1994) Annex 4, 110–34. In addition to this Declaration, there are other policy documents which are neither treaty law nor UN Resolutions and which have focused to some extent on the protection of children in armed conflict. The most detailed of these is probably the 'Children's Charter in Wartime of the United States Department of Labor Children's Bureau' (1942) (cited in Veerman (1992), 237–42). This refers, *inter alia*, to the concept of 'war vacations', which is incorporated into the Declaration of Amsterdam (Aldrich and van Baarda (1994), 117). See also the ICRC's 'Final Declaration of the Conference', in ICRC, *International Conference for the Protection of War Victims* (Geneva, 1993), 377, paras. 1 and 3.

[144] See Aldrich and van Baarda (1994), para. 8.5, 133.

The Amsterdam Declaration incorporates international humanitarian law regarding both child civilians and child combatants, although the emphasis is on the former. After the Preamble, it is separated into three sections: Part I, 'Recommendations on child-victims of war'; Part II, 'Recommendations on the humanitarian protection and assistance of civilians including children'; and Part III, 'Concluding paragraphs'.

Part I sets out a number of general provisions, including measures regarding non-discrimination; the distinction between civilians and combatants; and the importance of family unity during hostilities and of addressing the psychological impact of armed conflict. It then, in relation to particular categories of 'child-victims', focuses on measures regarding the treatment of, among others, unaccompanied, orphaned, or refugee children; child victims of mines and booby-traps; children born as a result of rape; and child prisoners of war. The final section of Part I goes on to deal with supervisory mechanisms, such as the Committee on the Rights of the Child, and it proposes, in some detail, the appointment within the UN of a Special Rapporteur on the Protection of Children in Armed Conflict.

In Part II, the Amsterdam Declaration sets out a number of general observations, arguing, for example, that the Declaration should apply in both international and non-international armed conflicts. Further, it deals with relief actions for the civilian population, emphasising, *inter alia*, the right of victims of armed conflict to prompt humanitarian assistance. As regards restrictions on the use of force, Part II then, for example, refers to the question of zones for the protection of civilians, as set out in 1949 GC IV and 1977 GP I. It argues that Articles 14 and 15 of 1949 GC IV should, 'by analogy', apply to non-international as well as international armed conflicts. Also emphasised here is the importance of humanitarian cease-fires, and of strengthening the 1980 Inhumane Weapons Convention. In relation to supervisory mechanisms, Part II concludes by looking, among other things, at the potential of the International Fact-Finding Commission (mentioned in section 6.2.2 below) to intervene in non-international armed conflicts, and at the possible role of Protecting Powers in relation to this Commission.

Finally, in Part III, this Declaration comments, *inter alia*, on the importance of the contribution of NGOs to standard-setting, and on the problem of the politicisation of humanitarian aid. It urges states to take the Declaration into account when applying or interpreting international humanitarian law.

The Amsterdam Declaration therefore incorporates many of the measures concerning child civilians already described in this book. In addition, it attempts to raise standards in a number of areas, for example by extending to non-international armed conflicts certain provisions applicable in international armed conflicts (such as Articles 14 and 15 of 1949 GC IV), and by proposing the appointment of a Special Rapporteur for the Protection of Children in Armed Conflict. This latter proposal is discussed more fully in section 8.3.4 below.

4.5 SUMMARY: THE LAW OF ARMED CONFLICT CONCERNING CHILD CIVILIANS

In summary, it is evident that the body of law described in this Chapter is fairly detailed, and covers most of the essential issues that affect child civilians in situations of armed conflict.

Thus the treaty law set out in 1949 GC IV and the 1977 GPs provides for the special treatment of children generally; for the establishment of zones for their protection; for the removal or evacuation of children from the combat arena; for the free passage of consignments; for family unity; and for restrictions on the imposition of the death penalty. Provision is made particularly for children in international armed conflict, including specific categories of children (such as those in occupied territory). However, the key provisions also apply in non-international armed conflict. In addition, the 1980 Inhumane Weapons Convention, to a limited extent, specifically addresses the problem of children's vulnerability to weapons such as landmines. The emphasis throughout is largely on the positive duty to assist children in situations of armed conflict, rather than on the negative duty simply not to harm them.

Further, much of this body of law is incorporated into Article 38 of the 1989 CRC although, as mentioned in section 4.2.5.3.1 above, there is some ambiguity about the specific provisions that apply to particular states.

In any event, this is clearly a substantial body of law, and its more diligent observance would alleviate the suffering of at least some children in situations of armed conflict. This point is relevant to later discussion, in Chapter 8, regarding the impact of this law, and whether it can best be strengthened by improved implementation of existing provisions, or by legislative reform.

5

Customary Law

The three preceding chapters have considered international human rights and humanitarian law, as set out largely in treaty and in other legal instruments, that is relevant to the treatment of child civilians in situations of armed conflict. However, a summary of this body of law would be incomplete without at least a brief consideration of the possible customary law status of certain of its provisions.

The customary status of particular norms is, of course, important, as this generally renders them binding on all states, even states that are not party to treaties that may articulate such norms.[1] Further, when they are enshrined in treaty, customary principles cannot, for example, be subject to derogation, reservation, or withdrawal.[2] In addition, as one authority has emphasised, 'the invocation of a norm as both conventional and customary adds at least rhetorical strength to the moral claim for its observance and affects its interpretation'.[3]

This Chapter will discuss the possible customary law status of the principle that child civilians in armed conflict are entitled to special treatment. A definitive examination of this complex and controversial question is beyond the scope of this book and would be a fruitful area for further research.

5.1 GENERAL ISSUES

Customary law in general, and specifically in relation to human rights and humanitarian principles, has been described and analysed by many writers.[4]

---

[1] See Meron (1989), 3. See also P. Sieghart, *The International Law of Human Rights* (Oxford, 1984), 11. The only exception to the universal application of customary law is that it does not normally apply to states that have persistently objected to a particular norm *ab initio*.

[2] See, for example, Meron (1989), 6 and 7. More generally, see 1969 Convention on the Law of Treaties (1969 Vienna Convention), UN Doc. A/Conf.39/27, 23 May 1969; 8 ILM 679 (1969), and I. Sinclair, *The Vienna Convention on the Law of Treaties* (2nd edn., Manchester, 1984).

[3] Meron (1989), 9.

[4] See particularly Gardam (1993), which deals with a subject of considerable relevance to the present book, namely the customary-law status of the norm of non-combatant immunity. On customary law in the context of humanitarian law, see, among others, Greenwood, in Delissen and Tanja (eds.) (1991), 93–114; Green (1993), 55–6; Meron 'The Geneva Conventions as Customary Law' (1987), and Meron (1989) generally. In relation to customary law and human rights norms see, *inter alia*, L. Hannikainen, *Peremptory Norms (Jus Cogens) in*

Further, it has been examined in major cases before the ICJ, such as the *Nicaragua Case*,[5] and the *North Sea Continental Shelf Cases*.[6]

For the purposes of this book it is necessary only to pinpoint certain relevant concepts concerning customary law, as analysed in these writings and judgments, which can throw light on the possible customary law status of principles pertaining to the protection of child civilians. The relevant general concepts are discussed in sections 5.1.1 to 5.1.3 below, before the possible customary principles relating to child civilians are examined in section 5.2.

5.1.1 Customary Law and Peremptory Norms (*Jus Cogens*)[7]

The first aspect of customary law to be considered here, in preparation for the discussion in section 5.2, is the relationship between customary law and peremptory norms. Both these terms are used by different writers in examining and categorising certain legal principles relevant to child civilians in situations of armed conflict. For the sake of clarity, therefore, these two terms are defined briefly below.[8]

However, the key issue under consideration in section 5.2 is whether or not particular principles pertinent to child civilians can be categorised as customary norms. Since all peremptory norms are likely to be customary law principles, the distinction between these two terms is not of crucial significance in this context.

First, the essential components of customary law have been described by the ICJ as follows: 'not only must the acts concerned amount to a settled practice, but they must also be such, or be carried out in such a way, as to

---

International Law: Historical Development, Criteria, Present Status (Helsinki, 1988), 425–520; Meron (1989), 79–135; Oraa (1992); and the American Law Institute, *Restatement of the Law Third, the Foreign Relations Law of the United States* (St Paul, Minn., 1987), para. 702. Concerning customary law in general, see, e.g., Sinclair (1984); Cheng (1965); M. Akehurst, 'Custom as a Source of International Law' 47 *BYIL* 1 (1974–5); A. A. D'Amato, *The Concept of Custom in International Law* (Ithaca, 1971); H. W. A. Thirlway, *International Customary Law and Codification* (Leiden, 1972), and the American Law Institute (1987). On the related subject of peremptory norms, see also Hannikainen (1988) generally.

[5] *Military and Paramilitary Activities in and against Nicaragua (Nicaragua* v. *The United States of America): Merits* [1986] ICJ Rep. 14.

[6] *North Sea Continental Shelf Cases* [1969] ICJ Rep. 3 (Judgment of 20 Feb.). These cases and the Nicaragua case have been discussed by many writers, including some of those cited in n. 4 above. See generally, e.g., Meron (1989); Hannikainen (1988) and Gardam (1993).

[7] In the interest of simplicity, and following the practice of Hannikainen, the terms *jus cogens* and 'peremptory norm' (as defined in the text of this sect.) are used interchangeably in this book, although Meron, among others, points out that in certain contexts peremptory norms may not be coterminous with *jus cogens*: Meron (1986), 197.

[8] A further category of international legal principles, which is also generally customary, does not require discussion here. This is obligations *erga omnes*, which are international obligations so basic that they apply to all states, and every state has a right to act in order to protect them. See, e.g., the discussion in Meron (1989), 188–200; Meron (1986), 173–87; and Sinclair (1984), 212–13.

be evidence of a belief that this practice is rendered obligatory by the existence of a rule of law requiring it'.[9] It is therefore seen to consist of two main elements: state practice and *opinio juris*.[10] The fact that customary law evolves through state practice and *opinio juris* means that, to quote one authority, it is 'perhaps the most "political" form of international law, reflecting the consensus of the great majority of states'.[11]

Some writers define state practice more broadly than others,[12] and the preference here is to follow a wide definition, in order to address a range of factors which may indicate such practice. Thus, in section 5.2 below, evidence of state practice will be sought, *inter alia*, in patterns of ratification or approval of international treaties and other legal instruments, including UN Resolutions;[13] commentaries on such international legal instruments; their *travaux préparatoires*; and the reports of international conferences. State practice as evidenced in the Iraqi conflicts will be more fully discussed in Chapter 7.

Peremptory norms may be distinguished from customary law generally in that they are particularly stringent norms which can crystallise from customary law principles. They are defined in Article 53 of the 1969 Vienna Convention as norms 'accepted and recognised by the international community of states as a whole as a norm from which no derogation is permitted and which can be modified only by a subsequent norm of general international law having the same character'.[14]

5.1.2 Relationship Between Treaty and Custom

The second aspect of customary law relevant to the present discussion is the relationship between treaty and customary law, since both these categories

[9] See the *North Sea Continental Shelf Cases* [1969] ICJ Rep. 3, 44. This quotation is described by one authority as the '*locus classicus* of the constitutive elements of international customary law': Meron (1989), 107. See also Art. 38(1)(b) of the Statute of the ICJ. (Annexed to the UN Charter, 1946–7 *Yearbook of the UN* 847).

[10] See Gardam (1993), 133–6 for an analysis of these elements in the context of the norm of non-combatant immunity. However, in a critique of Meron (1989), one writer states that too much emphasis can be placed on the 'orthodox "two-element theory" of custom' which, he argues, is in fact little supported in case law, although lip-service is paid to it: M. Koskeniemi, 'The Pull of the Mainstream', 8.6 *Michigan Law Review* 1946 (May 1990).

[11] Higgins (1963), 1.

[12] See, e.g., Gardam (1993), 133–5; Hannikainen (1988), 232–3; and Brownlie (1990), 5. For a narrower definition of state practice, see generally D'Amato (1971).

[13] On the customary law status of UN General Assembly and Security Council Resolutions, Hannikainen (1988), 232–3, argues that such resolutions, particularly when adopted consistently by a number of international organs, or repeatedly by one organ, seem to be evidence of the practice and the *opinio juris* of those states which vote for the resolutions. See also discussion in sect. 2.1.2.1 above.

[14] For discussion of the concept of peremptory norms/*jus cogens*, see particularly Meron (1986), 175–97; Meron (1989), 8–9; Sinclair (1984), 203–26; Brownlie (1990), 512–15; M. Whiteman, '*Jus Cogens* in International Law, With a Projected List', 7 *Georgia Journal of International and Comparative Law* 609 (1977), and Hannikainen generally.

of law articulate rules which concern the treatment of child civilians in situations of armed conflict.

Treaty and customary law principles may overlap and co-exist (as indicated, *inter alia*, at the beginning of this Chapter). Thus it is widely accepted that treaty provisions can be regarded as expressing customary norms, particularly (1) when they codify principles that were already customary law prior to the treaty, or (2) when they go beyond existing customary law, but the principles expressed in the treaty come to be accepted as generally applicable and therefore part of new customary international law.[15]

Accordingly international customary law can be generated by treaty,[16] and membership of a treaty can itself sometimes constitute state practice. On the latter point, the ICJ stated in the *North Sea Continental Shelf Cases* that, as regards provisions that are of a norm-creating character, 'very widespread and representative participation in the convention might suffice of itself, provided it included that of States whose interests were specially affected'.[17] This point is particularly relevant in considering the possible customary law status of principles articulated in widely ratified treaties such as the 1949 GCs and the 1989 CRC, as discussed in sections 5.2.2 to 5.2.4 below.

However, there is some controversy about the significance of treaty membership in the development of customary law. Thus, for example, one authoritative body, the Institute of International Law, is of the view that, when a country is party to a particular treaty, its practice in complying with those treaty provisions that may codify customary principles is, in itself, not convincing evidence of the existence of a customary norm.[18]

5.1.3 Inconsistent State Practice

Finally, the third aspect of customary law pertinent to the discussion in section 5.2 concerns the significance of inconsistent state practice and the

---

[15] Greenwood (1991), 96. The relationship between treaty and custom has been explored by writers such as Gardam (1993), 136–41; Higgins (1994), 28–37; Meron (1989), 4–8 and generally; D'Amato (1971), 103–66, and Greenwood (1991), 98–9. Further, this issue was examined by the ICJ in the *Nicaragua Case* (see, e.g., [1986] ICJ Rep., para. 218, regarding Common Art. 3) and the *North Sea Continental Shelf Cases* [1969] ICJ Rep. 41–5.

[16] See, e.g., Sinclair (1984), 23.

[17] [1969] ICJ Rep. 43. See also Gardam (1993), 137, and Meron (1989), 8.

[18] Institut de Droit International (Session de Lisbonne), *First Commission: Problems Arising From a Succession of Codification Conventions on a Particular Subject. Rev.1.* (N.p., Aug. 1995), 5. In this context, the Institute argues that 'the significance of an instance of State practice will be substantially enhanced if it is established that those concerned had been acting in the conviction that the practice was required by a rule of customary international law independently of the applicability of the convention': *ibid*. See also discussion of this question in Gardam (1993), 137–8.

relative weight to be placed, in this context, on *opinio juris* and on state practice. Again, this issue has been explored by a number of writers, and is only touched on here.[19]

The ICJ, too, examined this question in the *Nicaragua Case*, and it accepted that inconsistent state practice does not necessarily undermine the continuing existence of a customary norm, provided that certain criteria are met. These are that 'the conduct of States should, in general, be consistent with such rules, and that instances of State conduct inconsistent with a given rule should generally have been treated as breaches of that rule, not as indications of the recognition of a new rule'.[20]

One writer emphasises that, although the Court's approach here is 'highly controversial', it is nonetheless sound, particularly in relation to certain aspects of humanitarian law, such as the principle of non-combatant immunity. In support of the customary status of the norm of non-combatant immunity, she argues that:

there is a high level of contrary State practice in the area of humanitarian law, particularly with respect to non-combatant immunity. However, despite the common practice of failing to distinguish between civilians and combatants, states do not claim that they regard civilians as legitimate targets of attack. Quite the reverse.[21]

Clearly this argument applies equally to the protection of child civilians in situations of armed conflict, where, despite state practice to the contrary, no state would claim to regard child civilians, in particular, as legitimate targets of attack.

Another writer emphasises, in relation to humanitarian law generally, that 'in the violent situations addressed by the humanitarian Conventions, the gulf between the more enlightened norms and the actual practice of states may, to some extent, be expected to remain formidable'.[22] This statement acknowledges the inevitability of a degree of inconsistent state practice in the context of customary norms pertaining to situations of armed conflict.

5.2 RELEVANT CUSTOMARY NORMS

The above section considered certain pertinent terms and issues regarding customary law in general, and this section will now examine specific principles which relate to the protection of child civilians and which may be

[19] See, e.g., discussion in Gardam (1993), 133–5; Hannikainen (1988), 235; and Meron (1989), 58–60.
[20] The *Nicaragua Case* [1986] ICJ Rep. 98, para. 186.
[21] Gardam (1993), 135.
[22] Meron (1989), 44.

considered customary. These principles are found in both human rights and humanitarian law, and are as follows: (1) the right not to be arbitrarily deprived of life; (2) the entitlement of children to special treatment generally; (3) the entitlement of civilians to protection in situations of armed conflict; and (4) the entitlement of child civilians to special treatment in situations of armed conflict. As indicated in Chapters 2 to 4 above, the first two categories of principles are primarily to be found in human rights law, and the latter in humanitarian law.

5.2.1 The Right Not to be Arbitrarily Deprived of Life

Although much has been written on the possible customary nature of certain human rights norms and instruments, controversy remains about the precise principles that constitute customary human rights law.[23] Nonetheless, there does seem to be agreement on the status of certain norms, including a consensus that the right not to be arbitrarily deprived of life is a customary principle,[24] and arguably a peremptory norm.[25]

As a principle of customary human rights law, the prohibition on arbitrary deprivation of life can apply equally in times of peace and times of conflict, and even to states that are not party to treaties which express this norm. Accordingly, states are in principle obliged to observe this norm in all conflict situations, including internal disturbances, and, clearly, in relation to all those involved, whether adult or child.

In this context, it is of interest that, in a recent case, the Inter-American Commission on Human Rights held that the prohibition on the execution of juveniles is emerging as a customary international norm.[26] This judgment therefore supports the customary status of two relevant principles: the right to life and the entitlement of children to special treatment.

5.2.2 The Entitlement of Children to Special Treatment Generally

As regards the concept that children, as such, are entitled to special treatment generally, it is arguable that this is now a customary norm, or at

---

[23] E.g., there is even disagreement as to the customary status of the UDHR, as is evidenced by comments of writers such as Sieghart (1984), 53–4; R. Higgins, *Human Rights—Proposals and Problems* (Leeds, 1979), 7; and Oraa (1992), 215.

[24] See, e.g., Higgins (1976–7), 282; Hannikainen (1988), 436; and Meron (1989), 193–4. Further, see Human Rights Committee General Comment No. 24(52) on Reservations to the ICCPR. UN Doc. CCPR/C/21/Rev.1/Add.b, at 3 (1994). The right to be protected from torture and analogous treatment is also largely accepted as a customary norm, but, as already mentioned, that aspect of the relevant law is not being dealt with here.

[25] The peremptory status of the right to life is supported by Hannikainen (1988), 436 and 516–17.

[26] *Annual Report of the Inter-American Commission on Human Rights*, Res. No. 3/87, Case No 9647 (US), 172, para. 60.

least an evolving customary norm, although its detailed content may be ill-defined and subject to disagreement.

Evidence in favour of a customary norm supporting the special treatment of children may be gleaned from, *inter alia*, the wide acceptance within the international community of both human rights and humanitarian conventions which articulate the principle of special care and assistance for children; relevant UN resolutions; and the reports of international conferences (as discussed particularly in Chapters 2 and 4).[27] Further evidence comes in the form of government approval of and involvement in international organisations and other bodies concerned with children (see Chapter 6 below), and the prevalence of domestic legislation which provides for their special treatment.

Thus Chapters 2 and 4 above describe a pattern of international treaty ratification and the adoption of other legal instruments, which repeatedly affirm the notion that children should benefit from preferential treatment in a broad range of circumstances.

However, as indicated in section 5.1.2, there are differences of opinion on the significance that can be attached to state compliance with norms set out in treaties to which the state is party. Such compliance can be seen either simply as compliance with the treaty, or as recognition of a customary principle, or both, depending on the circumstances. For the purposes of the following discussion, it is argued only that it is significant, in indicating an acceptance of the underlying principle that children are entitled to special treatment generally, that so many states have ratified or unanimously supported the relevant legal instruments. It is not argued here that such ratification or support indicates acceptance, as customary norms, of the detailed content of such legal instruments.

Accordingly, as regards human rights law, it will be recalled that the main global human rights instruments (particularly the UDHR, the ICCPR, and the ICESCR) and all the regional instruments support, to a greater or lesser extent, the broad concept of special treatment for children. Further, both the 1924 and the 1959 Declarations of the Rights of the Child set out the general principle that children are entitled to special treatment, and the 1989 CRC crystallises this principle and elaborates on it. Indeed, the unanimous adoption of all three of these instruments specifically concerning children, and the exceptionally rapid and extensive ratification of the 1989 CRC, lend weight to the contention that the principle of the special treatment of children, which underlies the 1989 CRC and is expressed particu-

---

[27] Sect. 1.5 above also indicates that there is cross-cultural support for the notion that children require special treatment. However, since such treatment does not always entail a higher level of care and protection (as with circumcision or child marriage), cross-cultural practices are not relied on here as a source of custom.

larly in its core principles,[28] now represents at least evolving customary law. The same cannot be said for certain of the detailed provisions of the 1989 CRC, as they clearly represent an advancement on existing norms at this stage.[29]

In relation to humanitarian law, the broad ratification of 1949 GC IV and, to a lesser extent, the 1977 GPs, again indicates widespread support and possible customary status for the notion of special treatment of children, as expressed in many Articles in these treaties (see section 5.2.4 below).

Similarly, the reports and debates of the 1990 World Summit for Children, the 1992 Rio Conference, the 1993 Vienna Conference, the 1994 Cairo Conference, the 1995 Copenhagen Summit, and the 1995 Beijing Conference all reflect state practice, in recent international fora, which indicates a consensus that the special requirements of children must be considered and separately provided for.

Finally, there is evidence that states generally make provision in their domestic legislation for the particular requirements of children, as mentioned in section 1.5 above.

It is therefore arguable, perhaps particularly after the unprecedented state support for the 1989 CRC, that the concept that children are entitled to special treatment should now be accepted as, at least, an evolving norm of international customary law. Again, as a human rights norm it would generally apply in times of peace as well as in situations of armed conflict, and, importantly, in internal disturbances.

Acceptance of the customary status of a norm regarding the special treatment of children has certain consequences, for example in relation to UN intervention, and military strategy, in situations of armed conflict. This issue is considered further in section 8.2 below.

5.2.3 The Entitlement of Civilians to Protection in Situations of Armed Conflict

The entitlement of civilians to protection in situations of armed conflict is a further principle of international customary law which is, clearly, relevant to the treatment of child civilians in such situations. As already discussed, child civilians qualify for protection under international humanitarian law both as members of the civilian population generally, and as a particularly vulnerable and distinct category of civilian.

---

[28] As indicated above (sect. 2.2.2), there is no real consensus on the content of these core principles, but they arguably include Art. 3, on the best interests of the child, and Art. 12, concerning the wishes of the child.
[29] Examples of provisions which generally represent an advancement are Arts. 31 (the child's right to leisure, play and cultural activities) and 33 (protection from drug abuse).

General customary principles for the protection of civilians include the admonition that 'the right of belligerents to adopt means of injuring the enemy is not unlimited'.[30] They also incorporate the precepts of military necessity;[31] humanity,[32] and chivalry[33] which should be observed in the conduct of armed conflict. Broadly, these precepts establish a framework for the limitation of certain methods of armed conflict, as well as for the protection of civilians, including that they should not be directly attacked and that they should be shielded when possible from the effects of attack. The tension in particular between military necessity and humanitarian considerations is a continuing and major dilemma in armed conflict, and one that is most relevant to the protection of civilians, including children.[34] Indeed, one writer contends that 'it is the relation between these two forces which determines the contents of the law of armed conflict at any given moment'.[35]

In relation to the protection of civilians in armed conflict, another writer has meticulously researched the customary law status of the principle of non-combatant immunity, and has concluded that this is a customary norm in international armed conflict.[36] She specifically cites as customary, for example, the provisions of 1977 GP I Article 48 (the basic principle of distinguishing civilians from combatants and only targeting the latter), and certain paragraphs of Article 51 (measures for the protection of the civilian population). These paragraphs include Article 51(5)(b) (the proportionality principle); Article 51(2) (prohibiting the targeting and terrorising of civilians); Article 51(3) (providing for civilian immunity in the absence of direct participation in hostilities); Article 51(4)(a) and (b) (prohibiting certain kinds of indiscriminate attacks); and Article 51(7) (prohibiting

---

[30] Roberts and Guelff (eds.) (1989), 5. As will be recalled, this concept is expressed in 1907 Hague Convention IV and 1977 GP I (sects. 3.1.1. and 3.1.2.1).

[31] 'Military necessity' is defined as the principle that '[o]nly that degree and kind of force, not otherwise prohibited by the law of armed conflict, required for the partial or complete submission of the enemy with a minimum expenditure of time, life, and physical resources may be applied': Roberts and Guelff (eds.) (1989), 5. (The authors here cite the United States, Department of the Navy, Office of the Chief of Naval Operations, *The Commander's Handbook on the Law of Naval Operations* (Washington, DC, 1987), 5–1.)

[32] The principle of humanity prohibits '[t]he employment of any kind or degree of force not required for the purpose of the partial or complete submission of the enemy with a minimum expenditure of time, life and physical resources': *ibid.*

[33] The principle of chivalry forbids '[d]ishonourable (treacherous) means, dishonourable expedients, and dishonourable conduct during armed conflict': *ibid.*

[34] For discussion of these concepts see, e.g., A. Eide, 'The Laws of War and Human Rights—Differences and Convergences', in C. Swinarski (ed.), *Studies and Essays on International Humanitarian Law and Red Cross Principles in Honour of Jean Pictet* (Geneva, 1984), 681; G. Herczegh, *Developments of International Humanitarian Law* (Budapest, 1984), 150–60; and G. H. Aldrich, 'Establishing Legal Norms Through Multilateral Negotiation—The Laws of War', 9 *Case Western Reserve Journal of International Law* 13 (1977).

[35] Van Dongen (1991), 3.

[36] Gardam (1993), 132–62. See also Khushalani (1982), 150–1, regarding the possible *jus cogens* status of the principle of civilian protection in situations of armed conflict.

the use of civilians as a shield against attack).[37] This writer also considers that some customary rules for the protection of civilians apply in non-international armed conflicts, although these are less clearly defined or established.[38]

Other writers, too, have tackled this issue, and have found evidence in favour of the customary nature of certain principles for the protection of civilians in situations of armed conflict.[39] One such writer has, by tracing their origins in the Regulations annexed to 1907 Hague Convention IV,[40] identified certain specific provisions of 1949 GC IV as generally representing customary norms. These include, among others, Article 27 (entitling protected persons to humane treatment and respect); Article 32 (forbidding murder, torture, corporal punishment, and other brutality); Article 33 (prohibiting collective punishment, intimidation, terrorism, and reprisals); and Article 51 (restricting compulsory labour, including the prohibition for those under 18).[41] This writer also cites as possible customary principles certain Articles in 1977 GP I, such as Article 35(1) and (2) (limiting the means and methods of warfare); Article 51(2) (see this section, above); Article 57(2)(c) (advance warning of attacks which may affect civilians); Article 59 (non-defended localities); Article 60 (demilitarised zones); and Article 75 (fundamental guarantees).[42] Further, he describes as customary certain elements of Common Article 3. These are Article 3(1)(a) to (c), which provide for humane treatment, and prohibit violence to life and person, the taking of hostages, and outrages upon personal dignity.[43]

---

[37] Gardam (1993), 146–59. See also sect. 3.1.2.1 above.

[38] See Gardam (1993), 163–80. Greenwood (1991), 113, describes parts of 1977 GP II as customary, particularly Art. 4(1) and (2) (elaborating on the humane treatment principle of Common Art. 3) and Art. 6(2) (the right to due process). See also Van Dongen (1991), 196–7, who argues that the fundamental guarantees in Art. 4 of 1977 GP II (which includes the specific measures for children) reflect customary human rights norms and as such deserve recognition as customary.

[39] See, e.g., Greenwood, who notes that in the 1991 Gulf War the coalition states categorised as a customary rule the principle of distinction (as set out in 1977 GP I, Art. 48, 51(2), and 52(1)). C. Greenwood, 'Customary International Law and the First Geneva Protocol of 1977 in the Gulf Conflict', in Rowe (ed.) (1993), 88. Further, Greenwood points to practice in the 1991 Gulf conflict that 'reaffirms the customary law principle of proportionality in a way which other recent conflicts have failed to do': *ibid.* 79. He cites this principle as expressed in both Arts. 51(5)(b) and 57(2)(a)(iii): *ibid.* 88. In an earlier work, Greenwood ((1991), 108–11), identifies a number of provisions in 1977 GP I as customary, including, *inter alia*, Arts. 48, 51(2), 51(5)(b), and 51(7).

[40] In this context, it is of interest that the 1907 Hague Convention IV was declared, by the International Military Tribunal at Nuremberg, to represent customary law (*Trial of the Major War Criminals Before the International Military Tribunal*, Nuremberg 1946, Judgment, Vol. XXII, at 497). See also comment on this in, e.g., Gardam (1993), 19, and Meron (1989), 225.

[41] Meron (1989), 47.

[42] *Ibid.*, 64. The author cites an expert doing a study for the US Joint Chiefs of Staff as the source of this information.

[43] *Ibid.*, 34. He argues, too, that Common Art. 3(1)(a) (prohibiting violence to life and person) has attained the status of *jus cogens*: *ibid.*, 31.

Indeed, in the *Nicaragua Case* the ICJ found that Common Article 3 as a whole constitutes a 'minimum yardstick' applicable to international armed conflict, as well as applying to non-international armed conflict.[44] This aspect of the *Nicaragua* judgment is significant, in that it emphasises the customary nature of basic principles for the protection of civilians in all categories of armed conflict.

Further, a number of provisions in humanitarian law concerning the protection of civilians have been identified by one writer as peremptory norms, although he does, perhaps, cast his net rather wide. These include, as regards civilians in the power of an adversary in an international armed conflict, 1949 GC IV Articles 27, 32, 33 (see this section above), and 34 (prohibiting the taking of hostages).[45] They also encompass, in relation to interned civilians, certain peremptory obligations of the Detaining Power to ensure satisfactory minimum conditions.[46] Moreover, they include, for those in occupied territory, the peremptory obligation of the Occupying Power to prevent excessive use of force against the civilian population and to allow civilians to enjoy adequate housing, food, and medical care.[47] In addition, this writer categorises as peremptory certain Articles of 1949 GC IV and of 1977 GP I which guarantee special protection to vulnerable groups of civilians. These include 1949 GC IV Article 16 (respect for the wounded and sick, the infirm, and expectant mothers) and 1977 GP I Article 10 (special care for the wounded, sick, and shipwrecked).[48]

Finally, in relation to civilians in the theatre of operations, this writer cites as peremptory norms two principles which, he argues, apply in situations both of international and of non-international armed conflict, and are at the core of elementary humanitarian considerations regarding civilian protection. These are, first, the prohibition of direct attacks against civilians (as exemplified by Article 48 of 1977 GP I) and, secondly, the prohibition of annihilation or mass extermination of civilians, and of causing to them, on a massive scale, severe injuries of a permanent character.[49]

---

[44] [1986] ICJ Rep., para. 218. See discussion on this point in, e.g., Gardam (1993), 169–70; and Meron (1989), 27–34 (and see sect. 3.1.2.2 above). The *Tadić Case* (citing the *Nicaragua Case*) affirms that Common Art. 3 has become part of customary law: 35 ILM 63 (1996).

[45] Hannikainen (1988), 667–8. He also states that Arts. 40 (restricting compulsory labour), 51 (as above), and 147 (defining grave breaches of 1949 GC IV) 'appear peremptory': *ibid.* 669.

[46] These are set out in 1949 GC IV Arts. 27 (as above); 81 (provision of maintenance); 85 (provision of accommodation); 91 (provision of medical care); and 92 (provision of regular medical inspections): *ibid.*

[47] 1949 GC IV Arts. 27 and 29 (provision for humane treatment), and Arts. 55–60 (the provision of necessary facilities to civilians in occupied territories): *ibid.*, 670.

[48] *Ibid.* Measures concerning child civilians are also cited in this context, as discussed in sect. 5.2.4 below.

[49] Hannikainen (1988), 685–7. He also describes rape, which, as already mentioned, is commonplace in many situations of armed conflict, as a form of torture which is prohibited as a peremptory norm of international law: *ibid.*, 510.

It therefore appears, as regards the protection of civilians generally in situations of armed conflict, that there are a number of norms that are widely regarded as customary, even if there is some disagreement about their precise content.[50] These norms include, in particular, concepts such as the proportionality principle, and the fundamental rules that civilians are to be distinguished from combatants and must not be the object of attack, and that they are to be treated humanely. At the very least, there is consensus that the core principles expressed in Common Article 3, and perhaps especially in Common Article 3(1)(a) to (c), represent customary law applicable to non-combatants in both international and non-international armed conflict.

5.2.4 The Entitlement of Child Civilians to Special Treatment in Situations of Armed Conflict

The above discussion indicates the customary law status, or evolving customary law status, of a number of principles of international human rights and humanitarian law that relate to the protection of child civilians in situations of armed conflict. These are: the prohibition on the arbitrary deprivation of the right to life; the principle that children are in general entitled to special treatment by reason of their status as children; and various measures in humanitarian law providing for the protection of civilians in situations of armed conflict.[51]

The question then arises whether it can be argued that these principles, when taken together, amount to a customary norm, or evolving norm, to the effect that child civilians are entitled to special treatment in situations of armed conflict (as regards, for example, protection against loss of life). Clearly, it would be unsatisfactory to attempt to answer this question simply on the basis of the arguments above, and it therefore merits further discussion here.

5.2.4.1 Special Treatment of Child Civilians Generally

Judging by the disturbing statistical evidence of the numbers of children killed and injured in situations of armed conflict during the last few decades,

---

[50] The 'Intergovernmental Group of Experts for the Protection of War Victims' (see also sect. 6.3.1.2 below) recommended, *inter alia*, that the ICRC prepare a report on the customary rules of international humanitarian law applicable in international and non-international armed conflicts. See ICRC, 'Follow-Up to the International Conference for the Protection of War Victims', 304 *Int'l. Rev. of the Red Cross* 34 (Jan.–Feb. 1995). If this is accomplished, it should further clarify the content of this body of customary law.

[51] Interestingly, one writer lists three categories of violations of international law, which are particularly pertinent to the subject of this book, as 'categories of international offences that could be defined without exculpatory caveats'. This seems to be another way of describing peremptory norms, or at least customary norms. The categories listed are: offences against children; the use of biological and chemical weapons; and offences against non-belligerent civilians: T. M. Franck, 'Legitimacy in the International System', 82 *AJIL* 713 (1988).

state practice in this context does not provide encouraging evidence in favour of a customary norm that children are entitled to special treatment. Nonetheless, as mentioned in section 5.1.3, it is inevitable that in armed conflict the gap will be wide between international legal norms and state practice. Further, (as discussed above in section 5.1.3[52]), it is arguable (if still controversial) that inconsistent state practice does not necessarily negate the existence of a customary norm. Thus the norm can remain valid as long as the evidence indicates that failure to abide by it is not a denial of the norm, but rather a failure to observe it while nonetheless in principle accepting it.

Bearing this in mind, there is a considerable body of persuasive evidence pointing to, at least, an evolving customary norm in favour of the entitlement of child civilians to special treatment in situations of armed conflict. This can be found, for example, in the support given by governments to treaties such as the 1949 GCs, the 1977 GPs and the 1989 CRC; in the *travaux préparatoires* to and commentaries on such treaties; in UN resolutions and reports of recent international conferences; and in aspects of state practice as described in the Iraqi study in Chapter 7.

Given the uncertain significance, in terms of customary law, of state compliance with principles contained in treaties they have ratified (see section 5.1.2), the 1989 CRC is nonetheless worthy of attention in this context. As already mentioned (section 5.2.2), the speed and extent of its adoption indicate, at the very least, an acceptance by states of the underlying principle of children's entitlement to special treatment in many situations, including in armed conflict. Although certain measures articulated in the 1989 CRC clearly cannot claim customary law status at this point, it is arguable that Article 38, in confirming the obligation of governments to observe the relevant existing international humanitarian law, strengthens the customary status of such law.[53]

Moreover, although the *travaux préparatoires* to the discussions on Article 38(4) reveal that there was disagreement on the level of state obligation (see section 4.2.5.3.3), it is significant that there was no dispute about the fundamental principle that child civilians are entitled to particular protection in situations of armed conflict, in accordance with international humanitarian law.

Further support for a customary norm that child civilians merit special treatment can be found in the wide state ratification of the 1949 GCs and, to a lesser extent, the 1977 GPs, with their many Articles providing specifi-

---

[52] See particularly reference to the *Nicaragua* case (Sect. 5.1.3, n. 20) and, e.g., Gardam (1993), 142.

[53] Goodwin-Gill and Cohn (1994), 70, also argue that the text of Art. 38, 'which reflects a minimal "consensus", is nonetheless important for the consolidation that it brings to the rule of customary international law'.

cally for the protection of child civilians. Certain relevant Articles in 1949 GC IV are also incorporated and summarised in, for example, the British Manual of Military Law.[54] Military manuals of this nature are traditionally relied on as providing evidence of state practice in armed conflict.[55]

As mentioned above, a number of writers have commented on the customary law status of measures in 1949 GC IV and the 1977 GPs. In this context some have identified, as customary norms or evolving customary norms, various Articles in these conventions specifically concerning the treatment of child civilians. Thus the key Article 77 of 1977 GP I (the entitlement of children to special respect), and Article 78 (evacuation of children) have been cited by one authority as 'likely candidates to eventually reflect general practice recognised as law'.[56]

Another writer goes even further, arguing for peremptory status for certain Articles of 1949 GC IV and 1977 GP I which provide for special protection of vulnerable categories of civilians. In this context, he identifies Article 24 of 1949 GC IV (regarding the care of orphaned children or those separated from their families) and, again, the central Article 77 of 1977 GP I. He argues that '[t]here appears to be a general peremptory obligation to treat humanely particularly children, seriously sick or wounded civilians, as well as expectant mothers'.[57]

Accordingly, there is support from two prominent writers on customary law and peremptory norms for the notion that Article 77 of 1977 GP I, the pivotal Article in the humanitarian treaties on the entitlement of children to special treatment, enjoys at least the status of an evolving norm of customary law. This argument must now be strengthened in light of the overwhelming endorsement by the international community of the 1989 CRC, including its Article 38.

Other evidence in favour of a norm, or evolving norm, that child civilians merit special treatment in situations of armed conflict can be found, for example, in the passage by the UN General Assembly of Resolution 3318 (XXIX) (section 4.4.1 above) calling on states to observe international humanitarian law in relation to women and children in such situations. Additional support comes in the form of reports of the major international conferences discussed in sections 2.1.4 and 2.2.4, and particularly the reports of the 1995 Beijing Conference, the 1993 Vienna Conference, and the 1990 World Summit, all of which made specific recommendations on the protection of children in armed conflict.

[54] *The Law of War on Land, Part III of the Manual of Military Law* (London, 1958). This particularly emphasises measures regarding the treatment of orphans and children separated from their families. See, e.g., paras. 36 and 538.

[55] See Meron 'The Geneva Conventions as Customary Law' (1987), 361, and Greenwood (1991), 102–3.

[56] This assessment was made by a US Joint Chiefs of Staffs expert, cited by Meron (1989), 66.

[57] Hannikainen (1988), 670–1.

5.2.4.2 *Special Treatment of Children in Relation to Receipt of Necessities*

Moreover, as will be discussed in Chapters 7 and 8, there is evidence of state practice, at least in the 1991 Gulf War, which indicates that certain limited measures for the special treatment of child civilians may increasingly be observed as customary principles in some conflict situations. In particular, the evidence indicates respect for the notion that child civilians, as a vulnerable group within the civilian population, are entitled to priority in the receipt of necessities.

In this context, the 1989 CRC provides explicitly in Article 6(2) that States Parties must ensure 'to the maximum extent possible the survival and development of the child'. Further, under Article 24(c) of this Convention States Parties are, among other things, obliged to take 'appropriate measures' to provide children with adequate food and drinking water (see section 2.2.2 above). Thus the 187 States Parties to this Convention have a treaty obligation to endeavour to provide necessities to children within their jurisdiction. As already mentioned, in the absence of a derogation clause these obligations generally apply to children in situations of armed conflict as in times of peace. Further, the affirmation in the 1989 CRC of this duty to provide necessities may lend weight to its status as a customary norm.

States Parties to the widely ratified 1949 GC IV and to the 1977 GPs are also obliged to supply children with necessities in situations of armed conflict (for example, under Article 23 of 1949 GC IV), as mentioned above (sections 4.2.1.4 and 4.2.3).

The obligation to provide child civilians with special treatment particularly in relation to the provision of necessities is therefore both a treaty rule and, arguably, a customary norm. On the basis of the information and discussion presented here and in Chapters 2, 4, 7 and 8, this norm can be seen to consist, as a minimum, of two elements: (1) when children in situations of armed conflict are deprived of necessities, strenuous efforts must be made, by the government or others responsible, to remedy this, and (2) in circumstances where necessities are being supplied to civilians in situations of armed conflict, children must be among those given priority.[58] A government, or indeed an NGE, not acting in accordance with these principles should therefore be subject to intense international pressure and

---

[58] This book cannot enter into a wider discussion regarding humanitarian intervention generally. For further information on this, see, e.g., L. Minear, T. Weiss, and K. Campbell, *Humanitarianism and War: Learning the Lessons From Recent Armed Conflicts* (Providence, RI, 1991); G. Kent, *Rights to International Humane Assistance* (Hawaii, 1993) (and see references cited by this author: *ibid.*, n. 9, 15); L. Minear and T. Weiss, *Humanitarian Politics* (Pennsylvania, 1995), and L. Minear, *Humanitarianism Under Siege: A Critical Review of Operation Lifeline Sudan* (Trenton, NJ, 1991). As regards humanitarian aid specifically in relation to children, see, e.g., Aldrich and van Baarda (1994) 12, 13, 29, and 127–8, and frequent comment in Ressler, Tortorici, and Marcelino (1993).

censure, both through purely political channels and, possibly, through more formal complaints procedures, where available.[59]

5.3 SUMMARY: CUSTOMARY LAW

From the above discussion, it is clear that many strands of customary law, or evolving customary law, contribute to the concept that there is a customary norm that child civilians are entitled to special treatment in situations of armed conflict. Indirect evidence in favour of this norm stems from the customary law status of the prohibition on arbitrary deprivation of the right to life; the customary law, or evolving customary law, status of the principle that children are in general entitled to special treatment as children; and the customary law status of the concept of non-combatant immunity in situations of armed conflict.

More direct evidence in favour of a norm supporting the special treatment of child civilians can be found in the sources outlined in section 5.2.4 above, which indicate that *opinio juris* and, to a lesser extent, state practice seem to support such a norm. Further, that section points to the possible customary law status of the significant Article 77 of 1977 GP I.

On the basis of the arguments and evidence set out in this Chapter, it is submitted here that there is at least an evolving norm of customary law that child civilians are to be granted special treatment in situations of armed conflict. Further, the Iraqi study in Chapter 7 below provides evidence that this norm is particularly well-established as regards the provision of necessities to child civilians in such situations.

Accordingly, if and when it is clearly established as a customary norm, the principle in favour of special treatment of children in armed conflict can, as discussed, co-exist with treaty obligations; be binding on non-state parties to treaties expressing this norm; and, further, its existence in both customary and conventional law would enhance claims for its observance. Moreover, acceptance of this norm as customary has implications for the conduct of armed conflicts affecting children, for war crimes trials before both national and international tribunals, and for matters such as military training.

However, it must be borne in mind that acceptance of the customary status of principles regarding the special treatment of children, and their entitlement to necessities, would not mean that these principles could outweigh other norms pertinent to the conduct of armed conflicts. Certainly

---

[59] In relation to governments, these might indude, for example, complaints to the Commission on Human Rights under the Resolution 1503 procedure (discussed in sect. 6.1.2.3 below), or requests to the Committee on the Rights of the child to take measures under the 'Urgent Action' procedure (sect. 6.1.1.3 below).

such acceptance would add weight to these two precepts, and raise their profile as factors to be taken into account, for example in making military decisions. In that way, children may, in some armed conflicts, be better protected. Nonetheless, military decisions would, in the harsh reality of armed conflict, still be guided by, among others, the principle of proportionality[60] (which is itself a customary norm) and judgments as to military objectives.[61] These issues are mentioned further in Chapter 8 below.

[60] As already mentioned, the principle of proportionality prohibits attacks which could cause 'excessive' damage to civilians, in relation to the military advantage to be gained by the attack (see particularly 1977 GP I, Art. 51(5)(b), and, among others, Green (1993), 152). According to this principle, therefore, harm to civilians can be permissible, depending on the circumstances. A decision on proportionality tends to be subjective although, as Green points out ((1993), 331), 'it must be made in good faith, and may in fact come to be measured and held excessive in a subsequent war crimes trial'.

[61] As indicated in sect. 3.1.2.1 above, military objectives are lawful objects of attack. However, attacks on these objectives will be rendered unlawful if they cause excessive incidental damage, particularly in terms of harm to civilians or civilian objects (see, e.g., 1977 GP I, Art. 57(2)(b), and Green (1993), 120–1 and 330–1).

6

Monitoring, Implementation, and Enforcement of International Law Concerning Child Civilians

Chapters 2 to 5 above presented an overview of international human rights and humanitarian law relating to the treatment of child civilians in situations of armed conflict. Before examining the Iraqi conflicts for evidence of the impact of this body of law, this Chapter will look briefly at various organisations and legal mechanisms which have a role to play in its monitoring and/or implementation and/or enforcement.[1] These include the Committee on the Rights of the Child; certain principal organs of the UN and other bodies operating under its ægis; mechanisms for enforcing the laws of armed conflict; the ICRC; and relevant NGOs.

The focus here is on global international organisations and mechanisms, and regional mechanisms will therefore not be discussed.[2] Similarly, the role played by individual states is not described, although clearly they can be important in supervising and enforcing compliance with the pertinent international law, for example through diplomatic or legal action, and even, on occasion, military measures.[3]

In this Chapter, the Committee on the Rights of the Child is described and commented on more fully than the other mechanisms. This is because it is quite recently established, and is the only international monitoring body with the specific mandate, accepted by almost the entire international community as parties to the 1989 CRC, of regularly supervising state compliance with international humanitarian law concerning child civilians.

---

[1] For further information on pertinent implementation mechanisms in international law, see, among others, Meron (1989), 136–247; Hannikainen (1988), 301–11; Goodwin-Gill and Cohn (1994), 150–8; The American Law Institute (1987), para. 703; van Boven (1991), 3–10; B. G. Ramcharan, 'Strategies for the International Protection of Human Rights in the 1990s' 13 *Human Rights Quarterly* 156–7 (1991); and K. Vasak, 'The Distinguishing Criteria of Institutions', in Vasak (ed.) (1982), 215–28. Specifically as regards the right to life, see D. Weissbrodt, 'Protecting the Right to Life: International Measures Against Arbitrary or Summary Killings by Governments', in Ramcharan (ed.) (1985), 297–307.

[2] Nonetheless, some of the regional procedures are well established and in certain cases may be more effective than those available through the UN or other international mechanisms. Relevant procedures, within, e.g., the OAS and the Council of Europe include inter-state and individual complaint mechanisms regarding human rights violations.

[3] On the role of individual states see, e.g., Gasser, in Fox and Meyer (eds.) (1993), 15–44.

The first category of organisations and mechanisms to be examined below incorporates international governmental bodies, starting with the UN-based Committee on the Rights of the Child.

6.1.1 The Committee on the Rights of the Child

The work of the Committee on the Rights of the Child will be looked at in terms of its implementation mechanisms generally and its initiatives in relation to children in armed conflict, and, finally, there is an assessment of the work of the Committee in this context.

6.1.1.1 Implementation Mechanisms

The framework for the implementation mechanisms of the 1989 CRC is set out in Part II of this treaty. It starts with Article 42, which places a duty on states to make the 'principles and provisions of the Convention widely known, by appropriate and active means, to adults and children alike'. Among other things, Article 42 therefore obliges States Parties to the 1989 CRC to acquaint children themselves with rules of international humanitarian law concerning their status and treatment, in accordance with Article 38.

Article 43(1) then provides for the establishment of the Committee on the Rights of the Child, to monitor the progress made by States Parties in fulfilling their obligations under the Convention. This Committee consists of ten experts selected with regard to equitable geographic distribution, and serving in their personal capacity (see also section 2.2.2 above). At the time of writing, the States Parties to the 1989 CRC had recently adopted an amendment to the effect that the membership of the Committee should be increased to eighteen.[4] This had been endorsed by the General Assembly,[5] and would enter into force when accepted by two-thirds of the States Parties to this Convention (Article 50(2)).

The 1989 CRC sets out the election procedures for and terms of office of the Committee members, and provides, *inter alia*, that the Committee establish its own rules of procedure (Article 43(3)–(10)).[6] This Convention

---

[4] See UN Doc. CRC/C/SR.260 (10 Jan. 1996), para. 4, and paras. 10–12 for comment (by Committee member Mrs Santos Pais) on the implications of this amendment. On its financial ramifications, see UN Doc. CRC/SP.19 (28 Dec. 1995). Amendments to the 1989 CRC, such as this, require that the GA and the States Parties to the Convention agree to amend the Convention accordingly (Art. 50, mentioned later in this sect.).

[5] See UN GA Res. 50/155 (21 Dec. 1995).

[6] The Committee has now adopted its rules of procedure, discussed, e.g., in D. O'Donnell, 'Two Steps Forward . . . One Step Backward?' 8 *International Children's Rights Monitor* 5 (1991).

originally specified that the Committee was normally to meet annually (Article 43(10)), but its intense work schedule has now led, at the request of its members, to the Committee meeting three times per year.[7]

Two years after ratification and every five years thereafter, States Parties are to submit reports to the Committee describing measures adopted to give effect to the rights recognised in the Convention, and progress made in their realization (Article 44(1)).[8] Such reports should highlight difficulties which affect the capacity of states to fulfil their Convention obligations (Article 44(2)).[9] The Committee may request further information from States Parties (Article 44(4)), and it issues observations on the reports submitted. The more recent 'concluding observations' of the Committee identify both positive and negative aspects of the practice of particular states. In some instances the Committee has been very critical, while in others it has found the reports praiseworthy.[10]

A number of reports submitted inevitably come from countries embroiled in situations of armed conflict or internal disturbances, and the reports therefore address these problems to a greater or lesser extent. In 1994 Croatia, for example, presented as a separate annex a 'Report on the Violations of the Rights of Children During the War'.[11]

The 1989 CRC explicitly requires States Parties to make their reports widely available to the public in their own countries (Article 44(6)). In addition, the Committee on the Rights of the Child must itself submit, every two years, a report on its activities to the General Assembly (Article 44(5)).[12]

To facilitate implementation further, Article 45(a) provides for the Committee to be assisted by the participation and/or advice of other bodies, as

---

[7] See, e.g., UN Doc. CRC/SP.11 (31 May 1994) for the Committee's request to meet more frequently.

[8] For information, regularly updated, on the number of States Parties to the 1989 CRC and the status of submission of reports, see, e.g., UN Docs. CRC/C/44 (31 July 1995) and CRC/C/53 (11 Mar. 1996). For an overview of the reporting procedures generally, see UN Doc. CRC/C/33 (24 Oct. 1994).

[9] The Committee has prepared general guidelines for States Parties on the form and content of their reports. For guidelines on initial reports, see UN Doc. CRC/C/5. See also Committee discussion of 6 Mar. 1995 (UN Doc. CRC/C/SR.108). For a critical appraisal of these guidelines, see O'Donnell (1991), 7–8.

[10] The Committee was, e.g., rather critical of the UK report (see, among others, UN Docs. CRC/C/SR.204 (27 June 1995) and CRC/C/SR.206 (3 July 1995)), and enthusiastic about that of Burkina Faso (UN Doc. CRC/C/3/Add.19 (15 July 1993)). And see P. David, 'Burkina Faso Sets the Example to the Other States of the World', 11.2/3 *International Children's Rights Monitor* 22 (1994).

[11] See UN Doc. CRC/C/8/Add.19/Annex (2 Dec. 1994).

[12] For an example of a recent report, see *Report of the Committee on the Rights of the Child*, UN GAOR, 49th Sess., Supp. No. 41 (A/49/41) (1994). As well as these biennial reports, the Committee regularly publishes a compilation of its conclusions and recommendations, and reports on individual sessions. See, e.g., UN Doc. CRC/C/19/Rev.6 (5 Mar. 1996) and CRC/C/50 (22 Mar. 1996) respectively.

regards their particular areas of competence. These include the specialised agencies of the UN (such as the ILO, the World Health Organisation (WHO), and the UN Educational, Scientific, and Cultural Organisation (UNECSO))); UNICEF; other UN organs; and 'other competent bodies' (a term sufficiently broad to encompass NGOs).[13] These bodies may also be notified of state reports which indicate a requirement for technical advice or assistance (Article 45(b)).[14]

In addition, the Committee on the Rights of the Child is authorised to propose that the General Assembly ask the Secretary General to undertake studies on specific issues concerning the rights of children (Article 45(c)). The Committee has already acted under this provision in requesting a study on children in armed conflict, discussed in section 6.1.1.2 below.

Finally, this Committee may also make suggestions and recommendations based on information received under Articles 44 and 45, and these are to be communicated to the relevant State Party and to the General Assembly (Article 45(d)).[15]

Part III of the 1989 CRC deals with issues such as its ratification and entry into force (Articles 47 and 49), and provision is made for the Convention to be amended, thereby allowing for possible future changes (Article 50). Further, Part III includes guidance on reservations made to the 1989 CRC (Article 51). Such reservations could clearly have a considerable impact on the success, or otherwise, of its implementation. Indeed, there is controversy surrounding the sweeping reservations that have been made by certain States Parties to this Convention, which arguably render ratification almost meaningless.[16]

6.1.1.2 Initiatives of the Committee on the Rights of the Child in Relation to Children in Armed Conflict

Specifically as regards children in armed conflict, the Committee on the Rights of the Child has demonstrated a particular interest. Its positive

---

[13] Indeed, a group of NGOs drawn largely from the NGO Ad Hoc Group on the Drafting of the Convention on the Rights of the Child (the NGO Ad Hoc Group) had continued, after the adoption of the 1989 CRC, to work with the Committee: 6 *DCI Newsletter* 5–7 (May–June 1991). Further, the NGO Group for the Convention on the Rights of the Child has produced *A Guide for Non-Governmental Organisations Reporting to the Committee on the Rights of the Child* (Geneva, 1994), to facilitate such reports.

[14] For a summary of the Committee's recommendations on technical assistance to particular countries see, e.g., UN Doc. CRC/C/40/Rev.3 (5 Mar. 1996).

[15] In addition, the GA and other fora within the UN undertake work relevant to the mandate of the Committee on the Rights of the Child, and the Committee regularly keeps abreast of such work. See, e.g., UN Doc. CRC/C/Sr.77/Add.1 (27 Apr. 1994), and UN Doc. CRC/C/SR/195 (23 Jan. 1995).

[16] For a discussion of this problem, see O'Donnell (1992) and Kuper (1997). For declarations, reservations and objections made to the 1989 CRC up to 30 June 1995, see UN Doc. CRC/C/2/Rev.4 (1995).

initiatives in addressing this problem provide a useful model of the way in which UN bodies can monitor and attempt to encourage compliance with specific areas of the law. The main initiatives of the Committee in this context, and certain resulting actions within the UN generally, are therefore summarised below.

During its first session, the Committee resolved that it would devote its initial day of 'general discussion', to be held in its second session, to the topic of 'children in armed conflicts'. In so doing, the Committee acknowledged the importance it attached to this issue.[17]

The day of discussion on children in armed conflict was held on 5 October 1992, with the participation of representatives of a number of UN bodies, the ICRC, and NGOs. Mr Muntarbhorn, the Special Rapporteur on the Sale of Children, also took part.[18]

The discussion was wide-ranging, addressing issues such as: the effects of armed conflict on children, and their particular vulnerability; the efforts made by the various agencies to meet the needs of children in armed conflict; the difficulty of enforcing compliance with human rights and humanitarian law in situations of armed conflict; the problem of establishing and implementing legal measures for the protection of children in internal disturbances; the implications of the arms trade in relation to children; the appropriate age for recruitment and participation of children in the armed forces; the rehabilitation and reintegration of children affected by armed conflict; and the importance of preventive measures, both before and after the outbreak of hostilities.[19]

During the discussion a number of recommendations were put forward, including suggestions that the Committee play an active role in promoting wider state ratification of the relevant treaties; that the Committee take the 1989 CRC as a whole into account, and not just Articles 38 and 39, when examining reports from countries engaged in conflict; and that the Committee should prepare guidelines to define clearly the obligations of States Parties under Article 38.[20] Mr Muntarbhorn underlined the importance of educating the military, and children themselves, in international humanitarian law.[21]

On 9 October 1992, the Committee adopted its report on the general

[17] The Committee itself stated, in its report on this day of general discussion, that its decision to select the topic of children in armed conflict was based, first of all, on 'the outstanding importance of this issue in the context of the promotion and protection of children's rights': UN Doc. CRC/C/10 (13 Oct. 1992), para. 85.

[18] For the record of this discussion, see generally UN Docs. CRC/C/SR.38 (22 Jan. 1993) and CRC/C/SR.39 (12 Oct. 1992).

[19] See UN Docs. CRC/C/SR.38 (22 Jan. 1993) and CRC/C/SR.39 (12 Oct. 1992).

[20] These suggestions were made by Mr Macpherson (Quaker Peace and Service); Mrs Cohn (Henry Dunant Institute) (both cited in UN Doc. CRC/C/SR.38, paras. 12 and 22 respectively); and the author, Mrs Kuper (Rädda Barnen) (UN Doc. CRC/C/SR.39, para. 33).

[21] See UN Doc. CRC/C/SR.39, para. 8.

discussion of 5 October.[22] This highlighted five main areas of concern: the relevance and adequacy of standards set by existing international legal instruments; the need to reinforce measures which could prevent armed conflicts, or limit the participation of children in such conflicts; the necessity for ensuring effective protection of children in times of armed conflict; and, finally, the need to promote the recovery and reintegration of children affected by armed conflicts.

The Committee's report concluded with a number of 'follow-up' suggestions, in response to the 'outstanding and complex question of children in armed conflicts'.[23] The Committee proposed, for example, that it could develop more specific guidelines on Articles 38 and 39, and that an Optional Protocol could be drafted, raising the minimum age for child soldiers to 18.[24] It established a Working Group to consider these options.

In January 1993, after considering the report of its Working Group, the Committee again discussed children in armed conflict,[25] and resolved, *inter alia*, to ask the General Assembly to request that the Secretary-General 'undertake a special study on ways and means of protecting children in armed conflicts'.[26] The Committee duly made this recommendation to the General Assembly.[27]

The Committee's recommendation was noted by the Commission on Human Rights in its resolution of 10 March 1993 on 'Effects of Armed Conflict on Children's Lives'.[28] In its Preamble, this resolution emphasised the duty of states to 'take all possible measures to ensure special protection and suitable care . . . of children affected by an armed conflict'.

On 20 December 1993 the General Assembly adopted, without a vote, a resolution requesting that the Secretary-General appoint an expert to undertake a 'comprehensive' study on the situation of children affected by armed conflict, to cover the five main areas of concern identified by the Committee in its report of 9 October 1992.[29] Again, the Preamble to this resolution reinforced the concept of special protection for children in armed conflict.

---

[22] See UN Doc. CRC/C/10 (13 Oct. 1992).

[23] *Ibid.*, para. 106.

[24] The Committee subsequently prepared a preliminary Draft Optional Protocol on Involvement of Children in Armed Conflicts. See UN Doc. CRC/C/16—Annex VII. On this Protocol, see also below, in this sect.

[25] See UN Doc. CRC/C/SR.72 (2 Feb. 1993), regarding discussion of 28 Jan. 1993.

[26] *Ibid.*, para. 2.

[27] See UN Doc. CRC/C/16—Annex VI.

[28] Commission Res. 1993/83. See also sect. 6.1.2.3 below.

[29] UN GA Res. 48/157, 'Protection of Children Affected by Armed Conflicts', para. 7. See also subsequent related resolutions, such as UN GA Res. 49/209 (23 Dec. 1994) on children in armed conflict, and UN GA Res. 50/153 (21 Dec. 1995), 'The Rights of the Child'. The latter contains a section entitled 'Protection of Children Affected by Armed Conflicts', which expresses, *inter alia*, support for the UN study on children in armed conflict (para. 10).

This General Assembly resolution was, in turn, welcomed by the Commission on Human Rights in its further resolution of 9 March 1994 on 'Effects of Armed Conflicts on Children's Lives'.[30] Once more, this reiterated the notion of special protection.

At the time of writing, Graça Machel had been appointed as the expert entrusted with preparing the study on the impact of armed conflict on children, and was intending to present her final report to the UN Secretary-General in the autumn of 1996.[31] At a UNICEF meeting in November 1995, Ms Machel indicated that the study would make a number of concrete proposals to the General Assembly, including that children should be declared 'zones of peace', and that deliberately enlisting children into armed forces should become a crime against humanity; that there should be a complete ban on landmines; that there should be a continued commitment to humanitarian assistance, but with a broader mandate to maintain aid in order to rebuild communities after crises are resolved; and that the use of rape as a weapon in conflict should be categorised as a crime against humanity. The study will also apparently urge a 'long-term political agenda for the UN', with the aim of working towards a child-centered culture.[32]

Further, progress was being made on the drafting of the proposed Optional Protocol concerning child soldiers[33] (as well as one on the sale of children, child prostitution, and child pornography[34]), and members of the Committee had formally participated in this process.[35]

6.1.1.3 *Comment: The 1989 CRC in Relation to Children in Armed Conflict*

The 1989 CRC clearly contains many provisions which are directly or indirectly concerned with regulating and monitoring the treatment of child

---

[30] Commission Res. 1994/94. See also sect. 6.1.2.3 below.

[31] Study on the Impact of Armed Conflict on Children, *Scope of the Study of the Impact of Armed Conflict on Children* (Johannesburg, 1994). The study was to be guided by an Eminent Persons Group and a Technical Advisory Group of experts. The intention was to undertake wide-ranging consultations, and field visits to countries in different regions. On this study, see also DCI, 'An Opportunity to Effect Genuine Change?' 11.4/12.1 *International Children's Rights Monitor* 33 (1994–5), and El-Haj (Dec. 1995).

[32] El-Haj (Dec. 1995), 13.

[33] Commission Res. 1994/91 (9 Mar. 1994) asked ECOSOC to authorise 'an open-ended inter-sessional working group' to elaborate a draft Optional Protocol to the 1989 CRC regarding the involvement of children in armed conflicts. This working group met from 31 Oct.–11 Nov. 1994 and from 15–26 Jan. 1996, and, at the time of writing, the Optional Protocol had not yet been finalised. See R. Brett, *Report on the Working Group to Draft an Optional Protocol to the Convention on the Rights of the Child on Participation of Children in Armed Conflict* (Quaker UN Office, Geneva, 1994), and R. Brett, *Report on the Second Session of the Working Group to Draft an Optional Protocol to the Convention on the Rights of the Child on Participation of Children in Armed Conflict* (Quaker UN Office, Geneva, 1996).

[34] This Optional Protocol was being drafted in accordance with Commission Res. 1994/90, para. 17.

[35] See UN Doc. CRC/C/50, paras. 249–51.

civilians in situations of armed conflict. What, then, are some of the strengths and weaknesses of the Convention in this context? How much can be expected of it? The answers to these questions will become more apparent in years to come, bearing in mind that, at the time of writing, the Convention had been in force for less than six years.

Despite its relatively short life, much has already been written about the 1989 CRC generally.[36] It has, for example, been praised for providing 'a universal definition of the very concept of the rights of the child',[37] but has been criticised for the 'promiscuous proliferation' of children's rights,[38] and, on the other hand, for failing to include some rights![39] It has attracted approval for explicitly recognising the need, in some countries, for practical assistance as a prerequisite to securing certain entitlements for children (Article 45).[40] It has been censured for not sufficiently involving children, for example in its drafting or reporting procedures.[41] These and other views on the 1989 CRC as a whole will not be further described here.

Specifically as regards child civilians however, the 1989 CRC promises to have a positive impact in some respects, but falls short in others.

On the negative side, the most disappointing aspect of the 1989 CRC in relation to child civilians is the weak standard set by the pivotal Article, Article 38, as discussed in section 4.2.5 above. The drafting of Article 6, regarding the right to life, is also far from satisfactory, as mentioned in section 2.2.2. Indeed, the vague terminology of many Articles in the 1989 CRC could pose problems, for example in relation to the reporting process, as states attempt to comply (or possibly to evade compliance) with imprecise obligations.[42]

Moreover, it may be that this Convention's reliance on state reports,

[36] E.g., see chapters in Freeman and Veerman (eds.) (1992), including those by Lopatka, 47–52; Cohen, 53–70; Heintz, 71–8; and Johnson, 95–114. See also Olsen, in Alston, Parker and Seymour (eds.) (1992); 91/2 *Bulletin of Human Rights* (1992); J. Himes, *The UN Convention on the Rights of the Child* (Florence, 1993); B. Abramson, 'An Enormous Challenge', 9.3/4 *International Children's Rights Monitor* 24 (1992), and L. Theytaz-Bergman, 'Out of Time', 11.1 *International Children's Rights Monitor* 10 (1994).

[37] Rädda Barnen, *The Rights of the Child* (Sweden, 1990), 14.

[38] Fox, in Verhellen and Spiesschaert (eds.) (1989), 410.

[39] Cohen (1989), 1451. The rights omitted include, e.g., human rights protection for alien children; protection against medical experimentation; and protection for child victims of forced internal migration.

[40] Rädda Barnen pointed out that certain Arts. in the Convention specified the link between rights and assistance (e.g., Arts. 24(4), 28(3), and 45(a) and (b)), and argued that there should be higher demands on richer states: Rädda Barnen (1990), 11–12.

[41] See, e.g., P. Alston, and S. Parker, 'Introduction', in Alston, Parker and Seymour (eds.) (1992), p. xi, and D. Gomien, *Duties of Private Parties Under the Convention on the Rights of the Child: An Obstacle to Implementation?*, Paper from DCI Congress 'Working for Children's Rights' (Finland, 1989), 5–7.

[42] This point is also raised, e.g., by Gomien (1989), 5–7. Nonetheless, a certain lack of precision may be an inevitable consequence of the consensual process of drafting international legal instruments such as the 1989 CRC.

and its lack of any inter-state or individual complaints mechanism, will limit its capacity to strengthen state observance of international legal norms regarding, *inter alia*, children in armed conflict. Certainly there is an argument for periodically reviewing the necessity for a complaints mechanism. Ultimately it may be that an Optional Protocol should be adopted, allowing for such a mechanism, as is discussed in section 8.3.5 below.

Having said this, a number of writers see as a particularly positive feature of the 1989 CRC the fact that it relies on co-operation rather than coercion.[43] Indeed, it may be precisely because of its reliance on state reports rather than complaints mechanisms that this Convention has proved acceptable to so many states, and one of the strengths of the 1989 CRC must be that it has so rapidly attracted support from countries in all regions of the globe.

However, one writer has expressed concern regarding the performance of the Committee in monitoring state reports from countries embroiled in armed conflicts. His criticism focuses on the committee's apparent failure, when examining state reports from some such countries, to question the government representatives on their observance of the international law applicable in situations of armed conflict.[44] This is significant, since a lack of proper scrutiny by the Committee of country reports, particularly when grave violations of human rights and/or humanitarian law are taking place, will seriously undermine the purpose and impact of the reporting process in improving observance of the relevant standards.

It is to be hoped that in time the Committee will become increasingly rigorous in fulfilling this aspect of its mandate.[45] At the time of writing, the Committee was still experiencing difficulties in adjusting to, among other things, the avalanche of state reports, and in attempting to define the scope of its present and future work.[46]

However, on the positive side, the simple fact of the existence of the Committee means that there is for the first time a monitoring body within the UN, reporting regularly to the General Assembly, which has as part of its mandate the periodic review of state compliance with standards of international law applicable to children in armed conflict.

[43] See, e.g., Rädda Barnen (1990), 13 and O'Donnell (1991), 5.
[44] For a discussion of this issue, see Abramson (1993), 26. As Abramson points out, the Committee's weakness in this regard can also be seen as a failure of the NGO community sufficiently to brief the Committee.
[45] DCI, e.g., has submitted to the Committee a document (Abramson, *Children and War: A Background Paper* (1992)) which, *inter alia*, contains detailed suggestions concerning the Committee's role in monitoring state compliance with Arts. 38 and 39, including through the reporting process.
[46] The Committee's records reveal numerous discussions on the scope of its mandate. See, e.g., UN Doc. CRC/C.SR.42 (3 Mar. 1993), discussing urgent appeals concerning children, and UN Doc. CRC/C.19/Rev.1 (30 Mar. 1994), regarding, *inter alia*, the Committee's involvement in regional meetings and in establishing a Document Unit on children's rights.

Moreover, the Committee is to be commended for its sustained and serious efforts as regards, for example, initiating the day of discussion and the study on children in armed conflict, as described above. These initiatives may well bear fruit in terms of concrete measures to improve the protection of children in armed conflict, particularly after publication of the UN study on children in armed conflict and its recommendations.

Further, within the UN the work of the Committee has already prompted initiatives which support the principle that children are entitled to special treatment in situations of armed conflict. These include, for example, recent resolutions of both the General Assembly and the Commission on Human Rights which expressed this principle (section 6.1.1.2 above).[47]

Another constructive development in this context is the Committee's decision to undertake 'Urgent Actions' in relation to complaints received about serious government violations of Convention rights,[48] which could obviously include such violations committed against children in situations of armed conflict.

In any event, the Committee on the Rights of the Child clearly cannot, by itself, shoulder the whole burden of implementing the 1989 CRC. This task also requires commitment from governments, from the public, and from children's advocates including NGOs.

Bearing this in mind, however, both the 1989 CRC as such and the work of the Committee on the Rights of the Child are positive developments in the context of international law concerning children in armed conflict. Despite their failings, this Convention and the Committee provide a focus for international efforts to strengthen and monitor observance of the pertinent law, and this is to be welcomed.

6.1.2 The UN and its Principal Organs

In addition to the specific mandate of the Committee on the Rights of the Child, certain of the principal organs of the UN, to be discussed in this section, are directly or indirectly concerned with issues relating to the protection of child civilians in armed conflict. Other bodies connected with the UN that are significant in this context are mentioned separately in section 6.1.3 below.

There is a vast literature on the history, structure, and role of the UN,[49]

---

[47] See also, e.g., UN Doc. A/50/672 (24 Oct. 1995), containing a brief report by the Secretary-General on 'Promotion and Protection of the Rights of Children: Concrete Measures Taken to Alleviate the Situation of Children in Armed Conflict'.

[48] See discussion of this in Abramson, 'An Enormous Challenge' (1992). See also, e.g., summary of the Committee's 2nd Session, in UN Doc. C/CRC/10.

[49] See, e.g., Higgins (1963); Higgins, *Problems and Process* (1994), 169–85; UN (1994); Bowett (1982); Meron (1986); T. Weiss, D. Forsythe, and R. Coate. *The United Nations and Changing World Politics* (Boulder, Colo., 1994); P. Alston (ed.), *The United Nations and*

and therefore what follows only touches on aspects of particular relevance here.

The UN as a whole is mandated to promote and encourage respect for human rights and fundamental freedoms; to maintain international peace and security; to develop friendly relations among states; and to foster international co-operation in solving international problems.[50] Clearly, these broad functions of the UN have some relevance to children in armed conflict, particularly in emphasising the need for international peace and security, and respect for human rights. However, while much in the Charter is pertinent to the protection of such children, this treaty contains no specific reference to them.

In supervising state compliance with its purposes as set out in the Charter, including those pertinent to child civilians, the UN employs a variety of methods.[51] As well as political debate and decisions, for example within the General Assembly or the Security Council, such methods incorporate: the scrutiny of reports submitted to various UN bodies (such as ECOSOC, see section 6.1.2.3 below);[52] the hearing of inter-state complaints (for example, by the ICJ); the consideration of communications regarding human rights

---

Human Rights: A Critical Appraisal (Oxford, 1992); A. Roberts, and B. Kingsbury (eds.), *United Nations, Divided World* (2nd edn., Oxford, 1993); A. Cassese (ed.), *UN Law/Fundamental Rights: Two Topics in International Law* (Alphen aan den Rijn, 1979); F. Kirgis, *International Organizations in Their Legal Setting: Documents, Comments and Questions* (St Paul, Minn., 1977 and 1981 (Supp.)); L. Sohn, 'Human Rights: Their Implementation and Supervision by the United Nations', in Meron (ed.) (1984), 369–401; P. Wallensteen, 'The United Nations in Armed Conflicts: An Overview', in R. Dupuy (ed.), *The Development of the Role of the Security Council* (Dordrecht, 1993), 303–16; M. C. Bhandare, 'The Role and Machinery of the United Nations in the Field of Human Rights' 89/1 *Bulletin of Human Rights* 12 (1990); T. Van Boven, 'Reliance on Norms of Humanitarian Law by United Nations Organs', in Delissen and Tanja (eds.) (1991), 495–513; and M. Kamminga, *Inter-State Accountability for Violations of Human Rights* (N.p., 1990), 63–126. Particularly in relation to issues concerning children in the UN context, see Kubota (1989).

[50] These purposes of the UN are set out in Art. 1 of the UN Charter. For detailed analysis of this Charter generally, see B. Simma (ed.), *The Charter of the United Nations: A Commentary* (Oxford, 1995). Another important Charter Art. is, e.g., Art. 2. This sets out principles for UN action in pursuance of its purposes, including Art. 2(3) (encouraging dispute settlement by peaceful means), 2(4) (regarding the importance of territorial integrity), and 2(7) (emphasising the principle of non-intervention). Also significant in this context are the human rights provisions in the Charter (including Arts. 1(3), 13, 55, 56, 62(2), and 68), many of which relate to the functions of UN principal organs, such as the General Assembly and the Security Council, discussed later in this sect.

[51] The various supervisory and enforcement mechanisms of the UN are discussed more fully, e.g., in UN (1994), 303–45; Higgins (1990); Sohn, in Meron (ed.) (1984), and Vasak, in Vasak (ed.) (1982), 221–4.

[52] On the reporting mechanism generally, see, e.g., UN (1991), including the useful article by P. Alston, 'The Purposes of Reporting', *ibid.* 13. See also UN Doc. A/44/668 (8 Nov. 1989) on 'Effective Implementation of International Instruments on Human Rights, Including Reporting Obligations Under International Instruments on Human Rights' (also known as the 'Alston report').

violations (as under the Resolution 1503 procedure, outlined in section 6.1.2.3); and studies of particular problems, by, *inter alia*, Special Rapporteurs, or by the Secretary-General. The Secretary-General may also engage in efforts to resolve conflict situations, or advance human rights, as in the use of his good offices.[53]

Further, as regards human rights violations, the UN as a whole is not limited to pursuing patterns of gross violations, but can take action on behalf of (and against) individuals, obviously including individual children.[54]

However, despite its wide mandate and its potential to enhance the protection of human rights and international peace and security, the UN was, at the time of writing, subject to major criticisms.[55] These concerned, in particular, its perceived failures as regards action taken (or not taken) in Somalia, Rwanda, and the former Yugoslavia. Further, it was under financial pressure.[56] The role of the organisation was therefore in a state of flux and its future effectiveness somewhat unpredictable. Nonetheless, it clearly merits discussion here.

Of the six principal organs of the UN, the most pertinent as regards the monitoring and enforcement of international law concerning children in armed conflict are the General Assembly, the Security Council, and ECOSOC, all of which took action, to a greater or lesser extent, in the Iraqi conflicts, (see Chapter 7). The ICJ is also relevant, although it was not

---

[53] For further information, see J. P. de Cuellar, 'The Role of the UN Secretary-General', in Roberts and Kingsbury (eds.) (1993), 125–42. See also T. Franck and G. Nolte, 'The Good Offices Function of the UN Secretary-General', *ibid.*, 143–82.

[54] One writer comments, e.g., that Art. 55 of the Charter refers to human rights and fundamental freedoms *for all*, and that the UN has on occasion passed resolutions concerning named individuals: Kamminga (1990), 105. Further, nothing in the Charter prohibits the GA, ECOSOC, or the Commission on Human Rights from considering, at the request of a state, communications from individuals or organisations as the basis for public discussion: Sohn, in Meron (ed.) (1984), 391. In addition, Arts. 41 and 42 of the Charter do not preclude the possibility that individual responsibility should be borne by those who violate Charter provisions: Oppenheim (1952), 159.

[55] See generally, *inter alia*, Weiss, Forsythe and Coate (1994); Alston (ed.) (1992); Roberts and Kingsbury (eds.) (1993); Eriksson (1996); T. Weiss, 'The United Nations and Civil Wars', 17.4 *The Washington Quarterly* 139 (1994); B. Urquhart and E. Childers, *A World in Need of Leadership: Tomorrow's United Nations* (Uppsala, 1990); and R. Higgins, 'The New United Nations and Former Yugoslavia' 8.1 *Interights Bulletin* 19 (1994). For criticisms in the press, see, e.g., *Independent*, 2 June 1993, 18 June 1993, 16 July 1993, and 13 Oct. 1993; *Independent on Sunday*, 17 Apr. 1994; *Guardian*, 4 June 1994, 24 Sept. 1994, 8 June 1995, and 26 June 1995. See also comments by: General P. Morillon (former head of the UN Protection Force (UNPROFOR) in the former Yugoslavia), *Independent*, 16 Apr. 1993; M. Sahnoun (former UN special envoy to Somalia), *Independent*, 16 June 1993; the NGO Médecins Sans Frontièrs, *Guardian*, 8 Nov. 1993; C. Sammaruga, (president of the ICRC), *Guardian*, 18 Apr. 1994; and Major-General Dallaire (former commander of UN Rwanda observer mission) *Independent*, 24 Nov. 1994.

[56] See comment on UN finances in, e.g., *Guardian*, 29 May 1993, 13 May 1994, 12 Dec. 1995, and 27 Apr. 1996, and *Independent*, 14 Feb. 1995, 16 Feb. 1995, and 2 Apr. 1996.

active in relation to the Iraqi conflicts. These four UN organs are considered briefly below.[57]

6.1.2.1 The General Assembly

To start with the General Assembly, this consists of representatives of all the Member States of the UN (185 at the time of writing).[58] It is competent (under Articles 10 to 15) to address a wide range of issues, including many relevant to children in armed conflict.

An indication of the extent of its remit is found, for example, in Article 10, authorising the General Assembly to discuss 'any questions or any matters within the scope of the present Charter or relating to the powers and functions of any organs provided for in the present Charter'. Specifically in relation to human rights, it is authorised by Article 13(1)(b) to undertake studies and make recommendations.

In this context, the General Assembly regularly designates, as themes for forthcoming years, particular concerns which merit attention. Thus, for example, it proclaimed 1979 the International Year of the Child.[59] It has also recently appointed a High Commissioner for Human Rights,[60] and, as mentioned above, Graça Machel as the expert to undertake the study on children in situations of armed conflict.

Moreover, in certain circumstances the General Assembly can recommend, *inter alia*, 'measures for the peaceful adjustment of any situation, regardless of origin, which it deems likely to impair the general welfare' (Article 14). Further, the General Assembly has (under Article 22) established various subsidiary organs, including UNICEF, that can play a significant role in relation to children in armed conflict.[61]

Since it is the main forum for political debate within the UN, the General Assembly is obviously very significant as a focus for international policy and decision-making. As discussed in section 2.1.2.1 above, many of its resolutions assume a quasi-legislative role, and a number of such resolutions have a bearing on the subject under consideration here.[62]

---

[57] By Art. 7(1) of the Charter, the other two principal UN organs are the Trusteeship Council and the Secretariat.

[58] See UN Doc. ST/LEG/SER.E/13, 3.

[59] See UN GA Res. 31/169 (21 Dec. 1976).

[60] This post was established in Dec. 1993 by UN GA Res. 48/141. The High Commissioner, who must report annually to the Commission on Human Rights, has responsibility for a broad range of UN human rights activities. As mentioned in sect. 2.1.2.1 above, he has met with the Committee on the Rights of the Child, and emphasised the importance of promoting the rights of children. See also, e.g., UN Docs. CRC/C/38 (20 Feb. 1995), paras. 10–11, and CRC/C/SR.260 (10 Jan. 1996), paras. 2–9.

[61] For further information on the subsidiary organs, see, e.g., Bowett (1982), 56–8.

[62] In addition to key instruments such as the UDHR, see, e.g., UN GA Res. 3318(XXIX) (in sect. 4.4.1 above) and resolutions concerning the protection of civilians generally (sect. 3.1.3 above), as well as a resolution concerning Iraqi occupied Kuwait (sect. 7.3.2.3.1 below).

6.1.2.2 The Security Council

The Security Council can also play a pivotal role in relation to armed conflicts involving child civilians, since it is empowered to take action for the maintenance of international peace and security (Article 24). It can fulfil this function either through the pacific settlement of disputes likely to endanger international peace or, if that fails, the Security Council can take enforcement action.[63] As regards the latter, it may either take action which does not involve the use of armed force (under Article 41) or action which does (under Article 42).[64] In either case, action under Articles 41 and 42 must be preceded by a determination under Article 39 of 'the existence of any threat to the peace, breach of the peace, or act of aggression'.

However, the Security Council has tended to be highly politicised, and its effective functioning has, in the past, been thwarted by the exercise of the veto by one or more of the permanent members.[65] In the 'post-Cold War' era this may no longer be the case to the same extent, although the Security Council is still very much subject to political manœuvres.

In recent years Security Council resolutions have directly affected child civilians in situations of armed conflict (and, on occasion, have specifically referred to them), as illustrated in the Iraqi study (section 7.3.2 below), and also, for example, in relation to Somalia, the former Yugoslavia, and Rwanda.[66]

6.1.2.3 ECOSOC

ECOSOC, as the principal organ of the UN dealing with social and economic issues, also fulfils a multiplicity of functions, some of which deal directly with human rights and other issues pertinent to the protection of child civilians. This body incorporates the Commission on Human Rights and the Sub-Commission on the Prevention of Discrimination and Protection of Minorities, whose work also merits discussion here.

[63] See Ch. VI, 'Pacific Settlement of Disputes' (Arts. 33–38), and Ch. VII, 'Action with Respect to Threats to the Peace, Breaches of the Peace, and Acts of Aggression' (Arts. 39–51) of the UN Charter.

[64] One writer notes that the Security Council can pursue enforcement and conciliation simultaneously. Further, the enforcement provisions of the Charter are also applicable to states that are not UN members, and even to bodies not recognised as states: Oppenheim (1952), 164 and 166.

[65] On the veto, see Art. 27(3) of the Charter. The permanent members are, by Art. 23 of the Charter, China, France, Russia, the UK, and the US. However, at the time of writing it seemed likely that there would be changes in the Security Council, with the addition of more permanent members, possibly Japan and Germany. See *Independent*, 27 Jan. 1993 and 28 Jan. 1993, and *Guardian*, 24 Sept. 1994.

[66] Numerous Security Council Resolutions have been adopted concerning these conflicts, including, among others, the two providing for the establishment of war crimes tribunals in the latter two situations: UN Docs. S/RES/827, 25 May 1993 (regarding the former Yugoslavia) and S/RES/995, 8 Nov. 1994 (regarding Rwanda), mentioned further in sect. 6.2.1 below.

Looking first at ECOSOC as a whole, this may, under Article 62, make studies and recommendations, prepare draft Conventions, and call international conferences on matters falling within its mandate. Article 62(2) explicitly states that recommendations may be made regarding the promotion of human rights. ECOSOC is also empowered, under Article 64, to obtain reports regarding, *inter alia*, steps taken by member states to comply with its recommendations. Further, Article 71 makes provision for ECOSOC to consult NGOs on matters within its competence (and see section 6.3.2.1 below).

By Article 68, ECOSOC may set up commissions 'in economic and social fields and for the promotion of human rights'. It was by this authority that ECOSOC established, in 1946, the Commission on Human Rights, which is one forum within ECOSOC that can and does deal with issues concerning child civilians.[67]

The Commission on Human Rights, which functions as the centre of the institutionalised human rights work of the UN, is made up of fifty-three government representatives of UN member states, selected on the basis of an equitable geographic distribution. Being composed of government representatives, it is subject to criticism as 'not only a political organ, but a politicised one'.[68]

The tasks of the Commission encompass the preparation of studies, recommendations, and international instruments on human rights. Recent initiatives of the Commission broadly relevant in relation to child civilians in armed conflict include, among others, the appointment of a Special Rapporteur on Iraq, Max van der Stoel, and one on the former Yugoslavia, Tadeusz Mazowiecki, whose reports have highlighted the plight of children;[69] and the establishment in 1991 of a 'thematic' Working Group on the sale of children and child prostitution.[70] In addition, the Commission has

---

[67] The wide mandate of the Commission included, from the start, a concern with violations of human rights in situations of armed conflict. Thus one of its aims was to 'prevent recurrence of acts as monstrous as those which formed the prelude to World War II': L. Sohn and T. Buergenthal, *International Protection of Human Rights* (Indianapolis, Indiana, 1973), 756. For discussion of the Commission generally, see, e.g., P. Alston, 'The Commission on Human Rights', in Alston (ed.) (1992), 126–210; and H. Cook, 'The United Nations Commission on Human Rights—Some Recent Developments' 6.3 *Interights Bulletin* 44 (1991).

[68] Meron (1986), 276. The Iraqi study provides a clear example of the failure of the Commission, owing to political factors, to censure Iraq for its use of chemical weapons against the Kurds (sect. 7.3.1 below).

[69] See, e.g., a report on the former Yugoslavia by Mr Mazowiecki, which contains a substantial section devoted to the 'Situation of Children' (UN Doc. E/CN.4/1994/110, 33–43). This states, *inter alia*, that in 'the present conflict the human rights of children . . . have been completely disregarded' (para. 272).

[70] Thus, e.g., a report by Special Rapporteur V. Muntarbhorn on the rights of the child and sale of children particularly mentioned the problem of child soldiers: UN Doc. E/CN.4/1993/ 67 (12 Jan. 1993).

recently adopted various resolutions concerning children's rights, and children in armed conflict.[71]

The Commission is assisted by the Sub-Commission on the Prevention of Discrimination and Protection of Minorities, consisting of twenty-six experts elected by the Commission to act in their individual capacity.[72] The Sub-Commission, too, has undertaken work pertaining to the protection of children generally and in situations of armed conflict.[73]

Of some relevance as regards attempts to limit human rights violations involving children in situations of armed conflict is the power of the Commission, with the assistance of the Sub-Commission, to examine complaints of such violations through procedures authorised under ECOSOC Resolutions 1235 and 1503.[74] (Indeed, the Resolution 1503 procedure was invoked in relation to Iraq, as mentioned particularly in section 7.3.1 below.) Under Resolutions 1235 and 1503, the Commission and Sub-Commission can examine information contained in communications[75] concerning gross violations of human rights. They can then study those situations which reveal a consistent pattern of violations, with a view to making recommendations to ECOSOC, which may take action on such recommendations.[76] Although of some value, the Resolution 1503 procedure has been criticised, among other things, for its complexity and its largely confidential nature.[77]

However, in relation to human rights violations, the Commission may

---

[71] See, e.g., Commission Res. 1993/83; 1994/91, and 1994/94 (sect. 6.1.1.2 above).

[72] For further information on the Sub-Commission, see A. Eide, 'The Sub-Commission on Prevention of Discrimination and Protection of Minorities', in Alston (ed.) (1992), 211–64. See also comment on the Sub-Commission in, among others, Meron (1986), 275–6, and Bhandare (1990), 22–3.

[73] E.g., in 1991 the Sub-Commission considered a draft report by Mr Mazilu, its Special Rapporteur on the problem of 'human rights and youth', including (at 10) a brief section on children in armed conflict: UN Doc. E/CN.4/Sub.2/1991/42 (10 July 1991). It has also collected information regarding the education provided by governments to their police and armed forces on the subject of human rights in times of armed conflict: UN Doc. E/CN.4/Sub.2/1991/5 (12 July 1991).

[74] Res. 1235(XLII) was adopted by ECOSOC on 6 June 1967, meeting 1479: *UN Yearbook 1967*, 512. Res. 1503(XLVIII), which augments Res. 1235 (XLII), was adopted by ECOSOC on 27 May 1970, meeting 1693: *UN Yearbook 1970*, 530. For discussion of the history of and procedures under these two resolutions, see, e.g., UN (1994), paras. 2589–613; Bhandare (1990), 18–21; Kamminga (1990), 84–6; and Sohn, in Meron (ed.) (1984), 385–91.

[75] Such communications can originate from persons or groups that are victims of violations, or persons or groups with direct and reliable knowledge of the violations. Communications from NGOs are admissible if the organisation acts in good faith according to human rights principles: UN (1994), para. 2595.

[76] Accordingly, under resolutions 1235 and 1503 the UN may respond to violations which do not represent a threat to international peace and security, but are purely 'a consistent pattern of gross and reliably attested violations of human rights'. See comment in Kamminga (1990), 117.

[77] For criticisms of this procedure, see, among others, Sohn, in Meron (ed.) (1984), 391, and Meron (1986), 124.

also, *inter alia*, consider communications from individuals or organisations for public discussion.[78]

6.1.2.4 The ICJ

The fourth and final principal organ of the UN to be mentioned here is the ICJ. The role of this body, as the main judicial organ of the UN, is broadly relevant to the protection of child civilians in armed conflict, as evidenced, for example, by the rulings in the *North Sea Continental Shelf* and *Nicaragua* Cases, mentioned in section 5.1 above.

In general, however, as one writer emphasises, the ICJ (in contrast to the political organs of the UN, particularly the General Assembly, ECOSOC, and the Commission on Human Rights) has rarely been asked to adjudicate on whether particular member states should be held accountable for human rights violations allegedly committed under their authority.[79] Nor was the ICJ called upon to consider issues arising from the Iraqi conflicts discussed in Chapter 7 below, and it has heard only one case, in its history, focusing on child protection.[80] Interestingly, in this case Judge Lauterpacht argued that '[a]part from criminal law, it is difficult to conceive of a more appropriate and more natural object of *ordre public*, as generally understood, than the protection by the State of infants, especially when they are helpless, ill, in actual or potential danger'.[81]

In principle the ICJ can hear cases concerning the treatment of child civilians in situations of armed conflict, and such matters may come before this Court in the context of the case concerning *Bosnia and Herzegovina* v. *Yugoslavia*.[82] This case was, at the time of writing, subject to preliminary proceedings, including objections by Yugoslavia on admissibility and jurisdiction, and had not been heard. Accordingly, it will not be further discussed here.

In any event, the ICJ does not have automatic jurisdiction,[83] and consent

[78] Further, the Commission is also entitled publicly to discuss a situation which has previously been subject to the confidential resolution 1503 procedure. See A. Schwelb and P. Alston, 'The Principal Institutions and Other Bodies Founded Under the Charter', in Vasak (ed.) (1982), 275.

[79] Kamminga (1990), 88. He observes that issues concerning human rights have formed part of various ICJ judgments, but the question of state accountability *per se* has come indirectly before the ICJ only once, for an advisory opinion. See [1950] ICJ Rep. 70, cited in *ibid.*, 88 and 91. See also N. Rodley, 'Human Rights and Humanitarian Intervention: The Case Law of the World Court' 38 *ICLQ* 321 (1989).

[80] This was the *Case Concerning the Application of the Convention of 1902 Governing the Guardianship of Infants* (*Netherlands* v. *Sweden*) [1958] ICJ Rep. 55. See also discussion in Boothby, Ressler, Steinbock (1988), 239, 263–4 and 389.

[81] [1958] ICJ Rep. 90.

[82] *Application of the Convention on the Prevention and Punishment of the Crime of Genocide*: (*Bosnia and Herzegovina* v. *Yugoslavia* (*Serbia and Montenegro*)), ICJ Orders of 8 Apr. 1993; 16 Apr. 1993; 13 Sept. 1993; 7 Oct. 1993; 21 Mar. 1995; and 14 July 1995.

[83] Treaties provide for reference to the ICJ in a variety of ways. See discussion in Sohn, in Meron (ed.) (1984), 373.

by the offending state to adjudication is generally a prerequisite. In addition, only states can be party to contentious cases before the ICJ.[84]

Nonetheless, the Court may be asked for an advisory opinion on legal matters by the General Assembly, the Security Council, or other bodies authorised by the General Assembly. Advisory opinions of the ICJ do carry considerable weight, and it is in this capacity that the jurisdiction of the Court might most effectively be invoked to give guidance on issues concerning the treatment of child civilians in particular conflicts,[85] or in general.[86]

6.1.2.5 Comment: The UN and its Principal Organs

As the primary intergovernmental forum dealing with issues of peace and security and human rights, the mandate of the UN obviously covers much of relevance as regards the protection of children in situations of armed conflict. This applies to its work in law-making and standard-setting; to its monitoring and enforcement mechanisms in relation to the maintenance of peace and security; and to its human rights reporting and other supervisory procedures.

As discussed, the General Assembly, ECOSOC, and the Security Council have all taken action relevant to child civilians in situations of armed conflict, as has the ICJ, to a lesser extent. No doubt more could be done by the principal organs of the UN in this context, perhaps particularly within the ICJ and under the Resolution 1503 procedure, but this depends in large measure on states or NGOs, and/or others with *locus standi*, invoking the appropriate mechanism. Indeed, the ICJ may have an opportunity to affirm and clarify aspects of the pertinent international law, particularly in the context of allegations of genocide, in the *Bosnia and Herzegovina* application.

In any event, as regards issues involving children in armed conflict, the diversity and seeming fragmentation of relevant work among various organs within the UN give rise to some concern about the co-ordination of this work.[87] It may be that the Committee on the Rights of the Child or

---

[84] There is no access, e.g., to individuals or NGOs: Schwelb and Alston, in Vasak (ed.) (1982), 266.

[85] In this context, see arguments in favour of seeking an ICJ advisory opinion on legal aspects of the Israeli occupation of the West Bank and Gaza Strip: J. Dugard, 'Enforcement of Human Rights in the West Bank and Gaza Strip', in Playfair (ed.) (1992), 461–87.

[86] Regarding the importance of advisory opinions, (and for discussion of the ICJ more generally), see, *inter alia*, Higgins. *Problems and Process* (1994), 186–204. An ICJ advisory opinion was, e.g., recently requested concerning the legality of the use of nuclear weapons (see n. 46, Ch. 2 above: ICJ Verbatim Record CR–95/32 and ICJ Verbatim Record CR–95/34).

[87] L. Minear, U. Chelliah, J. Crisp, J. MacKinlay, and T. Weiss, (*United Nations Coordination of the International Humanitarian Response to the Gulf Crisis* (Providence RI, 1992), 3), warn that 'co-ordination' is the most over-used and least understood term in international parlance, and they set out a detailed definition of this term. Nonetheless, this term is used in this book in the sense in which it is commonly (even if imprecisely) understood.

other possible mechanisms discussed in Chapter 8 will provide the necessary focus.

6.1.3 Other Bodies Operating Under UN Auspices

As well as the principal organs of the UN, there are a number of bodies which operate, broadly, under the UN mandate and are concerned, directly or indirectly, with monitoring and/or implementing international law in relation to child civilians. Three of the most pertinent of these are mentioned below. These are UNICEF, UNHCR, and the Human Rights Committee.

There are other bodies set up in agreement with, or under the auspices of, the UN, that will not be described here although their work, too, touches on issues concerning child civilians in armed conflict. These bodies include 'specialised agencies' such as the WHO, UNESCO, and the ILO;[88] the Department of Humanitarian Affairs (DHA);[89] and the Department of Peacekeeping Operations.

The discussion here will also not encompass human rights treaty-monitoring mechanisms other than the Human Rights Committee, although the mandates of bodies such as the Committee Against Torture and the Committee on Economic, Social, and Cultural Rights encompass issues pertinent to child civilians in situations of armed conflict.[90]

6.1.3.1 UNICEF

First, to consider UNICEF,[91] this body was established under General Assembly Resolution 57(1) of 11 December 1946. It aimed to address concerns about the fate of children in armed conflict, particularly in response to the events of World War II, although its mandate was later extended.[92]

---

[88] E.g., in 1990 the ILO maintained two programmes (one in Afghanistan and one in Pakistan) for the rehabilitation of child victims of armed conflict: UN Doc. E/CN.4/Sub.2/1990/43, 20. Further, bodies such as the ILO, WHO, and UNESCO contribute to the work of the Committee on the Rights of the Child, and participate in its debates. See, e.g., UN Doc. CRC/C/SR.195 (23 Jan. 1995) and UN Doc. CRC/C/SR.203 (27 Jan. 1995).

[89] The DHA, established in 1992 and incorporating the UN Disaster Relief Organisation, has a wide mandate. *Inter alia*, it provides humanitarian aid in emergency situations, including situations of armed conflict; aims to implement early warning systems; and works with the Department of Peacekeeping Operations. See, e.g., 8 *DHA News* 35–46 (Mar./Apr. 1994), including information on the DHA's work in 1993 and 1994 on a 'Special Emergency Programme For Iraq': *ibid.*, 40.

[90] The Human Rights Committee is selected for discussion here by reason of its broad human rights mandate under the ICCPR; the wide ratification of the ICCPR, and because of the individual communications mechanism under the Optional Protocol.

[91] Regarding UNICEF generally, see UN (1994), paras. 1923–5.

[92] Under UN GA Res. 57(1), UNICEF was initially established as a temporary body to provide necessities 'for the benefit of children and adolescents of countries which were the victims of aggression' and 'for child health purposes generally'. In the 1950s its existence was

The work of UNICEF has traditionally been concerned with meeting the basic requirements of children, especially in relation to health care.[93] In this context, it must be credited with certain major achievements as regards children in armed conflict. Most notable among these was the negotiation of short-term cease-fires, in, particularly, El Salvador, Lebanon, and the Sudan, for the purpose of immunising children (and, in the Sudan, providing food and other relief supplies).[94] Further, in the context of its work on 'children in especially difficult circumstances' UNICEF has undertaken a number of other initiatives regarding children in armed conflict,[95] including commissioning a major study on such children which incorporates practical guidelines for addressing their needs.[96]

UNICEF was also, for example, instrumental in providing necessities to children in Iraq during the 1991 Gulf War (see Chapter 7). In this context it contributed to implementing measures in international law, as set out in 1949 GC IV and in 1977 GPI, concerning the provision of relief supplies to child civilians.

More recently, UNICEF seems to be increasingly directing its attention to issues concerning, broadly, the implementation of children's rights and advocacy on their behalf. Thus a 1990 article written by a UNICEF Senior Advisor stated that

UNICEF should extend its country-level strategies from their present focus on delivery of health, education and other services towards a new advocacy of child protection. This might involve UNICEF assistance in the drafting of certain types of legislation, law enforcement, judicial and social welfare measures, and new forms of citizens' empowerment.[97]

This change of direction has been evidenced by, *inter alia*, UNICEF's participation in the later stages of drafting the 1989 CRC, and by UNICEF's initiative in organising the 1990 World Summit for Children.

Further, UNICEF recently made clear the priority that it accords to children in armed conflict, when the organisation published, as a central feature of its report on *The State of the World's Children 1996*, its 'Anti-War

extended and its mandate expanded to include continued action on behalf of children in 'underdeveloped' countries, among others: UN GA Res. 417(V) (1 Dec. 1950) and UN GA Res. 802(VIII) (6 Oct. 1953). See also Ressler, Boothby, and Steinbock (1988), 270. For a summary of UNICEF's work in the 50 years since it was established, see UNICEF (1995), 43–73.

[93] The policy and primary concerns of UNICEF are summarised each year in its report, *The State of the World's Children.*

[94] Ressler, Tortorici, and Marcelino (1993), 92–4. UNICEF also endeavoured to negotiate such cease-fires in the conflict in the former Yugoslavia. See UN DOC. CRC/C/SR.38, para. 8.

[95] Thus UNICEF has, *inter alia*, prepared a number of reports and discussion papers on children in armed conflict, and organised a 1987 international conference on 'Children in Situations of Armed Conflict in Africa', discussed in Kent (1990), 21–2.

[96] This is the study by Ressler, Tortorici, and Marcelino (1993).

[97] V. Bosnjak, 'Children's Rights: New Directions for UNICEF?', 56 *UNICEF Intercom* 6 (Apr. 1990).

Agenda'.[98] This ten-point agenda highlights a number of key issues relevant to child civilians (issues mentioned also in Chapter 8 below). These issues concern, *inter alia*, the importance of taking measures to prevent conflict, and educating children for peace; the concept of 'zones of peace' for children; a total prohibition on landmines; taking specific steps to safeguard women and girls; supporting war crimes tribunals; and monitoring the effect of sanctions on children.

6.1.3.2 UNHCR

Unlike UNICEF, UNHCR[99] is, in its work with children, obviously primarily concerned with the situation of refugees. In this context, UNHCR specifically acknowledges the entitlement of children to 'special assistance' (see the following paragraph), and has published guidelines on the protection and care of refugee children.[100]

In 1993 UNHCR drafted its 'Policy on Refugee Children',[101] a detailed statement which emphasises the importance of addressing the distinct needs of refugees who are children (generally defined here as under 18 in accordance with the 1989 CRC). This document describes the history of recent UNHCR decisions and initiatives concerning refugee children (paragraphs 7, 8, 19, and 20), and cites three factors which 'contribute to the special needs of refugee children: their dependence, their vulnerability and their developmental needs' (paragraph 10). The document also sets out a basis for action, including a section on relevant legal principles (paragraphs 16 to 18). It outlines UNHCR policy (paragraphs 21 to 27), stating, *inter alia*, that UNHCR staff should try to ensure the recognition of children's rights, 'including their rights to personal security and special assistance' (paragraph 27).

The work of UNHCR means that this organisation is involved, both in the formulation of policy and in actual conflict situations, in evacuating children from situations of armed conflict[102] and in providing them with supplies and necessities. In this way, among others, it participates in the implementation of principles of international law concerning the protection of child civilians.

---

[98] UNICEF (1995), 40–1.

[99] Concerning UNHCR generally, see, e.g., UN (1994), paras. 154–61. Although this book does not discuss in any depth issues concerning child refugees, the work of UNHCR in assisting children in armed conflicts, and during their immediate aftermath, is relevant here.

[100] See UNHCR (1994), for the latest version of these. The initial guidelines were published in 1988: *ibid.*, 14. See also UNHCR, *The State of the World's Refugees* (New York, 1993). This contains, e.g., sections on the protection of refugees in times of armed conflict (67–82), and on 'Children in War' (73).

[101] UNHCR (1994), 163–76.

[102] See, e.g., the two UNHCR and UNICEF Joint Statements on the evacuation of children from former Yugoslavia: Ressler (1992), 25–32 (and mentioned above in sect. 4.2.1.3). See also summary of UNHCR activities as reported to the Committee on the Rights of the Child in 1994: UN Doc. CRC/C/SR.175 (13 Oct. 1994).

6.1.3.3 The Human Rights Committee

Last, but by no means least, a significant intergovernmental body linked with the UN and of relevance here is the Human Rights Committee, made up of eighteen members 'of high moral character and recognized competence in the field of human rights'.[103] Although an autonomous body established by States Parties to the ICCPR, its expenses are paid by the UN and its staff is provided by the UN Secretariat.

The Human Rights Committee fulfils a variety of functions, many of which are, at least in principle, pertinent in monitoring the observance of international law concerning child civilians.[104]

Thus, the Human Rights Committee can, in theory, assist in interstate disputes, where one State Party considers that another is not complying with its obligations under the ICCPR (Articles 41 to 43). However, this interstate procedure has been ineffective, as states have been unwilling to invoke it.

Of more practical significance for the protection of child civilians is the regular scrutiny by this Committee (under Article 40) of state reports. It thereby monitors compliance with the ICCPR, including, *inter alia*, compliance with Article 24 (right of the child to special treatment), Article 7 (prohibition of torture and other maltreatment), and Article 6 (right to life). Also relevant are the Human Rights Committee's influential 'General Comments', which clarify issues concerning interpretation of the ICCPR and the reporting obligations of states party to it.[105]

As regards state reports, there is no mechanism to enforce government compliance with views expressed by the Human Rights Committee. In response to such reports, this Committee can simply 'transmit its reports, and such general comments as it may consider appropriate, to the States Parties' (Article 40(4) of the ICCPR).[106] The State Party concerned need only submit 'observations' on any comments made by the Human Rights Committee (Article 40(5)). This problem is, however, addressed to some extent by the Human Rights Committee's power to question state representatives regarding issues arising from their reports. These exchanges, recorded in the summary records and annual reports of the Hu-

---

[103] Art. 28(2) of the ICCPR. Consideration is given to equitable geographic distribution of members, and they serve in their individual capacity (Arts. 31(2) and 28(3)).

[104] Fuller descriptions of the work of the Committee can be found, e.g., in T. Opsahl, 'The Human Rights Committee', in Alston (ed.) (1992), 369–443, and K. Das, 'United Nations Institutions and Procedures Founded on Conventions on Human Rights and Fundamental Freedoms', in Vasak (ed.) (1982), 334–48. See also generally Hampson (1992), regarding the role of the Committee in encouraging compliance with international humanitarian law.

[105] See reference to the Committee's General Comments on Arts. 6 and 24, in sects. 2.1.2.1 and 2.1.2.2 above.

[106] For criticism of this mechanism see, e.g., Meron (1986), 123–5.

man Rights Committee, can 'reflect satisfaction or disapproval with a situation prevailing within a particular state and are, therefore, significant'.[107] In addition, in March 1993 the Human Rights Committee decided to adopt, after the examination of each country report, comments on these reports, concluding with recommendations for improved observance of specific rights.[108] Such recommendations could encourage more rigorous state compliance with Articles in the ICCPR, such as Articles 6 and 24, relevant to child civilians.

Another aspect of the Human Rights Committee's mandate which is pertinent in relation to child civilians is the power of this Committee, under the Optional Protocol to the ICCPR, to consider individual complaints.[109] The state subject to the complaint must be a party to the Optional Protocol, and only states that are party to the ICCPR are eligible.[110]

Under Article 1 of the Optional Protocol, complaints must be submitted by individuals subject to the jurisdiction of a particular State Party who claim to be victims of a violation by that state of any of the rights articulated in the ICCPR.[111] Thus complaints must in general be made by victims themselves, and it is unclear whether a third party not directly linked to the victim, such as an NGO, could submit a claim on behalf of an individual.[112] In any event, under the Optional Protocol child civilians themselves or relatives on their behalf would have *locus standi* to submit complaints.

The cases are considered in private hearings, but are subsequently summarised in the annual report of the Human Rights Committee to the General Assembly.

---

[107] *Ibid.*, 125.

[108] See 'Human Rights Committee Adopts Country Specific Reports' 7.2 *Interights Bulletin* 22 (1992–3).

[109] For a useful summary of the differences between the Resolution 1503 procedure before the Commission on Human Rights, and the role of the Human Rights Committee under the Optional Protocol, see Bhandare (1990), 21, and UN (1994), 316–17. Complaints under the Optional Protocol cannot be dealt with if simultaneously under consideration in the Resolution 1503 procedure.

[110] As at 31 Dec. 1995 only 87 of the 132 parties to the ICCPR were party to the Optional Protocol: UN Doc. ST/HR/4/Rev.13, 10 (see sect. 2.1.2.1 above).

[111] The procedure for the consideration of communications is set out in the Optional Protocol, and the Human Rights Committee has also drawn up its own rules. For discussion of this, see, e.g., M. Schmidt, 'The Optional Protocol To The International Covenant on Civil and Political Rights: Procedure and Practice' 4.2 *Interights Bulletin* 27 (1989).

[112] See discussion on this point in Meron (1986), 101–4. See also T. Van Boven, 'United Nations and Human Rights: A Critical Appraisal', in Cassese (ed.) (1979), 131, and D. Weissbrodt, 'The Contribution of International Nongovernmental Organisations to the Protection of Human Rights', in Meron (ed.) (1984), 420, n. 83. Certain other treaty-monitoring bodies, such as the Committee Against Torture, accept communications from NGOs. See J. Voyame, 'United Nations Convention Against Torture and Other Cruel, Inhuman and Degrading Treatment or Punishment' 89/1 *Bulletin of Human Rights* 79 (1990).

The Human Rights Committee is not empowered to deliver binding judgments, and it has been criticised for its inability to enforce compliance in respect of individual communications under the Optional Protocol.[113] Nonetheless, it has now accumulated a substantial body of case law. One writer describes it as operating in a 'quasi-judicial fashion' and observes that 'its decisions under the Optional Protocol have been honoured by States Parties, *inter alia*, through changes in legislation, release of prisoners and payment of compensation to victims of human rights violations'.[114] Its decisions therefore carry some weight, and it could be a useful forum before which to bring cases regarding breaches of ICCPR provisions relevant to the treatment of child civilians.

6.1.3.4 *Comment: Other Bodies Operating Under UN Auspices*

From the above description, it is clear that UNICEF, UNHCR, and the Human Rights Committee all participate, to a greater or lesser extent, in monitoring and/or implementing aspects of international law relating to the treatment of child civilians in armed conflict.

UNICEF and UNHCR are involved both in practice and on a policy level in measures to protect such children (as in the evacuation of children from the former Yugoslavia) and in the provision of relief to children in many conflicts (including the intervention of UNICEF in the Iraqi conflicts (see Chapter 7)). Further, in its policy statement on refugee children, UNHCR specifically recognises the entitlement of child refugees to 'special assistance', as mentioned in section 6.1.3.2 above.

As regards the Human Rights Committee, the interstate complaints mechanism is currently a dead letter. However, it is worth emphasising that the individual complaints procedure under the Optional Protocol has considerable (and largely unrealized) potential as an avenue of redress for individual child victims of violations in conflict situations. Depending on the circumstances, such complaints could cite breaches of, *inter alia*, Articles 6, 7, and 24 of the ICCPR, as applicable.

In any event, the Human Rights Committee is well placed to use its reporting mechanism to encourage state compliance with the relevant standards in the ICCPR. The work of this Committee could thereby augment that of the Committee on the Rights of the Child, in stressing the importance of observing rules regarding the protection of children in armed conflict and in calling states to account.

---

[113] See, e.g., discussion in Meron (1986), 84 and 125–6.

[114] J. Martenson, 'Introduction' 89/1 *Bulletin of Human Rights*, at 2 (1990). However, the Human Rights Committee has recently expressed concern regarding the level of implementation of its views. UN GAOR, 46th Sess. Supp. 40/A/46/40 (1991) 173–4. For a collection of its decisions, see UN, *Selected Decisions of the Human Rights Committee Under the Optional Protocol* (New York, Vol. 1 (1985), and Vol. 2 (1990)).

6.2 WAR CRIMES TRIBUNALS AND TREATY PROVISION
FOR PUNISHMENT OF GRAVE BREACHES

In addition to the key intergovernmental bodies described above, there are a number of mechanisms and measures available to governments, and the international community as a whole, for punishing breaches of international law in situations of armed conflict, and in that way contributing to its enforcement and observance.

The available measures are discussed here in two main categories: international war crimes tribunals, and the provisions regarding grave breaches of the laws of armed conflict as set out in the 1949 GCs and 1977 GP I.[115] The latter procedures have not had much impact, owing primarily to lack of political will to implement them.[116] In any event, neither of these mechanisms applies specifically to children, although both clearly incorporate within their mandates violations committed against children in situations of armed conflict.

The aim here is to give a very general overview of this subject, and therefore the discussion below will not deal, for example, with matters such as the war crimes tribunals established after World War I.[117]

War crimes can be defined, in the words of the Charter of the Nuremberg Tribunal, as follows: 'violations of the laws or customs of war' including, but not limited to, 'murder, ill-treatment, or deportation to slave labour or for any other purpose of civilian populations of or in occupied territory, murder of hostages, plunder of public or private property, wanton destruction of cities, towns, or villages, or devastation not justified by military necessity'.[118]

Such crimes are often cited as an example of the universality principle. Thus all states have jurisdiction to try war crimes in that they threaten the international community as a whole and are criminal in all countries.[119]

---

[115] This simple categorisation is adequate for the purposes of this book. Regarding other possible categories, see, e.g., Hampson, 'Liability for War Crimes', in P. Rowe (ed.) (1993), 242. Further discussion on the issue of war crimes can be found, e.g., in McCoubrey (1990), 205–23; Oppenheim (1952), 566–88; Detter de Lupis (1987), 352–60; Van Dongen (1991), 48–58 and 97–109; Green (1993), 268–301; H. McCoubrey, 'Warcrimes: The Criminal Jurisprudence of Armed Conflict' XXI-1-2-3-4 *Revue de Droit Militaire et de Droit de la Guerre* 169 (1992); and D. Plattner, 'The Penal Repression of Violations of International Humanitarian Law Applicable in Non-International Armed Conflicts', 278 *Int'l. Rev. of the Red Cross* 410–13 (Sept.–Oct. 1990).

[116] This point is made by various authors, including Hampson (1992), 119–20; Kalshoven (1987), 67, and Van Dongen (1991), 130. See also J. Verhaegen, 'Legal Obstacles to Prosecution of Breaches of Humanitarian Law', 27 *Int'l. Rev. of the Red Cross* 607 (Nov.–Dec. 1987).

[117] These are discussed in Van Dongen (1991), 48–58, and M. C. Bassiouni, *Crimes Against Humanity in International Criminal Law* (Dordrecht, 1992), 199–204.

[118] See Art. 6, sect. II, of the Charter of the International Military Tribunal annexed to the 'Agreement for the Prosecution and Punishment of the Major War Criminals of the European Axis' (London, 8 Aug. 1945): (1951) 82 UNTS 280. See also Green (1993), 285, and definition in Oppenheim (1952), 566–7.

[119] M. Shaw, *International Law* (Cambridge 1986), 359. See also Sieghart (1984), 48.

6.2.1 International War Crimes Tribunals

International war crimes tribunals[120] are epitomised by those established after World War II at Nuremberg (November 1945 to October 1946) and Tokyo (May 1946 to November 1948). While these Tribunals may be criticised concerning the detail of some of their decisions, the Nuremberg Tribunal, in particular, was of considerable significance.[121]

Only the Nuremberg Tribunal will be considered briefly here, since it was important in the development of the relevant body of international law,[122] and, further, it considered numerous offences committed against child civilians. In addition, the existence and achievements of this Tribunal may have paved the way for the establishment of the Yugoslav and Rwandan Tribunals (mentioned later in this section).

The Nuremberg Tribunal was established on 8 August 1945, when the United States, the United Kingdom, France, and the USSR concluded their 'Agreement for the Prosecution and Punishment of the Major War Criminals of the European Axis'.[123] Annexed to this Agreement was the Charter which regulated the constitution, jurisdiction, and functions of the Tribunal.

Article 6, the first Article of Section II ('Jurisdiction and General Principles') of the Charter, defined the crimes coming within the jurisdiction of the Tribunal. These crimes, for which it was explicitly stated that there would be individual responsibility,[124] were: crimes against peace,[125] war crimes,[126] and crimes against humanity.[127]

---

[120] War crimes tribunals differ from human rights enforcement mechanisms in many respects. Thus, among other things, the latter deal with the civil responsibility of states *vis-à-vis* individuals within their jurisdiction, while the former concern the criminal responsibility of states and those acting on their behalf in relation to situations of armed conflict.

[121] Higgins, e.g., speaks favourably of the Nuremberg Tribunal ('The New United Nations' (1994), 21). For discussion of the Nuremberg and Tokyo tribunals generally, see, among others, Best (1994), 180–206.

[122] See discussion in Bassiouni ((1992), 528) regarding the development of the concept of 'crimes against humanity' in relation to the Charter of the Nuremberg Tribunal.

[123] See n. 118 above.

[124] McCoubrey ((1990), 214–15), argues that the Tribunal 'served a valuable purpose, not least in establishing that individuals can be called to account for crimes which they committed as members of governments'. See also, generally, L. Sunga, *Individual Responsibility in International Law for Serious Human Rights Violations* (Dordrecht, 1992).

[125] Defined in Art. 6 as 'planning, preparation, initiation, or waging of a war of aggression, or a war in violation of international treaties, agreements, or assurances, or participation in a common plan or conspiracy for the accomplishment of any of the foregoing'.

[126] See definition in sect. 6.2 above.

[127] Defined in Art. 6 as 'murder, extermination, enslavement, deportation, and other inhumane acts committed against any civilian population, before or during the war, or persecutions on political, racial, or religious grounds in execution of or in connection with any crime within the jurisdiction of the Tribunal, whether or not in violation of the domestic law of the country where perpetrated'. For discussion of the concept of crimes against humanity see, e.g., Bassiouni (1992).

In addition, this Article of the Charter stipulated that leaders and others participating in plans to commit any of the three listed categories of crimes were 'responsible for all acts performed by any persons in execution of such plan'. Articles 7 and 8 dealt further with the issue of responsibility for war crimes, including a warning that obedience to superior orders would not necessarily exonerate a defendant.

These principles set out in the Nuremberg Charter were subsequently reaffirmed in various resolutions of the UN General Assembly.[128]

The transcript of the proceedings of the Nuremburg Tribunal indicated that many of the crimes under consideration included offences committed against child civilians.[129] Further, both the Indictment and the Judgment of the Tribunal made specific mention of such offences,[130] and, in so doing, indicated the particular seriousness with which they were regarded.

More recently, there are the war crimes tribunals that have been established to hear cases concerning offences committed in the former Yugoslavia and in Rwanda.[131] The mandates of these tribunals do not specifically refer to children, except insofar as their jurisdiction extends explicitly to acts of genocide, as defined in the 1948 Genocide Convention to include measures concerning children (see section 2.1.2.1 above). Once again, however, children clearly come within the jurisdiction of these Tribunals as victims of any of the crimes listed.[132] At the time of writing, the work of both these tribunals was in its early stages, with neither having yet fully decided any cases (although the Yugoslav Tribunal had begun to hear

---

[128] See, e.g., UN GA Res. 95(1) (11 Dec. 1946) and UN GA Res. 177 (II) (21 Nov. 1947).

[129] *Trial of the Major War Criminals Before the International Military Tribunal, Nuremberg: Official Text in the English Language. Proceedings* (Nuremberg, 1947). E.g., Vol. ii, 125–6 (including the burning alive of children), and Vol. vi, 212–16 (including the gassing of children).

[130] *Ibid.*, Vol. i, 44 and 50 (setting out in the Indictment details of crimes committed against children in the USSR by the Nazis) and Vol. xxii, 540 (concerning, in the Judgment, the 'shipment' to Germany of 40,000–50,000 youths, aged 10–14).

[131] See UN Docs. S/RES/827 and S/RES/955. For further information on these tribunals, e.g. in relation to the former Yugoslavia, see Higgins ('The New United Nations' (1994)); C. Greenwood, 'The International Tribunal for Former Yugoslavia' 69 *International Affairs* 641 (1993); F. Hampson, *Violation of Fundamental Human Rights in the Former Yugoslavia: II The Case for a War Crimes Tribunal* (David Davis Memorial Institute, London, 1993); T. Meron, 'War Crimes in Yugoslavia and the Development of International Law', 8.1 *AJIL* 78 (1994); S. Grant, 'Protection Mechanisms and the Yugoslav Crisis' 8.1 *Interights Bulletin* 3 (1994), and S. Grant, 'Dispensing International Justice: The Yugoslav and Rwandan Criminal Tribunals', 9.2 *Interights Bulletin* 39 (Summer 1995).

[132] In relation to the former Yugoslavia (described, in the *Tadić Case*, (35 ILM, 55 and 56 (1996)), as being a mixed international and non-international armed conflict) these crimes are categorised as: grave breaches of the 1949 GCs; violations of the laws or customs of war; genocide and crimes against humanity. Arts. 2, 3, 4, and 5 of S/RES/827. As regards Rwanda, a non-international armed conflict, the categories are: genocide, crimes against humanity, and violations of Common Art. 3 of the 1949 GCs. Arts. 2, 3, and 4 of S/RES/955.

evidence).[133] Their case law on children cannot therefore be commented on here.

Indeed, during the Iraqi occupation of Kuwait, threats were made by a number of heads of state regarding the possible establishment of a war crimes tribunal in relation to Iraq. However, as mentioned in Chapter 7 below, this tribunal did not materialise.[134]

Further, the international community has recently been forging ahead with long-standing efforts to establish a permanent international criminal court, empowered to adjudicate on various crimes, including war crimes and crimes against humanity. On 11 December 1995 the UN General Assembly agreed to establish a preparatory committee to discuss the draft statute for this court, prepared by the International Law Commission.[135] In this context, the International Law Commission had produced a number of versions of its 'Draft Code of Crimes Against the Peace and Security of Mankind'.[136] A permanent international criminal court could clearly have considerable potential to hear cases regarding violations of the laws of armed conflict affecting child civilians. However, at the time of writing, this court had not yet been established, nor the Draft Code finalised. Accordingly it, too, will not be further discussed here.

6.2.2 Treaty Provisions for the Punishment of Grave Breaches as Set Out Under the 1949 GCs and 1977 GP I

As well as possibly being subject to adjudication before war crimes tribunals, grave breaches of humanitarian law in international armed

---

[133] The Rwanda Tribunal began work on 26 June 1995. 4 months earlier, on 13 Feb. 1995, the Yugoslav Tribunal had issued 'the first ever genocide indictment': Grant (Summer 1995), 39. The latter had also made decisions on preliminary and jurisdictional issues of some importance, particularly in the *Tadić Case*.

[134] As regards Iraq, one authority argues that '[a] historic opportunity was missed to breathe new life into the critically important concept of individual responsibility for laws of war violations': T. Meron, 'The Case for War Crimes Trials in Yugoslavia' 72.3 *Foreign Affairs* 124 (1993).

[135] See UN GA Res. 50/46 (11 Dec. 1995): 'Establishment of an international criminal court'. The draft statute is to be completed by the end of Aug. 1996, and in its session beginning in Sept. 1996 the GA will arrange an 'international conference of plenipotentiaries to finalize and adopt a convention on the establishment of an international criminal court' (*ibid.*, para. 5). For discussion on the drafting process, see *Guardian*, 30 Mar. 1996 and 16 Apr. 1996. See also generally 'International Criminal Tribunals', 9.2 *Interights Bulletin* 37 (Summer 1995); J. Crawford, 'The ILC Adopts a Statute for an Interntional Criminal Court', *ibid.*, 61; and C. K. Hall, *Challenges Ahead for the United Nations Preparatory Committee Drafting a Statute for a Permanent International Criminal Court: Reprint of an Article in AI UK Lawyers' Network Newsletter, No. 21 (Supplement, 1996)* (London, 1996).

[136] At the time of writing, the latest version was set out in UN GAOR, 50th Sess., Supp. No. 10 (A/50/10) 'Report of the International Law Commission on the Work of its Forty-Seventh Session' (2 May–21 July 1995). For comment on an earlier draft of this document and a summary of its long history (originating in a desire to perpetuate the work of the Nuremberg Tribunal), see AI, *Establishing a Just, Fair and Effective International Criminal Court* (London, 1994).

conflicts can be addressed under the provisions of the 1949 GCs and 1977 GP I.[137] These treaties all contain measures concerning grave breaches of their provisions, and such breaches clearly incorporate acts committed against children, although once again children are not specifically referred to.[138]

In brief, all four of the 1949 GCs contain similar Articles concerning grave breaches, and these oblige States Parties to these Conventions to ensure that such breaches are punished.[139] These provisions are additional to other measures encouraging compliance with the 1949 GCs, such as those regarding the role of the Protecting Power and/or the ICRC, and the duties of States Parties to 'respect and ensure respect for' the Conventions, in accordance with Common Article 1.

Under the 1949 GCs, grave breaches are defined broadly as acts committed against protected persons which involve 'wilful killing, torture or inhuman treatment, including biological experiments, wilfully causing great suffering or serious injury to body or health' (see, for example, Article 147 of 1949 GC IV). In relation specifically to civilians, under Article 147 of 1949 GC IV such breaches are further defined to include other prohibited acts, such as unlawful deportation, transfer, or confinement.[140]

The 1949 GC Articles on grave breaches generally oblige States Parties to enact legislation to provide effective penal sanctions for persons committing such breaches or ordering their commission. The parties are also required to search for persons involved in the commission of grave breaches, and to bring them before their municipal courts, or to hand them over for trial to another concerned party to the 1949 GCs, if the latter has made out a *prima facie* case.[141] Further, for example, an enquiry can be instituted, at the request of a party to the conflict, into alleged violations of these Conventions (as under Article 149 of 1949 GC IV).[142]

---

[137] The discussion in this sect. does not deal with non-international armed conflicts. In any event, as Green (1993), 312, points out, 1977 GP II 'is silent on the issue of breaches and their consequences', and accordingly both government and rebel authorities should treat acts of this kind according to national criminal law. See also Plattner (Sept./Oct. 1990). However, the *Tadić Case* comments on a developing trend to extend the grave breaches provisions of the GCs and 1977 GP I to non-international armed conflicts: 35 ILM 59 (1996).

[138] On the relationship between the law as expressed in the post World War II international military tribunals and the 1949 GC measures regarding grave breaches, Brownlie observes that '[t]he Conventions avoid the term "war crimes" in relation to "grave breaches" but there can be no doubt that the latter constitute war crimes': Brownlie (1990), 563.

[139] The main provisions are contained in 1949 GC I (Arts. 49, 50, and 51); 1949 GC II (Arts. 50, 51, and 52); 1949 GC III (Arts. 129, 130, and 131), and 1949 GC IV (Arts. 146, 147, and 148).

[140] In addition, as regards civilians, Art. 147 forbids 'compelling a protected person to serve in the forces of a hostile Power, or wilfully depriving a protected person of the rights of fair and regular trial prescribed in the present Convention, taking of hostages and extensive destruction and appropriation of property, not justified by military necessity and carried out unlawfully and wantonly'.

[141] See discussion on this in, e.g., McCoubrey (1990), 211.

[142] However, this provision is dependent on agreement between the parties. See discussion in Van Dongen (1991), 220.

1977 GP I, among other things, expands the 1949 GC definition of grave breaches, including that relating to attacks on the civilian population.[143] It also, *inter alia*, places a duty on parties to repress grave breaches which result from a failure to act (Article 86(1)), and it addresses the responsibility of superiors for acts of their subordinates (Article 86(2)). The parties are obliged to assist each other in relation to criminal proceedings regarding grave breaches (Article 88), and to co-operate with the UN in this context (Article 89). 1977 GP I also confirms that a party to the conflict can be liable to pay compensation if it violates the provisions of this Protocol or of the 1949 GCs (Article 91).

In addition, 1977 GP I extends the 1949 GC provisions for enquiry into alleged abuses, by allowing for the establishment of an International Fact-Finding Commission.[144] This Commission is entrusted with the task of enquiring into grave breaches or serious violations of the 1949 GCs or of 1977 GP I, and of restoring, through its good offices, respect for these treaties (Article 90(2)(c)). In other situations, the Commission may institute an enquiry at the request of a party to the conflict, but only with the consent of the other party or parties concerned (Article 90(2)(d)).

As mentioned above (section 4.4.2), the Amsterdam Declaration specifically referred to the potential of this Commission to investigate grave breaches concerning children in armed conflict situations. However, at the time of writing, the Fact-Finding Commission was fairly recently established (it came into existence in 1992),[145] and its potential unexplored.

6.2.3 Comment: Procedures for Punishing War Crimes and/or Grave Breaches

International war crimes tribunals and treaty provisions regarding grave breaches of the laws of armed conflict are, again, clearly relevant in enforcing international law relating to child civilians,[146] although resort to these mechanisms is relatively infrequent, and they generally contain no explicit reference to the protection of children.

---

[143] See Art. 85. This designates as grave breaches certain acts 'when committed wilfully, in violation of the relevant provisions of this Protocol, and causing death or serious injury to body or health' (Art. 85(3)). Such acts include, e.g., making civilians the object of attack or launching indiscriminate attacks affecting civilians. See Art. 85(3)(a) and (b).

[144] This Commission should consist of 'fifteen members of high moral standing and acknowledged impartiality' (Art. 90(a)). For further information on this Commission, see, e.g., F. Hampson, 'Fact-Finding and the International Fact-Finding Commission', in Fox and Meyer (eds.) (1993), 53–82.

[145] Green (1993), 274.

[146] One authority emphasises that war crimes trials, when properly conducted, have an educative effect. See Hampson, 'Liability for War Crimes', in Rowe (ed.) (1993), 260. In addition, they can fulfil a documentary and therapeutic role. See also Grant (1995), 41–2.

War crimes tribunals have played an important role in addressing violations of international law in certain armed conflict situations, as evidenced particularly by the Nuremberg Tribunal. It is to be hoped that the case law of those set up to investigate recent conflicts (as in the former Yugoslavia and in Rwanda) may contribute to the development of international law specifically regarding crimes committed against child civilians. In this context, it may not be unduly optimistic to assume, in the 1990s and thereafter, a greater awareness of the legal entitlements of children than prevailed at the time of the Nuremberg Tribunal.

On the other hand, existing humanitarian treaty mechanisms concerning grave breaches committed in international armed conflicts have been somewhat under-used. It may be, however, that improved implementation of these measures could be encouraged by the Committee on the Rights of the Child, in monitoring observance by States Parties of their obligations under Article 38(1) and (4) of the 1989 CRC (see, further, section 8.3.7.2.2). The Fact-Finding Commission could also possibly take action in relation to violations affecting children in armed conflict, although at the time of writing the likelihood of this seems rather remote.

6.3 NON-GOVERNMENTAL BODIES: THE ICRC AND NGOS

This Chapter has considered relevant work of the UN and bodies working within this organisation or under its auspices, including the Committee on the Rights of the Child, and has outlined mechanisms for punishing war crimes and grave breaches of international humanitarian law. It now remains to describe the work of international non-governmental bodies in implementing or monitoring compliance with international law concerning child civilians in situations of armed conflict.

6.3.1 The ICRC

The ICRC,[147] established in 1863, is a non-governmental body of great significance in monitoring, developing, and encouraging implementation of international law relevant to child civilians in situations of armed conflict. Its authority to undertake this task is derived from treaty, particularly the

---

[147] General information about the ICRC quoted here is derived largely from its own publications, including: ICRC, *The International Committee of the Red Cross (ICRC)* (Geneva, n.d.); ICRC, *The International Committee of the Red Cross: What it is, What it Does* (Geneva, n.d.); ICRC, *Presenting the ICRC* (Geneva, 1986); and ICRC, *Red Cross and Red Crescent: Portrait of an International Movement* (Geneva, n.d.). Further descriptions of the work of the ICRC can be found, e.g., in D. Forsythe, *Humanitarian Politics: The International Committee of the Red Cross* (Baltimore, Md., 1977); D. Forsythe, 'The International Committee of the

1949 GCs and 1977 GP I, and from its own statutes, resolutions, and well-established tradition. Largely owing to its treaty-based role, the ICRC can be seen as an organisation *sui generis*, although many writers describe it as an NGO.[148] It is accordingly considered here separately from the NGOs.

The structure and main functions of the ICRC are outlined briefly below, as is information concerning some of its work in relation to children generally. Certain initiatives of the ICRC specifically in relation to the Iraqi conflicts are mentioned later, in section 7.5.2.

6.3.1.1 Structure and Functions of the ICRC

The ICRC was originally established as a private Swiss organisation concerned to alleviate the suffering of victims of armed conflict. Although it now has an official treaty-based role, the organisation remains a private institution, funded by voluntary contributions, largely staffed by Swiss nationals, and based in Geneva.[149] It describes itself as neutral in relation to politics, religion, and ideology.

The ICRC was the founding institution of the International Red Cross and Red Crescent Movement (the Movement), consisting of three components: the ICRC itself, the National Red Cross and Red Crescent Societies, and the League of Red Cross and Red Crescent Societies (the governing body of the national societies).[150] These components normally meet every four years with the representatives of the States Parties to the 1949 GCs, at the International Conference of the Red Cross. This Conference is the highest deliberative assembly of the Movement. Decisions and resolutions of the Conference are significant, as they carry weight not only within the Movement, but also in influencing the governments, many represented at the Conference, that have signed the 1949 GCs.[151]

The ICRC engages in various humanitarian activities, all relevant to the protection of child civilians in situations of armed conflict. Thus it has been instrumental in drafting humanitarian conventions, including the 1949 GCs and the 1977 GPs. These treaties generally empower the ICRC to act 'as a

Red Cross', in Fox and Meyer (eds.) (1993), 83–103; A. Hay, 'The ICRC and International Humanitarian Issues', 238 *Int'l. Rev. of the Red Cross* 3 (1984); and D. Weissbrodt, 'Ways International Organisations Can Improve Their Implementation of Human Rights and Humanitarian Law in Situations of Armed Conflict', in E. Lutz, H. Hannum, and K. Burke (eds.), *New Directions in Human Rights* (Philadelphia, Penn., 1989), 78–86.

[148] One writer who seems to categorise the ICRC as an NGO is, e.g., Weissbrodt, in Meron (ed.) (1984).

[149] In addition, the ICRC has field operations set up in areas of conflict throughout the world: *The ICRC: What it is; What it does*, 12.

[150] Of these three components, only the role of the ICRC itself is outlined in this book.

[151] Meron, (*Human Rights in Internal Strife* (1987), 109), states, in relation to decisions of the Conference: 'The participation of states comprising virtually the entire international community in the adoption of resolutions and statutes gives them considerable importance.'

neutral intermediary between parties to conflicts, in order to bring protection and assistance to the victims',[152] and confer on it, *inter alia*, the right to take action (such as visiting prisoners of war),[153] and the right to negotiate directly with states (for example, in offering its humanitarian services).[154] It also runs the Central Tracing Agency.[155] In addition, the statutes and resolutions of the ICRC confer on it a right of humanitarian initiative in situations not covered by the 1949 GCs or the 1977 GPs,[156] so that the work of the ICRC can cover the entire spectrum of conflict situations.

The ICRC will not undertake fact-finding without the formal agreement of the relevant government,[157] nor, in general, does it make public its reports on its activities. The ICRC sees this principle of 'discretion' as essential to its continued and effective functioning. However, in cases of serious violations of international humanitarian law the ICRC may make public appeals.[158]

6.3.1.2 The Work of the ICRC Concerning Children in Armed Conflict Generally

According to a number of writers, the ICRC has consistently been concerned about the plight of children in situations of armed conflict, and has worked on their behalf.[159]

As early as 1919 the ICRC helped to set up the Save the Children Fund International Union, and in 1939 it was involved in drawing up the Convention for the Protection of Children in the Event of International Conflict or

---

[152] See Hay (1984), 5 and 6.

[153] For information regarding this aspect of the ICRC's role, see, e.g., D. Weissbrodt, and J. McCarthy, 'Fact-Finding by Non-Governmental Organisations' in B. G. Ramcharan (ed.), *International Law and Fact-Finding in the Field of Human Rights* (London, 1982), 199.

[154] The humanitarian role of the ICRC in international armed conflict is expressly authorised in, *inter alia*, Arts. 10, 63, and 142 of 1949 GC IV, and Art. 74 of 1977 GP I. Common Art. 3 of the 1949 GCs makes similar provision regarding non-international armed conflict.

[155] This Agency undertakes much work relevant to children, in that it traces missing persons, organises repatriations and family reunification, and facilitates the exchange of family messages. See sect. 4.2.1.3 above.

[156] For a description of the basis of the ICRC's right of humanitarian initiative in internal strife, see Meron, *Human Rights in Internal Strife* (1987), 105–17. See also 'ICRC Protection and Assistance Activities in Situations Not Covered by International Humanitarian Law', 28 *Int'l. Rev. of the Red Cross* 9 (Jan.–Feb. 1988).

[157] Weissbrodt and McCarthy, in Ramcharan (ed.) (1982), 193.

[158] *The ICRC: What it is; What it does*, 14. See also Meron, *Human Rights in Internal Strife*. (1987), 116. Further, although contrary to its normal practice, the ICRC may express an opinion on the use of a particular weapon, such as chemical weapons, if it gives rise to an 'exceptionally grave situation': ICRC, 'Action by the International Committee of the Red Cross in the Event of Breaches of International Humanitarian Law', 21 *Int'l. Rev. of the Red Cross* 76 (Mar.–Apr. 1981). A number of writers have commented on the limitations of the role of the ICRC. See, e.g., Meron. *Human Rights in Internal Strife* (1987), 117; Hampson, in Meyer (ed.) (1989), 70; and Forsythe, in Fox and Meyer (eds.) (1993).

[159] See, e.g., Plattner (1984), 2; Pictet (1958), 185–6; Krill (1986), 40; and Singer (1986), 24–5.

Civil War, which was later incorporated into 1949 GC IV (as mentioned in section 4.1 above). Further, on many occasions in World War II the ICRC apparently took action on behalf of children.

More recent initiatives include the 1991 ICRC conference on the protection of victims of war, which generated certain recommendations concerning the protection of children (see Note 143, Chapter 4). Subsequently, partly as a result of that 1991 conference,[160] the Twenty-sixth International Conference of the Red Cross, in 1995, adopted a resolution on the protection of civilians in armed conflict, which contains a section on children.[161]

The ICRC has, in one document, summarised in some detail its work and policy in relation to children in situations of armed conflict.[162] This starts from the assumption that '[c]hildren, being particularly vulnerable, should have priority in receiving protection and assistance' (page 1). As regards the treatment of children in armed conflict, the ICRC document refers to two resolutions of the XXVth International Conference of the Red Cross (1986): Resolution IX, dealing with the protection of children in armed conflicts, and Resolution XX, dealing with assistance to children in emergency situations (page 6). Reference is also made to the work of the ICRC in contributing to the drafting of the 1989 CRC. The document comments that, despite the 'legal panoply' of rules regarding children in armed conflict, 'there is no denying that children continue to be the innocent victims of armed conflicts' (page 9).

This ICRC document also discusses the ICRC role in providing medical and nutritional assistance to children in armed conflict, noting that here it assists children within the broader context of its assistance to all victims of conflict. However, it emphasises the specific needs of children regarding, for example, their dependence on adults; their particular nutritional requirements; and greater vulnerability to certain diseases (page 12). The ICRC document also comments on its role in visiting children detained as prisoners of war or as internees (page 19). Finally, this document emphasises the importance, as regards children, of the work of the Central Tracing Agency, and of the wide dissemination of international humanitarian law.

6.3.2 NGOs

In addition to the intergovernmental organisations and mechanisms considered above, and the ICRC, many international NGOs are actively

---

[160] See ICRC (1995), 38.

[161] ICRC, 'Resolutions of the 26th International Conference', 310 *Int'l. Rev. of the Red Cross* 60–8 (Jan.–Feb. 1996). The section on children emphasises, *inter alia*, the importance of providing them with 'the protection and assistance to which they are entitled under national and international law': *ibid.*, 63.

[162] ICRC, *ICRC and Children in Situation of Armed Conflict* (Geneva, 1987).

involved in efforts to monitor or encourage compliance with rules for the protection of child civilians in situations of armed conflict.[163] Such NGOs are described briefly below, before this Chapter looks in more detail at the work of one particular organisation (AI).

6.3.2.1 Structure and Functions of Pertinent NGOs

The relevant NGOs often consist of an international secretariat which is representative of national sections in different countries.[164] Some of these organisations aim largely to provide child civilians with material assistance, while others (such as AI) focus primarily on political lobbying and legislative changes. The work of organisations in the latter category is more pertinent to the subject of this research, and therefore one such organisation, AI, is later described here by way of example.

Certainly NGOs have played a vital and continuing role in developing and monitoring standards as regards both human rights and humanitarian law relevant to child civilians.[165] Thus, for example, one writer states, in assessing the human rights work of NGOs generally:

It would scarcely be possible to exaggerate the influence that NGOs have had on the development of international human rights law. Moreover NGOs are better placed than anyone else to monitor continuing performance—or lack of it—by national governments of the obligations by which they become bound in international law, and to pass their information on to the institutions called upon to supervise, interpret, apply, and enforce them.[166]

However, the work of NGOs is not above criticism. One authority notes that NGOs are of uneven quality, that the activism of NGOs has aroused some suspicion of them within the UN, and that their independence can be impugned.[167]

In fulfilling their functions, NGOs employ various strategies. Human rights NGOs have been described as;

[163] See, e.g., the 1984 NGO forum on 'Child Victims of Armed Conflicts': Rädda Barnen, *Report on Child Victims of Armed Conflicts: NGO Forum* (Stockholm, 1984). See also Singer (1986), 5.

[164] For further discussion of the structure of NGOs, see Weissbrodt, in Meron (ed.) (1984), 407–8.

[165] On the role of NGOs generally in this context, see, e.g., *ibid.* 403–38; Weissbrodt and McCarthy, in Ramcharan (ed.) (1982), 186–230; N. Rodley, 'The Work of Non-Governmental Organisations on the World-Wide Promotion and Protection of Human Rights' 90.1 *Bulletin of Human Rights* 84–93 (1992), and J. Shestack, 'Sisyphus Endures: The International Human Rights NGO', 24 *New York Law School Law Review* 89 (1978).

[166] Sieghart (1984), 442. Another writer describes 'the four wheels of the chariot of human rights' as composed of 'the United Nations bodies, the United Nations Secretariat, the States and the NGOs': Bhandare (1990), 25–6. See also comments in, e.g., A. Cassese, 'How Could Nongovernmental Organisations Use UN Bodies More Effectively' 1.4 *Universal Human Rights* 75 (1979), and Weissbrodt, in Meron (ed.) (1984), 411, 418, and n. 73.

[167] Weissbrodt, in Meron (ed.) (1984), 419 and 409. See also Cassese (1979) generally.

unofficial ombudsmen safeguarding human rights against government infringement, by such techniques as diplomatic initiatives, reports, public statements, efforts to influence the deliberations of human rights bodies established by intergovernmental organizations, campaigns to mobilize public opinion, and attempts to affect the foreign policy of some countries.[168]

In this context, many NGOs operate within the UN generally,[169] and some have consultative status with bodies such as ECOSOC, the ILO, and UNESCO.[170] Thus, as mentioned in section 4.2.5, NGOs were deeply involved, within ECOSOC, in drafting and debating proposed Articles of the 1989 CRC.[171] NGOs have also, to some extent, played a continuing role in the work of the Committee on the Rights of the Child (as mentioned in section 6.1.1.1 above). Further, certain NGOs concerned with children's rights issues have now formed the Child Rights Caucus,[172] with the aim of co-ordinating their efforts to influence UN policy, as formulated in international conferences and other such fora.

6.3.2.2 AI

AI,[173] established in 1961, is an example of an NGO that has done a great deal of work on issues relating to the protection of children, and on Iraq. Its structure and main functions are described briefly here, as are certain of its activities generally regarding children. Its work in relation to the Iraqi conflicts is outlined in section 7.5.1 below.

6.3.2.2.1 Structure and Functions

AI is one of the largest human rights NGOs, with over a million members, subscribers, and supporters in over 150 countries and territories.[174] People

---

[168]   Weissbrodt, in Meron (ed.) (1984), 404.

[169]   Within the UN, NGOs can, e.g., make oral and written interventions, and exercise informal influence by providing human rights research, or participating in drafting sessions: Weissbrodt, in Meron (ed.) (1984), 419 and 429.

[170]   Weissbrodt in Meron (ed.) (1984), 406–7. As regards ECOSOC, various NGOs whose work relates to the protection of child civilians have consultative status with this body. These include AI, the Friends World Committee for Consultation, the International Save the Children Alliance, Rädda Barnen, DCI, and the Minority Rights Group. Art. 71 of the UN Charter, which specifically allows ECOSOC to consult NGOs, was implemented by ECOSOC resolution 1296 (XLIV) of 23 May 1968. This divides NGOs into three categories, each entitled to differing degrees of participation in the work of ECOSOC: Bowett (1982), 69.

[171]   See, e.g., Cohen (1983), 387, and N. Cantwell, 'Non-Governmental Organisations and the United Nations Convention on the Rights of the Child' 91/2 *Bulletin of Human Rights* 16 (1992).

[172]   This Caucus was formed by the NGOs during preparations for the Copenhagen Summit: I. Newmark, 'The Child Rights Caucus: A New Kid On The Block' UNICEF. First Call for Children 10 (Jan.–Mar. 1995).

[173]   General information quoted here is derived from AI, *Amnesty International Handbook* (London, 1992); E. Larsen, *A Flame in Barbed Wire* (New York, 1978); AI, *What Makes Amnesty International Work?* (Colombo, 1988); and AI, *What Does Amnesty International Do?* (Mitcham, 1985).

[174]   AI (1992), 116.

who support the goals of AI may become members, and many members belong to local groups and take part in AI activities. The local groups generally operate within national sections, which are established in almost fifty countries.[175]

The work of the members, groups, and sections of AI is conducted under the ægis of the International Council, and various committees and bodies accountable to it. This Council, consisting of representatives of all sections, normally meets every two years. It is the principal governing body of AI and determines the organisation's mandate and policy.[176]

AI is funded almost entirely through money raised by its groups and sections. The organisation prides itself on its 'independence, universality and impartiality' and follows strict guidelines, including those on its funding policy, in order to preserve these qualities.[177]

AI's work frequently either includes or concentrates particularly on children, often in situations of conflict, although children are not specifically given priority in the AI mandate.[178] The mandate has traditionally focused on the treatment of prisoners, including 'prisoners of conscience'[179] and political prisoners.

More recently, AI's concerns have been extended to incorporate other situations which could be pertinent as regards child civilians. These now encompass extrajudicial killings, including in situations of armed conflict,[180] and arbitrary killings, torture, and hostage-taking by political opposition groups (although government violations are still the main focus).[181] Further, the organisation interprets its mandate to authorise action on behalf of victims of 'disappearances', as well as some categories of refugees.

AI employs various techniques in fulfilling its mandate. Detailed research, sometimes involving fact-finding missions, is an essential component of its work.[182] The information thus ascertained can be channelled, for example, into case work on behalf of particular prisoners and/or into general campaigns and/or into 'Urgent Action' campaigns, involving immediate appeals in emergency situations.

AI also engages in work at the UN, and with other international organisations, to develop and strengthen international law relevant to its mandate.[183]

---

[175] *Ibid.*, 47–8.   [176] *Ibid.*, 116–20.

[177] *Ibid.*, 17.

[178] The AI mandate is contained in Art. 1 of the Statute of Amnesty International: *ibid.*, 23–42 and 131.

[179] These are defined as people detained because of their beliefs, colour, sex, ethnic origin, language, or religion, and who have not used or advocated the use of violence. For further discussion, see *ibid.*, 24–9, 131, and 141.

[180] *Ibid.*, 25 and 36–7, and *What Does AI Do*, 21.

[181] *Ibid.*, 25, 29, and 40.

[182] *Ibid.*, 18–19 and 57–8.

[183] *Ibid.*, 11–13 and 53.

6.3.2.2.2 AI's Work Specifically Regarding Children

Although AI has, in its history, acted to some extent on behalf of children who came within its mandate, it is only in recent years that this aspect of its work has become more prominent.[184]

The organisation incorporates a separate section, Young Amnesty, for younger members. Further, a number of the national sections (for example, in Britain, France, Denmark, and Australia) have established groups working specifically on behalf of children.[185]

AI was one of the NGOs that actively participated in the working group responsible for drafting the 1989 CRC. It was particularly involved as regards Articles which touched on its concerns, such as the prohibition on child 'disappearances' and on the use of the death penalty for juveniles, the status of child refugees, and the right to rehabilitation after torture.[186]

Other examples of AI initiatives regarding children include its choice, in both 1989 and 1992, of 'children' as the theme for its annual 'Prisoner of Conscience Week', thus ensuring that for those weeks Amnesty groups were taking action on the organisation's concerns relating to children.[187] Further, on the eve of the World Summit for Children in 1990, AI issued a public appeal to stop the torture and killing of children generally.[188]

Moreover, this organisation has produced a number of publications regarding violations committed against children. For example, in 1989 AI published information on the imprisonment, torture, and killing of children in a wide range of countries, including Iraq.[189] Also in 1989 it published information regarding the use of the death penalty worldwide, showing, *inter alia*, that this penalty was still inflicted on children in many countries, again including Iraq.[190] More recently, the organisation has, among other things, published information about action which it has taken in relation to children in nineteen countries,[191] and about grave human rights violations against children generally.[192]

---

[184] See 'Amnesty International: Working for Children', 56 *Childright* 16 (May 1989), and AI, *Childhood Stolen: Grave Human Rights Violations Against Children* (London, 1995), 1.

[185] 'Amnesty International: Working for Children' (May 1989).

[186] See M. Crowley, 'Suffer Little Children', 41 *Amnesty* 10 (Oct.–Nov. 1989).

[187] 'Amnesty Spotlights Children', 60 *Childright* 4 (Oct. 1989), and 'POC Week—For Children', 58 *Amnesty Journal (British Section)* 1 (Oct.–Nov. 1992).

[188] See, e.g., report in *Independent*, 25 Sept. 1990.

[189] AI, 'The Youngest Victims: Children Jailed, Tortured and Killed', XIX.10 *Focus* 3 (Oct. 1989).

[190] AI, *When The State Kills . . . The Death Penalty v Human Rights* (London, 1989). See also D. Hadden, 'The Death Penalty: When the State Kills Young People', 59 *Childright* 7–8 (Sept. 1989).

[191] AI, *Children: Victims of Human Rights Violations* (London, 1990).

[192] See AI (1995). See also AI. *Focus* (Oct. 1992 and Jan. 1994).

6.3.2.3 Other Relevant NGOs

Many other NGOs are involved, to some extent, in work concerning children in situations of armed conflict. Most notable among these is the International Save the Children Alliance, and especially its Swedish branch, Rädda Barnen. Like DCI, the Geneva-based international children's rights organisation, Rädda Barnen was very active in the NGO group that contributed to the drafting of the 1989 CRC, and was particularly involved in the drafting of Article 38. These three organisations are all child-centred, and have been responsible for many international conferences and publications concerning children generally, as well as working on issues specifically concerning children in conflict situations.[193]

Other NGOs which have done, and/or are doing, work relevant to children in armed conflict include, for example, the Quaker organisation, Friends World Committee for Consultation; Human Rights Watch; Médecins Sans Frontièrs; Oxfam; and the Minority Rights Group. Of these, the Geneva office of the Friends World Committee for Consultation especially participated in the drafting of Article 38 of the 1989 CRC, and has been active in its opposition to the use of child soldiers.

6.3.3 Comment: The ICRC and NGOs, particularly AI

As regards international non-governmental bodies, the work of the ICRC and of certain NGOs forms an essential element in monitoring compliance with and attempting to raise standards in international law pertaining to child civilians. However, such organisations cannot themselves enforce this body of law, since that task must ultimately rest with governments and intergovernmental organisations.

The ICRC is particularly significant in this context, given its treaty-based role, most notably in the widely-ratified 1949 GCs. Despite criticisms that have been levelled at aspects of its practice, the ICRC has played an essential part in a variety of conflicts, over many years, and it has undoubtedly contributed to saving numerous children from the worst effects of such conflicts. This organisation operates from the explicit assumption that children in armed conflict are entitled to priority in the receipt of protection and assistance (see section 6.3.1.2 above).

In a different manner, the work of a number of NGOs, both on a practical level and in shaping law and policy, has contributed to the protection of child civilians in accordance with international law. AI serves as a useful example of one such NGO. However, the work of the various NGOs does sometimes duplicate that of other NGOs and, on occasion, may duplicate

---

[193] See, e.g., discussion on the drafting of Art. 38 (sect. 4.2.5 above), and the many publications by, particularly, Rädda Barnen and DCI, cited in this book.

aspects of the work of the ICRC and of certain UN bodies.[194] This problem is mentioned further in Chapter 8 below.

6.4 SUMMARY: MONITORING, IMPLEMENTATION, AND ENFORCEMENT MECHANISMS

In summary, the organisations and mechanisms outlined in this Chapter all have a role to play in the monitoring, implementation, and/or enforcement of international law regarding child civilians in situations of armed conflict, although many of these do not explicitly refer to children as included within their mandate.

The existing mechanisms (with the possible exception of the Committee on the Rights of the Child and certain non-governmental bodies) are not generally used as fully or effectively as they could be. Some of these, that could have a significant impact, seem particularly under-used (for example, applications to the Human Rights Committee under the Optional Protocol to the ICCPR, or international humanitarian law provisions concerning grave breaches). Again, the existence of the 1989 CRC and the work of the Committee on the Rights of the Child may encourage greater awareness of the potential of these mechanisms as possible avenues of redress for child civilians who suffer violations in situations of armed conflict.

In any event, the number of available mechanisms and organisations, and an obvious degree of overlap in their work, indicate the need for a way to be found of co-ordinating and making better use of all the possibilities. Suggestions for tackling this problem are set out in Chapter 8.

---

[194] See, e.g., discussion in Forsythe, in Fox and Meyer (eds.) (1993), 90; Weissbrodt, in Lutz, Hannum and Burke (eds.) (1989), 85–6; and Minear, Chelliah, Crisp, Mackinley and Weiss (1992), 34. See also criticisms of the co-ordination of the work of certain NGOs and UN agencies in Eriksson (1996) at, *inter alia*, 30–1, 46–7, and 57–9.

7

The Law in Practice: Three Conflicts

As mentioned in Chapter 1, the object of this book is not simply to describe the international law regarding child civilians in armed conflict, and those bodies and fora involved in its implementation. Such an exercise, while of some value, is like assembling the components of an engine without seeing how it functions. The concern here is to see how the 'engine' can best be mobilised. Accordingly, a further objective of this book is, in this Chapter, to attempt to assess the effectiveness of the relevant law, and, in Chapter 8, to make recommendations to enhance its effectiveness if this seems appropriate and possible.

First, to define what is meant by the 'effectiveness' of this body of law. This is measured, as stated in section 1.1 above, by the extent to which it seems to be observed, and the consequences of such observance. Do these laws appear to be respected, in terms of action taken or not taken, even if they are not specifically referred to? Are they invoked, in the sense that they are specifically referred to, even if not implemented? Are they implemented, being both explicitly invoked and acted upon? Finally, if the law is observed in any of these ways, does this have, even to a limited extent, the effect of preventing or ameliorating the existing or probable future harm to the child civilians concerned?

It is then necessary to address the question of how the effectiveness of this body of law is to be assessed. What evidence can be relied upon, and what criteria can be used? One approach is to take as an example a cluster of recent related conflicts, in order to gauge the extent to which the law regarding child civilians (as set out in Chapters 2 to 5 above) appears to have had any impact. This strategy will be followed here. The example to be discussed consists of the three conflicts involving Iraq, between 1987 and 1991.[1] The focus of this discussion remains the legal issues relating to child civilians in armed conflict, and accordingly it will not include a detailed historical and/or factual analysis of these conflicts.[2]

---

[1] Although they could be differently categorised, the events involving Iraq described in this Ch. are treated as 3 conflicts distinguished from each other partly according to their chronology, and partly according to the applicable body of law. Thus the two international armed conflicts which were so closely interlinked are considered as one, although the occupation of Kuwait could have been analysed as a conflict separate from the 1991 Gulf War.

[2] Such analyses of the Iraqi conflicts can, in any event, be found elsewhere. See, e.g., Rowe (ed.) (1993); M. F. Sluglett and P. Sluglett, *Iraq Since 1958: From Revolution to Dictatorship* (London, 1990); D. Korn, *Human Rights in Iraq* (New York, 1990); E. Karsh and I. Rautsi,

The three conflicts to be considered are, as mentioned in section 1.1: (1) the use of chemical weapons against the Iraqi Kurds in 1987 and 1988; (2) the 1990 occupation of Kuwait by Iraq and the 1991 Gulf War which this precipitated; and (3) the Kurdish (and Shia) uprisings of 1991 and their immediate aftermath.[3] In this context, certain indicators are selected as tools with which to try to measure the impact of the relevant law. The four indicators selected (of which the first two are the more significant) are: (1) the actual experiences of children in the three conflicts; (2) relevant decisions and debates within principal organs of the UN; (3) the work of certain UN-related bodies in the three conflicts; and (4) pertinent work of AI and the ICRC.

All three conflicts under consideration had devastating consequences for child civilians. Children were directly affected in that they were killed or wounded in large numbers. They were indirectly affected by the consequences of the conflicts, including starvation or malnutrition, disease, upheaval from home and family, material deprivation, and the general psychological and emotional trauma of their experiences. In this respect, the suffering of children in these conflicts was much like that of children in any conflict, and to some extent it is, sadly, possible to substitute for Iraq the names of other countries that have witnessed recent conflicts (such as Somalia, Afghanistan, the Sudan, Chechnya, Mozambique, the former Yugoslavia, Angola, or Rwanda), and to reach fairly similar conclusions.

Inevitably, however, the larger picture that emerges in this Chapter (given that it exmines a series of conflicts involving one particular country) cannot be conclusive, and will be, in some ways, impressionistic. Nor can these examples encompass all the legal possibilities.[4]

Moreover, it is clearly difficult to attempt to assess the effectiveness of

Saddam Hussein: A Political Biography (London, 1991); J. Miller and L. Mylroie, *Saddam Hussein and the Crisis in the Gulf* (New York, 1990); J. Bulloch and H. Morris, *Saddam's War* (London, 1991); J. Simpson, *From the House of War* (London, 1991); and A. Darwish and G. Alexander, *Unholy Babylon* (London, 1991). Particularly in relation to the Kurds of Iraq see, e.g., M. van Bruinessen, *Agha, Sheikh and State* (Utrecht, 1978); E. Ghareeb, *The Kurdish Question in Iraq* (Syracuse, NY, 1981); G. Chaliand, *People Without A Country* (London, 1980); D. McDowall, *The Kurds: The Minority Rights Group Report No. 23* (London, 1991); S. M. Resool, *Forever Kurdish* (H. Zahawi and L. Rashid (pub.)), (N.p., USA, 1990), and J. Bulloch and H. Morris, *No Friends But The Mountains* (London, 1992). Other relevant texts are cited in footnotes below, concerning particular aspects of the three Iraqi conflicts.

[3] Subsequent developments in relation to the 1991 Gulf crisis are not examined in this research. Such developments include, *inter alia*, minor military skirmishes between Iraqi and members of the coalition forces, particularly the US and Kuwait; the periodic negotiations with Turkey to renew the mandate of the forces protecting the Kurds in northern Iraq; the in-fighting between the two main Kurdish political parties in the north of Iraq; and the work of the UN team entrusted with inspecting and limiting Iraq's weapon capability.

[4] The examples selected here do not address, *inter alia*, legal problems concerning child civilians in situations of prolonged belligerent occupation, such as the occupation by Israel of the Palestinian territories (see sect. 4.2.2.1 above). It is not the aim of this research, nor, perhaps, is it feasible, to examine the legal impact of the whole range of conflicts involving child civilians, and to attempt to reach definitive conclusions.

the applicable law in the context of conflicts in which there was an almost total disregard for basic human rights and humanitarian principles, as in the 1987–8 chemical weapon attacks. It is also difficult to isolate factors indicating the impact of international law from other closely interrelated factors, such as political considerations, which may also lead to action on behalf of child civilians.

Despite these problems, lessons can be learned from an examination of the pertinent law in the context of the Iraqi conflicts, and it has proved possible to identify certain principles of this body of law that came into play in one or more of the three conflicts under consideration.

This Chapter accordingly first summarises the provisions of international law pertaining to the three conflicts. It then sets out the evidence revealed under the separate headings of the four indicators, and comments on the apparent impact of the applicable law in each case. From this, some conclusions are drawn, as set out in section 7.7.

7.1 APPLICABLE LAW IN THE THREE CONFLICTS

By way of background to the evidence examined in section 7.2 below, this section will note very briefly certain main areas of the law, as set out in Chapters 2 to 5 above, which are most pertinent to the three conflicts involving Iraq. In this context, it is worth noting that, at the time of these conflicts, Iraq was party to at least two of the key relevant international treaties: the ICCPR (as mentioned in section 2.1.5, since 25 January 1971) and the 1949 GCs (since 14 February 1956). The 1989 CRC was not directly relevant to any of the conflicts under consideration, as it was either in draft form, or adopted but not widely ratified, during the period in question.

First, the 1987–8 chemical weapon attacks on the Iraqi Kurds can be seen as taking place in the context of an internal disturbance, and therefore falling below the level at which humanitarian law generally applies.[5] Alternatively, it is arguable that these attacks occurred in the context of a non-international armed conflict (the continuing hostilities between the Iraqi Kurds and the Iraqi government[6]). In this case, the affected Kurdish civilians, adult and child, would clearly be entitled to humane treatment and other measures specified in Common Article 3 of the 1949 GCs.[7] In any event, children subjected to the chemical weapon attacks qualified for

---

[5] However, see arguments in sect. 3.1.2.2 above that the provisions of Common Art. 3 of the 1949 GCs should apply in any event, as customary law and basic minimum standards.

[6] These hostilities are described in the texts regarding the Kurds cited in n. 2 above.

[7] At the time of these attacks (and at the time of writing), Iraq had not ratified the 1977 GPs (see n. 12 below). In any event, for the purposes of this discussion, it is assumed that the 1987–8 chemical weapon attacks on the Iraqi Kurds could not be categorised as occurring in the course of a war of national liberation for the purpose of self-determination. Hence the

protection under many of the provisions of international human rights treaty law summarised in Chapter 2 above. These provisions include the right to special treatment and the right not to be arbitrarily deprived of life as articulated, for example, in the ICCPR and the UDHR. Further, customary law principles would apply, such as, again, those articulating the right to life and, arguably, the evolving norm regarding the special treatment of children generally (section 5.2.2 above). Also pertinent here is, at least, the 'first use' ban on employing chemical weapons (section 3.2 above),[8] and possibly the prohibition of genocide (section 2.1.2.1 above).[9]

Secondly, the invasion of Kuwait by Iraq and the 1991 Gulf War were both international armed conflicts. They were therefore, in principle, subject to the full panoply of legal safeguards, articulated in the 1949 GCs, pertaining to civilians generally, to child civilians specifically,[10] and (as regards Kuwait) to occupied territory.[11] To a lesser extent (owing to non-ratification by many of the key parties[12]), these conflicts were, in addition, subject to the provisions of 1977 GP I. Also applicable were humanitarian law principles relevant to international armed conflict and expressed in various other treaties, such as 1907 Hague Convention IV (see section 3.1.1),[13] and in customary law generally (sections 5.2.3. and 5.2.4). So too,

provisions of Art. 1(4) of 1977 GP I enabling this to be considered an international armed conflict, and other related provisions, will not be considered here. See discussion of this point in J. Connors, 'Humanitarian Legal Order and the Kurdish Question' (unpublished).

[8] As mentioned in sect. 3.2 above, the use of chemical weapons (and particularly their 'first use') is arguably prohibited, under customary principles, even in internal disturbances. Regarding non-international armed conflict, see also, e.g., ICRC (1993), 415, and Hannikainen (1988), 707 and 711–12. Further, Iraq is party to the 1925 Geneva Protocol.

[9] Korn supports the findings of P. Galbraith and C. Van Hollen, (*Chemical Weapons Use in Kurdistan: Iraq's Final Offensive: A Staff Report to the Senate Committee on Foreign Relations* (Washington, DC, 21 Sept. 1988)), that the policy of Iraq towards its Kurdish citizens 'has the characteristics of Genocide': Korn (1990), 177.

[10] Thus, e.g., during these conflicts was an attempt made to establish hospital or safety zones (1949 GC IV, Art. 14)? Was the free passage of essential foodstuffs and clothing permitted to children (1949 GC IV, Art. 23)? Was special provision made for orphaned children, or those separated from their families, or for family reunification (1949 GC IV, Arts. 24 and 26)?

[11] Questions to be addressed concerning children in Kuwait include: were the particular provisions regarding children in occupied territory observed, such as measures regulating their treatment generally (1949 GC IV, Art. 50), and/or their treatment if interned (1949 GC IV, Arts. 81, 82, 89, and 132), and/or the prohibition on the death penalty regarding offences committed by those under 18 (1949 GC IV, Art. 68)? As already mentioned in sect. 4.2.2.1, in situations of prolonged belligerent occupation (clearly not applicable to Kuwait), such as the Israeli occupation of the Palestinian territories, the provisions of human rights law could become increasingly relevant as the situation stabilised.

[12] Non-ratifying parties included Iraq, the US, the UK, France, Australia, and Egypt. See C. Greenwood, in Rowe (ed.) (1993), 64. Nonetheless, the US, e.g., has officially accepted, including in the 1991 Gulf War, that most rules in 1977 GP I regarding civilian immunity, and particularly the proportionality principle in Art. 51, express customary law: Middle East Watch, *The Bombing of Iraqi Cities* (New York, 6 Mar. 1991), 2–3. (This acceptance would arguably extend to Art. 77, setting out the core principle regarding the special treatment of children.)

[13] In any event, principles expressed in 1907 Hague Convention IV are now widely regarded as customary (see sect. 5.2.3).

once again, were principles of international human rights treaty and customary law regarding, *inter alia*, the special treatment of children and their right to life.

Finally, the 1991 Kurdish (and Shia) uprisings in the aftermath of the Gulf War could possibly be regarded as a continuation of an international armed conflict (the 1991 Gulf War) and therefore subject to the body of law applicable to such conflicts.[14] However, if, as seems more accurate, the uprisings are viewed as a separate conflict arising after the cessation of the international armed conflict, these could then fall within the limited protection granted to non-international armed conflicts under Common Article 3 of the 1949 GCs. Alternatively, they could be seen simply as internal disturbances, and therefore largely unregulated by international humanitarian law.[15] Whatever their categorisation in international humanitarian law, human rights customary law and non-derogable treaty provisions again apply regarding, *inter alia*, the right to life and the entitlement of children to special treatment.

The three conflicts under consideration here will now be examined for evidence of the impact of the relevant law, as outlined above. This examination will begin by looking at the actual experiences of the children involved.

7.2 THE EXPERIENCES OF CHILDREN IN THE
THREE CONFLICTS, AND IMPACT OF
THE APPLICABLE LAW

The three conflicts are examined here in chronological order, starting with the 1987–8 chemical weapon attacks.

7.2.1 The Experiences of Children in the 1987–8 Chemical Weapon Attacks

Prior to the chemical weapon attacks of 1987 and 1988, many children in Iraq, and particularly Kurdish children, were reported already to have experienced harsh treatment at the hands of the Iraqi government.[16]

[14] In this context, the question arises, regarding the establishment of 'safe havens' by certain governments in the allied coalition, of the legal status of those governments in northern Iraq at that time. E.g., was northern Iraq occupied territory (see sect. 7.2.4.3 below), or (and this seems unlikely in the circumstances) were those governments assisting the civil authorities?

[15] Middle East Watch, e.g., prefers to categorise the uprisings as a non-international armed conflict: (*Endless Torment: The 1991 Uprising in Iraq and its Aftermath* (New York, June 1992), 33–4), while the ICRC saw these as internal disturbances (see sect. 7.5.2 below).

[16] This is contrary to the statement, in Iraq's second periodic report to the Human Rights Committee in 1986, that it 'regards children as a basic pillar of society, and, accordingly, makes a special effort to ensure their welfare': UN Doc. CCPR/C/37/Add.3 (18 July 1986), para. 43.

Thus, a 1989 AI publication chronicled a history of serious human rights violations committed against children by the Iraqi government.[17] AI characterised children in Iraq, and especially Kurdish children, as 'innocent victims of political repression'.[18] Its report on these children recorded brutal treatment in prison; arbitrary arrest; detention without trial; the holding of children as 'hostages' in lieu of their relatives; torture by security forces (sometimes resulting in death); execution (often without prior trial or with summary trial);[19] 'disappearances';[20] and deliberate killings by government forces. It listed the names of 344 children and young people detained by the Iraqi government, and of thirty-one executed. The report pointed out that these acts were not only in breach of Iraq's international treaty obligations, but also of its own domestic legislation.[21]

In relation to the 1987–8 chemical weapon attacks, Iraq is reported to have started using these weapons against its Kurdish population in April 1987, and to have continued to do so on a fairly regular basis until at least October 1988.[22] Under the command of Ali Hassan Al-Majid, a cousin of Saddam Hussein, Iraqi forces apparently first used chemical weapons against Kurdish civilians in seven villages on 15 April 1987.[23]

On 16 April 1987 several other Kurdish villages were attacked with chemical weapons. In one of these, Sheikh Wassanan, 121 civilians were reported to have been killed, of whom seventy-six were children 'aged between one day and eight years'.[24] These attacks were alleged to have been followed by others over a period of at least six days, in which hundreds of people were left dead or injured.[25] Reports indicated that the majority of those killed were civilians, mainly women and children.

There were further chemical weapon offensives against Iraqi Kurds in May and June of 1987, and these attacks continued intermittently into the

[17] AI, *Iraq. Children: Innocent Victims of Political Repression* (London, 1989).

[18] *Ibid.*, 3.

[19] See *ibid.*, 7–8, 25 and 28, and Korn (1990), 105–7.

[20] See, e.g., AI, *Iraq: Children* (1989), 20. In relation to later 'disappearances', see 'Table of the Disappeared in the Anfal Operation' (including at least 359 children), in Middle East Watch, *Genocide in Iraq: The Anfal Campaign Against the Kurds* (New York, 1993), 365–7. See also, e.g., Middle East Watch and Physicians for Human Rights, *Unquiet Graves: the Search for the Disappeared in Iraqi Kurdistan* (N.p., USA, Feb. 1992).

[21] AI, *Iraq: Children* (1989), 3–5.

[22] The use of chemical weapons by Iraq during this period was well-documented. See, e.g., Galbraith and Van Hollen (Sept. 21, 1988); AI, *Iraq. Children* (1989), 30; and Korn (1990), 151. See also Physicians for Human Rights, *Winds of Death: Iraq's Use of Poison Gas Against Its Kurdish Population* (New Haven, Conn, Feb. 1989).

[23] D. Ala'Aldeen, *Death Clouds: Saddam Hussein's Chemical War Against the Kurds* (London, 1991), 11 and 13.

[24] *Ibid.*, 14. See also AI, *Iraq: Children* (1989), 28.

[25] Ala'Aldeen (1991), 15–16.

spring of 1988. According to one authority, between 15 April 1987 and the 16 March 1988 offensive against Halabja, such attacks took place on twenty-one different occasions.[26] In 1987 the chemicals used in the attacks were a form of mustard gas which was not as lethal as the toxic nerve gases, whose effect was more immediate, that began to be employed in 1988 as part of the 'Anfal Operations'.[27]

It was this more lethal gas that was used in Halabja on 16 and 17 March 1988, when publication of photographs of the victims finally brought the plight of the Iraqi Kurds to the attention of the international community. The attack on Halabja is estimated to have caused over 6,000 deaths and 9,000 injuries.[28] Again, a large number of the victims were women and children.

Despite the publicity attracted by the Halabja attack, and a degree of condemnation of Iraq by the international community, no effective sanctions were invoked and there were renewed chemical weapon offensives against the Iraqi Kurds later that same month,[29] and again in April, May, July, and early August of 1988.[30]

Then, after the August 1988 ceasefire in the Iran–Iraq war, major chemical weapon attacks were launched against the Iraqi Kurds between 25 August and 1 September, in what one writer described as 'the Bahdinan holocaust'.[31] Thousands of people died, thousands became refugees (fleeing largely to Turkey, and also to Iran[32]), and thousands were captured and placed in camps.[33]

In many of these attacks, the majority of those killed were, once more, reported to be civilians—the elderly, women, and children.[34] One account describes how, after the chemical explosions, many villagers ran to streams

[26] *Ibid.*, 33–4. This contains a table setting out the names of villages attacked, dates of attacks, and some data about victims.

[27] *Ibid.*, 17. The Anfal Operations were a series of major military offensives against the Kurds, starting in Feb. 1988. It has been estimated that between 50,000–100,000 people, 'many of them women and children', died in these attacks: Middle East Watch, *Genocide in Iraq* (1993), xiv. Specifically regarding children, see also *ibid.*, 18 and 178. For further information on the Anfal, see, e.g., Middle East Watch, *The Anfal Campaign in Iraqi Kurdistan: The Destruction of Koreme* (New York, 1993). The latter contains many references to the deaths of children, including at 50, 59, 60, and 68.

[28] Ala'Aldeen (1991), 18. See also AI, *Iraq: Children* (1989), 29, and AI, *Amnesty International Report* (London, 1989), 258.

[29] See AI, *Iraq: Children* (1989), 29.

[30] See Korn (1990), 161; Ala'Aldeen (1991), 35–6; and AI, *Amnesty International Report* (London, 1990), 127.

[31] Ala'Aldeen (1991), 25.

[32] Korn (1990), 145, cites an estimate of 60,000–100,000 refugees.

[33] Ala'Aldeen (1991), 25. According to this writer, over 70 children died within the first few weeks in one camp.

[34] The able-bodied men who were the Kurdish fighters (or 'Peshmerga') were in encampments around the villages. However, it was apparently the villages themselves that were normally the target of Iraqi attack. See also Middle East Watch, *Genocide in Iraq* (1993), 12.

to escape the effects of the gas, but those who could not run, 'mostly the very old and the very young, died'.[35]

The attacks of late August and early September 1988 provoked an international outcry (see section 7.2.4.1 below) but, in the absence of effective action, the Iraqi government used chemical weapons against the Kurds again in October 1988,[36] and possibly even into 1989, before the Anfal Operation finally ceased.

7.2.2 The Experiences of Children During the Occupation of Kuwait and the 1991 Gulf War

Unlike the 1987–8 chemical weapon attacks described above, the 1990 Iraqi occupation of Kuwait and the ensuing 1991 Gulf War were widely publicised conflicts and need be only briefly outlined in this section, to highlight aspects relevant to the subject of this research.[37]

Child civilians were primarily caught up in these events in four different contexts: (a) in Kuwait, as inhabitants of Kuwait after the Iraqi occupation; (b) in Kuwait and Iraq, as Western hostages of Iraq after the invasion of Kuwait; (c) in Iraq, as inhabitants of Iraq during the occupation of Kuwait and the 1991 Gulf War; and (d) in Israel, as inhabitants of Israel attacked by Iraq during this period.

The applicable international law will be examined here only in relation to the two situations involving the largest numbers of children, namely: child civilians who were inhabitants of Kuwait during the Iraqi occupation ((a) above) and those in Iraq during the occupation of Kuwait and the 1991 Gulf War ((c) above).[38]

This section starts with a brief summary of relevant events in the occupation of Kuwait and the 1991 Gulf War,[39] before looking separately at the experiences of children in Kuwait and in Iraq.

[35] Galbraith and Van Hollen (1988), 14–15. In one incident alone, in Aug. 1988, chemical weapons were apparently dropped on Kurdish refugees sheltering near the Turkish border, and over 5,000 people, again primarily women and children, were estimated to have been killed: Korn (1990), 146.

[36] See Korn (1990), 161; Ala'Aldeen (1991), 37, and discussion in J. Connors, 'International Law and the Kurds of Iraq: A Review of the Instruments', 3 *Kurdistan Liberation* 16 (Mar. 1991). Some commentators put the date for the end of the Anfal Operation as late as June 1989: Middle East Watch, *Genocide in Iraq* (1993), 333.

[37] For further information, see, *inter alia*, Karsh and Rautsi (1991); Miller and Mylroie (1990); Bulloch and Morris (1991); Bulloch and Morris (1992); Simpson (1991); and Darwish and Alexander (1991).

[38] For the purposes of this research, it is not necessary to consider the particular legal status of foreign national children generally in Kuwait and Iraq during the relevant period.

[39] Where the information describing the occupation of Kuwait and the 1991 Gulf war is unattributed, it is largely drawn from Karsh and Rautsi (1991). Direct quotations from their book are attributed, as is information cited from other sources. For a chronology of the 1991 Gulf crisis, see D. Tavers, 'A Chronology of Events', in Rowe (ed.) (1993), 3–28.

7.2.2.1 Background: Occupation of Kuwait and 1991 Gulf War

The Iraqi invasion of Kuwait took place on 2 August 1990, and was completed within seven hours. When a British Airways flight *en route* to India landed in Kuwait, its crew and passengers, including a number of children, were taken prisoner by the Iraqi forces.

The following day, the United States announced that the 82nd Airborne Division was being sent to Saudi Arabia, thus inaugurating 'Operation Desert Shield'. Saddam Hussein responded on 8 August by proclaiming the annexation of Kuwait.[40]

On 18 August, Iraq threatened that foreigners in Iraq, specifically including babies, were to share the deprivations that would be suffered by Iraqi children under the economic blockade that had been imposed by the UN.[41] A few days later, Saddam Hussein appeared on television with a number of Western hostages, among whom were two young boys. This 'blatant use of children, old men and women'[42] provoked public outrage in many countries. Then, on 29 August, the day after Iraq officially declared Kuwait to be its nineteenth province, the Iraqi government released the women and children hostages.

In early September 1990, Saddam Hussein announced that Iraqi children were dying as a result of the UN-imposed trade embargo.[43] Pressure mounted for the total embargo on food and other necessities to be lifted, and the Security Council began to debate a resolution to that effect, which directed that particular attention be paid to, *inter alia*, the needs of 'children under 15'. This resolution (Resolution 666) was passed on 13 September.[44] Despite this resolution, sanctions had apparently begun to bite to the extent that, on 4 December 1990, the Iraqi Health Minister, calling for the lifting of sanctions, declared that 1,000 children had died through lack of medicine.[45]

During this period, many Kuwaitis fled their country.[46] Those Kuwaitis and foreigners remaining, among whom were many children, experienced a regime of terror under an administration led by Ali Hassan Al Majid, already notorious for his treatment of the Kurds.[47] There were consistent reports of atrocities committed by the Iraqi army in Kuwait.[48] This gave rise

---

[40] Bulloch and Morris (1991), 110–11.

[41] *New York Times*, 19 Aug. 1990. The pertinent UN decisions and debates concerning this conflict are described later in this Ch.

[42] Bulloch and Morris (1991), 112.

[43] *Independent*, 6 Sept. 1990.

[44] See sect. 7.3.2.1 below. See also *Independent*, 10, 11, and 13 Sept. 1990.

[45] Darwish and Alexander (1991), 304.

[46] AI, (19 Dec. 1990, cited in Karsh and Rautsi (1991), 228), estimated this figure at approximately 300,000 Kuwaitis.

[47] Bulloch and Morris (1991), 120.

[48] See, e.g., *Independent*, 22 Nov. 1990, and evidence presented to the UN Security Council (UN Doc. S/PV.2959 (27 Nov. 1990), discussed, e.g., in sect. 7.2.2.2. below).

to speculation that the Iraqis should ultimately be brought before a 'Nuremberg-style' war crimes tribunal.[49]

However, four months passed in relatively fruitless negotiations and initiatives by governments, individual politicians, and the UN, during which time Iraq also launched a number of attacks on Israel. Finally, on 12 January 1991 the US Congress authorised President Bush to use force to evict Iraq from Kuwait. On 17 January, about twenty-six hours after the expiration of a UN deadline,[50] US-led allied planes attacked political, strategic, and military targets throughout Iraq.

In the following weeks, Iraq was subjected to aerial bombardment by the forces of the allied coalition. Despite news restrictions, it became increasingly clear by late January 1991 that, among other effects of this strategy, the civilian population of Iraq, adult and child alike, was suffering considerable hardship and many casualties.[51] As the conflict progressed, reports of Iraqi civilian casualties intensified,[52] and the conditions in which they lived were becoming intolerable. A joint UNICEF/WHO mission was launched to bring emergency medical and other supplies primarily to Iraqi children (see section 7.2.2.3.2 below).[53]

Then, on 13 February 1991, American bombers destroyed an air-raid shelter in the Ameriyya area of Baghdad, killing about 310 civilians, among whom were 130 children.[54] This brought widespread censure, and military efforts were subsequently increasingly focused on the Iraqi troops in Kuwait. By 26 February the Iraqis had relinquished control of Kuwait, and six weeks after the start of the 1991 Gulf war (or 'Operation Desert Storm'), on 28 February 1991, the war finally came to an end.

7.2.2.2 The Experiences of Children in Occupied Kuwait

In relation to the experiences of children in Kuwait during the 1990–1 Iraqi occupation, selected examples are outlined below.[55] The ex-

---

[49] See *Independent*, 5, 16, 17, 21, and 23 Oct. 1990.

[50] The deadline of 15 Jan. 1991 was imposed by Resolution 678 (29 Nov. 1990), mentioned in sect. 7.3.2.1 below.

[51] See, e.g., *Guardian*, 22 and 24 Jan. 1991, and *Independent*, 8 Feb. 1991.

[52] See *Independent*, 12 and 15 Feb. 1991. See also *Guardian*, 12 Feb. 1991. One journal estimated a total of 5,000–15,000 Iraqi civilians killed during this period: 244 *The New Internationalist* 30 (1991).

[53] *Independent*, 1 and 11 Feb. 1991. See also Vittachi (1993), 51–7, who describes the UNICEF/WHO mission as the only instance of a corridor of peace in an international armed conflict.

[54] This was the estimate of Iraqi officials: Middle East Watch, *The Bombing of Iraqi Cities* (1991), 3. Another estimate was of 300 civilians killed, of whom 91 were children: *Independent*, 15 Feb. 1991. For a legal analysis of the legitimacy of the attack on this shelter, see Hampson, 'Means and Methods of Warfare in the Conflict in the Gulf', in Rowe (ed.) (1993), 96–7.

[55] A more detailed description of the many abuses suffered by these children can be found, e.g., in AI, *Iraq/Occupied Kuwait: Human Rights Violations Since 2 August 1990* (London, Dec. 1990). See also Middle East Watch, *The Conduct of Iraqi Troops in Kuwait* (New York, 1990).

periences of children in Iraq itself are addressed in the following section (7.2.2.3).

In general, numerous child civilians as well as adult civilians in occupied Kuwait were reported to have 'disappeared' and to have been tortured, killed, mutilated, and raped. Young Kuwaiti males suspected of resistance to the occupation were targeted. One report stated: '[a]rrest and torture threatened every individual. Young men were shot near their homes and in front of their families, and this method was used to terrorise the people and to eliminate the young men on the pretext that they worked in the resistance.'[56] Similarly, young girls were subjected, in particular, to sexual assaults.[57] Child civilians in occupied Kuwait also suffered acutely from food shortages, the lack of health care, schools, and other services, and the severe trauma of their experiences.

One witness who gave evidence to a UN Security Council hearing on 27 November 1990, regarding human rights abuses in occupied Kuwait, reported that: '[f]ive weeks ago in one town the Iraqis came with a list of boys between the ages of 13 and 20 years. Thirty-five young boys were arrested and tortured . . . only five of them have been released.'[58] Children were also tortured to force their parents to reveal information.[59]

AI quoted, as a typical example of the experiences of young civilians arrested in occupied Kuwait, that of a 16-year-old boy arrested for breaking the curfew:

I was asked about my father, brothers and friends. During interrogation a second person would punch me or beat me with a belt. Each session usually lasted about half an hour. After five days my left arm was marked with the letter H using a hot skewer. I was told that if I got into any more trouble it would mean certain death.[60]

The AI report comments that '[i]ncidents such as these, as well as the prevailing climate of fear, also took their toll on younger children.' One witness commented to AI that these tactics caused children to live in 'a permanent state of fear', and many developed stutters or became incontinent.[61]

Children were also the victims of executions, many of them extrajudicial. AI cites examples, such as the extrajudicial execution of a 12-year-old girl,[62] and other killings caused by deprivation of essential medical

[56] Quoted from a memorandum prepared by the Kuwaiti Red Crescent: AI (Dec. 1990), 2.

[57] AI cites rape as one of the common forms of torture used by the Iraqis in Kuwait: *ibid.* 37–8. See also Kuwaiti presentation to the UN Security Council, referring to the rape of young girls in occupied Kuwait (UN Doc. S/PV.2959, 31).

[58] UN Doc. S/PV. 2959, 51.

[59] E.g., one witness described to the Security Council the torture of her 1-year-old child to elicit information from her husband: *ibid.*, 26.

[60] AI (Dec. 1990), 16.

[61] *Ibid.*, 16.

[62] *Ibid.*, 43.

treatment.[63] A doctor who gave evidence to the Security Council stated: '[t]he hardest thing was burying the babies. Under my supervision 120 newborn babies were buried in the second week of the invasion.'[64] There were also reports before the UN of 'deformed' and epileptic children being evacuated from hospitals or deprived of treatment, many of them dying as a result.[65]

Similar evidence of Iraqi atrocities in Kuwait was presented in a report to the Commission on Human Rights on 7 February 1991. This report cited these acts as being in breach of the 1949 GCs, and it again repeatedly referred to violations committed against children.[66] It emphasised that these abuses had 'obviously drastically affected the psychological state of Kuwaiti children . . . Thousands of children have fled the country with their families to escape the daily torture.'[67]

7.2.2.3 The Experiences of Children in Iraq

A different set of factors came into play in relation to the experiences of child civilians in Iraq during the period dating from the invasion of Kuwait until the end of the 1991 Gulf War.

One difference was that, during the 1991 Gulf War the allied coalition was at pains to present itself as complying with standards of international law. In practice this had a limited beneficial impact on the situation of Iraqi child civilians, although these children nonetheless suffered enormously as a result of the UN sanctions imposed following the invasion of Kuwait, and of the 1991 Gulf War itself.

The following section will outline separately both the direct and indirect effects of these hostilities, as experienced by Iraqi child civilians during the period under consideration.

7.2.2.3.1 Direct Effects on Children of the 1991 Gulf War

As regards the direct effects, many children were killed or wounded in the allied aerial bombardment of Iraq, although it is not at this stage (and may never be) possible to have an accurate estimate.[68] It is probable that such deaths and injuries occurred on a greater scale than was portrayed in

---

[63] It was alleged, e.g., that babies died after Iraqi soldiers removed them from incubators: *ibid.* 43–56. There was, however, controversy regarding this allegation, and doubt has been cast on it. See, e.g., *Independent*, 12 Jan. 1992, and *New York Times*, 6 Feb. 1992. See also Hampson. 'Liability for War Crimes', in Rowe (ed.) (1993), 248.

[64] UN Doc. S/PV.2959, 37.

[65] *Ibid.*, 33–5 and 37–8.

[66] UN Doc. E/CN.4/1991/70 (7 Feb. 1991), 'Situation of Human Rights in Occupied Kuwait'. See 5–14 for examples of arrest, torture, arbitrary killing, rape, and similar abuses committed against children.

[67] *Ibid.*, 4.

[68] See *Guardian*, 28 Mar. 1991, quoting the UNICEF director in the Middle East to the effect that UNICEF could not estimate the numbers of children who died in the 1991 Gulf War.

the Western media, which were in any event subject to reporting restrictions.

Within the first week of the 1991 war, for example, there were apparently many civilian casualties in Iraq, including children.[69] Indeed, given that it is estimated that more than half of Iraq's population is under 18,[70] and 20 per cent of the population consists of children under 5,[71] any suffering inflicted on the civilian population would inevitably affect large numbers of children.

This applies, for example, to the allied raid on a bridge in Iraq in early February 1991, which was reported to have caused the death of forty-seven civilians and wounded 102 others, including children.[72]

Shortly after this raid, a former US Attorney-General, Ramsay Clark, who had visited Iraq, alleged that the allied bombing had caused such extensive civilian casualties (in the region of 6,000–7,000) that he accused the United States of committing war crimes.[73] In the same period it was reported that Massoud Barzani, leader of the Kurdistan Democratic Party (KDP), had estimated 3,000 civilians killed in Kurdish areas as a result of inaccurate bombing,[74] and Iraq alleged that thousands of civilians had been killed in allied bombardments on houses, schools, and neighbourhoods.[75] The most publicised single incident in which allied bombs hit civilian targets was, of course, the 13 February 1991 attack on the air-raid shelter in Baghdad (section 7.2.2.1 above).

The Iraqi representative, Mr Al-Abari, addressing the UN Security Council on 3 April 1991, alleged that the majority of targets hit by US aircraft during the 1991 Gulf War were not military, and that they in fact 'hit civilian targets, causing the deaths of tens of thousands of women and children and the elderly'.[76]

[69] See *Guardian*, 22 Jan. 1991, for reports of civilian casualties, and evidence of 'many coffins . . . some of them small'.

[70] See *Independent*, 1 Feb. 1991.

[71] See WHO/UNICEF, *Joint WHO/UNICEF Team Report. A Visit to Iraq. February 16–21 1991* (UN Doc. S/22328, 4 Mar. 1991), 6. This report also estimated that 4% of the Iraqi population of 18 million was children under the age of a year.

[72] One newspaper commented that the allied policy of rendering roads and bridges impassable 'is evidently killing and wounding an increasing number of Iraqi civilians': *Independent*, 8 Feb. 1991. This report specifically mentioned one 10-year-old killed in the Feb. attack on the bridge.

[73] See *Independent*, 12 Feb. 1991. See also R. Clark and Others, *War Crimes: A Report on United States War Crimes Against Iraq* (Washington, DC, 1992).

[74] See *Independent*, 12 Feb. 1991.

[75] See *Guardian*, 12 Feb. 1991, and *Independent*, 13 Feb. 1991.

[76] UN Doc. S/PV.2981 (3 Apr. 1991), 23–6. According to one estimate, at least 25,000 people died in the 1991 Gulf War (it is not specified whether these are purely military casualties): *Independent*, 17 July 1991. However, it was reported in 1992 that a US Census Bureau demographer, Ms Daponte, alleged that her superiors 'tried to suppress information about Iraqi deaths from the war for political reasons'. She originally estimated that '86,194 men, 39,612 women and 32,195 children were killed by the allies in the war, in rebellions afterwards, or by disease and deprivation', but later stated that these estimates were too low: *Independent*, 14 Apr. 1992.

7.2.2.3.2 *Indirect Effects on Children of the 1991 Gulf War*

In relation to the indirect effects of the 1991 Gulf War, children were affected by shortages of food and other necessities, initially as a result of the UN-imposed sanctions. These shortages were exacerbated by the devastation caused to the country during the 1991 allied bombing campaign, which also disrupted many services, including schools and hospitals, used by Iraqi children.

As already mentioned (section 7.2.2.1), in September 1990 Saddam Hussein alleged that Iraqi children were dying as a result of the UN-imposed embargo, and concern about the effect of the embargo on children and other civilians culminated in the passing of Security Council Resolution 666 (1990).

The WHO/UNICEF mission to Iraq from 16 to 21 February 1991 reported that 'normal life had come almost to a halt' in Baghdad,[77] owing to lack of basic amenities such as water, food (including baby milk), electricity, and gas. Women and children were particularly affected by these shortages. In addition, schools were closed, health services seriously disrupted, and the war had caused psychological disturbances, such as a fear of being alone, in many children.[78] The report, widely circulated to UN members, concluded that if action was not taken particularly regarding water and sanitation 'there could be a catastrophe in Iraq'.[79]

The WHO/UNICEF mission was limited to providing medical and health supplies specifically to children and mothers. It was not permitted to bring in food supplies, even baby milk, as the United States feared that such shipments could be used by the Iraqi army. The decision not to bring in food was controversial, and the then UN Secretary-General, Perez de Cuellar, was quoted as saying, 'If there is a doubt, [it] is important to preserve the lives of children. The grown-ups can have political ideas but the children have not, we should not expose them to starvation.'[80]

In the immediate aftermath of the 1991 Gulf War concern was expressed in the UN regarding a pending health catastrophe in Iraq,[81] and by late March 1991 UN officials stated publicly that five million children in the region risked spending their formative years in deprived circumstances as a result of the Gulf War.[82] In late April 1991 concern intensified after a report to the UN Security Council by the Undersecretary-General, Marti Ahtisaari, which referred to the 'devastation' which had befallen Iraq, with 'near apocalyptic results upon . . . the economic infrastructure' causing massive problems regarding food, water, health, and other necessities.[83]

---

[77] WHO/UNICEF (Feb. 1991), 2.   [78] *Ibid.*, 2–9.   [79] *Ibid.*, 16.
[80] See *Independent*, 11 Feb. 1991.
[81] See, e.g., *Independent*, 4 Mar. 1991.
[82] *Guardian*, 28 Mar. 1991.
[83] UN Doc. S/PV.2981 (3 Apr. 1991). See also *Independent*, 24 Apr. 1991.

In July 1991, the UN reported that the bulk of Iraq's population, of whom nine million were children under 16, could not obtain basic nutrition,[84] and a Harvard Univerity team warned that 'at least 170,000 young children under five years of age will die in the coming year' owing to the delayed effects of the war.[85] A subsequent report by the Harvard team, in late September 1991, estimated that by that stage child deaths in Iraq had trebled, as a result of malnutrition, epidemics, and lack of medicines, since the imposition of sanctions and the 1991 Gulf War.[86] In November 1994, UNICEF estimated that, again, approximately three times as many children had died since the beginning of 1991 as in the previous three years.[87]

Indeed, the combined effect on the health of the Iraqi population of the 1991 Gulf War and the imposition of sanctions has been a continuing cause of concern among commentators up to the time of writing.[88] Thus, a 1996 report by researchers from Harvard University and the London School of Economics apparently supported claims by the WHO that over 500,000 Iraqi children may have died in the previous six years, due to the sanctions.[89]

7.2.3 The Experiences of Children in the 1991 Kurdish (and Shia) Uprisings in Iraq, and Their Aftermath[90]

The experiences of children during the 1987–8 chemical weapon attacks and during the occupation of Kuwait followed by the 1991 Gulf War, have been

---

[84] *Independent*, 3 July 1991. See also UN Doc. S/22799 (17 July 1991). This included an annexed report on humanitarian needs in Iraq, which commented, *inter alia*, that, '[a]s usual, it is the poor, the children, . . . the most vulnerable amongst the population who are the first to suffer': *ibid.*, 6. The report estimated that 300,000 children under 6 were malnourished (10% of the population of that age group): *ibid.*, 27.

[85] *Independent*, 12 July 1991. The report of the Harvard University team was contested by a Tuft University report commissioned by UNICEF (but from which UNICEF later distanced itself): *Independent*, 11 July, 1991.

[86] See *Independent*, 20 Sept. 1991. This study examined the effect of the conflict on 6,000 Iraqi households in 200 representative neighbourhoods.

[87] UNICEF–UK, *News in Brief* (London, Nov. 1994), 3.

[88] See, e.g., *Independent on Sunday*, 8 Jan. 1995. Among other things, this article cites child psychologist, M. Raundalen, describing Iraq as having the most traumatised child population he had encountered, and as a 'land where childhood is dead'. See also J. G. Gardam, 'Noncombatant Immunity and the Gulf Conflict', 32, *Virginia Journal of International Law* 813, n. 1 (1992); N. El Saadawi, 'The Impact of the Gulf War on Women and Children', in Clark and Others, (1992), 180–3, and UN Doc. E/CN.4/1993/77 (21 Jan. 1993) summarising Iraqi statistics regarding increases in under-5 mortality attributed to the effects of sanctions.

[89] *Guardian*, 18 May 1996. See also M. O'Kane, 'The Wake of War', *Guardian Weekend*, 18 May 1996.

[90] Where the information in this sect. is unattributed, it is derived from newspaper reports in the *Independent* during the relevant period. Direct quotations from this newspaper and detailed points are, however, attributed in the footnotes. Information from publications other than the *Independent* is also attributed.

considered above. It now remains to examine here their experiences in the 1991 uprisings and their aftermath.

These uprisings against Saddam Hussein's government were staged by Iraqi Kurds and Shia, to some extent encouraged by certain politicians in the allied coalition.[91] They erupted shortly after the 28 February 1991 ceasefire.

The Kurdish uprising and its consequences, particularly in relation to Kurdish children, will be the focus here. This is not to underestimate the significance of the Shia uprising. However, a discussion of the Kurdish uprising follows on from that regarding the use of chemical weapons against the Kurds, and also allows for comparison of the response of the international community to the events of 1991 as opposed to those of 1987–8.

The period covered here encompasses the uprisings in March 1991, and the aftermath of these as manifested in the mass exodus of refugees in April and May. The immediate response of the international community is also outlined to the point at which the 'rapid reaction force' was established in mid-July 1991. These events are first summarised below, and the specific experiences of the children involved are then described.

7.2.3.1 Background: 1991 Uprisings and Their Aftermath

The popular uprisings against the government of Saddam Hussein started in early March 1991, after the declaration of the 1991 Gulf War ceasefire. They spread from the Shia in the south of Iraq to the Kurds in the north. By mid-March full-time armed forces of the KDP and the Patriotic Union of Kurdistan (PUK) were drawn into the conflict, and Kurdish leaders were claiming that half a million of Iraq's four million Kurds were in 'liberated areas'.[92] Massoud Barzani, as Commander-in-Chief of the Kurdish forces, urged the allied coalition, which had not intervened on their behalf, 'to abandon their indifference towards the suffering and merciless killing of Iraqi civilians'.[93]

However, by 13 March the Shia rebellion was being crushed. Fighting continued in the north, and a PUK spokesman publicised an Iraqi government threat to kill thousands of Kurdish hostages, 'mostly women and children'.[94] Thousands of Iraqis fled to Iran to escape the fighting, and there were allegations that napalm had been used against them by government forces.[95]

---

[91] See, e.g., comments by President Bush quoted in *The Times*, 4 Apr. 1991, and in Simpson (1991), 361.

[92] See quotation from Jalal Talabani, leader of the PUK, in *Independent*, 9 Mar. 1991.

[93] See *Observer*, 10 Mar. 1991.

[94] See *Independent*, 13 Mar. 1991.

[95] See *Independent*, 20 Mar. 1991.

As the Shia rebellion crumbled, the Kurds took Iraq's primary oil city, Kirkuk, and on 28 March 1991 the Iraqis launched a massive attack on Kirkuk. However, they refrained from employing chemical weapons, which would almost certainly have brought intervention by the allied coalition. An estimated 5,000 civilians and military were killed or wounded in the assault on Kirkuk. Reports increasingly emerged of massacres of Kurdish villagers, 'including many women and children' in other parts of the north, and of other atrocities committed against them.[96] There were severe shortages of food, fuel, and essential services.

With the Kurdish areas being retaken by the Iraqis, thousands of Kurds began to leave Iraq for shelter in Iran or Turkey. By 1 April 1991, 50,000 refugees had apparently arrived in Iran, and an estimated 2,000 more were arriving each day. The Kurds were also fleeing to Turkey at a similar rate. They were fiercely pursued by the Iraqi army which, according to a Kurdish spokesman, was 'using all its might and muscle against Iraqi civilians, including women and children'.[97]

The hardships of the journey, the bitter weather, and the inadequately equipped refugee camps took their toll. The refugees, particularly old people and children, were dying in their hundreds. Faced with this catastrophe and mounting criticism of their inaction, the allied coalition started to formulate a response.

By the end of the first week of April, an estimated 580,000 Kurdish refugees were camped on the borders of Iran and Turkey, with an estimated two million *en route*.[98] International relief efforts were underway, but as yet with little effect.[99]

At this stage, the allied coalition began to discuss the establishment of temporary 'safe havens' in northern Iraq to shield the Kurds from further attacks, and in mid-April 1991 the United States and Britain announced their decision to do so.[100] By 17 April, troops from the United States, Britain, and France had flown into Iraq entrusted with the task of setting up the safe camps. At this time, it was estimated that the death rate of the refugees (now from disease as well as cold and hunger) had 'stabilised' at about six per 10,000, or about 510 a day among the 850,000 refugees.[101] However, by the end of April, although a number of safe camps were

---

[96] *Independent on Sunday*, 31 Mar. 1991 See also, e.g., Middle East Watch, *Endless Torment* (1992), regarding the uprisings generally, and *ibid.*, p. vii, concerning the arrest and killing of young men.

[97] See *International Herald Tribune*, 2 Apr. 1991.

[98] *Independent on Sunday*, 7 Apr. 1991.

[99] These relief operations were limited to refugees in Iran and Turkey. The only international organisation operating within Iraq itself at this point was the ICRC: *Independent*, 10 Apr. 1991.

[100] The intention was to buttress civil aid with a military presence, and to turn the running of these camps over to the UN as soon as possible.

[101] See *Independent*, 24 Apr. 1991.

established, UN officials reported that the refugees, overwhelmed by conditions on the borders, were returning home at the rate of almost 20,000 a day.[102]

A US government agency, the Centre for Disease Control, estimated that between 25 March and 29 May 1991 approximately 6,700 Iraqi refugees, most of whom were children under 5, died in mountain camps along the Turkish border alone.[103]

By late June 1991 the allied coalition had agreed to establish a 'rapid reaction' force, to be based in Turkey, for the protection of the Kurds in northern Iraq. In mid-July the allied forces began their withdrawal from northern Iraq and a residual force regrouped in Turkey. Thus ended three months of 'Operation Provide Comfort', and thus began 'Operation Poised Hammer'.

7.2.3.2 The Experiences of Children During the 1991 Uprisings and their Aftermath

The experiences of children in the 1991 uprisings and their aftermath were, to a large extent, documented in harrowing detail. In particular, from quite an early stage the Western media were able to observe and describe events as they unfolded in the exodus of Kurdish refugees following the unsuccessful uprisings.

During the uprisings themselves, Kurdish civilians suffered numerous casualties, as in the recapture of Kirkuk, and they experienced shortages of food, medicines, and other necessities.[104] Reports from Kurdish areas spoke of extreme acts of violence committed by Iraqi government forces, including the killing of women and children, even of babies, and the taking of young Kurdish male hostages.[105]

However, it was in the exodus of refugees following the uprisings that the plight of the Kurdish children involved was particularly evident. As the Kurds streamed out of northern Iraq into Iran and Turkey, newspaper reports repeatedly emphasised the suffering of the children. Thus, one commentator protested at 'the slaughter of innocent children from helicop-

---

[102] See *Independent*, 30 Apr. 1991.

[103] See *Guardian*, 8 June 1991. Another estimate placed at 30,000 the number of refugees who died in the period immediately after the 1991 Gulf War, and at 4,000–16,000 the number of 'other civilian dead'. 224 *New Internationalist* 30 (1991).

[104] Accounts, e.g., of the Iraqi recapture of Kirkuk spoke of 'savagery visited upon the civilian population', and of 'rapidly deteriorating conditions . . . with little food or medicine and a devastated infrastructure': *Guardian*, 30 Mar. 1991, and see also *Independent*, 22 Mar. 1991.

[105] See *Guardian*, 30 Mar. 1991, describing events in Karahanjir, where Iraqi forces allegedly killed the inhabitants, including babies, and took young male hostages. See also *Independent on Sunday*, 31 Mar. 1991, for accounts of the torture and killing of Kurdish children, and others, by Iraqi forces, and the taking of hostages.

ter gunships',[106] while others observed, for example, that 'refugee children are dying in their hundreds',[107] or that '[c]hildren are dying. Why is it always the children?' (quoting an adult refugee).[108]

Day after day Western newspapers carried photographs of desperate Kurdish refugees, and sometimes of the bodies of the dead, many of whom were children.[109] Day after day reports emerged of the sheer number of child refugees and of their misery; of child deaths and illness in the harsh conditions of the mountains. For example, one account in mid-April commented, in relation to Cukura camp on the Iraqi–Turkish border: '[m]ost striking was the fact that half of this group of 500,000 refugees on the Turkish-Iraqi border are children.' This report also stated that children under 7 were the majority of up to 100 people dying each day in Uzumlu camp.[110] Another wrote of several dozen corpses on the floor of the mosque in Cukura, twenty of which were 'no more than three feet long'.[111]

Later accounts spoke of 80 per cent of the children arriving in Iran as suffering from dysentery;[112] of hypothermia, typhoid, malnutrition, and shock 'being common among women and children';[113] and of Iraqi Kurds, 'mostly children or the elderly, who froze to death' in Piranshahr camp in Iran.[114]

Some child refugees arriving in Iran also apparently lost limbs from mines, remnants of the Iran–Iraq war, which were on the Iraqi side of the border.[115] In mid-April, one reporter was moved to write:

The most terrible reality of all is that children are the ones who are suffering, and dying, the most ... One would like to believe that if leaders such as President George Bush or John Major could witness this, they might find a way through diplomatic barriers and rush ... tents, food and medicine to western Iran.[116]

In fact, by mid-April 1991 the allied coalition and the UN had begun to supply aid to Kurdish refugees, although primarily to those in Turkey, as part of 'Operation Provide Comfort'.

---

[106] *The Times*, 4 Apr. 1991.
[107] See *Guardian*, 6 Apr. 1991. See also *Independent*, 5 Apr. 1991.
[108] See *Guardian*, 6 Apr. 1991.
[109] See, e.g., *Guardian*, 6 Apr. 1991; *Independent*, 10 and 12 Apr. 1991; *Independent Magazine*, 13 Apr. 1991; and *Independent on Sunday*, 14 Apr. 1991.
[110] *Independent*, 8 Apr. 1991.
[111] *Independent*, 12 Apr. 1991. This report also described the shape of 'childish heads' visible in the home-made shrouds.
[112] *Independent on Sunday*, 14 Apr. 1991.
[113] UK Committee for UNICEF, *Gulf Crisis Update 3* (London, 13 May 1991).
[114] *Independent on Sunday*, 14 Apr. 1991. This report described 300 children lying on the floor of the mosque, many likely to die.
[115] *Independent*, 17 Apr. 1991. See also Middle East Watch, *Hidden Death: Land Mines and Civilian Casualties in Iraqi Kurdistan* (New York, 1992).
[116] *Independent*, 15 Apr. 1991.

7.2.4 Comment: The Experiences of Children in the Three Conflicts. Evidence of the Impact of the Relevant Law

The above description summarised the experience, in practice, of child civilians in the three conflicts involving Iraq. The question to be considered now is whether, in this context, there was evidence that international law regarding the treatment of child civilians in armed conflict appeared to have been observed to any extent. Sections 7.3 to 7.5 below will then look at other indicators of the impact of the relevant law, such as UN debates and decisions.

7.2.4.1 Comment: Impact of the Law in Practice: 1987–8 Chemical-weapon Attacks

In the 1987 and 1988 Iraqi chemical weapon attacks, children were clearly killed and injured in large numbers. They were not in any way offered special protection (as children), or treated humanely (as civilians). Nor was their right to life respected (as a fundamental, if not absolute, human right). Indeed, even the prohibitions on the 'first use' of chemical weapons and, arguably, on genocide, were not observed.

Moreover, children seem to have suffered disproportionately in the chemical weapon attacks, partly due to their greater vulnerability as children. Thus, for example, young children's bodies may not be strong enough to withstand these weapons to the same extent as the bodies of healthy adults, nor can children run to safety as quickly as an adult, or necessarily know what measures to take to minimise the effects. It is important to emphasise that these are precisely the sort of considerations that underlie existing international legal rules aiming to offer children special treatment generally, and specifically in situations of armed conflict.

In practice, therefore, in the 1987–8 chemical weapon attacks there was no evidence of observance by Iraq of international law pertaining to the protection of child (or other) civilians either in situations of non-international armed conflict or in internal disturbances. Perhaps this is not surprising, in that the direct targeting of civilians is in itself a flagrant violation of numerous fundamental precepts of international human rights and humanitarian law, both customary and as set out in treaty. A government prepared to flout international legal norms to the extent of using chemical weapons against its own citizens in this way is unlikely to concern itself with legal niceties in relation to children.

In terms of the reaction of the international community, there were some protests regarding Iraq's use of chemical weapons. For example, on 8 September 1988 the US State Department publicly condemned Iraq's use of chemical weapons against the Kurds. Despite US evidence based on intelligence sources (intercepts of Iraqi military communiqués) Iraq issued a denial.[117] The twelve Member States of the European Community also made a declaration censuring Iraq's actions.[118] Further, in mid-September 1988, at the behest of the United States, the USSR, and eleven other countries, the UN Secretary-General asked permission of Iraq and Turkey to send a team of UN experts to investigate the alleged attacks. Both governments rejected this request.[119]

Moreover, Iraq's use of chemical weapons against the Kurds prompted, in September 1988, the then US President, Ronald Reagan, to call in the UN General Assembly for an international conference on chemical weapons. However, this conference, which took place in January 1989, did not censure Iraq for its attacks on the Kurds, and the Kurds were not permitted to attend the conference, even as observers.[120]

The international response to the 1987–8 chemical weapon attacks may nonetheless indirectly have contributed to discouraging further use of chemical weapons by Iraq against the Kurds. The publicity surrounding the deaths of women and children, particularly in the attack on Halabja, provoked a public outcry, in addition to the criticisms voiced by various governments. While no effective measures were in fact taken, these protests may have precipitated the cessation of Iraqi chemical weapon attacks against the Kurds. It is, however, more likely that the attacks ceased simply because they had largely achieved their aim of paralysing the Kurdish resistance.

In any event, it is notable that, despite the very real possibility that Iraq would resort to the use of chemical weapons in the 1991 Gulf War, it seems largely not to have done so.[121]

7.2.4.2 Comment: Impact of the Law in Practice: Children in Iraqi-occupied Kuwait and Children in Iraq

In relation to children in Iraqi-occupied Kuwait, the examples discussed in section 7.2.2.2 above indicate that they were in practice not treated in accordance with the many legal provisions relevant to their circumstances. Thus these children were denied the protection theoretically accorded to them in international human rights treaty law and in customary law generally. Further, they did not benefit from the humanitarian treaty

---

[117] Korn (1990), 147.
[118] See 4 *European Political Cooperation Bulletin*, 92 (1988).
[119] Korn (1990), 152.
[120] *Ibid.*, 201.
[121] This may have been due to allied threats of a proportionate response. See *Independent*, 29 Nov. 1991, and *Guardian*, 28 Sept. 1991. Although there has been speculation that Iraq may have used chemical agents during the 1991 Gulf War, resulting in the 'Gulf War Syndrome', this seemed, at the time of writing, increasingly unlikely. See, e.g., *Guardian*, 11 Feb. 1994, 4 Apr. 1996, and 18 Apr. 1996, and the *Independent on Sunday*, 26 Mar. 1995.

provisions pertaining to the treatment of children in situations of international armed conflict, and particularly in occupied territory (as summarised in section 7.1 above).

The fact that even the most fundamental of the applicable legal rules (such as the right not to be arbitrarily deprived of life) were not in any sense observed by Iraq as the Occupying Power in Kuwait is, again, not surprising in a context in which Iraq rode roughshod over many of the cardinal precepts of international law, not least by invading a sovereign country.[122] Thus the violations committed in relation to child civilians in occupied Kuwait were, once more, only one feature of a situation involving numerous gross breaches of international law. However, unlike the 1987–8 chemical weapon attacks, the occupation of Kuwait ultimately triggered direct military intervention by the allied coalition. To the extent that this intervention put a stop to the abuses committed against children in Kuwait, it indirectly enforced certain of the laws relating to their protection. Nonetheless, the decision of the allied coalition to intervene was made on the basis of a host of economic and political considerations, and cannot be considered in any sense as an example of action taken to enforce international law regarding the treatment of child civilians.

The 1991 Gulf War precipitated by the occupation of Kuwait was significant as the first major international armed conflict since World War II. Further, it was the only one, at the time of writing, which had, since World War II, galvanised concerted military action based on the consensus of a wide range of governments.[123] Given that the 1991 Gulf War was based on this level of consensus, and that it took place in the optimistic atmosphere of the immediate 'post Cold War' period, it may be that state practice, as manifested in this conflict, represented the 'best that mankind has to give', at this point in time, in terms of compliance with international law regarding the protection of child civilians in situations of armed conflict. However, it may also mean that this conflict was so atypical as to make it unreliable as a guide to future state practice. Indeed, both these possibilities may apply.[124]

Children in Iraq during the period of the 1991 Gulf War clearly ex-

---

[122] However, for most of this period Iraq maintained that Kuwait was one of its provinces, and therefore categorised the conflict as an internal disturbance.

[123] This distinguishes the 1991 Gulf War from the conflict in the former Yugoslavia, where military intervention by the international community had, at the time of writing, been limited and characterised by prevarication and discord.

[124] The 1991 Gulf War is seen by a number of writers as providing significant evidence of recent state practice in situations of armed conflict. See, e.g., Minear, Chelliah, Crisp, Mackinley, and Weiss (1992); Greenwood, in Rowe (ed.) (1993); Hampson, 'Means and Methods of Warfare in the Gulf', in Rowe (ed.) (1993); O. Schachter, 'United Nations Law in the Gulf Conflict', 85 *AJIL* 452 (1991), and Gardam (1993), 144. The latter refers repeatedly to state practice in the 1991 Gulf War as contributing to evidence of certain customary principles: *ibid.*, 147, 148, 151–3, 155–6, 161–2, among others.

perienced (and, at the time of writing, are apparently still experiencing) considerable suffering as an indirect result of the imposition of sanctions and of the 1991 Gulf War itself. Further, many provisions of international human rights and humanitarian law designed to protect child civilians from the more direct effects of international armed conflict were, again, not observed. These arguably included fundamental rules, such as the proportionality principle, as well as more detailed provisions, such as those regarding the creation of zones (Articles 14 and 15 of 1949 GC IV).

Nonetheless, in this international armed conflict there is some evidence of respect for certain principles of international law regarding child civilians.[125] Although the relevant law was not cited directly in any detail,[126] in actuality both the allied coalition and the UN seemed largely to accept in principle that children were entitled to a degree of special protection in this conflict, and certainly that they should in particular have priority (with other vulnerable groups) in receiving food, clothing, and medicine (in accordance with Article 23 of 1949 GC IV), and should not be targeted in military attacks (in accordance with both customary law and treaty provisions such as Article 27 of 1949 GC IV).

In practice this meant, *inter alia*, that as early as September 1990 Presidents Bush and Gorbachev agreed that food supplies should be flown into Iraq, giving 'special priority . . . to meeting the needs of children',[127] and that the important UN Resolution 666 (1990) was passed, as well as others invoking 'humanitarian' considerations (see section 7.3.2.1 below). Similarly, the February 1991 UNICEF/WHO 'aid corridor' was authorised to take medical supplies into Iraq for children and mothers. Further, in the context of continuing discussions regarding the possibility of easing sanctions on Iraq, President Bush, for example, was quoted in July 1991 as being in favour of this specifically on the grounds that the United States 'is not going to see the suffering of innocent women and children there' (Iraq) as a result of the economic sanctions.[128]

At the time of writing, however, the sanctions remained largely in place, although agreement had just been reached in principle, under Security Council Resolution 986 (1995)[129] that Iraq could sell oil to the value of two billion dollars, over a six-month period, in order to purchase essential

---

[125] Perhaps it is not surprising to find at least some such evidence, given that this was an international armed conflict, in which context international law concerning child civilians is most developed. Further, a degree of compliance with this body of law may be expected in the planned and public armed conflict that was the 1991 Gulf War. As one commentator aptly stated, this was 'a war by appointment . . . a war by invitation . . . a war with a published programme': L. Freedman, 'Baghdad Stunned by Science', *Independent*, 18 Jan. 1991.

[126] See, e.g., discussion in sect. 7.3.2.1 below, regarding pertinent UN resolutions.

[127] See *Independent*, 10 Sept. 1990.

[128] See *International Herald Tribune*, 24 July 1991.

[129] UN Doc. S/RES/986 (1995), 14 Apr. 1995.

food and medical supplies under UN supervision.[130] Given the appalling suffering of the Iraqi population since the 1991 Gulf War, as a combined result of the UN sanctions and of Saddam Hussein's intransigence in nego-tiations concerning the easing of these, the question remains whether the imposition of such sweeping sanctions can be justified when the conse-quences for children and others may be catastrophic (see further section 8.2 below).

Finally, the allied coalition took great pains throughout to stress that it was concerned to avoid injury to civilians generally and to minimise 'collat-eral damage'.[131] As already mentioned, the extent to which it succeeded in this is debatable.[132] Nonetheless, the public outcry following the bombing of the Ameriyya shelter in Baghdad, in which many Iraqi women and children were killed, may have embarrassed the coalition to the extent that it seemed to mark a shift of focus in its strategy.[133] Again, this shift may have indicated some awareness of the need to minimise civilian casualties, even if it was arguably too little and too late.

7.2.4.3 Comment: Impact of the Law in Practice: Children in the 1991 Uprisings and Their Aftermath

In the aftermath of the 1991 Gulf War, children again suffered extensively, and for many weeks little was done to ameliorate their suffering or to comply with any of the applicable international law (as summarised in section 7.1 above). This situation was finally addressed by 'Operation Safe Haven'. However, it is impossible to gauge precisely the extent to which this initiative and subsequent UN and allied actions in aid of the Kurds were motivated by international concern to protect the children involved. What is clear is that the plight of the starving and dying Kurdish children, relentlessly publicised in the western media, was a major factor in igniting

---

[130] *Guardian*, 21 May 1996. Prior to this, the Iraqi government had maintained that it found the conditions imposed by Security Council Res. 986 (1995) unacceptable. See, e.g., *Guardian*, 11, 14 Dec. 1995, 18, 20 Jan. 1996, and 10 Mar. 1996; and *Independent*, 17 and 19 Jan. 1996.

[131] See Air Vice-Marshall Tony Mason, 'Morale and Civilian Death', *Guardian*, 7 Feb. 1991. See also D. Garrat, 'The Role of Legal Advisers in the Armed Forces', in Rowe (ed.) (1993), 55–62; *United States Department of Defence Report to Congress on the Conduct of the Persian Gulf War—Appendix on the Role of the Law of War: (April 10, 1992)* 31 ILM 612 (1992); and *Independent*, 17 Jan. 1992.

[132] See particularly Middle East Watch, *Needless Deaths in the Gulf War* (New York, 1991), 4. See also Middle East Watch, *The Bombing of Iraqi Cities* (1991), 2; Schachter (1991), 466, and Gardam (1992). The latter argues (834–5) that coalition state practice indicated respect only for minimal legal standards, such as the prohibition on direct targeting of civilians. Further, a 1992 Pentagon analysis of the performance of certain allied missiles in the 1991 Gulf War revealed a considerably lower accuracy rate than had previously been maintained: *Guardian*, 11 Apr. 1992, and *Independent*, 14 Apr. 1992.

[133] For justification, by the US Department of Defense, of the attack on the Baghdad shelter, see *United States Department of Defense Report* (10 April, 1992), 626–7.

public concern to the pitch at which the United States, France, and the United Kingdom, as well as the UN, felt obliged to intervene.

This point was repeatedly emphasised in the Western press. In early April 1991, one commentator described Western members of the Security Council, discussing strategies for assisting the Kurdish refugees, as '[r]eeling from the worldwide anger at the failure of the United Nations to prevent the bloody repression of the Kurds'.[134] Others specifically linked this public outrage to 'the horror, the pity, of the dying Kurdish children'.[135] Another report firmly placed US moves to aid the Kurds against the backdrop of 'television pictures of dying Kurdish babies' which 'steadily arouse public opinion'.[136] Yet another article described, as the most enduring recent image on British television, pictures of Kurdish women in the snow 'made desperate by their freezing children's hunger, pleading for Western help that never came'.[137]

When the United States did decide to assist the Kurds, President Bush apparently cited as a reason for this his 'frustration' at the slaughter of innocent civilians,[138] and emphasised that 'the lives of hundreds of thousands of innocent men, women and children' were at stake.[139]

In terms of the international legal protection of child civilians, the Western and UN intervention in the aftermath of the uprisings thus demonstrates the complex interface between public opinion, political action, and international law. Again, it is not possible to maintain that this intervention was undertaken solely, or even primarily, to enforce the relevant international law concerning child civilians. However, it is arguable that the intervention was to some extent motivated by public concern specifically in relation to children, and that the actions taken by the United States, the United Kingdom, France, and the UN indicated a rather belated implicit acknowledgement of a number of international legal principles, both customary and conventional, pertaining to the treatment of child civilians in armed conflict. These include general principles such as the requirement for humane treatment of civilians, and prohibitions on targeting them. Arguably, some respect was also evidenced for the principle that children are entitled to special treatment, and at least must be supplied, as a priority, with necessities such as food and shelter.

Certainly, the Western and UN humanitarian interventions in Iraq after the uprisings constituted an exceptional interference, and on dubious legal grounds, in the internal affairs of a sovereign state. However, this particular situation had some unique features, including that the sovereign state in question had recently been vanquished and was in no position to retaliate.

---

[134] *Independent*, 5 Apr. 1991.
[135] *Independent on Sunday*, 7 Apr. 1991.
[136] *Independent*, 10 Apr. 1991.
[137] *Independent on Sunday*, 14 Apr. 1991.
[138] *Independent*, 5 Apr. 1991.
[139] *Guardian*, 6 Apr. 1991.

In this context, it may perhaps be arguable that northern Iraq could be regarded as occupied territory during the period of the establishment of the safe havens (Note 14 above).[140] If so, the 1949 GC IV measures concerning occupied territory would have been applicable, and, indeed, some of the actions taken by the United States, the United Kingdom, and France at that time (as in the provision of food and shelter) were broadly in compliance with relevant measures.

7.3 UNITED NATIONS DECISIONS AND DEBATES CONCERNING THE THREE CONFLICTS. IMPACT OF THE RELEVANT LAW

The preceding section attempted to assess the effectiveness of the pertinent international law as reflected in the experiences of child civilians in these conflicts. This section will now seek evidence of the impact of the relevant law through an analysis of the deliberations and decisions of the UN. The focus here will be on the extent to which UN debates and resolutions reflected any awareness of international law concerning the treatment of child civilians, and any intention to enforce such law. Only certain of the main UN decisions and discussions relevant to each conflict will be examined.[141]

Practical action taken by the UN in the context of these conflicts is not generally discussed here, and relevant action was in any event largely mentioned in the previous section.[142]

The following section will look at the UN response to each of the three conflicts in turn, before section 7.4 briefly considers the response of UNICEF and of the Human Rights Committee.

7.3.1 UN Decisions and Debates Concerning the 1987–8 Chemical Weapon Attacks

UN debates and resolutions concerning the 1987–8 chemical weapon attacks against the Kurds originated largely in the Sub-Commission on the

---

[140] This argument is put forward for the sake of completeness, but somewhat tentatively, since, strictly speaking, it would presume the continuation of the international armed conflict until mid-July 1991, and this is highly debatable. Nonetheless, the question remains as to the legal rules applicable in northern Iraq during the period of the establishment of the safe havens.

[141] For a more detailed collection of documents, including UN resolutions and Summary Records of Security Council debates, regarding the occupation of Kuwait and its repercussions, see generally E. Lauterpacht, C. Greenwood, M. Weller, and D. Bethlehem, *The Kuwait Crisis. Basic Documents* (Cambridge, 1991), and M. Weller (ed.), *Iraq and Kuwait: The Hostilities and their Aftermath* (Cambridge, 1993).

[142] For a critique of UN humanitarian action in relation to the 1991 Gulf crisis, see generally Minear, Chelliah, Crisp, Mackinley and Weiss (1992).

Prevention of Discrimination and Protection of Minorities and in its parent body, the Commission on Human Rights, mainly under the Resolution 1503 procedure. Although such debates took place in 1988 and in 1989, it was only in 1990 and 1991 that these bodies were able to reach a decision to take action that reflected concern regarding the chemical weapon attacks.

Thus, the meetings of the Sub-Commission in 1988 and 1989 considered a draft resolution which, among other things, expressed concern about human rights in Iraq and the use of chemical weapons by Iraq against its own citizens, and which called for a UN study of human rights in Iraq and the possible appointment of a Special Rapporteur. In both these meetings, a motion was successfully passed which resulted in no action being taken on the draft resolution.[143] However, in 1990 a draft resolution concerned with human rights both in Iraq and in occupied Kuwait met with greater success, and was adopted by a secret ballot. This resolution again, *inter alia*, drew attention to the use by Iraq of chemical weapons, and called for the Commission on Human Rights to study human rights in Iraq and to appoint a Special Rapporteur.[144]

In the Commission on Human Rights, proceedings followed a similar pattern. A closed session in 1988 considered a draft resolution concerning the human rights situation in Iraq and decided that this was 'no longer under consideration under Council resolution 1503 (XLVIII)'.[145] In 1989, the debate resulted in a 'roll-call' in favour, once again, of taking no decision on a draft resolution which concerned the human rights situation in Iraq, and which specifically referred to chemical weapon attacks against the Kurds. Interestingly, on this occasion it was the Iraqi representative who successfully moved that no decision be taken.[146]

At its meeting in February 1991 the Commission on Human Rights was criticised by representatives of various NGOs for its inaction regarding Iraq.[147] Then in March 1991 this Commission finally adopted a resolution on the 'Situation of Human Rights in Iraq' which cited, *inter alia*, 'the fact that chemical weapons have been used on the Kurdish civilian population' and which referred to the massive forced displacement and deportation of Kurds and the destruction of their towns. It specifically called on Iraq to abide by its obligations under the 'International Covenants', and requested the appointment of a Special Rapporteur on human rights in Iraq. This request was subsequently approved by

---

[143] See UN Doc. E/CN.4/1988/45, 99, and UN Doc. E/CN.4/Sub.2/1989/58, 71.

[144] See UN Doc. E/CN.4/Sub.2/1990/59, 17 and 35. The voting on the secret ballot was 18 to 1, with 4 abstentions.

[145] See UN Doc. E/CN.4/1988/82–8, 244.

[146] UN Doc. E/CN.4/1989/75–86, 178, 243–5, and 249. The vote on the 'roll-call' was 17 to 13, with 9 abstentions. For further information on this discussion, see UN Doc. E/CN.4/1989/SR.55/Add.1, 18.

[147] See UN Doc. E/CN.4/1991/SR.34, 8–21.

ECOSOC[148] (see section 6.1.2.3 above, regarding Special Rapporteur Max van der Stoel).

7.3.2 UN Decisions and Debates Regarding the Occupation of Kuwait and the 1991 Gulf War

In comparison with its unimpressive performance as regards the chemical weapon attacks against the Kurds, the UN galvanised a 'historic response'[149] to the occupation of Kuwait in particular. Numerous resolutions were adopted, which orchestrated the international reaction, culminating in the 1991 Gulf War itself.

In the context of the occupation of Kuwait and the ensuing Gulf War, the focus of UN decision-making was primarily the Security Council, although there were other pertinent initiatives, particularly in the General Assembly and within ECOSOC. The discussion below will therefore centre primarily on certain Security Council resolutions, and debates concerning them, during the period under consideration here. These resolutions are first summarised, and those with a particular bearing on the protection of child civilians are then discussed more fully.

7.3.2.1 Occupation of Kuwait and 1991 Gulf War:
Security Council Resolutions

The relevant Security Council resolutions are as follows: Resolution 660 (1990)[150] (condemning the Iraqi occupation of Kuwait); Resolution 661 (1990)[151] (imposing economic sanctions—discussed below); Resolution 662 (1990)[152] (declaring null and void the Iraqi annexation of Kuwait); Resolution 664 (1990)[153] (primarily regarding the safety of third-state nationals in Kuwait); Resolution 665 (1990)[154] (imposing a naval blockade); Resolution 666 (1990)[155] (dealing with the availability of food in Iraq and Kuwait—discussed below); Resolution 667 (1990)[156] (regarding Iraqi acts against diplomatic premises in Kuwait); Resolution 669 (1990)[157] (dealing with requests for assistance under Article 50 of the UN Charter); Resolution 670 (1990)[158] (regarding restrictions on air flights to Iraq and

---

[148] ECOSOC, Commission on Human Rights, Report of the 47th Sess. 1991. Supp. No 2, UN Doc. E/CN.4.1991/91, Res. 1991/74, 12, 167, and 260.
[149] To quote UN Secretary-General de Cuellar (1990), 11.
[150] UN Doc. S/RES/660 (1990), 2 Aug. 1990.
[151] UN Doc. S/RES/661 (1990), 6 Aug. 1990.
[152] UN Doc. S/RES/662 (1990), 9 Aug. 1990.
[153] UN Doc. S/RES/664 (1990), 18 Aug. 1990.
[154] UN Doc. S/RES/665 (1990), 25 Aug. 1990.
[155] UN Doc. S/RES/666 (1990), 13 Sept. 1990.
[156] UN Doc. S/RES/667 (1990), 16 Sept. 1990.
[157] UN Doc. S/RES/669 (1990), 24 Sept. 1990.
[158] UN Doc. S/RES/670 (1990), 25 Sept. 1990.

Kuwait—discussed below); Resolution 674 (1990)[159] (regarding Iraqi actions in Kuwait—discussed below); Resolution 677 (1990)[160] (regarding protection of the Kuwaiti population register); Resolution 678 (1990)[161] (setting the 15 January 1991 deadline for Iraqi compliance with these resolutions); Resolution 686 (1991)[162] (marking the end of the Gulf War); and Resolution 687 (1991)[163] (dealing, *inter alia*, with Iraq's international legal obligations concerning the use of chemical and biological weapons, Iraq's liability in relation to compensation and return of property to Kuwait, and prohibitions on the supply of products to Iraq—discussed below).[164]

Of these fourteen resolutions, five in particular are significant as regards legal principles relating to the treatment of child civilians, and are discussed below. However, in only one of these, Resolution 666 (1990), is the reference to children explicit.

Thus, Resolution 661 (1990), adopted only four days after the invasion of Kuwait, imposed economic sanctions on Iraq and Kuwait, but specifically excluded 'supplies intended strictly for medical purposes and, in humanitarian circumstances, foodstuffs'. Similarly, in imposing sanctions on the provision of funds to Iraq or Kuwait, the resolution excepted 'payments exclusively for strictly medical or humanitarian purposes and, in humanitarian circumstances, foodstuffs'. Although these provisos do not expressly mention children, the reference to 'humanitarian circumstances' clearly incorporates consideration of their needs, as was made explicit in Resolution 666 (1990). Resolution 661 (1990) also set up a Committee entrusted with the task of implementing its provisions.

Resolution 666 (1990), adopted on 13 September 1990 as concern intensified regarding the effect of sanctions on vulnerable categories of civilians, is the Security Council Resolution of particular interest here, in that it specifically referred to the needs of children. Citing Resolution 661 (1990), it acknowledged in its Preamble that circumstances may arise when food should be supplied to civilians in Iraq or Kuwait 'in order to relieve human suffering'. The resolution called for the Committee established under Resolution 661 (1990) to decide, on the basis of information to be supplied by the Secretary-General, whether such circumstances had now arisen. It explicitly

---

[159] UN Doc. S/RES/674 (1990), 29 Oct. 1990.
[160] UN Doc. S/RES/677 (1990), 28 Nov. 1990.
[161] UN Doc. S/RES/678 (1990), 29 Nov. 1990.
[162] UN Doc. S/RES/686 (1991), 2 Mar. 1991.
[163] UN Doc. S/RES/687 (1991), 3 Apr. 1991.
[164] There were subsequent Security Council resolutions concerning this conflict, including Resolution 688 (1991), which dealt with the uprisings and is discussed in sect. 7.3.3 below. In addition, there were, *inter alia*, Security Council Resolutions 689 (1991); 692 (1991); 699 (1991); 700 (1991); 705 (1991); 706 (1991); 707 (1991); 712 (1991); and 715 (1991), which addressed problems concerning the less immediate aftermath of the 1991 Gulf War and related issues, and will not be discussed here.

requested that, in the provision of information to the Committee, 'particular attention shall be paid to such categories of persons who might suffer specially, such as children under 15 years of age, expectant mothers, maternity cases, the sick, and the elderly'.[165] Thus, Resolution 666 (1990) points to some acceptance by members of the Security Council of principles concerning, for example, the provision of food and other necessities to children and other vulnerable civilians (as in Article 23 of 1949 GC IV) and the entitlement of children to special protection (as in Article 24 of the ICCPR; Article 26 of the UDHR; and Article 77 of 1977 GP I), although this Resolution does not directly cite the specific legal provisions.

Resolution 670 (1990) responded to Iraqi maltreatment of Kuwaitis and others, and imposed an embargo on air traffic to and from Iraq and Kuwait with the exception of the transport of 'food in humanitarian circumstances'. It also expressly affirmed that 'the fourth Geneva Convention' applied to Kuwait and that, as a party to that Convention, Iraq was bound to comply fully with all its terms and was subject to its provisions regarding grave breaches.

Resolution 674 (1990), in response to further Iraqi abuses in Kuwait, again cited 1949 GC IV and certain other international treaties (such as the UN Charter), and demanded, *inter alia*, that Iraq ensure access to food and other essentials for Kuwaitis and third-state nationals.[166]

Neither of these last two resolutions thus specifically referred to child civilians, or, indeed, to detailed measures regarding occupied territory. However, both resolutions implicitly incorporated child civilians (including in occupied territory) in that they acknowledged Iraq's duty to comply with 'all' the terms of 1949 GC IV, and were concerned with the provision of essential supplies to the civilian population.

The lengthy Resolution 687 (1990) (nicknamed the 'Mother of all Resolutions') is the last of the five resolutions under consideration here. This, *inter alia*, referred to certain of Iraq's international legal obligations specifically in relation to the use of chemical weapons (citing, for example, the 1925 Geneva Protocol), in the context of calling for the destruction of Iraq's arsenal of such weapons. It also, once again, while continuing the prohibition on the supply of 'products' to Iraq, allowed for the passage of food-

---

[165] It seems likely that, in Res. 666 (1990), the Security Council set 15 as the upper age limit for children in accordance with the usage in Art. 23 of 1949 GC IV, among others. It is regrettable that the Security Council did not take this opportunity to apply the age limit of 18, which is arguably the emerging norm for defining childhood, as discussed in sect. 1.3.

[166] This resolution also referred to the need to hold Iraq accountable for grave breaches of, *inter alia*, 1949 GC IV, and requested that states collect evidence of such breaches (paras. 1 and 2). These would, as discussed above (sect. 6.2.2) include serious violations committed against children.

stuffs and other 'materials for essential civilian needs', thereby implicitly acknowledging the needs of children, among others.

7.3.2.2 Occupation of Kuwait and the 1991 Gulf War: Security Council Debate

Not surprisingly, some of the Security Council discussions of these five relevant resolutions echo the themes outlined above, in relation to child civilians.[167] Thus these discussions demonstrate concern regarding the provision of necessities to vulnerable civilian groups, specifically including children, and a general awareness of some aspects of international humanitarian law, particularly 1949 GC IV.

For example, the provisional verbatim records of the Security Council debate on Resolution 666 (1990) contain a number of references to the specific needs of children, underlining, *inter alia*, the importance of 'special emphasis' being given to 'the situation of children and mothers . . . and all who are experiencing special suffering as a result of the aggression'.[168]

Awareness of this issue was also evident in the November 1990 Security Council discussion on the audio-visual presentation concerning atrocities committed by the Iraqi forces in Kuwait, many of which involved children (section 7.2.2.2 above). In debates on this presentation, reference was repeatedly made to Iraq's non-compliance with the 1949 GCs, and especially with 1949 GC IV.[169]

Similar references were made in other pertinent Security Council debates, such as those concerning Resolution 674 (1990)[170] and Resolution 678 (1990).[171]

Another relevant discussion on the situation of child civilians took place on 20 December 1990 within the Security Council Committee established by Resolution 661. The discussion concerned distribution of food and medical supplies within Iraq and Kuwait, and the Committee acknowledged that priority must be given to those who might particularly suffer, as set out in Security Council Resolution 666 (1990). One representative made the point

---

[167] For extracts from a number of Security Council debates between 2 Aug. and 29 Nov. 1990 concerning the occupation of Kuwait generally, see Lauterpacht, Greenwood, Weller and Bethlehem (1991), 99–176.

[168] UN Doc. S/PV.2939 (14 Sept. 1990), 56. The quotation is from the UK representative, Sir David Hannay. Similar sentiments were expressed by, among others, the representatives of Zaïre, the US, and the USSR.

[169] See, e.g., UN Doc. S/PV.2959 (27 Nov. 1990), para. 13; UN Doc. S/PV.2960 (27 Nov. 1990), paras. 12, 16, 25, and 31; and UN Doc. S/PV.2962 (28 Nov. 1990), paras. 3, 10, and 17 (the last including an account of the killing of two boys, cited as a grave breach of the 1949 GCs).

[170] See, e.g., UN Doc. S/PV.2950 (27 Oct. 1990), paras. 3–5, including reference by the Kuwaiti representative to the murder of 'innocent children', and UN Doc. S/PV.2951 (29 Oct. 1990), para. 86.

[171] See UN Doc. S/PV.2963 (29 Nov. 1990), para. 78.

that the 'balance of concern had now shifted to the needs of Iraqi and Kuwaiti children'.[172] Other representatives added their support to this suggestion and emphasised the plight of children.[173]

7.3.2.3 Occupation of Kuwait and the 1991 Gulf War. Initiatives of the General Assembly and ECOSOC

As already mentioned, the Security Council was the primary, but not the sole, forum in the UN that gave rise to resolutions and debates concerning the occupation of Kuwait and the 1991 Gulf War. Discussions in the other fora will not be considered below, with the exception of certain particularly relevant initiatives within the General Assembly and ECOSOC.

7.3.2.3.1 The General Assembly

In the period under consideration, the General Assembly adopted only one resolution, Resolution 45/170 of 18 December 1990, which merits consideration here, concerning human rights in occupied Kuwait.[174] It made reference specifically to child civilians, and repeatedly expressed concern at the treatment of civilians generally in occupied Kuwait (although it did not cite any of the detailed international law concerning either children or occupied territory).

The resolution condemned Iraq for the torture, arrest, summary execution, and disappearance of civilians in Kuwait 'in violation of the UN Charter, the International Covenants on Human Rights and other relevant human rights instruments and relevant instruments of humanitarian law'. It went on expressly to affirm that 1949 GC IV applied to Kuwait and that Iraq must comply 'fully' with it.

Of particular note here is this resolution's expression of 'grave concern' at the living conditions in occupied Kuwait 'of women, children, the elderly and third-state nationals, which are becoming increasingly difficult'. It thus specifically paid attention to the needs of children, among others.

The resolution also, *inter alia*, requested that the Commission on Human Rights consider the situation of human rights in occupied Kuwait, and the Commission complied with this request (see section 7.3.2.3.2 below).

7.3.2.3.2 ECOSOC

Within ECOSOC, the Commission on Human Rights in February 1991 considered a report on the 'Situation of Human Rights in Occupied

---

[172] UN Doc. S/AC.25/SR.21 (20 Dec. 1990), 7. The quotation is from the UK representative, Mr Richardson, who described children as a priority since the numbers of foreigners in Iraq and Kuwait had diminished.

[173] Thus, e.g., the Cuban representative described children as 'the most vulnerable group in Iraq and Kuwait': *ibid*. 8 and 9.

[174] UN GA Res. 45/170 (18 Dec. 1990), 'The Situation of Human Rights in Occupied Kuwait'. The vote on this resolution was 144 in favour, one (Iraq) against, and no abstentions: UN, *Resolutions and Decisions Adopted by the General Assembly During the First Part of its Forty-Fifth Session: 18 Sept. to 21 Dec. 1990*, 517.

Kuwait'. The report described the 'barbaric acts' of Iraqis in Kuwait as constituting a 'flagrant violation of the Geneva Conventions of 1949' and recounted numerous abuses suffered by Kuwaiti children, among others, at the hands of the Iraqis.[175]

The following month, the Commission on Human Rights adopted a resolution on the 'Situation of Human Rights in Kuwait under Iraqi Occupation'. Among other things, this resolution referred to the suffering of the civilian population in Kuwait and condemned Iraq for 'grave human rights violations' there. It also criticised Iraq for its failure to respect international law, 'in particular with reference to the protection of the civilian population'. The resolution concluded with a decision to appoint a Special Rapporteur to examine Iraqi human rights violations in Kuwait,[176] and this decision was approved by ECOSOC.[177]

At the same session of the Commission, it also finally adopted its resolution on the 'Situation of Human Rights in Iraq' which incorporated condemnation of the chemical weapon attacks on the Kurds (see section 7.3.1 above).

Further, the Commission on Human Rights provided the forum for a speech made in May 1991 concerning child civilians in the context of the Gulf War. In a debate on the 'Status of the Convention on the Rights of the Child' the Iraqi representative, Mr Al-Kadhi, pointed to the 1989 CRC as enshrining the 'general principles of humanitarian law, in time of war and peace, as they affected children'. He described Iraq as a victim of aggression which violated these principles, and referred to the economic blockade and bombing of Iraq as contravening Article 24 (regarding the rights of children to food and health). In addition, he complained that Iraq suffered from a violation of Article 38, regarding the application of international humanitarian law to children. Mr Al-Kadhi argued that these 'serious violations reflected the flagrant contradiction between the laws which protected children in times of armed conflict and their application in practice'.[178] While it is heartening to see this very valid point being made in a UN debate, it is perhaps ironic, in the context of the conflicts under consideration here, that it should have been made by the Iraqi delegate.

Moreover, under the ægis of ECOSOC, the Special Rapporteur on Iraq, Max van der Stoel, had, at the time of writing, prepared eleven separate

---

[175] UN Doc. E/CN.4/1991/70, 2 and generally.
[176] UN Doc. E/CN.4/1991/91, 154, Res. 1991/67 (6 Mar. 1991).
[177] *Ibid.*, 10.
[178] UN Doc. E/CN.4/1991/SR.45 (10 May 1991), 11. Iraq actually acceded to the 1989 CRC on 15 June 1994. See UN Doc. CRC/C/2/Rev.4 (1995), 6.

reports regarding human rights in Iraq.[179] His major reports in 1992 and 1994, for example, both contained a separate section on women and children,[180] emphasising that in Iraq they were suffering from serious human rights violations committed against them, and were also suffering by reason of violations committed against their adult male relatives.

7.3.3 UN Decisions and Debates Concerning the 1991 Uprising and its Aftermath

The uprisings of the Kurds and Shia after the 1991 Gulf War and the exodus following their defeat gave rise to few formal resolutions within the UN. This is because the response of the international community to this crisis sprang largely from initiatives taken by certain members of the allied coalition (particularly the United States, France, and the United Kingdom), and thus tended to sidestep the formal UN machinery. There were, nonetheless, numerous discussions within the UN about its role in responding to these events, with the Secretary General and others questioning UN authority to intervene, while the United States and others maintained that the existing Security Council resolutions provided the requisite mandate.[181] These discussions did not focus particularly on child civilians, and will not be described here.

During the relevant period, the Security Council adopted one substantive resolution, Resolution 688 (1991),[182] regarding in particular the Kurdish uprising and its aftermath. This resolution expressed UN concern, *inter alia* at the 'magnitude of the human suffering involved'. It condemned the repression of the Iraqi civilian population, 'including most recently in Kurdish populated areas', asserting that the consequences of this 'threaten[ed] international peace and security in the region.' The resolution called on Iraq to end this repression, and for an 'open dialogue' to ensure respect for the human and political rights of Iraqi citizens. It also demanded that Iraq allow access by international humanitarian organisations, and

---

[179] See, *inter alia*, UN Docs. E/CN.4/1992/3 (18 Feb. 1992); E/CN.4/1993/45 (19 Feb. 1993); and E/CN.4/1994/58 (25 Feb. 1994). At the time of writing, the latest such report was UN Doc. E/CN.4/1996/61 (4 Mar. 1996). The General Assembly had also adopted resolutions on human rights in Iraq which, *inter alia*, condemned Iraq for human rights violations and referred to the reports of the Special Rapporteur. See, e.g., UN GA Res. 47/145 of 18 Dec. 1992 and UN GA Res. 48/144 of 20 Dec. 1993.

[180] UN Docs. E/CN.4/1992/3 and E/CN.4/1994/58, paras. 84–6 and 87–90 respectively.

[181] These debates mainly concerned the authority of the UN to assist in establishing the safe havens and to provide protection for the refugees. See, e.g., *Independent*, 10 Apr. 1991, 18 Apr. 1991, and 26 Apr. 1991.

[182] UN Doc. S/RES/688 (1991), 5 Apr. 1991. For comment on the implications of this resolution as regards humanitarian intervention, see D. Scheffer, 'Towards a Modern Doctrine of Humanitarian Intervention', 23 *University of Toledo Law Review* 267 (1993).

called on the Secretary General to report on the plight of Iraqi civilians, particularly the Kurds, and to use all available resources to meet the needs of refugees.

Although Resolution 688 (1991) did not refer specifically to child civilians, the Security Council debate on it revealed some concern for the children caught up in these events. Delegates repeatedly referred to the fact that, for example, the 'defenceless civilians' fleeing Iraq included 'many . . . women and children'.[183] However, support for this resolution was not unanimous, with Cuba, for example, making the point that, despite legitimate concern for the plight of civilian 'women, children, and the elderly' within the Security Council, the UN Charter does not allow the Security Council to intervene in questions of a humanitarian nature. Nonetheless, the Resolution was passed.[184]

Another debate relevant to child civilians immediately after the 1991 Gulf War took place on 3 March 1991 within the Committee established by the Security Council under Resolution 661 (1990). This debate concerned the delivery of food, medicines, and hospital equipment to Iraq, and again contained a number of references to the specific needs of children.[185] A letter from the Secretary General to the Committee was quoted in the debate, in which he stated that 'there was a clear need to . . . meet the nutritional requirements of the Iraqi population, especially women and children'.[186]

7.3.4 Comment: UN Debates and Decisions Concerning the Three Conflicts. Evidence of the Impact of the Relevant Law

Sections 7.3.1 to 7.3.3 above considered various UN decisions and debates relating to the three Iraqi conflicts. The issue to be examined now is the extent to which these yielded evidence of the impact of the relevant law.

7.3.4.1 Comment: Impact of the Law in UN Decisions and Debates—1987–8 Chemical Weapon Attacks

In relation to the 1987–8 chemical weapon attacks against the Kurds, it is clear from the above discussion that UN action was ineffectual, and indeed it appears that no pertinent UN resolution was passed, even within ECOSOC, until after the 1990 invasion of Kuwait. This response must be

---

[183] UN Doc. S/PV. 2982 (5 Apr. 1991). This comment came from the Turkish delegate (6). Similar comments were made by delegates from: Pakistan (9); Iran (12); Yemen (26); France (53); Austria (56); USA (57); Russia (59); the UK (63); and Luxembourg (73).

[184] *Ibid.*, 46–7 and 52. The Resolution was passed with 10 in favour, 3 against, and 2 abstentions.

[185] UN Doc. S/AC.25/SR.31 (2 Apr. 1991). See references to the needs of children at 2, 3, and 4.

[186] *Ibid.*, 3.

seen in the context of an equally ineffectual response from the international community generally, as described in section 7.2.4.1 above. Further, it is partly explained by the politicised nature of the Commission on Human Rights, and to a lesser extent the Sub-Commission on the Prevention of Discrimination and the Protection of Minorities, which enabled Iraq to muster support in resisting censure.[187]

It is also the case that, when the Commission on Human Rights and the Sub-Commission did eventually adopt resolutions expressing concern at the chemical weapon attacks against Kurdish civilians, this concern was voiced in relation to the civilian population in general. No particular mention was made of child civilians as such.

7.3.4.2 Comment: Impact of the Law in UN Decisions and Debates—The Occupation of Kuwait and the 1991 Gulf War

In the context of the occupation of Kuwait and the 1991 Gulf War, the five Security Council resolutions discussed in section 7.3.2.1 above showed a degree of concern to take into account the humanitarian needs of the civilian population of Iraq and Kuwait. However, only one of these, Resolution 666 (1990) referred directly to the needs of children. Nonetheless, bearing in mind that Security Council resolutions constitute mandatory decisions binding on all UN members,[188] the importance of Resolution 666 (1990), in referring specifically to the needs of child civilians, should not be underestimated.

Some of the Security Council Resolutions discussed in section 7.3.2.1 also explicitly confirmed the relevance of the 1949 GCs and other international treaties, although again not referring directly to provisions concerning child civilians.[189] These resolutions thus indicated a limited acknowledgement by the Security Council of certain basic principles of international law regarding the treatment of civilians generally in armed conflict. Further, in various debates on these resolutions, and particularly on Resolution 666 (1990), there was evidence of concern predominantly as regards the provision of food and other necessities to vulnerable civilians, including children (section 7.3.2.2 above).

General Assembly Resolution 45/170 on occupied Kuwait was significant in that this called in general terms for respect for relevant human rights and humanitarian treaties, as well as specifically drawing attention to the

---

[187] See Korn (1990), 218–20, regarding UN lobbying by Iraqi representatives.

[188] Under Art. 25 of the Charter, decisions of the Security Council (obviously including its resolutions) are legally binding on all UN members, as they thereby 'agree to accept and carry out the decisions of the Security Council'.

[189] Indeed, as one writer has commented, the resolutions of the Security Council regarding the 1991 Gulf War generally make scant reference to the laws of armed conflict: E. Suy, 'International Humanitarian Law and the Security Council Resolutions on the 1990–1 Gulf War', in Delissen and Tanja (eds.) (1991), 517.

plight of, among others, child civilians. Given that the General Assembly is more representative of the international community as a whole than is the Security Council, it is noteworthy that this resolution, the only pertinent General Assembly resolution adopted during the period under consideration here, explicitly singled out child civilians as the object of 'grave concern'.

In relation to ECOSOC activity concerning child civilians in occupied Kuwait and the 1991 Gulf War, this did not, apart from Mr Al-Kadhi's speech (and certain subsequent reports of Special Rapporteur Max van Der Stoel), indicate a particular awareness of the suffering of children in this crisis, and/or the need for their special protection. The relevant resolutions of the Commission on Human Rights regarding both Iraq and Kuwait did not refer specifically to child civilians. However, clearly children were incorporated within the resolutions' general expression of concern for the civilian population, as well as in the demands that Iraq abide by its international legal obligations.

7.3.4.3 Comment: Impact of the Law in UN Decisions and Debates. The 1991 Uprisings and Their Aftermath

As regards UN decisions and debates in response to the uprisings and their aftermath, the organisation again indicated a limited awareness of the need for special protection of child civilians. This was manifested particularly in the discussion on Security Council Resolution 688 (1990), which took place in early April 1991 against the backdrop of public outrage at UN inaction regarding the suffering of the mainly Kurdish refugees, among whom children were prominent (see section 7.3.3 above). It is therefore only to be expected that the discussion reflected some of this public concern, although the resolution itself provided for children simply as part of the civilian population, and did not refer directly to them.

Thus it seems, from the evidence of the UN decisions and debates referred to above, that the impact of international law concerning child civilians was different in each of the three Iraqi conflicts, but was most apparent in the context of the international armed conflicts represented by the invasion of Kuwait and the 1991 Gulf War. This evidence is further summarised in the concluding section of this Chapter.

7.4 WORK OF CERTAIN UN-RELATED BODIES IN THE IRAQI CONFLICTS: THE HUMAN RIGHTS COMMITTEE AND UNICEF

Section 7.3 above considered the attitude of certain principal UN organs to the relevant international law, and the work of other bodies associated with the UN now deserves mention in the context of the Iraqi conflicts. The two selected for a brief discussion below are the Human Rights Committee and UNICEF, as, respectively, examples of an important treaty monitoring body and of a UN agency working on behalf of children.[190]

7.4.1 The Human Rights Committee

It is of interest here that the third periodic report of Iraq was submitted to the Human Rights Committee in June 1991.[191] The Iraqi report contained a number of references to the experiences of Iraqi child civilians as a result of the 1991 Gulf War and the imposition of sanctions. Thus the report claimed that sanctions under Resolution 661 (1990) 'jeopardised the right to life' so that 'hundreds of children died as a result of shortages of milk and vaccines' (page 3). It gave examples of the effect of the economic blockade, including reference to a January 1991 announcement by the Iraqi Ministry of Health of 'the death of 2,400 children because of shortages of food and medicine', and it mentioned a raid by coalition forces on a baby-milk plant '[a]t a time when the children of Iraq were suffering a severe shortage of milk'. The report claimed that the war limited the ability of Iraq 'to carry out its responsibilities *vis-à-vis* children, the group most affected by the war' (pages 9 and 10).

During subsequent sessions in 1991, the Human Rights Committee discussed this report with Iraqi representatives at some length.[192] The Iraqis were also asked to respond in greater detail to issues raised under, *inter alia*, Article 6 (right to life), Article 7 (prohibition on torture), and Article 27 (rights of minorities), although a more detailed response on Article 24 (rights of the child) was not requested.

The Committee periodically expressed strong criticism both of the nature of the Iraqi regime[193] and of Iraq's unsatisfactory compliance with the ICCPR, as evidenced in its report and discussion with the Committee.[194] Among others things, Iraq was censured for its use of chemical weapons;[195]

[190] Other UN-related bodies, such as UNHCR, were also active in these conflicts, but all such bodies cannot be considered here. For further information see, e.g., Minear, Chelliah, Crisp, Mackinley, and Weiss (1992), generally, and, regarding UNHCR specifically, see UNHCR (1993), 84–5.

[191] UN Doc. CCPR/C/64/Add.6 (24 June 1991).

[192] The records of the relevant sessions can be found in UN Docs. CCPR/C/SR.1080 (23 July 1991); CCPR/C/SR.1081 (18 Oct. 1991); CCPR/C/SR.1106 (4 Nov. 1991); CCPR/C/SR.1108 (4 Nov. 1991); CCPR/C/SR.1082 (14 Nov. 1991); and CCPR/C/SR.1107 (31 Dec. 1991).

[193] See, e.g., UN Docs. CCPR/C/SR.1080, 7, 12, and 14, and CCPR/C/SR.1082, 5, 11, and 13.

[194] See, e.g., UN Docs. CCPR/C/SR.1080, 8; CCPR/C/SR.1082, 9, 10, 11, and 13; CCPR/C/SR.1106, 6; and CCPR/C/SR.1108, 6–7.

[195] See UN Doc. CCPR/C/SR.1080, 8–12.

its treatment of the Kurds generally;[196] and of Kurdish and other children specifically.[197] Indeed, in his concluding remarks the Chairman of the Committee referred to the difficult conditions in Iraq which threatened the health of its citizens, 'and more particularly its children'.[198]

7.4.2 UNICEF

As regards UNICEF, in December 1990, shortly before the 1991 Gulf War, this organisation made one of the few emergency shipments of that period to Iraq. The shipment consisted largely of vaccines for children.[199]

During the 1991 Gulf War, UNICEF attempted to persuade the allied coalition and Iraq to agree to the establishment of a 'relief corridor' into Iraq, to channel food and medicines to civilians, particularly children, in line with its successful initiatives in other conflicts (as in the Sudan, El Salvador, and the Lebanon). Although UNICEF did not succeed in establishing a continuing 'relief corridor' as such during the Gulf War (and this may have been partly due to the war's brevity), by addressing this issue it contributed to raising awareness of the needs of child civilians in Iraq.[200] In any event, as already mentioned, UNICEF, in conjunction with the WHO, managed, during the 1991 Gulf War, to bring into Iraq one shipment of fifty-four tonnes of basic medical and health supplies. This took place in the context of the February 1991 WHO/UNICEF 'Special Mission to Iraq', which also gave rise to an influential report.

Other UNICEF actions in this context included, in April 1991, the publication of a further report on children and women in Iraq. This asserted that their situation was 'growing more critical every day', and that three million children under five in the region as a whole would face a period of extreme difficulty in relation to their health.[201]

7.4.3 Comment: The Human Rights Committee and UNICEF. Evidence of the Impact of the Relevant Law

In relation to the Human Rights Committee, the Iraqi report and the debate on it highlight certain strengths and weaknesses of the Human Rights Committee's reporting mechanism in encouraging observance of the

---

[196] See, e.g., UN Doc. CCPR/C/SR.1108, 13, and CCPR/C/SR.1082, 5.
[197] See, e.g., UN Doc. CCPR/C/SR.1080, 14, and CCPR/C/SR.1082, 13.
[198] UN Doc. CCPR/C/SR.1108, 14.
[199] UK Committee for UNICEF (13 May 1991).
[200] Further, in discussions concerning the proposed relief corridor, Mr Grant, then Executive Director of UNICEF, was reported to have reminded international leaders of the commitments they had made in the 1990 World Summit regarding 'periods of tranquillity and special relief corridors' for children in armed conflict: *Independent*, 1 Feb. 1991.
[201] UN Doc. E/ICEF/624 (Apr. 1991), 2 and 3.

ICCPR.[202] More specifically, this report and discussion also illustrated some awareness, on both sides, of the particular problems faced by Iraqi children as a result of the 1991 Gulf conflict, and of their entitlement to special treatment as children, in accordance with Article 24 of the ICCPR. Although the Committee missed the opportunity to obtain more detailed information specifically on Iraqi compliance with that Article, the impression is that both the Committee and Iraq, to a limited extent in their discussion, acknowledged the particular difficulties faced by Iraqi children.

The work of UNICEF during the Iraqi conflicts reveals that this organisation acted in accordance with principles of international law regarding child civilians, although it did not appear to make specific reference to them. Certainly UNICEF's actions in providing aid to children in Iraq immediately before and during the 1991 Gulf War were in accordance with Article 23 of 1949 GC IV, as well as with numerous other principles of international human rights and humanitarian law described in Chapters 2 to 5 above.

Moreover, UNICEF's efforts to secure a 'relief corridor' contributed to the notion of children as 'zones of peace', an important idea linked to the 1949 GC IV concept of 'hospital and safety zones' (Article 14 of 1949 GC IV), as discussed further in section 8.2.1 below.

7.5 AI AND THE ICRC: THEIR WORK IN THE THREE CONFLICTS

Having examined, for evidence of the effectiveness of the relevant law, the experiences of children in the three Iraqi conflicts, certain UN decisions and debates, and relevant work of UNICEF and the Human Rights Committee, it remains now to consider the work of non-governmental bodies, exemplified by the ICRC and AI. Both organisations were extremely active in the context of the Iraqi conflicts, and it is only possible here to touch on certain aspects of the work undertaken.

7.5.1 AI

AI's work in the context of the 1987–8 chemical weapon attacks included, *inter alia*, issuing on 8 September 1988 an 'unprecedented' public appeal to the UN to stop the massacres.[203] It also issued an Urgent Action Appeal to

[202] Clearly Iraq was concerned to appear to comply with the ICCPR and was obliged to be accountable to some extent under this instrument. The Committee did not appear satisfied that Iraq had fulfilled its obligations, but its role was limited to voicing criticisms and attempting to elicit information.

[203] AI, *Iraq: Children* (1989), 30.

AI members, which emphasised, *inter alia*, that the dead included many women and children.[204] Further, in the autumn of 1988 the organisation appealed to the UN Security Council regarding the chemical weapon attacks, and to the Turkish government on behalf of the Kurdish refugees.[205]

Perhaps the single most significant AI publication in this context was the major report *Iraq—Children: Innocent Victims of Political Repression* (see section 7.2.1 above), which referred to certain international legal instruments specifically concerning children (such as the 1959 Declaration and the then draft Convention on the Rights of the Child).[206] In February 1989, when this report was published, AI appealed to the Iraqi government regarding its 'politically motivated brutal treatment of children and young people'.[207]

In addition, in 1988, 1989, and 1990 AI was active in international fora, including the Commission on Human Rights and the Sub-Commission on the Prevention of Discrimination and the Protection of Minorities, in relation to its concerns in Iraq.[208]

In the context of the invasion of Kuwait and the 1991 Gulf War, AI, for example, in December 1990 published a substantial report on human rights violations in occupied Kuwait.[209] The body of the report described in some detail abuses committed by Iraqi forces in Kuwait against the civilian population, many of the victims being children.[210] AI also called publicly on the Iraqi government to end the gross human rights violations committed by its forces in Kuwait.[211]

In relation to the Kurdish uprising and its aftermath, AI again published another major report, in July 1991, based on interviews conducted in Kuwait, Iran, Turkey, and northern Iraq, and setting out the organisation's concerns regarding Iraq since the uprising.[212] The report emphasised that unarmed civilians, among them women and children, were targeted even in

---

[204] AI, *Urgent Action, Iraq: Deliberate Killings of Unarmed Kurdish Civilians* (London, 2 Sept. 1988).

[205] AI, *Report* (1989), 260.

[206] AI, *Iraq: Children* (1989), 3–4.

[207] AI, *Report* (1990), 128.

[208] E.g., in 1988 AI submitted information on Iraq to the Commission under the Resolution 1503 procedure, and addressed the Sub-Commission concerning Iraq's attacks on Kurdish 'unarmed civilians, including women and children': AI, *Iraq: Oral Statement to the United Nations Sub-Commission on Prevention of Discrimination and Protection of Minorities* (London, Aug. 1988). On child civilians, see 3 and 4. In 1989 and 1990, AI again addressed the Commission about Iraq: AI, *Report* (1990), 128, and AI, (London, 1991), 125.

[209] AI (Dec. 1990).

[210] *Ibid.* See 16, 20, 27, 29, 31, 38, 42, 43, 44, 53, 56, and 58.

[211] AI, *Report* (1991), 125.

[212] AI, *Iraq: Human Rights Violations Since the Uprising: Summary of Amnesty International's Concerns* (London, July 1991).

situations outside the context of armed conflict, and it referred to a number of violations committed specifically against children.[213]

Other action taken by AI in this context included a public appeal on 4 April 1991 to world governments to protect the fleeing Kurdish and other refugees, and a similar appeal to the UN. Further, on 16 April the organisation wrote to the Iraqi government, calling, *inter alia*, for Iraq to put an end to violations committed against the refugees, and to abide by its obligations under, for example, the ICCPR and the 1949 GCs.[214]

In July 1991 AI also published a substantial document on the need for further UN action to protect human rights in Iraq and ensure that Iraq complied with its international obligations.[215]

7.5.2 The ICRC

The ICRC provided aid to some of those affected by the three conflicts, and made a number of public statements and appeals. For example, in response to the 1987–8 chemical weapon attacks, the ICRC made a public statement on 23 March 1988, condemning the use of chemical weapons.[216]

In relation to the occupation of Kuwait and the 1991 Gulf War, the ICRC, on the day of the Iraqi invasion of Kuwait, reminded the parties to the conflict of their obligations under the 1949 GCs.[217] The organisation also requested authorisation to intervene in Kuwait to provide protection and assistance for those in need, and Iraq's refusal of this request drew criticism from the UN, among others.[218]

Again, on 14 December 1990, in anticipation of the outbreak of hostilities after the adoption of Resolution 678 (1990) (setting the 15 January 1991 deadline), the ICRC called on the States Party to the 1949 GCs to respect international humanitarian law in relation, among other things, to the protection of civilians.[219]

When hostilities broke out, the ICRC once more reminded the parties to

---

[213] *Ibid.*, 1 and 10–13.

[214] *Ibid.*, 3 and 4.

[215] AI, *Iraq. The Need for Further United Nations Action to Protect Human Rights* (London, July 1991). This document stressed AI's concern for the lives and safety of the many Kurds, Shia, and others at risk of violations in Iraq, and again specifically cited incidents of abuses committed against children: *ibid.* 2 and 3.

[216] ICRC Press Release No. 1567, 23 Mar. 1988 (Geneva).

[217] ICRC, *Bulletin No. 181* (Geneva, Feb. 1991), 1 and 4. On ICRC involvement in the 1991 Gulf conflict generally, see M. Meyer, 'The Role of the International Red Cross and Red Crescent Movement: Problems Encountered', in Rowe (ed.) (1993), 224–40.

[218] See ICRC, *The Annual Report of the International Committee of the Red Cross 1990* (Geneva, Mar. 1991), 22. For UN criticisms of Iraq's position, see, e.g., UN Doc. S/PV.2939 (14 Sept. 1990), 58, and UN GA Resolution 45/170.

[219] ICRC, *Annual Report* (Geneva, 1991), 22. See also ICRC, 'International Humanitarian Law and the Middle East Conflict', 184 *ICRC Bulletin* 2 (May 1991).

the conflict of their 1949 GC obligations, particularly in relation to safe-guarding civilians, and also as regards the use of, *inter alia*, chemical weapons.[220] Similar appeals followed on 1 February and 24 February 1991. The latter appeal urged the belligerents to conclude agreements establishing neutralised zones, and specifically reminded them to allow evacuation of non-combatants 'especially the most vulnerable categories such as the wounded, sick, children and the elderly'.[221]

In the context of the Kurdish uprising and its aftermath, the ICRC concentrated on the provision of relief and related services, rather than on the implementation of international humanitarian law. This was because the organisation classified the Shia and Kurdish uprisings in Iraq as an internal disturbance, and accordingly one in which humanitarian law had limited relevance.[222] Nonetheless, in early April 1991 the ICRC publicly drew attention to the plight of civilians in Iraq, again specifically mentioning children, and called on the 'concerned authorities', *inter alia*, to 'adopt humanitarian measures'.[223]

7.5.3 Comment: AI and the ICRC. Evidence of the Impact of the Relevant Law

Although AI is not an organisation specifically representing children, its work in relation to the three Iraqi conflicts paid considerable attention to abuses committed against them. In this work, the organisation also sought to invoke certain treaties to which Iraq is party, including the ICCPR and the 1949 GCs. Thus, the organisation indicated its awareness of various legal measures relevant to the treatment of child civilians generally in armed conflict, and it worked to strengthen observance of these. Further, at least one of its relevant publications (the 1989 report on children in Iraq) referred to some provisions of international law specifically regarding the treatment of children.

The ICRC was particularly active in encouraging the observance of international humanitarian law, especially in relation to the occupation of Kuwait and the 1991 Gulf War, both of which were international armed conflicts in which it was free fully to exercise its mandate. In this context, the ICRC, in at least one appeal (24 February 1991) made specific reference to legal principles directly relevant to the protection of children, namely the possibility of allowing for their evacuation, and reference to the need to establish neutralised zones. Without actually citing the relevant provisions

[220] ICRC Press Release No 1658, 17 Jan. 1991 (Geneva).
[221] ICRC Press Release No 1661, 24 Feb. 1991 (Geneva).
[222] ICRC, *ICRC Bulletin* (Geneva, May 1991), 1 and 2. See also ICRC, *ICRC Communications to the Press* No 91/29, 10 Apr. 1991 (Geneva), and No 91/30, 17 Apr. 1991 (Geneva).
[223] ICRC Press Release No 1668, 5 Apr. 1991 (Geneva).

in the 1949 GCs, the organisation acknowledged children as a particularly vulnerable group within the civilian population, as well as emphasising the need to shield civilians as a whole from the effects of the hostilities. Further, in relation to the 1991 uprisings and their aftermath, the organisation made a public statement (in April 1991) specifically referring to the plight of child civilians.

7.6 OTHER POSSIBLE INDICATORS

Finally, in addition to the evidence revealed by the four main indicators considered above in sections 7.2 to 7.5, it is relevant to note that there are a number of other factors that could serve as indicators regarding the extent to which the applicable international law had any impact in the three conflicts under consideration.

Such factors include, among others: individual government initiatives; instructions issued by governments to their armed forces in the 1991 Gulf War;[224] the numerous threats of a war crimes trial to adjudicate on the actions of Saddam Hussein and his government;[225] and the role played by the media.[226] However, these factors are not generally as pertinent or revealing as the four indicators already discussed, and will not be considered further.

7.7 SUMMARY: THE LAW IN PRACTICE

The aim of this Chapter has been to consider, by examining certain indicators in the context of three conflicts involving Iraq, the apparent effectiveness (as defined at the beginning of this Chapter) of international law concerning child civilians in armed conflict.

---

[224] In this context, e.g., a representative of the UK Foreign and Commonwealth Office confirmed, in correspondence with the author, that the confidential Instructions issued to UK military personnel in relation to the 1991 Gulf War 'reflected the applicable rules of international law on the protection of civilian persons and objects', but that he 'certainly cannot remember any specific singling out of children in this context': correspondence dated 21 July 1991. (The representative preferred not to be named.)

[225] See, e.g., *Independent*, 16 Oct. 1990, 28 Feb. 1991, 5 Oct. 1991, 17 Oct. 1991, and 23 Oct. 1991, and *Guardian*, 22 Jan. 1991. See also Security Council Resolution 674 (sect. 7.3.2.1 above), regarding Iraq's responsibility for grave breaches of, *inter alia*, 1949 GC IV.

[226] The role of the media was particularly influential in relation to the aftermath of the 1991 uprisings (described above, sect. 7.2.3.2). On the media and the 1991 Gulf crisis as a whole, see H. Mowlana, G. Gerbner, and H. Schiller, *Triumph of the Image: The Media's War in the Persian Gulf—A Global Perspective* (Boulder, Colo., 1992), and *Independent on Sunday*, 3 July 1994. See also, more generally, R. Rotberg and T. Weiss, *The Media, Humanitarian Crises, and Policy-Making* (Cambridge, Mass., 1995).

It is hard to summarise without oversimplification the complexities revealed by this examination of the extent of observance of the relevant international law.[227] It is also difficult, as anticipated, to distinguish with any certainty those factors that indicate the impact of this body of law, as opposed to other possible influences. Despite these difficulties, certain trends can be identified, and these are significant.

The picture that emerges from this examination is one of very limited observance of certain principles of the relevant law.

In some situations, and particularly as regards the 1987–8 chemical weapon attacks, it is possible to say without exaggeration that this body of law was honoured mainly in the breach. This is despite the fact that the 1987–8 chemical weapon attacks provided a classic illustration of children's particular vulnerability to death and injury in situations of armed conflict, a vulnerability that is the rationale underlying many of the measures for their protection in the international law considered in this book.

In other situations, most notably in the context of various actions taken in relation to the 1991 Gulf War and its aftermath, there is evidence of respect for some pertinent legal principles.[228] The discussion in 1991 between the Human Rights Committee and Iraq and the latter's report under the ICCPR, for example, indicated a degree of awareness of the plight of children affected by this armed conflict. More specifically, certain debates within the Security Council and ECOSOC; Security Council Resolution 666 (1990); and arguably General Assembly Resolution 45/170 (see Section 7.3.2); as well as initiatives such as the UNICEF/WHO mission to Baghdad, all indicate acceptance of the precept that child civilians require special respect and protection, especially in terms of the distribution of food and other necessities. As posited in Chapter 5 above, children's entitlement to necessities in armed conflict situations could arguably be considered a customary norm, particularly given that *opinio juris* appears to support it and, in the 1991 Gulf War (and possibly in the aftermath of the 1991 uprisings), state practice in honouring this principle seemed fairly consistent, if belated and inadequate.

In addition, in the context of the 1991 Gulf War and the 1991 uprisings, there was evidence of respect, at least in theory, for the principle that the civilian population in general, and child civilians as a significant sector of that population, should not be directly targeted in armed conflict. This

---

[227] Indeed, one writer has commented that, as regards state practice generally in the context of armed conflict, this is difficult both 'to discover (given the secrecy which generally surrounds the wartime activities of States) or to evaluate (since the nature of armed conflict means that the gulf between principle and practice is likely to be particularly marked)': Greenwood, in Delissen and Tanja (eds.) (1991), 99.

[228] As already mentioned (sect. 7.2.4.2), the degree of consensus manifested by the international community in the 1991 Gulf War may make it either an unreliable guide to future state practice or an example of best practice, or perhaps both.

concept is already well-established in conventional and customary law, but the evidence of these two conflicts seems to indicate that violations committed against children (such as direct attacks on them) evoke a particularly strong public response, which can generate pressure to strengthen the observance of this principle in practice. This was manifested to a degree in the actions of the allied coalition during the 1991 Gulf War (for example, its apparent change of strategy after the public outcry at the bombing of the Baghdad air-raid shelter). It was also evident in the intervention of certain governments on behalf of the Kurds after the 1991 uprisings, culminating in the establishment of the safe havens.

In any event, these two precepts, that child civilians should not be deprived of necessities and should not be targeted in attacks, received considerable support in principle during the 1991 Gulf War and the intervention after the 1991 uprising. They were referred to in UN debates and resolutions; by governments individually or in coalition; and to some extent they were invoked by the major NGOs active in this context. They were fiercely propounded by the media. This in itself is significant, as acceptance in principle must precede implementation in practice.

However, despite evidence of respect for aspects of the relevant law, in all three conflicts the protection actually afforded to child civilians was without exception too little and too late. This was so even in relation to the most spectacular humanitarian intervention, 'Operation Safe Haven', and other initiatives taken in the wake of the uprisings.

Further, the examination of these three conflicts shows that the precise law regarding child civilians in armed conflict seems shrouded in ignorance. Almost nowhere in the relevant debates, resolutions, individual government actions, or NGO initiatives was the legislation regarding child civilians specifically cited.[229] Even when reference was made to principles set out in, for example, 1949 GC IV (as in Resolution 666 (1990), regarding the provision of necessities), the relevant Article (particularly 1949 GC IV, Article 23, in that case) was not referred to. Nor was mention generally made of international human rights law regarding children, such as Article 24 of the ICCPR; the 1924 and 1959 Declarations of the Rights of the Child; or even the 1989 CRC, which after all came into force in September 1990, during the occupation of Kuwait and before the 1991 Gulf War and its aftermath.

Accordingly, what conclusions can be drawn from this (predictably impressionistic) attempt to assess the effectiveness of international law con-

---

[229] As should be evident from this Ch., such legislation appears to have been directly cited in the relevant UN fora on only one occasion, and this was by the Iraqi representative in the Commission on Human Rights, some months after the end of the 1991 Gulf War, during a debate on the 1989 CRC (see sect. 7.3.2.3.2). This is, however, a hopeful sign that the existence of the 1989 CRC will increasingly encourage specific reference to the law concerning child civilians.

cerning child civilians in the context of the three conflicts involving Iraq? First, during the period under consideration, the relevant body of law was never specifically referred to in any context of significance, and was therefore never fully implemented, in the sense of being both invoked and acted upon. Nor was it simply invoked, by being referred to without being acted upon.

Nonetheless, although it was largely not explicitly cited, there was evidence of awareness and/or observance of some of the underlying precepts of this body of law. This was apparent in certain practical actions taken (as in the 1991 WHO/UNICEF mission, and the establishment of the 'safe havens'); in debates and decisions within the UN and related bodies; and in work done by organisations such as AI and the ICRC. To the extent that these precepts were observed in practice, as in the provision of food and necessities, and intervention to halt military action against civilians, they of course benefited child civilians. However, in all three conflicts under consideration, relief came only after enormous numbers of children had suffered death, injury, and/or the many other devastating consequences of armed conflict.

8

Conclusion

In a 1990 UNICEF lecture, the speaker commented that '[i]n the past it was soldiers who died in war . . . The present reality is that modern man wages war against children.'[1] Despite the plethora of laws designed to protect children in armed conflict, the description in Chapter 7 of the three Iraqi conflicts indicates that this speaker's comment was largely accurate.

Obviously, international law alone cannot provide a solution. It reflects and is limited by social and political values and realities. Moreover, as discussed in section 3.1.2, the law concerning child civilians in armed conflict contains significant lacunae (as in relation to children in internal disturbances), and this body of law is also uncomfortably vague in places.[2] Nonetheless, it is substantial, and one can be forgiven for asking why, with so much law, it seems generally so ineffective.

A central problem here, as with many other areas of international law and particularly humanitarian law, is that of implementation and enforcement,[3] despite the many organisations and procedures that play a role in this context (see Chapter 6).[4]

Further, insufficient attention has been paid to safeguarding child civilians, even though most governments express support in principle for the

---

[1] L. Palme, *Nations Touch at their Summits: 1990 UNICEF Lecture* (London, 20 Nov. 1990), 9. In the same vein, Rädda Barnen comments that children 'pay the highest price for . . . our wars': *The Rights of the Child* (1990), 14. See also Vittachi (London, 1993), 136.

[2] Thus, even the key norm that children 'shall be the object of special respect' (Art. 77(1) of 1977 GP I) can clearly be interpreted in a multitude of ways. Moreover, the absence in certain Arts. of fixed age limits can leave children subject to the whim of, e.g., an Occupying Power, as in relation to family accommodation of those interned or detained (Art. 77(4) of 1949 GC IV).

[3] Aldrich suggests 3 factors that are largely responsible for failure of compliance with international humanitarian law: (1) ignorance of the law; (2) cynicism due to a belief that compliance cannot be coerced and violations effectively punished; and (3) an absence of effective monitoring, fact-finding, and dispute-settlement mechanisms: G. H. Aldrich, 'Compliance with the Law: Problems and Prospects', in Fox and Meyer (eds.) (1993), 4.

[4] Many writers have commented on the issue of enforcement and implementation. For example, Franck (1980), 707, observes: 'The surprising thing about international law is that nations ever obey its strictures or carry out its mandates' in that 'the international system is organised in a voluntarist fashion, supported by so little coercive authority.' However, another writer argues that observance of international law is based on a perceived 'reciprocal advantage in cautioning self-restraint' (Higgins, *Problems and Process* (1994), 16), and that the main role of international institutions lies not in the imposition of sanctions but 'in the mobilisation of shame and in providing international scrutiny': Higgins (1979), 18.

entitlement of children in armed conflict to special protection and assist-ance,[5] and politicians and the media manipulate their plight for its emo-tional and symbolic value.

Clearly the law regarding child civilians operates in extreme circum-stances, and cannot fully achieve its aim of protecting children from the brutalities and upheavals of armed conflict. By their very nature, armed conflicts reflect human beings at their most ruthless and dangerous. In these situations, there may ultimately be no mercy even for children, despite the wide acknowledgement of their particular status.[6] Moreover, it is arguable that in some instances children are targeted in armed conflict precisely because they are so valued, in that they represent the future of a people or of a political ideology.[7]

Accordingly, there are inherent limits to the possible effectiveness of international law concerning child civilians. Nonetheless, within those limits there is scope for strengthening the impact of this body of law. This Chapter sets out possible strategies for doing so, after first summarising the contents of this book, and its core points.

8.1 SUMMARY

This book has attempted to address many aspects of international law concerning child civilians in situations of armed conflict. The chapters contain within them summaries of their main conclusions, and these will not be repeated here in any detail. What follows is therefore a brief description of the central points in each chapter.

First, Chapter 1 outlined the structure of the book and its three main aims: to describe the law concerning children in armed conflict and those mechanisms relevant to its implementation; to assess its impact; and to make recommendations for strengthening this. It then endeavoured to clarify certain key concepts and issues, such as 'childhood' and 'child', and to place these in the context of philosophical debates concerning the notion of children's rights, and in a cross-cultural perspective.

---

[5] This support is evidenced, e.g., by the wide ratification of the 1989 CRC and of other treaties (such as the ICCPR, the 1949 GCs, and the 1977 GPs) setting out special entitlements for children, as well as by the participation of so many governments in events such as the 1990 World Summit for Children, and other initiatives described in Chs. 2 and 4.

[6] The only certain solution to the problem of children becoming victims of armed conflict would be the eradication of armed conflict itself. Although this is a laudable aspiration, it seems, at least in the foreseeable future, too remote to merit serious consideration here (but see, e.g., J. Rotblat, 'Going to War on War', *Guardian*, 23 Jan. 1996). In any event, as one writer has pointed out, efforts to achieve world peace and to ameliorate the worst effects of armed conflict can co-exist: Hammarberg, in Aldrich and van Baarda (1994), 14.

[7] This point is also made by Kent (1990), 4. See also G. Kent, *Children in the International Political Economy* (Basingstoke, 1995), 83–4, quoting N. Boothby, 'Children and War', 10.4 *Cultural Survival Quarterly* 28 (1986).

Chapter 2 summarised international human rights law, global and regional, general and child-specific, pertinent to child civilians in situations of armed conflict. This chapter indicated that the principal human rights legal instruments all acknowledge to some extent the entitlement of children to special treatment as children, and, *inter alia*, their right not to be arbitrarily deprived of life.

The next two chapters examined relevant provisions of international humanitarian law in relation to child civilians, first (in Chapter 3) those concerning the civilian population generally, and then (in Chapter 4) those specifically referring to children. From these two chapters it was evident that there is a large body of law and many detailed provisions regarding the treatment of child civilians, particularly in the context of international armed conflict. These provisions impose both negative and positive obligations on belligerents, although the emphasis as regards child civilians is on the positive duty to protect, or actively assist, them. Central to these provisions are Article 77(1) of 1977 GP I, expressing the fundamental precept that children are entitled to 'special respect' in situations of international armed conflict, and the analogous, rather understated, Article 4(3) of 1977 GP II, applicable in non-international armed conflict.

Chapter 5 considered the status in customary law of various legal principles pertinent to the treatment of child civilians in situations of armed conflict. It argued that there is a customary norm, or developing customary norm, that such children are entitled to special treatment generally, and that this norm is particularly well-established in relation to the receipt of necessities.

The next chapter then described the numerous organisations and legal mechanisms that play a part in the monitoring, implementation, and/or enforcement of the law regarding child civilians. Of particular relevance here is the work of the Committee on the Rights of the Child. This chapter indicated, among other things, that a number of the pertinent supervisory mechanisms are under-used. Further, while there are advantages to the existence of so many possible avenues of redress, there may also be drawbacks, such as inefficiency, overlap, and possible gaps in provision.

Chapter 7 attempted to gauge the effectiveness of international law relevant to child civilians by examining three recent conflicts involving Iraq. The evidence here demonstrated, *inter alia*, that while specific legal provisions seemed to be little known or cited, a few of the underlying legal principles concerning child civilians were respected to some extent in certain of the situations considered. These underlying principles included the precepts that child civilians must, once more, be granted special treatment especially in the receipt of necessities, and that they must not be directly targeted.

8.2 CORE POINTS

In the chapters outlined above, one theme has particularly emerged from the analysis and description of the relevant human rights, humanitarian, and customary law principles, and state practice as manifested in the three conflicts involving Iraq. This theme, which gathered momentum from chapter to chapter, was the constant reference, in all these contexts, to the entitlement of children to special treatment.[8]

In examining that theme in terms of its customary status, this book has tended to adopt a rather cautious approach, arguing that it represents a norm, or emerging norm, that children in armed conflict are entitled to special treatment, at least in the provision of necessities.

However, international lawyers can, and perhaps should, take a more positive and active role in their interpretation of legal principles.[9] Adopting that approach, this book could have put forward a bolder argument in identifying, as the preferred option, the key customary norm regarding child civilians. Accordingly, although it was beyond the scope of this research to develop in depth the debate regarding relevant customary law, it is submitted here that it could arguably be considered a norm of customary law that children in armed conflict are entitled to special treatment as children generally,[10] and not just in relation to the receipt of necessities, such as food and medicine. In any event, the indications are that this more general entitlement is, at least, an emerging norm.[11]

In support of this contention, there is the strong evidence of the existence of a well-established legal principle—set out in various human rights and humanitarian legal instruments, and articulated, *inter alia*, in recent international conferences—that children, as such, are entitled to special treatment

---

[8] As already mentioned (sect. 1.5), this entitlement seems to be based on a variety of considerations including the particular vulnerability of children, their significance as the generation of the future, and their lack of access to political and economic power.

[9] See, e.g., Ramcharan, (in Ramcharan (ed.), (1985), 1), who argues, in relation to the international human rights lawyer, that if he 'is doing his job well, he has to be ahead of his colleagues in postulating new theories, in advocating the recognition of new norms and in advancing new forms of action for promoting . . . human rights.' See also Gardam (1993), 95.

[10] This entitlement to special treatment could, by analogy, be extended to children in other 'extremely difficult circumstances', but that argument cannot be considered in the context of this book.

[11] In sounding a note of caution regarding the efforts of international human rights lawyers to expand existing categories of customary norms (such as the arguments put forward here), Koskeniemi ((May 1990), 1962), observes that human rights principles may in fact be weakened by transformation into legal rules. He states that '[b]y remaining in the periphery, in the field of largely subconscious, private, moral-religious experience that defies technical articulation, human rights may be more able to retain their constraining hold on the way most people, and by extension, most states behave.' This is a valid point. Nonetheless, the fact remains that people and states frequently fail to make adequate provision for the protection of children in armed conflict, and therefore it may not suffice to leave this to their 'moral-religious experience'.

(see Chapters 2 and 4 above). Instruments such as the 1924 Declaration of the Rights of the Child emphasise that this entitlement particularly applies in situations of danger, and Article 77(1) of 1977 GP I expressly affirms this principle in relation to children in international armed conflict.[12] However, state practice, as represented in the three conflicts involving Iraq, is less convincing. Nonetheless, in certain of these conflicts the precept that children merited special treatment was honoured in principle, and, on occasion, in practice. In any event, without reiterating the arguments already presented in section 5.1.3 above, contrary state practice is not necessarily an insurmountable obstacle to the existence of a customary norm.

If it is accepted that there is a norm, or emerging norm, that children are entitled to special treatment in situations of armed conflict, this is, realistically, unlikely to result in a dramatic amelioration of their suffering, given the brutal reality of such conflicts. Further, as mentioned in section 5.3 above, this norm would not negate or outweigh other precepts regarding the conduct of armed conflict, such as the principle of proportionality or the concept of military objectives. However, acceptance of this norm may at least contribute to saving the lives of, or reducing injury and/or trauma to, some children in some armed conflicts.[13] Even if this were achieved only to a very limited extent, it would be worthwhile. As one authority notes regarding the laws of armed conflict generally, 'each even partial success means that a prisoner will not have been tortured or put to death, a handgrenade not blindly lobbed into a crowd, a village not bombed into oblivion: that, in a word, man has not suffered unnecessarily from the scourge of war'.[14]

In practical terms, wider acceptance of a norm that children are entitled to special treatment in armed conflict has implications, for example, in the training of military advisors and soldiers,[15] and in planning preventive strategies to safeguard children in such situations (as mentioned further in section 8.3 generally). Consideration should also be given to emphasising, as one component of this norm, the particular vulnerability of female children to sexual abuse, and their need for additional protection and care in this respect.[16]

---

[12] Nevertheless, 1977 GP I is not universally ratified, nor is Art. 77(1) firmly established as customary (see sect. 5.2.4).

[13] Further, if the entitlement of children to special treatment generally is accepted as a customary norm in human rights law, this entitlement could apply equally to children in situations of internal disturbance, even when the state concerned is not party to the relevant human rights treaties.

[14] Kalshoven (1987), 160. See also van Dongen (1991), 2, and Cassese (1986), 255.

[15] Certainly the eventual inclusion of such a norm in military manuals would be a significant step, and a goal worth aspiring to.

[16] There are strong arguments in favour of explicitly categorising rape, in the context of armed conflict, as a war crime (and see Graça Machel's comments in sect. 6.1.1.2. above).

In any event, regardless of the status of a norm concerning the special treatment of child civilians generally, it is submitted here that the entitlement of children to such treatment at least in the receipt of necessities can be regarded as a customary norm. As discussed in section 5.2.4, this norm currently consists of at least two elements: (1) an obligation on governments or others responsible to make strenuous efforts to provide necessities to children who are deprived of these in situations of armed conflict, and (2) a requirement that children must be among those given priority in circumstances where necessities are being supplied to civilians in situations of armed conflict. Governments, NGOs, and others concerned with children in armed conflict should endeavour to build on these precepts, and to exert pressure on those states or NGEs acting in breach of them, so that the practice of respecting children's entitlement to basic necessities in armed conflict becomes increasingly inviolable.

In this context, one writer argues that states should be under a positive duty to offer aid to children deprived of basic nutrition in armed conflict, whether or not their government requests this[17] (although, realistically, the issue of consent, particularly of the belligerents, would need to be addressed). In the same vein, another authority contends that food and other necessities for children should be exempted from measures imposing economic sanctions, or alternatively that sanctions should not be imposed at all without first evaluating their possible effect on children.[18] In addition, for example, the Programme of Action of the Copenhagen Summit (section 2.1.4 above) called for effective mechanisms for targeting necessities, in disaster situations, particularly to women and children.[19] These proposals all have merit, and indicate support for the concept that children in armed conflict are particularly entitled to receive necessities. Conversely, acceptance of this concept as a customary norm would increase pressure on states to give priority to the needs of children in armed conflict in any of the ways suggested in these proposals.

8.3 RECOMMENDATIONS

This Chapter has summarised, above, the contents of this book and certain core points. A number of recommendations regarding the relevant law will now be proposed. In formulating these, it is useful to begin by setting clear

[17] G. Kent, *Strategy for Implementing Nutrition Rights* (Hawaii, 1994), 20.

[18] Hammarberg, in Aldrich and van Baarda (1994), 12. The effect of sanctions on children in Iraq has already been outlined in sect. 7.2.2.3 as commented on in sect. 7.2.4.2 above. For further information on the effect of sanctions on children, see, e.g., UNICEF (1995), 22. See also recommendations of the Platform for Action of the 1995 Beijing Conference (para. 145(i)). [19] UN Doc. A/CONF.166/L.1, para. 41(f).

objectives and then identifying ways of achieving them.[20] Starting, then, with the objective: broadly, this is to strengthen the impact of international law regarding child civilians in armed conflict, so that it can more frequently achieve its aim of providing such children with a measure of special treatment, and minimising their risk of death and injury. Strategies for achieving this objective are discussed here in the context of each recommendation.

The suggestions set out below are not intended to be exhaustive either in terms of listing all conceivable possibilities or of examining each one in depth. Rather, they represent an exploration of certain ideas which may be more fully researched in later work, and which could contribute to the continuing effort to enhance the protection of child civilians in armed conflict. Given the orientation of this book, the wider question of non-legal strategies will not generally be addressed here.[21] Such strategies, which are of considerable importance, include, for example, political pressure and other such measures to control the arms trade; the manipulation of aid as a means of limiting armed conflict; the clearing of existing minefields;[22] and efforts to prevent armed conflicts by addressing their root causes.

The recommendations discussed in sections 8.3.1 to 8.3.8 below incorporate measures for the establishment of zones, and the concept of prevention more generally; a possible Liaison Group; a more active role for children themselves; an Ombudsman for Children and/or Special Rapporteur for Children in Armed Conflict; legislative reform; wider dissemination and ratification of the relevant law; and more effective use of certain other existing mechanisms.

8.3.1 Zones and the Concept of Prevention

In addition to a possible customary norm regarding special treatment, another concept of key importance in relation to children in armed conflict

---

[20] Thus the questions posed are: What is the goal? How can it be achieved? By whom? Where? The importance of proceeding from clearly articulated objectives is emphasised by G. Kent, *Implementing the Rights of Children in Armed Conflict* (Draft) (Hawaii, 21 May 1991), 7. See also Kent (1995), 98–9.

[21] For discussion of certain non-legal strategies regarding children in armed conflict, see, e.g., Abramson, *Children and War.* (1992), 4–14; Goodwin-Gill and Cohn (1994), 72–8 (in relation to child soldiers), and Ressler, Tortorici, and Marcelino generally. In this context, one appealing proposal (made by Dr Z. Ostrowski at a meeting of the NGO Committee on UNICEF) is that arms-producing countries contribute 10% of income from the production of arms to a Special Fund for Child Victims of Armed Conflict: D. Woods, *Children Bearing Military Arms* (Quaker UN Office, Geneva, Dec. 1993), 4. Many relevant proposals, both legal and non-legal, were also made at the 1994 Amsterdam conference on children in armed conflict, summarised in Aldrich and van Baarda. In addition, see the Anti-War Agenda of UNICEF (1995), 40–1, and the recommendations of the Intergovernmental Group of Experts for the Protection of War Victims: ICRC (1995), 33–8.

[22] Regarding this issue, see, e.g., Hammarberg, in Aldrich and van Baarda (1994), 13–14.

is that of establishing various types of zones for their protection. However, the establishment of zones should clearly not be at the expense of, or as a substitute for, efforts to create legal or political frameworks for the resolution of particular conflicts.

Indeed, the dangers of relying too heavily on the notion of safe areas, or of establishing these in inappropriate circumstances, have been amply demonstrated by the conflict in the former Yugoslavia, where some such zones have, in many respects, failed to fulfil their primary function of safeguarding their civilian inhabitants.[23] Nonetheless, the failure of these particular safe areas does not invalidate the concept of zones as such, and, even in the conflict in the former Yugoslavia, they may have saved many lives. This concept is accordingly discussed further below.

It will be recalled that in certain customary traditions, such as in some parts of Africa, fighting took place outside villages housing civilians, or civilians were removed to safe areas (section 4.1). The concept of zones for the protection of civilians may accordingly be rooted in the customary law of many peoples and is not simply a product of modern, or Western, international humanitarian notions.

As envisaged in 1949 GC IV and 1977 GP I, the different kinds of zones impose positive obligations to remove or protect those within them from the dangers of combat. If fully implemented, these provisions potentially offer child civilians a greater measure of protection than that available under most other relevant provisions of international humanitarian law, which aspire largely to improve aspects of the treatment of child civilians while they are embroiled in the armed conflict situation.

The distinction between the law concerning zones and that relating to the general treatment of child civilians is, nonetheless, not absolutely clear-cut. There is, for example, a degree of overlap between provisions regarding certain types of zones (such as 'hospital and safety zones' under Article 14 of 1949 GC IV) and those for the evacuation of children, in that both envisage the removal of children from the combat arena. Further, the concept of zones as set out in 1949 GC IV and 1977 GP I has become somewhat blurred in reality as it merges with the UNICEF concept of 'corridors of peace'. As already mentioned (section 4.2.1.2), these latter normally entail a short-term lull in the combat for a specific purpose, such

---

[23] The failure of these safe areas is due primarily to flaws in the UN mandate in former Yugoslavia. As one authority put it, 'to seek to establish a UN operation dedicated to ancillary relief . . . without a ceasefire in place is futile'. Further, 'we have chosen to respond to major unlawful violence, not by stopping that violence, but by trying to provide relief to the suffering': Higgins, 'The New United Nations' (1994), 19. Extensive coverage of inadequate UN protection of the 'safe areas' in former Yugoslavia (initially referred to by one newspaper as a 'Kurdish-style protection operation': *Guardian*, 28 Nov. 1992) can be found, e.g., almost daily in the *Guardian* in July 1995.

as the delivery to children of food, immunisation programmes, and/or medicines generally.

Despite these complications, the concept of zones, even in its more limited manifestation as 'corridors of peace', may in appropriate circumstances be particularly effective in alleviating the plight of child civilians.[24] This is not only because such zones, as indicated above, can remove or defend children entirely from the armed conflict situation, even if only for a short period.[25] It is also because there is increasingly the precedent that 'corridors of peace', as advocated strongly by UNICEF,[26] have been established and respected in a number of recent conflicts, not least to a limited extent in the 1991 Gulf War. The importance of instituting such 'special relief corridors' was also acknowledged in the 1994 Amsterdam Declaration and in the Declaration adopted at the 1990 World Summit, which, as already described, was endorsed by a large number of governments.[27] It therefore seems that efforts could and should be made to build on this concept, and increasingly establish, as a minimum, 'corridors of peace' in current and future conflicts involving children.

Moreover, there are strong arguments for governments, NGOs, and others concerned with child civilians in armed conflict to work towards the establishment of zones proper, as envisaged in 1949 GC IV and 1977 GP I. Depending on the circumstances, such zones may, by reason of their more permanent character, have the potential to provide child civilians with greater protection than the short-term 'corridors of peace'. Further, for similar reasons, provision for such zones should be extended to non-international armed conflicts where possible.[28]

As already mentioned (section 4.2.1.2), certain types of zones, such as neutralised zones (Article 15 of 1949 GC IV), are generally established once hostilities have erupted.[29] Preferably, however, attention should increasingly be directed towards procedures for setting up zones which can be established in times of peace, such as 'hospital and safety' and demilitarised

[24] See arguments in favour of the establishment of such zones in, e.g., Ressler, Tortorici, and Marcelino (1993), 30–1, 110, and 128. See also July 1987 UNICEF conference in Nairobi on children in armed conflict (n. 95, Ch. 6 above). Among other things, this conference passed a resolution to the effect that the safety of women and children should be the overriding concern, and African governments and the OAU were urged to promote children as zones of peace: Kent (1990), 21–2.

[25] In any event, initiatives such as immunisation and/or the supply of necessities in short-term cease-fires can clearly have a longer-term beneficial effect on child health.

[26] See, e.g., UNICEF (1995), 34–6.

[27] The ICRC also supports this concept. See ICRC (1995), 34–6.

[28] This was also recommended in the 1994 Amsterdam Declaration (sect. 4.4.2 above).

[29] Special agreements between the belligerents can also usefully be employed to create zones in these circumstances, and indeed to enhance the level of protection afforded to child civilians generally in particular armed conflicts (see sect. 3.1.2 above). A proposal calling for greater use of such agreements was made at the 1994 Amsterdam conference: Aldrich and van Baarda (1994), 78.

zones.[30] Agreements, in times of peace, providing for the establishment of zones, could be incorporated into preventive measures taken generally by governments, the UN, and others in attempting to anticipate future, or imminent, armed conflicts.[31]

The UN itself seems increasingly aware of the need for preventive measures.[32] This was evidenced, for example, in General Assembly Resolution 46/182,[33] adopted on 19 December 1991, not long after the uprisings in Iraq and their aftermath, and partly as a reaction to the perceived failures of the international community in responding to that crisis. Among other things, this resolution aimed to improve the ability of the UN to come to the aid of 'victims of disasters and emergency situations' (Preamble), and it repeatedly stressed the importance of preparedness and of prevention. It called for the UN to 'intensify efforts . . . for the systematic pooling, analysis and dissemination of early-warning information . . . on . . . emergencies' (paragraph 19)[34] emphasising that the UN should use the early-warning capacities of states, inter-governmental organisations and NGOs. Further, this resolution stated that, when the anticipated emergency was an armed conflict, attempts to prepare for and respond to this more effectively should include planning for the establishment of 'days and zones of tranquillity' and temporary relief corridors (paragraph 35(d)).[35]

Resolution 46/182 was followed, in June 1992, by the UN Secretary General's *Agenda For Peace*,[36] which, again, strongly emphasised the notion of prevention. This document specifically mentioned the usefulness of establishing demilitarised zones in conflict situations (paragraph 33).

In the context of prevention, for example, the Committee on the Rights

[30] The concept of 'hospital and safety' zones is particularly relevant here. This is because zones of this type specifically incorporate children under 15 (as well as other easily identifiable categories of vulnerable civilians), and are therefore perhaps more likely to be agreed in non-international armed conflicts, which are now the most prevalent form of armed conflict (see sect. 3.1 above).

[31] See, e.g., the work of International Alert, a fairly recent NGO which includes in its mandate preventive strategies in relation to armed conflicts: 'International Alert Objectives', 4 *International Alert Update* 2 (Nov. 1994).

[32] The notion of preventive measures in relation to armed conflict and human rights generally is also increasingly widely recognised. See particularly B. G. Ramcharan, *The International Law and Practice of Early-Warning and Preventive Diplomacy: The Emerging Global Watch* (Dordrecht, 1991). See also, e.g., recommendations of the ICRC conference on victims of war (ICRC, (1993), 429); Ramcharan, 'Strategies for the International Protection of Human Rights' (1991) generally, and Van Boven, in OMCT/SOS-Torture (1992), 183–192.

[33] UN GA Res. 46/182 (19 Dec. 1991).

[34] As already mentioned (sect. 6.1.3), certain UN bodies such as the DHA have as part of their mandates the operation of early-warning systems. However, the UN early-warning systems have recently been criticised for their failure, e.g., in relation to the Rwanda genocide, and changes have been recommended: See Eriksson (1996), *inter alia* 49 and 56–7.

[35] For an earlier GA resolution referring to the need for 'relief corridors for the distribution of emergency medical and food aid', see UN GA Res. 45/100 (14 Dec. 1990), para. 6.

[36] UN Doc. S/24111 (17 June 1992).

of the Child, in monitoring country reports, may glean information of use in identifying conflicts particularly affecting or likely to affect children. The Committee would then be in a position to make its concerns known within the UN more generally, and to question the parties regarding their strategies for protecting children, including through the establishment of zones.

Further, preventive measures can also be taken by those involved in military planning generally. To some extent, possible future conflicts can be anticipated.[37] In the interests of child civilians (and others), preparation for such conflicts should include discussion concerning the establishment of zones for their protection. Even if formal agreements do not result, the fact that the issue of zones has been addressed in principle may hasten their establishment if and when hostilities erupt (although, in actual conflict situations, the establishment of zones would be balanced against other military considerations (and see section 5.3 above)).

8.3.2 Liaison Group

Another concept which merits consideration here as a possible mechanism for strengthening the impact of the law regarding child civilians is that of a 'Liaison Group'. This body would be mandated to monitor developments, and to co-ordinate, oversee, and encourage action by existing organisations in relation to children in situations of armed conflict.

. A proposal to set up such a group was adopted at a 1991 international conference regarding children in armed conflict.[38] It has also been discussed by writers concerned at deficiencies and overlap in the work of organisations involved with children in armed conflict, and at gaps in their mandates.[39]

One writer in particular emphasises that there are no viable structures to safeguard children's rights in armed conflict and points to the constraints imposed, by their mandates, on the work of organisations such as UNICEF, the ICRC, and UNHCR.[40] In this context, the task of a Liaison Group

---

[37] E.g., in early 1992 reports appeared in national UK and US newspapers of a list drawn up by the Pentagon of seven possible wars (including anticipated military action against Iraq) in which the US might be embroiled in the following decade. See *Independent*, 18 Feb. 1992, referring to a report in the *New York Times*.

[38] Raoul Wallenberg Institute of Human Rights and Humanitarian Law, *Children of War: Report from the Conference on Children of War* (Lund, 1991), 45.

[39] See, e.g., Kent (1990), 25 and 26, and Kent (1995), 102. Another writer argues for the establishment of a new NGO if the task of enforcing human rights and humanitarian law generally in armed conflicts cannot be performed by those bodies already in existence. Hampson (1992), 137. A similar point is made by Brett: *Recruitment of Children* (1994) para. 3.2.3.

[40] Thus, e.g., the ICRC is concerned with armed conflict but not particularly with children, while UNICEF has traditionally been concerned with children but not specifically in armed conflict (although that may now be changing), and armed conflict forms only one part of the mandate of the Committee on the Rights of the Child: Kent (1990), 25.

would include that of strengthening the existing work of relevant organisations, and of exploring the possibilities of innovative action. Meeting once a year, it could bring together representatives of governments, international organisations, and NGOs, and 'go beyond formal rights and their associated instruments' to consider political, legal, and other measures for the protection of children in armed conflict.[41]

In the legal context, if a Liaison Group were to be established, it could also, for example, encourage the taking of cases regarding children in armed conflict before appropriate regional and international tribunals; the codification and/or revision of pertinent legislation; and the dissemination of information concerning existing law, perhaps with particular emphasis on the two key concepts discussed above (regarding children's entitlement to special treatment and the establishment of zones). Further, it could monitor and encourage wider participation in relevant debates and resolutions within the UN and other fora, with a view to increasing awareness of legal and other issues regarding children in armed conflict.

8.3.3 The Role of Children

In addition to measures such as an increased use of zones and the establishment of a Liaison Group, possible strategies to enhance the impact of international law regarding child civilians must include one factor which has been underplayed in this book: the role of children themselves.

There has been little discussion of this point here for the simple reason that the laws of armed conflict are drafted and enforced by adults, that armed conflicts are largely conducted by adults and at their instigation, and that children generally are excluded from decision-making in situations of armed conflict and tend to be powerless in these situations.

Nonetheless, a large number of those categorised under international law as 'children' are in fact perfectly competent to understand and participate in initiatives concerning children in armed conflict. Certainly, older children (up to the age of 18, according to the 1989 CRC definition) are normally competent in this respect. This was demonstrated, for example, by the intervention, in the Working Group drafting Article 38 of the 1989 CRC, of the Swedish Red Cross Youth (section 4.2.5.3.3 above). Indeed, Article 38 itself embodies the contradiction that it permits those classified by the Convention as 'children' (that is, from the age of 15) to be entrusted with the considerable responsibility of actively engaging in armed conflict as soldiers. Surely they must then be equally competent to engage in other issues concerning armed conflict.

In view of measures in the 1989 CRC regarding, for example, the importance of disseminating its provisions (Article 42) and of educating children

---

[41] *Ibid.*, 26.

for peace (Article 29(d)), it is to be hoped that children will increasingly be informed of the laws applicable to them in armed conflict, and be drawn into the debate regarding the part they play in such conflicts.[42] Article 29(d) is significant in this context, in emphasising the need for children to be educated to live responsibly 'in the spirit of understanding, peace, tolerance, equality of sexes, and friendship among all peoples'.[43]

Moreover, it may be that, in time, children will be encouraged to contribute directly to the work of the Committee on the Rights of the Child. This Committee could, for example, institute procedures whereby children themselves provide it with information and comment on country reports,[44] as well as possibly hearing cases concerning children under an individual complaints mechanism (see section 8.3.5 below).

8.3.4 Ombudsman for Children and/or Special Rapporteur on Children in Armed Conflict

Related to the concept of children participating directly in initiatives concerning their role in armed conflict is that of establishing, within the UN, an international Ombudsman for Children.[45]

The holder of this office would be charged with overseeing all issues of importance regarding children in the international context, including their protection in situations of armed conflict. In addition, such an Ombudsman could serve as a channel through which children, or those representing them, could put their concerns before international fora.

If an individual complaints mechanism were to be established under the 1989 CRC (see section 8.3.5 below), the need for an Ombudsman for Children would clearly be diminished. However, even in those circumstances, and depending on the evolution of the role of the Committee on the Rights of the Child, such an Ombudsman could still augment the work of that Committee by keeping abreast of wider political issues concerning children and placing such issues before the UN or other fora. An Ombudsman for Children could also be complementary to a possible Liaison Group which would focus entirely on co-ordinating work of existing organisations

[42] In countries where it is feasible to do so, they may then themselves publicise this issue, and put pressure on their governments to comply with international legal standards, in addition to possibly participating in international initiatives.

[43] The importance of educating children and others for peace is emphasised, e.g., in Vittachi (1993), 104–19.

[44] One writer argues for such mechanisms to be available to private parties generally: Gomien (1989), 5–7. Indeed, there is no bar in the 1989 CRC to a child becoming a member of the Committee on the Rights of the Child.

[45] Other writers have mentioned this possibility. See, e.g., Van Bueren (1995), 411–12. National ombudsmen could also perform a useful role, and indeed a number are already in existence. However, domestic initiatives such as this will not be discussed further here.

involved with children in armed conflict, while the role of the Ombudsman would be broader.

A variation on the concept of the more general Ombudsman is that of a UN Special Rapporteur on Children in Armed Conflict, specifically focusing on such children. The appointment of such a Rapporteur was recommended by the 1994 Amsterdam conference on children in armed conflict, and detailed proposals made.[46] These outlined the possible mandate of the Special Rapporteur, including tasks such as the gathering and dissemination of information concerning children in situations of armed conflict; authority to enter territory of a party to a conflict in order to verify alleged breaches of humanitarian law involving children, and in order to interview such children; the capacity to make his/her good offices and expertise available to the authorities concerned; and to make recommendations, which could be published, to such authorities. The recommendations made by the Special Rapporteur could include, among others, that the authorities concerned investigate the facts; that they halt the violations; and that they organise trials for those responsible, and/or pay compensation to the victims.

As a measure to strengthen the impact of legal rules concerning child civilians in armed conflict, the concept of such a Special Rapporteur has much in its favour. In this context, it is more directly relevant than a general Ombudsman for Children. These two roles could possibly co-exist and be complementary, but a proliferation of bodies with similar roles should be avoided, or problems may arise as regards overlapping and inefficient use of resources.

8.3.5 Legislative Reform

In addition to the possibilities considered above, legislative reform could contribute to improving the effectiveness of international law regarding child civilians in armed conflict.[47] This development could take the form of a new Optional Protocol to the 1989 CRC or, possibly, an entirely new treaty on children in armed conflict.

As already discussed, Article 38 of the 1989 CRC is profoundly disappointing in terms of raising standards in this area of the law. Nonetheless,

---

[46] See Aldrich and van Baarda (1994), 18, 67–9, and 124–6.

[47] Legislative reform aiming to enhance the impact of human rights and/or humanitarian law more generally is not discussed here. This would include, e.g., the establishment of a reporting system for international humanitarian law (B. G. Ramcharan, 'A Reporting System for International Humanitarian Law?', in E. Bello and B. Ajibola (eds.), *Essays in Honour of Judge Taslim Olawale Elias* (Dordrecht, 1992), 125–33); setting up an independent body to pronounce on the existence and nature of particular armed conflicts (R. Brett, *Recruitment of Children* (1994), 7; and see also Meron, *Human Rights in Internal Strife* (1987), 50), and numerous recommendations made in ICRC (1993).

this Article is only one facet of the large body of international law which relates to child civilians. The question then arises as to whether the limited impact of this body of law is due to failure to implement existing provisions or to the inadequacy of these provisions. Given that the pertinent measures are numerous and cover most legal issues regarding the treatment of child civilians in armed conflict, it seems, on balance, that their limited impact is largely attributable to failure to implement. A number of writers support this view.[48]

On the other hand, there are deficiencies in the body of existing law regarding child civilians, including vague terminology and certain lacunae (as emphasised in the introduction to this Chapter). Further, this law is confusingly dispersed throughout a number of treaties, both human rights and humanitarian, and is also rooted in customary law principles. This being the case, there is a strong argument for, at least, an attempt to codify all the existing law so that it is accessible and hence more readily understood and put into practice. For example, as matters stand, it may be no easy task for the Committee on the Rights of the Child, or perhaps certain governments themselves, to ascertain, for the purpose of state reports, the detailed content of 'international humanitarian law applicable to them in armed conflicts which are relevant to the child' under Article 38(1) of the 1989 CRC.

However, codification would be no simple undertaking. Any attempt at this would have to begin by tackling the question of how wide to cast the net. At the very least, the resulting treaty should contain existing provisions directly relevant to child civilians as set out in 1949 GC IV and the 1977 GPs (described above, in Chapter 4). At the other extreme, a more ambitious remit could include relevant customary principles and a wider range of humanitarian law, as well as human rights law. This more ambitious task would undoubtedly prove controversial.

In either case, whether the law is simply codified or is revised, an Optional Protocol to the 1989 CRC or a new treaty would be required.[49] As mentioned above (section 6.1.1.2), two Optional Protocols to the 1989 CRC are, at the time of writing, under consideration in the UN. However, when the possibility of a new treaty regarding children in armed conflict was mooted at an international conference on this subject in 1991, concern was voiced that attempts to extend the scope of Article 38 might precipitate

---

[48] See, e.g., Ressler, Tortorici and Marcelino (1993), 24, and Aldrich and van Baarda (1994), 94. A similar point is made concerning international humanitarian law generally in ICRC, 184 *ICRC Bulletin* 2 (May 1991).

[49] One authoritative document expresses a qualified preference for adopting protocols to existing treaties rather than drafting new treaties: UN Doc. A/44/668 (8 Nov. 1989) (the 'Alston Report', n. 52, Ch. 6 above), paras. 32 and 189–92. This also argues for implementation to be the priority (paras. 24 and 25), and for the drafting of non-binding standards, rather than new treaties (para. 28).

initiatives by some states to tamper with other Articles in the Convention, and the whole process could become counter-productive. The obvious point was also made that states unwilling to comply with the higher standards would simply not ratify the new instrument.[50]

It may be, therefore, that the task of drawing up a major new instrument regarding children in armed conflict should wait, while efforts are made to strengthen enforcement of the existing body of law, and to improve standards in domestic legislation. Indeed, according to a UN policy document, '[i]n the UN context more resources devoted to standard setting might also mean less resources available for other activities, including implementation.' This document accordingly argues for a feasibility study to be undertaken before the drafting of new instruments,[51] and it would seem advisable to conduct such a study in the present instance.

Nonetheless, it is likely that the time will come to formulate a new treaty, or Protocol to the 1989 CRC, on the international law concerning children in armed conflict. An instrument of this nature should clearly codify the existing law, and emphasise key elements, such as the entitlement of children to special treatment and the concept of establishing zones for their protection. Even if it only codified the law, this treaty could also usefully aim to incorporate the highest standards expressed in the relevant instruments.[52]

Assuming, however, this new instrument may go beyond codification and may revise and augment the existing law to some extent, it seems worth making a few preliminary suggestions here. These are set out below simply as questions which would obviously require full debate in the drafting process.

First, should a new treaty concerning children in armed conflict incorporate an individual complaints system, analogous to the Optional Protocol to the ICCPR? If so, it would then be open to children, or those acting on their behalf,[53] to present cases alleging violations of the relevant law to the Committee on the Rights of the Child or other designated body. This complaints system could apply to all the provisions of the new instrument. Alternatively, it could relate only to certain provisions, for example those of central importance (such as the prohibition against direct targeting of child civilians) or those which may particularly require independent monitoring (such as the treatment of child internees). There is already a precedent for a selective complaints mechanism in the Inter-American system, which

---

[50] Raoul Wallenberg Institute (1991), 43. Although the conference discussion focused on child soldiers, the points outlined here apply equally to child civilians.

[51] UN Doc. A/44/668, paras. 23–8 and 146–70.

[52] See reference to this issue in Cohn (1991), 105–6. Discussion by governments of such a document, even one limited to codifying existing obligations, could in itself raise awareness of this body of law and possibly give rise to a fruitful debate.

[53] Explicit provision could be made here for NGOs to have *locus standi*.

features a complaints procedure that applies only to certain Articles.[54] The drawback with this proposal generally, however, is that states are, in practice, highly unlikely to agree to subject themselves to a complaints procedure concerning abuses suffered by children in situations of armed conflict.[55]

Secondly, should this new law provide for a right to compensation for children unlawfully injured in armed conflict and/or those claiming on their behalf or on behalf of children unlawfully killed? A study making recommendations to this effect as regards serious human rights violations is, at the time of writing, under consideration within the UN.[56] It is certainly arguable that rights to compensation should apply, or be extended to, civilian victims of serious violations of human rights and humanitarian law committed during situations of armed conflict.[57]

Thirdly, should this treaty contain one set of rules which would be applicable to children in both international and non-international armed conflict? As already mentioned (Note 26, Chapter 3), a number of international lawyers feel that the distinction between these two categories of conflict cannot be justified in international humanitarian law generally, and this argument may have particular force as regards the protection of children (although, again, it could prove unpopular with governments).

Fourthly, should new legislation regarding children in armed conflict incorporate provisions explicitly dealing with the protection of such children in internal disturbances? Given that many conflicts involving child civilians are categorised as internal disturbances, and bearing in mind the subjectivity of such categorisation, there is an element of urgency in drafting rules concerning these. As mentioned above (section 3.1.2), progress has been made in so doing, although the existing draft rules do not exclusively focus on children. On the other hand, it must be borne in mind that, in the drafting of the 1989 CRC, attempts to include provision regarding internal disturbances met with total failure, largely owing to the reluctance of governments to permit international scrutiny of such situations.

[54] See, e.g., the individual petition system under the ADRDM, which applies only to certain rights, such as the right to life, liberty, and personal security (Art. I): Buergenthal, Norris, and Shelton (1990), 5–6.

[55] In this context states would tend to invoke in their defence the argument of military necessity. Further, states might well feel that their military activities are sufficiently curtailed by existing sanctions, such as possible UN enforcement action; provisions concerning grave breaches in the 1949 GCs and 1977 GPs (which would apply to flagrant violations involving children); and other measures outlined in Ch. 6 above.

[56] UN Doc. E/CN.4/Sub.2/1993/8 (2 July 1993), 'Study Concerning the Right to Restitution, Compensation and Rehabilitation for Victims of Gross Violations of Human Rights and Fundamental Freedoms'.

[57] Concerning compensation for children in armed conflict, see recommendation of the 1994 Amsterdam conference (sect. 8.3.4); ICRC (1993), 438, and, in the context of nutrition rights, Kent (1994), 8 and 9.

Fifthly, should the new treaty shift the burden of proof and incorporate a presumption of guilt on the part of a particular State Party, in circumstances where allegations were made against that state of grave violations of international law concerning child civilians, and fact-finding efforts by the international community are blocked? (This was the scenario, for example, in relation to the 1987–8 chemical weapon attacks on the Iraqi Kurds (section 7.2.4.1 above)). If so, this presumption could possibly then lead to the imposition of selective sanctions (taking account of the needs of children and other civilians) and/or other measures as appropriate. Again, an analogous procedure exists in the inter-American system, where the Inter-American Committee on Human Rights has established that, if a government does not respond within a certain period to an allegation regarding serious breach of its obligations, the Committee will assume that the facts alleged are true.[58]

These are, then, five concepts which would, among others, merit closer consideration if new legislation regarding children in armed conflict were to be formulated.

More generally, an Optional Protocol to the 1989 CRC, which established a complaints procedure regarding the provisions of the Convention as a whole, would clearly also be of benefit as regards children in armed conflict. A number of writers have discussed this possibility.[59] In the context of enhancing the impact of international law concerning child civilians, it is submitted here that an Optional Protocol of this nature would be a positive development, and particularly so in the absence of a new instrument specifically for children in armed conflict.

Further, in the context of legislative reform, a ban on the production, use, and export of landmines would substantially contribute to limiting the harm caused to children and other civilians by armed conflicts and their aftermath. Although such a ban was rejected at both the 1995 and 1996 conferences to review the 1980 Inhumane Weapons Convention, there will undoubtedly be renewed efforts to enact it in future.

Finally, in relation to the drafting of new law concerning children in armed conflict, mention must be made of the potential of regional and/or domestic legislation. Although this question cannot be discussed here, since the focus is on global organisations and mechanisms, it is worth noting that new regional and domestic instruments may, in the interim, prove the most effective method for working towards consolidation and revision of this

---

[58] See Art. 42 of the Regulations of the Inter-American Commission on Human Rights, regarding default judgments: OAS, *Basic Documents Pertaining to Human Rights in the Inter-American System* (Washington, DC., 1988), 90.

[59] See, *inter alia*, Van Bueren (1995), 410. Rights of individual petition are increasingly found in analogous treaties. Thus, at the time of writing, work was under way within the UN on drafting such an Optional Protocol to the 1979 CEDAW. See also provision in the ACRWC for the submission of communications (sect. 2.2.3.2 above).

body of law, since it may be some time before new international legislation is drafted. Individual governments, organisations, and others concerned with this issue could therefore fruitfully focus their efforts on domestic and regional fora at this stage.[60]

8.3.6 Dissemination and Ratification

Another strategy which is an essential step towards strengthening the impact of international law regarding child civilians is the wider dissemination of this body of law[61] and more extensive ratification of the relevant treaties.

Of particular importance here is the task of disseminating, to soldiers and others in the military establishment, the fundamental principles of international law regarding child civilians.[62] Information given in this context could start by emphasising that children in situations of armed conflict should generally be entitled to special treatment, and then elaborate on this by specifying the more detailed provisions of international humanitarian law discussed above in Chapter 4.

The need for improved training of soldiers has been amply demonstrated by the numerous reports of corruption and/or abuse (specifically including abuse of children) attributed to soldiers, including those serving in UN forces,[63] in a variety of different armed conflicts. Indeed, international humanitarian law itself imposes a duty on States Parties to the various treaties to make their provisions known to both the military and civilians (as

[60] The ACRWC (although not exclusively concerned with children in armed conflict, and, at the time of writing, not in force), clearly illustrates the usefulness of regional treaties as a means of raising standards in the relevant law.

[61] Indeed, this is intended as one of the primary functions of this book. The importance of dissemination of international humanitarian law generally has been emphasised by a number of writers. See, e.g., Goodwin-Gill and Cohn (1994), 180; Aldrich and Gasser, in Fox and Meyer (eds.) (1993), 13 and 25 respectively; ICRC (1993), 378–9; and many references in Ressler, Tortorici, and Marcelino (1993), including 20, 24, 35, 76, 77, and 130.

[62] In relation to children in armed conflict, the importance of educating the military in the relevant law has been raised, e.g., by Mr Muntarbhorn with the Committee on the Rights of the Child (sect. 6.1.1.2 above), and was mentioned in the 1994 Amsterdam conference: Aldrich and van Baarda (1994), 77. See also UNICEF (1995), 40, and ICRC (1995), 35.

[63] As regards UN forces, AI, e.g., has published a report referring to the failure of UN peacekeepers to respect human rights in some cases, and has made recommendations concerning this issue: AI, *Peace-Keeping and Human Rights* (London, 1994). See also Aldrich and van Baarda (1994), 129–30; A. Arnig, 'Child Prostitution in Cambodia: Did the UN Look Away?', 10.3 *International Children's Rights Monitor* 4 (1993); 'Graça Machel Joins DCI's Concern', 11.4 *International Children's Rights Monitor* 33 (1994/5); 'Sexual Exploitation of Children by UN Blue Helmets: A Case in Liberia', *ibid.*, 46; K. Maier, 'New World Disorder', *Independent Magazine*, 31 July 1993 (photograph of UN soldier beating a child); *Independent*, 27 Aug. 1993 and *Guardian*, 12 Jan. 1995 (regarding corruption among UN troops); and *Independent on Sunday*, 13 Nov. 1994 (regarding the torturing to death of a 16-year old Somali by UN troops).

in Article 144 of 1949 GC IV and Article 83 of 1977 GP I). Moreover, military training should ensure that soldiers are informed of their possible personal liability for the commission of grave breaches,[64] obviously including those affecting children.

In this context it is also of interest that military lawyers meet every three years for the International Congress of the International Society for Military Law and the Law of War. This could provide a useful forum for discussion and dissemination of key issues in international law regarding child civilians or children in armed conflict generally.

Moreover, awareness of this body of law is equally essential among members of armed opposition groups. Governments, political bodies, NGOs, and others who have friendly relations with such groups could encourage them to observe, among other things, international law regarding child civilians.[65] Indeed, in situations where an NGE is externally financed, pressure could be brought to bear on the supporting country to make such finance dependent on NGE compliance with the law.[66]

Further, wider dissemination of this body of law could be achieved through the international law-making process itself. Thus, for example, the central provisions regarding child civilians, such as their entitlement to special protection as articulated in Article 77 of 1977 GP I, could be identified and invoked, where applicable, in new international legal instruments. In addition, such provisions could be specifically cited in relevant UN resolutions, for example in relation to current armed conflicts, as was so conspicuously not done in relation to the three conflicts involving Iraq.

As one authority observes, '[t]he repeated invocation of rights assists in the perception of them as normative, and assists in turn in their implementation', so that '[i]nvocation is one of the building blocks of compliance.'[67] It is axiomatic that, as the relevant provisions become more widely known, the likelihood of their being implemented increases.

In this regard, the significance of public education must not be underestimated. One writer argues for the publication of information concerning children in armed conflict as part of the 'politics of embarrassment'.

---

[64] See Green (1993), 275 and 292. Further, this writer refers to a Model Agreement prepared by the UN Secretary General (May 1991) to the effect that governments must ensure that their forces serving in the UN are acquainted with, *inter alia*, the provisions of the 1949 GCs and the 1977 GPs: *ibid.*, 325.

[65] A similar proposal is made by Woods in relation to child soldiers: Woods (1993), 12.

[66] See, e.g., Rädda Barnen, *Position Paper on Children in War* (Stockholm, June 1990), 6, and Raoul Wallenberg Institute (1991), 46. See also Goodwin-Gill and Cohn (1994), 65 and 77.

[67] R. Higgins, 'Some Thoughts on the Implementation of Human Rights', 89/1 Bulletin of Human Rights, at 61 (1990). See also R. Higgins 'Encouraging Human Rights' 2 *London School of Economics Quarterly* 250 (1988); Cassese (1986), 279, and Meron (1989), 76.

He observes that public education should show what can be done to address the relevant problems, rather than being entirely negative, and that '[r]emarkably few of the studies and reports on children and war even mention the legal dimensions'.[68] Channels such as the ICRC (see further discussion in section 8.3.7.4 below), the media, NGOs generally, and reports of international conferences[69] can usefully contribute to wider dissemination of pertinent information, including legal principles.

As a basis for more effective action on behalf of child civilians, it is essential, too, that an effort is made systematically to collect reliable information on current armed conflicts affecting such children (which would probably be all current armed conflicts); the approximate numbers of such children; and the ways in which they are affected. Ideally, a central international database should be established, as has recently been accomplished in relation to child soldiers.[70]

Finally, another factor that could contribute to strengthening observance of the law regarding child civilians would be increased ratification of all the relevant legal instruments, although some of these (for example, the 1949 GCs and the 1989 CRC) are already almost universally ratified. Such instruments would include the 1977 GPs; the ICCPR and its Optional Protocol; as well as regional treaties such as the ACRWC, all of which, as has been seen, contain relevant provisions of importance.

8.3.7 Existing Mechanisms

As well as wider dissemination and ratification of the relevant law as a strategy to enhance its impact, better use could be made of existing mechanisms generally. Such mechanisms would include the principal organs of the UN, in addition to UN-related bodies such as the Human Rights Committee and the Committee on the Rights of the Child, which are discussed below in this context. Inter-state accountability and the ICRC and NGOs are then considered. The focus is on global mechanisms, although, again, regional and domestic procedures are clearly also significant.

---

[68] Kent (1991), 9. Another writer comments that humanitarian law seems less well-known than human rights law, and that this applies even to NGOs working with children in armed conflict: Hampson (1992), 136.

[69] E.g., the Declaration and Plan of Action of the 1990 World Summit for Children (while not referring to specific legal provisions) emphasised the key concepts that children in 'especially difficult circumstances', including situations of armed conflict, require special protection, and that there should be a commitment to take action to that end, such as establishing 'corridors of peace' (sect. 2.2.4 above).

[70] See Rädda Barnen. 1 'Children of War: A Newsletter on Child Soldiers from Rädda Barnen' (Oct. 1995). Information gathering was also proposed by the 1994 Amsterdam Conference as one of the possible functions of the Special Rapporteur on Children in Armed Conflict (sect. 8.3.4 above).

8.3.7.1 The UN Generally

As regards making better use of existing mechanisms, the UN obviously has a role to play, despite the many pressures, difficulties, and criticisms it faces.[71] Central here, of course, would be a greater awareness of the plight of child civilians and the relevant law in the context of UN action taken in respect of various armed conflicts and/or at their conclusion. Thus, during armed conflicts, it may not be unduly optimistic to expect that the situation of children could increasingly be one of the factors taken into account in UN decisions concerning, for example, sanctions, mediation, and the establishment of safe areas. At the cessation of hostilities, this consideration should again feature in UN decisions, for example, as regards peace-keeping strategies.

In relation to the more routine work of the UN, states could be encouraged regularly to initiate public discussions, in fora such as the General Assembly, regarding children in particular situations of armed conflict.[72] Indeed, there could be regular items included on the agendas of appropriate UN bodies, concerning, for example, 'Human Rights in Armed Conflict'.[73] Further, governments, other concerned bodies such as UNICEF, and NGOs could intensify their efforts to ensure that the issue of children in armed conflict is raised whenever pertinent to matters already on the agenda of the different UN fora, and perhaps particularly within the Sub-Commission on the Prevention of Discrimination and Protection of Minorities, the Commission on Human Rights, the General Assembly, and the Security Council.[74] The High Commissioner for Human Rights also has a role in this context. Discussions concerning children in armed conflict could be useful simply in raising international awareness of such children and of the pertinent law.[75] However, it would be preferable for such discussions to be sharply focused, with clearly-defined and achievable goals for action on behalf of child civilians, among others.

[71] Nonetheless, as has recently been so graphically demonstrated in the former Yugoslavia, the UN is far from omnipotent and 'can move no further than the individual Members allow the Organisation to go': T. van Boven, 'United Nations and Human Rights: A Critical Appraisal', in Cassese (ed.) (1979), 120.

[72] As already mentioned (sect. 6.1.2), such discussions can be initiated by communications from organisations, or even individuals, as long as a state requests the discussion.

[73] A proposal to this effect, in relation to the Commission on Human Rights, was made by R. Brett, *Report on the 1994 UN Commission on Human Rights: 31 January to 11 March 1994* (Quaker UN Office, Geneva, 1994), 14.

[74] This is especially important within the GA, where majority resolutions reflect the consensus of a large segment of the international community, and in the Security Council, given the binding nature of its resolutions and its role in enforcing peace and security. Indeed, the Vienna Declaration recommended that matters concerning children's rights be regularly reviewed by relevant UN organs and mechanisms. UN Doc. A/CONF.157/24 (Part 1) Chap. III, para. 281.

[75] This process seems already to be under way, to the extent that e.g., a recent UN General Assembly resolution (UN GA Res. 50/153 (see n. 29, Ch. 6)) calls, *inter alia*, for states to respect Arts. in 1949 G.C. IV, the 1977 GPs, and the 1989 CRC 'which accord children affected by armed conflict special protection and treatment' (para. 7).

8.3.7.2 *UN-Related Bodies*

In addition to the principal organs of the UN, certain other bodies connected with the UN or operating under its ægis could be particularly influential in enhancing the effectiveness of international law regarding child civilians. The two to be considered below in this context, by way of example, are the Human Rights Committee and the Committee on the Rights of the Child, although bodies such as UNICEF also have an important role to play.

8.3.7.2.1 *The Human Rights Committee*

The Human Rights Committee could undoubtedly perform a more active role in monitoring compliance with aspects of international law concerning child civilians, both through its scrutiny of state reports and through the individual complaints system under the Optional Protocol. This Committee could also, in principle, act in inter-state disputes (see further section 8.3.7.3 below).

Through the reporting system the Human Rights Committee is empowered to interrogate states involved in armed conflicts about, *inter alia*, the protection they afford to child civilians both in practice and in theory. As mentioned above (section 6.1.3.3), in scrutinising reports of such states, the Human Rights Committee could emphasise the importance of ICCPR provisions regarding, for example, the child's right to special protection (Article 24), in conjunction with the general right to life (Article 6) and the prohibition against torture (Article 7). NGOs and others again have a role here, in providing receptive Committee members with information about the situation of child civilians in specific countries, and in indicating questions which could be put to particular governments.[76]

In relation to the Optional Protocol, the Committee's role, while important in influencing state practice, is circumscribed by a number of factors. These include the fact that states involved in situations of armed conflict may not be party to this Protocol even if they are party to the ICCPR. Further, the Committee is limited by the complaints that find their way to it, and thus does not necessarily have the opportunity to hear cases relating to child civilians. Finally, the Committee's powers of enforcement under the Optional Protocol are somewhat restricted (see section 6.1.3.3).

Nonetheless, there is good reason to make the fullest possible use of the human rights machinery established under the ICCPR and its Optional

---

[76] Given the obvious role of the Committee in relation to human rights issues arising from situations of armed conflict, one writer questions why NGOs have not made greater use of the ICCPR reporting system to bring pressure to bear on governments regarding violations of both humanitarian and human rights law: Hampson (1992), 136. Another writer makes a number of proposals for more active involvement of NGOs in the work of the Committee: Cassese (1979).

Protocol, to address violations of human rights and, indirectly, humanitarian law, regarding child civilians in situations of armed conflict. There is clearly considerable overlap between some of the key provisions of international human rights and humanitarian law.[77] Further, since there is currently no individual complaints mechanism as such in humanitarian law, the Optional Protocol could usefully fulfil this role in appropriate circumstances.

8.3.7.2.2 *The Committee on the Rights of the Child*

As regards strengthening observance of the law concerning child civilians, the Committee on the Rights of the Child has already made constructive use of its powers under the 1989 CRC, particularly in proposing the UN study on children in armed conflict.[78] There are many possibilities for its continuing to do so.[79]

Certainly the reporting system under the 1989 CRC, as with that under the ICCPR, affords much scope for the Committee on the Rights of the Child to take an active role in monitoring state compliance with international law concerning child civilians in armed conflict. Indeed, given that the 1989 CRC, unlike the ICCPR, focuses specifically on children in armed conflict, the potential inherent in the Committee on the Rights of the Child is even greater.

Thus, although Article 38 is deeply flawed, the 1989 CRC does enable the Committee on the Rights of the Child to question states on their compliance with 'international humanitarian law applicable to them in armed conflicts which are relevant to the child' (Article 38(1)). States must also satisfy the Committee that they have taken 'all feasible measures to ensure protection and care of children who are affected by an armed conflict' (Article 38(4)). In this context, the Committee could remind governments, *inter alia*, of existing treaty mechanisms regarding responsibility for grave breaches of international humanitarian law (for example, under the 1949

[77] Hampson argues strongly for the use of human rights instruments to expose violations of humanitarian law. She observes that deliberate or reckless injury in armed conflict to any person who is not a lawful object of attack could amount to a violation of, e.g., the prohibition on cruel and inhuman treatment under the ICCPR, unless it was for the benefit of the victim: Hampson (1992), 133–4.

[78] It is to be hoped that the publication of this study and its recommendations will have a considerable impact on this area of law and its implementation. (See sect. 6.1.1.3 above.)

[79] In addition to the possibilities outlined in the text here, one writer has made detailed recommendations to the Committee on the Rights of the Child regarding ways of addressing the problem of children in armed conflict. See generally Abramson, *Children and War* (1992), and particularly 30–7. See also, e.g., suggestions made by Brett (*Recruitment of Children* (1994), 7) that the Committee should consider 'the way in which the provisions of the 1989 CRC are translated into domestic legislation, and the legal penalties attached to breaches of them', and that its mandate be expanded 'to enable it to investigate and pronounce on alleged violations of the Convention'.

GCs), and of the importance of military training in this body of law particularly as it concerns children (and see section 6.2.3 above).

The Committee on the Rights of the Child could also assist in clarifying the content of international humanitarian law regarding children in armed conflict, and therefore the task of states reporting under Article 38, by issuing a General Comment on this (see section 6.1.1.2).

Moreover, although the 1989 CRC does not at this stage incorporate individual or interstate complaints mechanisms, many of its existing implementation provisions can serve to put pressure on States Parties for greater compliance with the body of law concerning child civilians. These provisions include: the obligation of states to publicise their reports widely in their own countries (Article 44(6)), and to make the contents of the Convention known (Article 42); as well as the publication of the Committee's comments on state reports (under Article 45(d)) and its biennial report to the General Assembly (Article 44(5)).

In addition, the Committee could in future request, via the Secretary General and the General Assembly, further studies on the situation of children in armed conflict or on particular aspects of this problem (under Article (45(c)). Also, under Article 45(a) of the 1989 CRC the Committee may facilitate, for example through the convening of meetings or workshops, the provision of advice and technical assistance to governments desiring to improve implementation of international standards for the protection of child civilians.[80]

Nonetheless, despite the many opportunities presented by the 1989 CRC for enhancing the impact of international law regarding child civilians, it is necessary to be realistic about its potential in this sphere. After all, the question of children in armed conflict is only one of the many pressing issues that this Convention, and the overburdened Committee on the Rights of the Child, must address.

8.3.7.3 Inter-state Accountability Generally

In terms of existing mechanisms for strengthening the impact of international law regarding child civilians, there is also the vexed question of inter-state accountability for fundamental violations of this body of law. Certainly such violations can include the killing, wounding, or other serious abuse of child civilians in situations of armed conflict. Grave abuses of this kind could amount to *erga omnes* violations such that other states may legitimately take action against the offending state.[81] Indeed, in the context

---

[80] As mentioned in sect. 6.1.1.1, such meetings could call on the expertise of the specialised agencies, UNICEF, and 'other competent bodies'.

[81] As already mentioned (n. 8, Ch. 5), *erga omnes* violations injure all states so that every state is competent to bring actions against the breaching state. Such violations have been defined to include torture and arbitrary killing: Meron (1989), 194.

of the 1991 Gulf War and its aftermath there was much talk of the duty of states to intervene in situations where another state seriously breaches human rights and/or humanitarian law (see Chapter 7).

In this context, states can call each other to account within the UN generally (section 8.3.7.1 above). Other possible inter-state complaints mechanisms could include those set out in the ICCPR (where it currently remains a dead letter) or proceedings before the ICJ. Indeed, in the event of breaches of international law concerning child civilians, effective recourse to any of the existing inter-state mechanisms discussed in Chapter 6 would clearly strengthen the impact of this body of law. Thus, for example, in relation to international humanitarian law, such mechanisms would include the duty of States Parties, under Article 1 of the 1949 GCs, to respect and ensure respect for these Conventions in all circumstances;[82] measures in the 1949 GCs and the 1977 GPs regarding grave breaches of their provisions; perhaps the work of the International Fact-finding Commission (Article 90 of 1977 GP I); and the establishment of international military tribunals.[83] As regards the latter, it is to be hoped, as already mentioned, that such tribunals and other courts, such as the ICJ, will, in their case law, increasingly contribute to a greater awareness of international law concerning child civilians, and to its observance.

Moreover, in relation to both international humanitarian law and human rights law, another possible mechanism for inter-state accountability would be through an international criminal court, when (and if) established (section 6.2.1 above).

8.3.7.4 NGOs and the ICRC

In considering existing mechanisms that could assist in strengthening the impact of international law concerning child civilians in armed conflict, further mention must be made of NGOs and the ICRC. The role of NGOs generally has already been referred to in this Chapter, for example in the context of contributing to a Liaison Group; providing information to UN bodies; and facilitating dissemination of the relevant law.

The focus here is therefore mainly on the ICRC, which merits particular attention as the non-governmental body most explicitly and actively concerned with dissemination of international humanitarian law. However, despite its prominent role in this field, the ICRC's Press Releases and other public statements concerning the three conflicts involving Iraq rarely made

---

[82] In this context, one writer suggests, e.g., that a third-party state could act on its obligation to 'ensure respect' for the 1949 GCs by invoking the jurisdiction of the ICJ: Gasser, in Fox and Meyer (eds.) (1993), 41. For comment on the importance of complying with Art. 1, 1949 GC IV, see, e.g., Hampson (1992), 137; Rädda Barnen (June 1990), 8, and Woods (1993), 10.

[83] On this point, Meron, e.g., emphasises, as regards the war crimes tribunal for the former Yugoslavia, that '[a] successful war crimes tribunal for Yugoslavia will enhance deterrence in future cases: failure may doom it': Meron (1993), 127.

specific mention of the situation of child civilians (section 7.5.2 above). This may be due to the ICRC policy of generally incorporating child civilians in its work with the civilian population as a whole. Nonetheless, there are strong arguments in favour of the ICRC more frequently invoking the law regarding child civilians, where applicable, in its public statements and other initiatives. Not least among these is the gravity of the situation of child civilians in many armed conflicts, and the general lack of awareness of the relevant legal provisions.[84]

Further, the four-yearly International Conference of the Red Cross, in which the majority of governments participate, is an influential forum in which to continue efforts to strengthen observance of international humanitarian law affecting child civilians.[85] Discussions and resolutions could focus on ways of achieving more effective implementation of certain key concepts, such as, first, the developing norm of children's entitlement to special treatment generally in armed conflict and, secondly, the establishment of safety zones and/or 'corridors of peace'. As discussed in section 6.3.1.1 above, resolutions passed at these ICRC conferences carry considerable weight, and, in a political context, participating governments could be held accountable for non-compliance with these.[86]

8.3.7.5 1999 Hague Peace Conference

Finally, as regards existing mechanisms that could enhance the effectiveness of international humanitarian law concerning child civilians, mention should be made of the Hague Peace Conference. These conferences take place very rarely,[87] and they constitute a significant gathering of states for the purpose of discussing and revising international humanitarian law.

One such conference may take place in 1999 (the centenary of the first such conference), and here again key issues could be debated and disseminated regarding child civilians in armed conflict, such as the possible customary status of a norm providing for their special treatment, and the implications of this; and the importance of appropriate military training. Governments, NGOs, and others concerned with improving implementation of this body of law could accordingly work to include, on the agenda of such a conference, these and other pertinent topics.

---

[84] Indeed, the same arguments would apply equally to public statements made and initiatives taken by any NGO in this context.

[85] As mentioned in sect. 6.3.1.2 above, the 26th International Conference of the Red Cross passed a resolution referring, in part, to children in armed conflict. Moreover, the ICRC can, and does, host other conferences on pertinent subjects, such as the 1991 conference on war victims (n. 143, Ch. 4 above).

[86] National Red Cross and Red Crescent Societies, too, could be encouraged, within their own countries, to raise awareness of the plight of child civilians, and of the relevant law.

[87] To date only two such conferences have been held, the first in 1899, and the second in 1907.

8.3.8 Preferred Options

In summary, any of the recommendations outlined above would enhance the effectiveness of the law concerning child civilians, and all merit serious consideration. Some of the suggestions made, such as those regarding zones, build on important existing concepts.

In terms of new initiatives which seem likely to have the greatest impact, it is submitted here that the most useful could be the establishment of a Liaison Group; the appointment, within the UN, of a Special Rapporteur on Children in Armed Conflict; the eventual drafting of a new instrument concerning children in armed conflict; and, where feasible, greater involvement of children themselves in this issue.

8.4 CAVEATS

Before concluding this book, a point should be made concerning difficulties with the language used. As already mentioned in section 1.4.1 above, too much emphasis on phrases such as 'children's rights' reduces the concept to a cliché. Other, more precise language must be used and other ways must be found of expressing the child's various entitlements generally, and in armed conflict. This challenge has not been altogether successfully met here, or in much of the literature regarding the legal, social, and political status of children.

Further, this book has, to some extent, a Western bias. Although efforts have been made to counter this, these, too, have not been wholly successful. For example, in relation to the Iraqi conflicts, the material relied upon came largely from Western sources. The conclusions drawn, particularly concerning those conflicts, must therefore be regarded in that light.

8.5 FINAL COMMENT

Finally, as already mentioned (Note 61), one objective of this book is simply to make the law regarding child civilians better known, and thereby contribute to its implementation. It is to be hoped that it will at least succeed in this respect.

However, it is more strongly to be hoped that the proposals set out here will ultimately assist in achieving a further objective, which is a degree of compliance with this body of law that results in greater protection for child civilians in situations of armed conflict.[88] This aspiration should not prove

---

[88] Change may come slowly, but there is reason to hope that it will come. As one writer points out in relation to international human rights law, the principal lesson to be learned is patience: Bilder (1969), 607.

wholly unrealistic. Certain of the proposals outlined above, such as those regarding the establishment of zones or 'corridors of peace', are well-defined and demonstrably achievable, even if the law concerning child civilians, like most law, will inevitably remain flawed, inadequately observed, and in need of constant revision to reflect world events. In the end, at the risk of sentimentality, perhaps it can be said that if, as the result of this book, even one child civilian is spared death or injury, it will have achieved its aim.

Children in situations of armed conflict will never receive 'the best that mankind has to give', but perhaps they may be better shielded from the worst.

Afterword

During the time that has elapsed between the writing of this book and its final typesetting for publication, there have been a number of significant developments relevant to its subject matter. Some relate to world events, others to legal and policy initiatives.[1] This Afterword will refer briefly to the most pertinent of these, paying particular attention, in its initial section, to the contents of the UN study on children in armed conflict (Section 6.1.1.2 above),[2] presented to the UN General Assembly on 11 November 1996.

Notwithstanding these developments in the political, legal, and social landscape, the body of international human rights and humanitarian law described and analysed in this book remains unchanged, and may well undergo little substantive change for many years to come.

A) THE UN STUDY ON THE IMPACT OF ARMED CONFLICT ON CHILDREN

The UN study on the impact of armed conflict on children is both substantial and wide-ranging. After its introduction (Part I), the bulk of the report (in Part II) considers ways of mitigating the effects of armed conflict on children. This issue is examined in relation to child soldiers; refugees and internally displaced children; sexual exploitation and gender-based violence; landmines and unexploded ordnance; sanctions; health and nutrition; promoting psychological recovery and social reintegration, and education.[3] The study then looks (in Part III) at the relevance and adequacy of existing standards, including human rights and humanitarian law, for the

---

[1] Further, as is to be expected, various books of interest have been published since work on this manuscript was completed. Among others, these include: D. Fleck (ed.), *The Handbook of Humanitarian Law in Armed Conflicts* (Oxford, 1995); K. English and A. Stapleton, *The Human Rights Handbook: A Practical Guide to Monitoring Human Rights* (Essex, 1995); W. D. Angel, *The International Law of Youth Rights* (Dordrecht, 1995); R. Brett, M. McCallin and R. O'Shea, *Children—The Invisible Soldiers* (Stockholm, 1996); and D. McDowall, *A Modern History of the Kurds* (London, 1996). A useful collection of articles on customary human rights law can be found in 25. 1/2 *Georgia Journal of International and Comparative Law* (1995/1996).

[2] See UN Doc. A/51/306 (26 Aug. 1996).

[3] The discussion below on Part II of the report refers to most of these issues, with the exception of two that are peripheral to the subject of this book. These are: child soldiers, and the promotion of psychological recovery and social reintegration.

protection of children. The next three sections, before the conclusion (Part VII), consider reconstruction and reconciliation (Part IV); conflict prevention (Part V); and implementation mechanisms (Part VI).

In the introduction, Ms Machel, the appointed expert, emphasises the collaborative nature of this report, which incorporated contributions from six regional consultations held to determine regional priorities relating to children in armed conflict (paragraph 12).[4] Ms Machel also visited areas affected by armed conflict in Angola, Cambodia, Colombia, Northern Ireland, Lebanon, Rwanda, Sierra Leone, and Yugoslavia (paragraph 14). The study was guided by advice from a group of 'eminent persons' and 'technical experts', and supported by governments, regional bodies, intergovernmental organisations, and NGOs, as well as UN bodies (paragraphs 15 and 16).

The scope of the UN study is, of course, different from that of this book in that, for example, it also considers child soldiers. Further, discussion of the relevant international law forms a relatively small part of this study. It is equally concerned to examine political, social, and economic factors pertinent to children in armed conflict. Given its origins and mandate, this broad approach seems appropriate.

The report possesses certain other noteworthy, and positive, features. For example, it includes NGEs in the scope of its discussions and recommendations; it gives a high profile to gender-related issues, stressing both the vulnerabilities and the strengths of women and girl children affected by armed conflict; similarly, it emphasises the particular needs and attributes of adolescents affected by armed conflict. Further, it highlights a number of instances in which humanitarian intervention has done more harm than good,[5] and the need to guard against this.

The discussion below will refer to only some of the most pertinent aspects of the UN study, in the order in which it addresses these.

To start with Part II, its broad scope is evident from one of its opening paragraphs, stating that this section of the study

attempts to demonstrate that the impact of armed conflict on children cannot be fully understood without looking at the related effects on women, families and communities. It strives to illustrate how children's well-being is best ensured through family and community-based solutions to armed conflict and its aftermath. . . . Young people should be seen . . . as survivors and active participants in creating solutions, not just as victims or problems. (Paragraph 32).

[4] The 6 regions were: the Horn, Eastern, Central and Southern Africa; the Arab Region; West and Central Africa; Asia and the Pacific; Latin America and the Caribbean; and Europe. Statements from these consultations are included as Annexes to the study. See UN Doc. A/51/306/Add. 1.

[5] E.g., in discussing refugees and internally displaced children, the report points out that a possible negative side-effect of establishing centres (such as orphanages) for unaccompanied children is that such centres can actually encourage an increase in numbers of these children. Parents struggling to feed their children may leave them in these centres, attracted by the food

In relation to refugees and internally displaced children, the study comments, for example, that at least half of all refugees and displaced people are children (paragraph 66); that in flight from conflict children continue to be exposed to danger and 'are the first to die'; and that girls in this situation are particularly vulnerable to sexual abuse (paragraph 68). The recommendations in this section emphasise, *inter alia*, the importance of procedures for the survival and protection of unaccompanied children; of family unity, and of the avoidance of inappropriate adoptions (paragraph 90(a) and (b)).

Concerning sexual exploitation and gender-based violence, the study refers, among other things, to the hazards these pose particularly for women and girls who, in situations of armed conflict, may be victims not only of rape but also of 'prostitution, sexual humiliation and mutilation, trafficking and domestic violence' (paragraph 91). It also refers to one of the possible negative consequences of humanitarian intervention, namely that '[c]hildren may also become victims of prostitution following the arrival of peacekeeping forces' (paragraph 98, and see Note 63, Chapter 8 above). The study therefore recommends, for example, that 'humanitarian responses in conflict situations must emphasize the special reproductive health needs of women and girls'; that all military personnel should be instructed on their responsibilities to women and children; and that the 'treatment of rape as a war crime must be clarified, pursued within military and civilian populations, and punished accordingly' (paragraph 110(a), (b), and (d)).

In its section on landmines and unexploded ordnance, the report graphically describes the particular threat posed to children by these weapons (paragraphs 111–18), and stresses the importance of mine clearance, mine awareness programmes, and rehabilitation programmes (paragraph 119). It recommends, *inter alia*, that governments should enact national legislation to ban the production, use, trade in, and stockpiling of landmines, and should support the campaign for a worldwide ban; that, where relevant, their reports to the Committee on the Rights of the Child should address this issue, and that countries and companies profiting from the sale of mines should contribute funds to mine-clearance and mine-awareness programmes (paragraph 126(a), (b), and (e)).

As regards sanctions, the study comments that, although in theory 'most sanctions regimes exempt critical humanitarian supplies from general embargoes', this principle is ambiguous and difficult to apply consistently in practice, so that shortages often result, causing particular harm to children (paragraph 128, and see Section 7.2.2.3.2 above). In this context, the study refers to the Iraqi experience (paragraph 129). It argues for the cessation of

and health care they provide. Instead, family separation should be prevented by providing support to vulnerable families (para. 72).

comprehensive economic sanctions without safeguards for children and other vulnerable groups, and the substitution of measures such as arms embargoes, the freezing of overseas assets, and the suspension of air links (paragraph 130). The report therefore recommends, for example, that sanctions must only be imposed if they provide for 'humanitarian, child-focused exemptions' with effective monitoring mechanisms, and if they are precisely targeted at those whose behaviour the international community wishes to change (paragraph 135(a) and (c)).

Concerning health and nutrition, the study supports the important concept of children's entitlement to basic necessities in situations of armed conflict (see Sections 5.2.4 and 8.2 above). It discusses the hazards faced by children in situations of armed conflict, such as the spread of communicable diseases; disability; destruction of health facilities; disruption of food supplies, and malnutrition. In this context, the study recommends, *inter alia*, that the parties to a conflict 'must ensure the maintenance of basic health systems and services and water supplies' (paragraph 165(a)). Further, it recommends that governments support ' "days of tranquillity" or "corridors of peace" to ensure continuity of basic child health measures and delivery of humanitarian relief', and that NGEs should be encouraged to co-operate in such efforts (paragraph 165(c), and see Sections 4.2.1.2 and 8.3.1 above).

The final section of Part II of the study, regarding education, affirms the value of education for children in situations of armed conflict, in that it represents a 'state of normalcy'; provides contact with friends and teachers, and benefits the community as a whole (paragraph 185). The importance of education for such children is, as already mentioned, widely recognised in international humanitarian law (see, for example, Sections 4.2.1.3, 4.2.2.1.3, and 4.2.3 above). The study therefore recommends, *inter alia*, that '[a]ll possible efforts should be made to maintain education systems during conflicts' (paragraph 203(a)).

In its Part III, the study looks at the relevance and adequacy of existing standards for the protection of children. It makes the point that, in supporting the 1989 CRC, States Parties have recognized that

the protection of children is not just a national issue, but a legitimate concern of the international community. This is especially important since many of the most serious violations of children's rights are taking place in situations of conflict, such as Liberia and Somalia, where there is currently no functioning national government. (Paragraph 205).

The study emphasises that relief and protection measures should specifically include child-centred actions (paragraph 206) and again encourages the creation of 'corridors of peace' and 'days of tranquillity' (paragraph 208). It also argues that, in addition to the duty of states to comply with human rights law, NGEs should be 'treated as though they are bound by relevant human rights standards', and that there should be clear channels of accountability as regards the compliance of NGEs with human rights norms (paragraph 220).

This section of the report briefly summarises the pertinent human rights and humanitarian law, before focusing on the potential of the 1989 CRC as the most fruitful channel to provide comprehensive legal safeguards for children in situations of armed conflict. It maintains that if this treaty were to be 'fully implemented during armed conflicts, this would go a long way towards protecting children' (paragraph 229), and urges non-ratifying governments to 'do so immediately' (paragraph 240(a)). It argues that NGEs should be encouraged to make formal commitments to abide by the standards set out in the 1989 CRC (paragraphs 230 and 240(f)).[6] Also emphasised is the need for these standards to be 'widely known, understood, and implemented by policy makers, military and security forces and professionals dealing with the care of children', and to be known and asserted by children themselves (paragraphs 232 and 240(c) and (e), and see Sections 8.3.3 and 8.3.6 above). Further, governments are advised to adopt national legislative measures to implement the relevant standards (paragraph 240(b)). Another factor highlighted here is the need for accountability of governments and others through effective monitoring (paragraph 235). This monitoring is to be undertaken by, among others, the Commission on Human Rights (paragraph 236), treaty-monitoring bodies (particularly the Committee on the Rights of the Child (paragraph 237)), and, interestingly, those working for humanitarian agencies (paragraphs 239 and 240(d)).

In Part IV, the study looks at reconstruction and reconciliation. In relation to the latter, the study argues that it 'is difficult, if not impossible, to achieve reconciliation without justice', and that 'the international community should develop more systematic methods for apprehending and punishing individuals guilty of child rights abuses' (paragraph 248). The report acknowledges that in dealing with the most grave abuses, such as genocide, international law can provide more appropriate remedies than can national action. In this regard, while it welcomes the Rwanda and Yugoslav Tribunals, the study expresses concern regarding their resources and powers, and supports the establishment of an international criminal court (paragraph 249, and see Section 6.2.1 above).

Part V of the study describes conflict prevention as the most effective way to protect children, and it urges the international community to address root causes of violence (paragraph 253). In this context, it advocates

---

[6] The study points out that many NGEs 'aspire to form governments and to invoke an existing Government's lack of respect for human rights as a justification for their opposition', and that they should therefore establish their commitment to children by formally agreeing to implement the 1989 CRC standards. It cites 'encouraging precedents', including in Sudan in 1995 (para. 230).

programmes of education for peace, for adults as well as children (paragraphs 255–8); demilitarisation (paragraphs 259–62), and improved early warning systems and stand-by capacity, stressing that 'early warning must be linked to early action to be of any use' (paragraphs 263–5, and see Section 8.3.1 above).

In Part VI the study examines implementation mechanisms. It recommends the appointment of a special representative of the Secretary General on children and armed conflict (paragraph 266, and see Section 8.3.4 above, making a similar recommendation), and outlines the role of this representative (paragraphs 267–9). This section of the study then proposes some detailed, and some more vague and aspirational, follow-up actions to be undertaken by governments, regional and subregional organisations, the UN and bodies operating under its ægis (including the Committee on the Rights of the Child), and civil society organisations. For example, governments are urged to improve their international co-operation, political commitment, and action regarding children in armed conflict (paragraph 270); to ratify and implement the 1989 CRC and other pertinent international treaties (paragraphs 271–2), and to give priority to preventive measures (paragraph 273). As regards the UN and related bodies, the follow-up actions proposed are particularly lengthy and detailed (paragraphs 281–305). The introductory paragraphs here start by emphasising the Vienna Conference's recommendation that matters relating to the rights of children should regularly be reviewed by the relevant bodies within the UN and the specialised agencies. Further, child protection 'must be central to the humanitarian, peacemaking and peacekeeping policies of the United Nations, and should be given priority within existing human rights and humanitarian procedures' (paragraph 281). The study also makes a specific suggestion concerning the work of civil society organisations (such as NGOs, cultural organisations, and religious communities), that these organisations hold an international meeting on children in armed conflict, to take place in September 2000 (paragraph 311).

The report concludes by referring to the continuing 'mobilization work' that is already being undertaken, in the form of national and regional meetings, to implement its proposals. It acknowledges that it could not deal with all issues of relevance, and that work remains to be done (paragraph 315). It affirms that it is 'above all else . . . a call for action' (paragraph 317); that children must be claimed as 'zones of peace'; and, finally, that moral outrage should be transformed into concrete action since '[p]eace is every child's right' (paragraph 318).

It is evident from the above that this UN study is both thorough and ambitious. A number of the recommendations made in this book and discussed in Section 8.3 above (for example, regarding the establishment of zones, and other preventive measures; a more active role for children; the appointment of a UN official exclusively concerned with children in armed conflict; and wider dissemination and ratification of the relevant law) also appear in the study. As already stated, these could, if put into effect, shield many children from some of the devastating consequences of armed conflict. As with so many other international initiatives, time will tell just how influential this study has been. However, given the resources it has already mobilised and the commitment it already represents, there is certainly reason for, at least, cautious optimism.

B) LEGAL INITIATIVES

Another recent development that deserves mention is the ICJ *Advisory Opinion on the Legality of the Threat or Use of Nuclear Weapons.*[7]

Although this Opinion touches on many broadly relevant issues relating to human rights and humanitarian law, only one point of particular interest as regards children in armed conflict will be highlighted here: that concerning the right to life (Section 2.1 above).

In its Advisory Opinion, the ICJ stated that some 'proponents of the illegality of nuclear weapons have argued that such use would violate the right to life as guaranteed in Article 6 of the International Covenant on Civil and Political Rights, as well as in certain regional instruments for the protection of human rights. . . . In reply, others contended that the International Covenant on Civil and Political Rights made no mention of war or weapons, and it had never been envisaged that the legality of nuclear weapons was regulated by that instrument. It was suggested that the Covenant was directed to the protection of human rights in peacetime, but that questions relating to unlawful loss of life in hostilities were governed by the law applicable in armed conflict' (paragraph 24).

In deciding this issue, the ICJ commented that the provisions of the ICCPR remained applicable in times of armed conflict, although by operation of its Article 4 some of its provisions could be derogated from in times of national emergency. The Court observed that Article 6 was not derogable under Article 4, and therefore that

[i]n principle, the right not arbitrarily to be deprived of one's life applies also in hostilities.[8] The test of what is an arbitrary deprivation of life, however, then falls to be determined by the applicable *lex specialis*, namely, the law applicable in armed conflict which is designed to regulate the conduct of hostilities. Thus whether a

---

[7] ICJ. *Advisory Opinion on the Legality of the Threat or Use of Nuclear Weapons* (8 July 1996), 35 ILM 809 (1996).

[8] In their Dissenting Opinions, various judges of the ICJ also referred to this point. See particularly Judge Weeramantry and Judge Koroma, who both affirmed that the human rights principle regarding the right to life was a relevant consideration in determining the legality of the use of nuclear weapons (Dissenting Opinion of Judge Weeramantry, 52–3: 33 ILM 906–7 (1996); Dissenting Opinion of Judge Koroma, 16: 35 ILM 932 (1996)).

particular loss of life, through the use of a certain weapon in warfare, is to be considered an arbitrary deprivation of life contrary to Article 6 of the Covenant, can only be decided by reference to the law applicable in armed conflict and not deduced from the terms of the Covenant itself. (Paragraph 25).

This section of the Advisory Opinion is useful in confirming that the right not to be arbitrarily deprived of life, as articulated in human rights law (represented by the ICCPR), does apply in situations of armed conflict, although in such situations the test of arbitrary deprivation is to be found in the laws of armed conflict. The Advisory Opinion therefore highlights the convergence of humanitarian and human rights law in relation to this principle. This emphasises the importance, in appropriate cases, of using human rights monitoring mechanisms, such as applications to the Human Rights Committee, to censure those responsible for violations of the right to life in situations of armed conflict (see Section 6.1.3.3 above).

C) WORLD EVENTS

In considering recent political events of relevance, it is appropriate to mention the renewal of hostilities in Iraq in 1996.[9] As this book deals in depth only with certain conflicts involving Iraq between April 1987 and July 1991, this Afterword is clearly not the place in which to embark on a detailed discussion of the events in 1996. What follows is therefore a brief description of these events,[10] and of problems that are highlighted by them concerning child civilians and their protection under international law.

The 1996 hostilities in Iraq resulted from an eruption of tensions between the two main Kurdish political parties, the PUK and the KDP. At the beginning of September, KDP armed forces, backed by Iraqi troops, seized control from the PUK of Irbil, in the mainly Kurdish territory of northern Iraq. This territory was one of the two 'no-fly zones' imposed on Iraq, and patrolled largely by US forces, that had been established to shield the Kurds (in the north) and the Shia (in the south) from Iraqi attack in the wake of the 1991 uprisings.

On 3 September, the United States responded to the seizure of Irbil by attacking air defence and command and communications centres in south-

---

[9] Another development of interest in this context is the publication of press reports indicating that there may have been limited deployment of chemical weapons by Iraq against the allied coalition in the 1991 Gulf War (see *Guardian*, 22 Sept. 1996). This may, in part, explain the 'Gulf War Syndrome' (Sect. 7.2.4.1 above), although other evidence now suggests that this malaise could also have been caused by the exposure of allied troops to a combination of vaccinations, anti-nerve-gas tablets, and organophosphate pesticide poisoning (see *Independent*, 6 Oct. 1996 and 14 Oct. 1996, and *Guardian*, 10 Oct. 1996).

[10] Unattributed information set out here regarding the 1996 hostilities has been gleaned from both the *Independent* and the *Guardian* in Sept. and Oct. 1996. Specific quotations from these newspapers, and from other sources, are cited in the footnotes.

ern Iraq, despite a lack of support for this action on the part of many of the United States' former allies in the 1991 Gulf War. By 5 September the United States signalled an end to its involvement in the Iraqi crisis, as Iraqi troops were reported to be withdrawing from Irbil. However, on 10 September the KDP forces, again allegedly supported by Iraq, captured the key city of Sulamaniyah from the PUK. In effect, this extended Iraqi government influence into a substantial portion of northern Iraq. Refugees were reported to be fleeing to Iran, and the United States issued a warning that new air and missile strikes against Iraq were imminent. However, further US military action was not forthcoming. Then, on 13 October 1996 a PUK counter-offensive ousted the KDP from Sulamaniyah, amid speculation that the PUK was receiving assistance from Iran. In the following few days, the PUK recaptured two more towns from the KDP, and, by 17 October, the PUK apparently controlled 60 per cent of northern Iraq. At the time of writing (mid-November 1996) the KDP and the PUK were reported to have agreed a ceasefire, as of 24 October.

The above greatly simplified account of these events illustrates, among other things, the volatile and unpredictable nature of Iraqi politics, which may well generate further upheavals in the not too distant future. The key question to be addressed here is: what effect did these hostilities have on children in northern Iraq, and what did they reveal regarding international law and practice in relation to such children?

It is obvious that children caught up in the 1996 hostilities in Iraq would inevitably have experienced many of the damaging effects of armed conflict referred to in Section 1.1 above. Even in this relatively short-lived conflict, such effects would have included physical and emotional harm, as well as possible separation from families, displacement from home, shortages of food and other necessities, and missed schooling. It is of interest that, in sharp contrast to the 1991 Gulf War and its aftermath, in this instance little concern was expressed, either in the UN or by individual governments or the media, about the plight of children in northern Iraq, nor were attempts made to invoke or implement international law for their protection.[11]

Further, a particularly worrying aspect of these events in relation to children in northern Iraq, and indeed in Iraq as a whole, was that in early September the UN responded to the Iraqi-backed seizure of Irbil by

---

[11] Clearly the 1996 hostilities were a very minor conflict in comparison with the 1991 Gulf War. Further, it was no doubt easier to champion the Kurds when they were attacked by the Iraqi government than when Kurdish casualties were the result of internecine strife. Moreover, in the autumn of 1996 political and media scrutiny was increasingly focused on the humanitarian crisis that was looming in Zaïre and Rwanda. Nonetheless, given the considerable attention paid to the plight of Kurdish children, particularly in the aftermath of the 1991 uprisings (Sect. 7.2.3.2 above), it is a sign of the fickle nature of governments (individually and as represented in the UN) and of the media that, during the 1996 hostilities, no questions appear to have even been asked concerning the welfare of these children.

suspending the May 1996 agreement whereby Iraq was to sell two billion dollars worth of oil over a six-month period to pay for essential food and oil supplies (Section 7.2.4.2 above).[12] Moreover, on 3 September the United States apparently demanded reconsideration of the agreement as it related to relief in the Kurdish areas, thereby further deferring its implementation. Prior to these initiatives, the 'oil-for-food' agreement had, after numerous delays, been due finally to come into effect in late September 1996. In any event, by 1 October 1996 it was reported that the UN was hoping to approve this agreement 'in a matter of weeks'.[13]

The result of these tactics by the UN and the United States was that civilians in Iraq, and children in particular, were continuing further to suffer the effects of acute shortages of basic necessities. By September 1996, there were apparently 5,000 new cases of malnutrition in Iraq each month.[14] Given the particular vulnerability of children, combined with the high proportion of children in the Iraqi population, it is safe to assume that a large number of those new cases of malnutrition were children. Moreover, in September 1996 the WHO estimated that 500,000 Iraqi children had died as a direct result of six years of sanctions.[15]

Once again, it seems in this instance that questions concerning the effectiveness of economic sanctions as a strategy to weaken the Iraqi government, and the impact of such sanctions on vulnerable civilians such as children, were not given proper consideration by the UN or the United States. Recent reports on Iraq confirm that those bearing the brunt of the sanctions are the civilian population, while Saddam Hussein and his retinue continue to live in comfort.[16]

In summary, it seems that during the 1996 hostilities in Iraq children were once more exposed to the hazards of armed conflict, and the international community took scant notice of their particular needs and/or entitlements under international law. Moreover, economic sanctions against Iraq were again extended, to the detriment of these children and with little or no political effect.

The 1996 hostilities also raise issues concerning, for example, the legality of the US intervention, and the categorisation of this conflict in international humanitarian law (see Section 3.1.2 above). It is, however, beyond the scope of this brief Afterword to consider these more general issues here.

---

[12] One newspaper article described this as 'a policy switch that will attract further international controversy, because of its humanitarian implications': *Guardian*, 4 Sept. 1996.

[13] *Guardian*, 1 Oct. 1996.

[14] This was the estimate of the British Red Cross: *Guardian*, 5 Sept. 1996.

[15] *Ibid.*

[16] See, e.g., *Guardian Weekend*, 19 Oct. 1996.

Bibliography

The Bibliography below lists books, articles, and reports that are used as sources in this research, and are cited in the footnotes. Detailed information regarding sources not listed in the bibliography (such as documents of international organisations, untitled articles in journals, or newspaper cuttings), is given in the footnotes. When a footnote first refers to one of the sources included in the Bibliography, full bibliographic information is given. When reference is made to a source as a whole, pages are not cited. For repeat references, the footnote mentions only the surname of the author, date of publication, and page numbers (where relevant). Where several works by a particular author (or authors) were published in the same year, the title of the work referred to appears in abbreviated form in the footnote.

ABI-SAAB, R., 'Humanitarian Law and Internal Conflicts: The Evolution of Legal Concern', in A. J. M. Delissen and G. J. Tanja (eds.), *Humanitarian Law of Armed Conflict* (Dordrecht, 1991), 209–23.

ABRAMSON, B., *Children and War: A Background Paper with Recommendations for the Committee on the Rights of the Child and its Working Group on Children in Armed Conflict* (Geneva, 1992).

——'An Enormous Challenge' 9.3/4 *International Children's Rights Monitor* 24 (1992).

——'Children's Rights in the Age of Landmines: Part One' 11.2/3 *International Children's Rights Monitor* 35 (1994).

——'Children's Rights in the Age of Landmines: Part Two' 11.4/12.1 *International Children's Rights Monitor* 25 (1994–5).

AHLSTRÖM, C., *Casualties of Conflict* (Uppsala, 1991).

AKEHURST, M., 'Custom as a Source of International Law' 47 *BYIL* 1 (1974–5).

AL-HAQ., *Punishing a Nation: Human Rights Violations During the Palestinian Uprising, December 1987–December 1988* (West Bank, 1988).

ALA'ALDEEN, D., *Death Clouds: Saddam Hussein's Chemical War Against the Kurds* (London, 1991).

ALDRICH, G. H., 'Establishing Legal Norms Through Multilateral Negotiation—The Laws of War', 9 *Case Western Reserve Journal of International Law* 13 (1977).

——'Compliance with the Law: Problems and Prospects', in H. Fox and M. Meyer (eds.), *Armed Conflict and the New Law: Vol. II—Effecting Compliance* (London, 1993), 3–14.

——and VAN BAARDA, TH. A., *Conference on the Rights of Children in Armed Conflict* (The Hague, 1994).

ALLOTT, A. N., 'Legal Personality in African Law', in M. Gluckman (ed.), *Ideas and Procedures in African Customary Law* (London, 1969), 179–95.

ALSTON, P., 'The Purposes of Reporting', in UN, *Manual on Human Rights Reporting* (New York, 1991), 13–16.

——'The International Covenant on Economic, Social and Cultural Rights', in UN, *Manual on Human Rights Reporting* (New York, 1991), 39–77.

——(ed.), *The United Nations and Human Rights: A Critical Appraisal* (Oxford, 1992).

——'The Commission on Human Rights', in P. Alston (ed.), *The United Nations and Human Rights: A Critical Appraisal* (Oxford, 1992), 126–210.

——'The Legal Framework of the Convention on the Rights of the Child' 91/2 *Bulletin of Human Rights: The Rights of the Child* 1 (1992).

——(ed.), *The Best Interests of the Child* (Oxford, 1994).

——and PARKER, S., 'Introduction', in P. Alston, S. Parker, and J. Seymour (eds.), *Children, Rights and the Law* (Oxford, 1992), pp. vi–xii.

————and SEYMOUR, J. (eds.), *Children, Rights and the Law* (Oxford, 1992).

AMNESTY INTERNATIONAL, *What Does Amnesty International Do?* (Mitcham, 1985).

——*Urgent Action. Iraq: Deliberate Killings of Unarmed Kurdish Civilians* (London, 2 Sept. 1988).

——*What Makes Amnesty International Work?* (Colombo, 1988).

——*Iraq: Oral Statement to the United Nations Sub-Commission on Prevention of Discrimination and Protection of Minorities* (London, Aug. 1988).

——'Amnesty International: Working for Children', 56 *Childright* 16 (May 1989).

——'Amnesty Spotlights Children', 60 *Childright* 4 (Oct. 1989).

——'The Youngest Victims: Children Jailed, Tortured and Killed', XIX.10 *Focus* 3 (Oct. 1989).

——*When The State Kills . . . The Death Penalty v. Human Rights* (London, 1989).

——*Iraq. Children: Innocent Victims of Political Repression* (London, 1989).

——*Amnesty International Report* (London, 1989).

——*Iraq/Occupied Kuwait: Human Rights Violations Since 2 August 1990* (London, Dec. 1990).

——*Children: Victims of Human Rights Violations* (London, 1990).

——*Amnesty International Report* (London, 1990).

——*Iraq. The Need for Further United Nations Action to Protect Human Rights* (London, July 1991).

——*Iraq: Human Rights Violations Since the Uprising: Summary of Amnesty International's Concerns* (London, July 1991).

——*Amnesty International Report* (London, 1991).

——*Amnesty International Handbook* (London, 1992).

——*Establishing a Just, Fair and Effective International Criminal Court* (London, 1994).

——*Peace-Keeping and Human Rights* (London, 1994).

——*Childhood Stolen: Grave Human Rights Violations Against Children* (London, 1995).

——(UK), 'Landmines: The Blind Sentinels', *Working Group for Children Newsletter* 1 (Spring 1996).

AN-NA'IM, A. A. (ed.), *Human Rights in Cross-Cultural Perspectives* (Philadelphia, Penn., 1992).

—— 'Introduction', in An-Na'im, A. A. (ed.) *Human Rights in Cross-Cultural Perspectives* (Philadelphia, Penn., 1992), 1–15.

ANAND, R. P. 'Attitude of the Asian-African States Toward Certain Problems of International Law' (1966) 15 *ICLQ* 55.

ANKUMAH, E., 'Towards an Effective Implementation of the African Charter', 8.3 *Interights Bulletin* 59 (1994).

APOSTEL, PROF. DR L., 'Children's Rights and Needs or/and Human Rights and Needs', in E. Verhellen and F. Spiesschaert (eds.), *Ombudswork for Children* (Leuven, 1989), 47–85.

ARCHARD, D., *Children: Rights and Childhood* (London, 1993).

ARIES, P., *Centuries of Childhood* (New York, 1962).

ARNIG, A., 'Child Prostitution in Cambodia: Did the UN Look Away?' 10.3 *International Children's Rights Monitor* 4 (1993).

BASSIOUNI, M. C., *Crimes Against Humanity in International Criminal Law* (Dordrecht, 1992).

BAXTER, R. R. and BUERGENTHAL, T., 'Legal Aspects of the Geneva Protocol of 1925', 64 *AJIL* 853 (1970).

BELEMBAOGO, A., 'The Best Interests of the Child—The Case of Burkina Faso', in P. Alston (ed.), *The Best Interests of the Child* (Oxford, 1994), 202–26.

BELLO, E., *African Customary Humanitarian Law* (Geneva, 1980).

——and AJIBOLA, B. (eds.), *Essays in Honour of Judge Taslim Olawale Elias* (Dordrecht, 1992), Vol. ii.

BEN SALEM, H., 'The African System for the Protection of Human and Peoples' Rights' 8.3 *Interights Bulletin* 55 (1994).

BENNETT, W., 'A Critique of the Emerging Convention on the Rights of the Child', 20 *Cornell International Law Journal* 1 (1987).

BERNHARDT, R. (ed.), *Encyclopedia of Public International Law: Vol. 3: Use of Force: War and Neutrality, Peace Treaties* (Amsterdam, 1982).

BEST, G., *Humanity in Warfare* (London, 1980).

——*War and Law Since 1945* (Oxford, 1994).

BHANDARE, M. C., 'The Role and Machinery of the United Nations in the Field of Human Rights' 89/1 *Bulletin of Human Rights* 12 (1990).

BILDER, R., 'Rethinking International Human Rights: Some Basic Questions' II *Human Rights Journal* 557 (1990).

BOSNJAK, V., 'Children's Rights: New Directions for UNICEF?', 56 *UNICEF Intercom* 6 (April 1990).

BOSSUYT, M., *Guide to the 'Travaux Préparatoires' of the International Covenant on Civil and Political Rights* (Dordrecht, 1987).

BOTHE, M., PARTSCH, K., and SOLF, W., *New Rules for Victims of Armed Conflicts* (The Hague, 1982).

BOUCAUD, P., *The Council of Europe and Child Welfare: the Need for a European Convention on Children's Rights* (Strasbourg, 1989).

BOWETT, D. W., *The Law of International Institutions* (London, 1982).

BOYLE, C. K., 'The Concept of Arbitrary Deprivation of Life', in B. G. Ramcharan (ed.), *The Right to Life in International Law* (Dordrecht, 1985) 221–45.

BRETT, R., *Discussion Paper on Ways of Improving the Implementation of Human Rights and Humanitarian Law* (Quaker UN Office, Geneva, Jan. 1994).

——*Recruitment of Children: The International Legal Standards and How They Could be Improved* (Quaker UN Office, Geneva, 1994).

——*Report on the Working Group to Draft an Optional Protocol to the Convention on the Rights of the Child on Participation of Children in Armed Conflict* (Quaker UN Office, Geneva, 1994).

—— *Report on the 1994 UN Commission on Human Rights: 31 January to 11 March 1994* (Quaker UN Office, Geneva, 1994).

—— *Report on the Second Session of the Working Group to Draft an Optional Protocol to the Convention on the Rights of the Child on Participation of Children in Armed Conflict* (Quaker UN Office, Geneva, 1996).

BROWNLIE, I., *International Law and the Use of Force by States* (Oxford, 1963).

—— *Principles of Public International Law* (4th edn., Oxford, 1990).

—— *Basic Documents in International Law* (4th edn., Oxford, 1995).

B'TSELEM, *Annual Report 1989: Violations of Human Rights in the Occupied Territories* (Jerusalem, 1989).

—— *Closure of Schools and Other Setbacks to the Education System in the Occupied Territories* (Jerusalem, 1990).

—— *The Killing of Palestinian Children and the Open-Fire Regulations* (N.p. June, 1993).

—— *Khan Yunis December 1992: Case Study No 2* (Jerusalem, 1993).

—— *Renewal of Deportation of Women and Children from the Occupied Territories on Account of 'Illegal Residency'* (Jerusalem, n.d.).

—— *Violations of Human Rights in the Occupied Territories 1990/1991* (Jerusalem, n.d.).

—— *Violations of Human Rights in the Occupied Territories 1992/1993* (Jerusalem, n.d.).

BUERGENTHAL, T., 'To Respect and to Ensure: State Obligations and Permissible Derogations', in L. Henkin (ed.), *The International Bill of Rights: The Covenant on Civil and Political Rights* (New York, 1981), 32–71.

—— 'The Inter-American Court, Human Rights and the OAS' 7 *Human Rights Law Journal* 157 (1986).

—— NORRIS, R., and SHELTON, D., *Protecting Human Rights in the Americas* (3rd edn., Kehl, 1990).

BULLOCH, J., and MORRIS, H., *Saddam's War* (London, 1991).

—— and —— *No Friends But The Mountains* (London, 1992).

CAMPBELL, T. D., 'The Rights of the Minor: As Person, as Child, as Juvenile, as Future Adult', in P. Alston, S. Parker, and J. Seymour (eds.), *Children, Rights and the Law* (Oxford, 1992), 1–23.

CANTWELL, N., 'Non-Governmental Organisations and the United Nations Convention on the Rights of the Child' 91/2 *Bulletin of Human Rights* 16 (1992).

CASSESE, A. (ed.), *UN Law/Fundamental Rights: Two Topics in International Law* (Alphen aan den Rijn, 1979).

—— 'How Could Nongovernmental Organisations Use UN Bodies More Effectively' 1.4 *Universal Human Rights* 73 (1979).

—— *International Law in a Divided World* (Oxford, 1986).

CERNA, C. M., 'Promotion and Protection of Human Rights by the Inter-American System', 5.1 *Interights Bulletin* 3 (1990).

CHALIAND, G., *People Without A Country* (London, 1980).

CHANLETT, E., and MORIER, G. M., 'Declaration of the Rights of the Child' XXII(22) *International Child Welfare Review* 4 (1968).

CHENG, B., 'United Nations Resolutions on Outer Space: "Instant" International Customary Law?' 5 *Indian Journal of International Law* 23 (1965).

CHILDREN'S RIGHTS DEVELOPMENT UNIT, *Civil and Political Liberties: Consultation Document* (London, May 1993).

CLARK, R., and Others. *War Crimes: A Report on United States War Crimes Against Iraq* (Washington DC, 1992).

COHEN, C. P., 'The Human Rights of Children', 12 *Capital University Law Review* 369 (1983).

—— 'United Nations Convention on the Rights of the Child: Introductory Note' 28 ILM 1449 (1989).

—— 'The Relevance of Theories of Natural Law and Legal Positivism', in M. Freeman and P. Veerman (eds.), *The Ideologies of Children's Rights* (Dordrecht, 1992), 53–70.

COHEN, E. R., *Human Rights in the Israeli-Occupied Territories 1967–1982* (Manchester, 1985).

COHN, I., 'The Convention on the Rights of the Child: What it Means for Children in War' 3.1 *International Journal of Refugee Law* 100 (1991).

—— *Comments to the UN Committee on the Rights of the Child, 5 October 1992: Children and Armed Conflict* (Geneva, 1992).

CONNORS, J., 'International Law and the Kurds of Iraq: A Review of the Instruments' 3 Kurdistan Liberation 16 (Mar. 1991).

—— 'Humanitarian Legal Order and the Kurdish Question' (unpublished).

COOK, H., 'The United Nations Commission on Human Rights—Some Recent Developments', 6.3 *Interights Bulletin* 44 (1991).

COUNCIL OF EUROPE, *The Protection of Minors Under the European Convention on Human Rights: Analysis of Case Law* (Strasbourg, 20 June 1990).

CRANSTON, M., *What Are Human Rights?* (New York, 1973).

CRAWFORD, J., 'The ILC Adopts a Statute for an Interntional Criminal Court', 9.2 *Interights Bulletin* 61 (Summer 1995).

CROWLEY, M., 'Suffer Little Children', 41 *Amnesty* 10 (Oct./Nov. 1989).

D'AMATO, A. A., *The Concept of Custom in International Law* (Ithaca, NY, 1971).

DARWISH, A., and ALEXANDER, G., *Unholy Babylon* (London, 1991).

DAS, K., 'United Nations Institutions and Procedures Founded on Conventions on Human Rights and Fundamental Freedoms', in K. Vasak (ed.), *The International Dimensions of Human Rights* (Westport, Conn., 1982), 303–62.

DASBERG, L., 'What is a Child and What are its Rights', in E. Verhellen and F. Spiesschaert (eds.), *Ombudswork for Children* (Leuven, 1989), 35–46.

DAVID, P., 'Burkina Faso Sets the Example to the Other States of the World', 11.2/3 *International Children's Rights Monitor* 22 (1994).

—— 'Tracing Work is a Delicate Affair', 11.2/3 *International Children's Rights Monitor* 9 (1994).

DEFENCE FOR CHILDREN INTERNATIONAL, *Memorandum: Article 38 of the Draft Convention on the Rights of the Child and the Participation of Children in Armed Conflicts* (Geneva, Mar. 1989).

—— 'An Opportunity to Effect Genuine Change?', 11.4/12.1 *International Children's Rights Monitor* 33 (1994/1995).

DE CUELLAR, J. P., *Report of the Secretary-General on the Work of the Organisation* (Geneva, 1990).

—— 'The Role of the UN Secretary General', in A. Roberts and B. Kingsbury (eds.), *United Nations, Divided World* (2nd edn., Oxford, 1993), 125–42.

DE LANGEN, M., 'The Meaning of Human Rights for Children', in M. Freeman and P. Veerman (eds.), *The Ideologies of Children's Rights* (Dordrecht, 1992) 256–64.

DE MAUSE, L. (ed.), *The History of Childhood* (New York, 1974).

—— 'The Evolution of Childhood', in L. de Mause (ed.), *The History of Childhood* (New York, 1974), 1–52.

DE LUPIS, I. D., *The Law of War* (Cambridge, 1987).

DELISSEN, A. J. M., and TANJA, G. J. (eds.), *Humanitarian Law of Armed Conflict* (Dordrecht, 1991).

DETRICK, S. (ed.), *The United Nations Convention on the Rights of the Child: A Guide to the Travaux Préparatoires* (Dordrecht, 1992).

DIALLO, Y., *African Traditions and Humanitarian Law: Similarities and Differences* (Geneva, 1976).

DINSTEIN, Y., 'The International Law of Belligerent Occupation and Human Rights' 8 *Israel Yearbook on Human Rights* 104 (1978).

—— 'The Right to Life, Physical Integrity, and Liberty', in L. Henkin (ed.), *The International Bill of Rights: The Covenant on Civil and Political Rights* (New York, 1981), 114–37.

—— 'Human Rights in Armed Conflict', in T. Meron (ed.), *Human Rights in International Law: Legal and Policy Issues* (Oxford, 1984), 345–68.

DOSWALD-BECK, L., 'The Value of the 1977 Geneva Protocols for the Protection of Civilians', in M. Meyer (ed.), *Armed Conflict and the New Law* (London, 1989), 137–72.

'Draft European Convention on the Exercise of Children's Rights', 121 *Childright* 9 (Nov. 1995).

DRAPER, G. I. A. D., 'Humanitarian Law and International Armed Conflicts', 13 *Georgia Journal of International and Comparative Law* 253 (1983).

DUGARD, J., 'Enforcement of Human Rights in the West Bank and Gaza Strip', in E. Playfair (ed.), *International Law and the Administration of the Occupied Territories: Two Decades of Israeli Occupation of the West Bank and Gaza Strip* (Oxford, 1992), 461–87.

DUPUY, R. (ed.), *The Development of the Role of the Security Council* (Dordrecht, 1993).

DUTLI, M. T., *Enfants-Combattants Prisonniers: Extract from the International Review of the Red Cross* (Geneva, Sept.–Oct. 1990).

DWORKIN, R., *Taking Rights Seriously* (London, 1978).

EIDE, A., 'The Laws of War and Human Rights—Differences and Convergences', in C. Swinarski (ed.), *Studies and Essays on International Humanitarian Law and Red Cross Principles in Honour of Jean Pictet* (Geneva, 1984), 675–97.

—— 'The Sub-Commission on Prevention of Discrimination and Protection of Minorities', in P. Alston (ed.), *The United Nations and Human Rights: A Critical Appraisal* (Oxford, 1992), 211–64.

—— ALFREDSSON, G., MALANDER, G., REHOF, L. A., ROSAS, A., and SWINEHART, T., *The Universal Declaration of Human Rights: A Commentary* (Drammen, 1992).

EL SAADAWI, N., 'The Impact of the Gulf War on Women and Children', in R. Clark and Others, *War Crimes: A Report on United States War Crimes Against Iraq* (Washington DC, 1992), 180–3.

ELAHI, M., 'The Rights of the Child Under Islamic Law: Prohibition of the Child Soldier', 19 *Columbia Human Rights Law Review* 259 (Spring 1988).

ELIAS, T. O., *The Nature of African Customary Law* (Manchester, 1956).

EL-HAJ, T. A., 'The Impact of Armed Conflict on Children', 122 *Childright* 12 (Dec. 1995).

ERIKSSON, J., *The International Reponse to Conflict and Genocide: Lessons from the Rwanda Experience. Synthesis Report. Joint Evaluation of Emergency Assistance to Rwanda* (Copenhagen, 1996).

FARSON, R., *Birthrights: A Bill of Rights for Children* (New York, 1974).

FENRICK, W. D., 'New Developments in the Law Concerning the Use of Conventional Weapons in Armed Conflict' 19 *The Canadian Yearbook of International Law* 229 (1981).

FLEKKØY, M. G., 'Attitudes to Children—Their Consequences for Work for Children', in M. Freeman and P. Veerman (eds.), *The Ideologies of Children's Rights* (Dordrecht, 1992), 135–47.

—— 'Children as Holders of Rights and Obligations', in D. Gomien (ed.), *Broadening the Frontiers of Human Rights: Essays in Honour of Asbjørn Eide* (Oxford, 1993), 97–120.

FORSYTHE, D., *Humanitarian Politics: The International Committee of the Red Cross* (Baltimore, Maryland, 1977).

—— 'The International Committee of the Red Cross', in H. Fox and M. Meyer (eds.), *Armed Conflict and the New Law: Vol. II—Effecting Compliance* (London, 1993), 83–103.

FOX, H., and MEYER, M. (eds.), *Armed Conflict and the New Law: Vol. II—Effecting Compliance* (London, 1993).

FOX, S., 'The Convention on the Rights of the Child: Risks and Potential', in E. Verhellen and F. Spiesschaert (eds.), *Ombudswork for Children* (Leuven, 1989), 409–25.

FOX, V., 'Historical Perspectives on Children's Rights', in E. Verhellen and F. Spiesschaert (eds.), *Ombudswork for Children* (Leuven, 1989), 297–311.

FRANCK, T. M., 'Legitimacy in the International System', 82 *AJIL* 705 (1988).

—— and NOLTE, G., 'The Good Offices Function of the UN Secretary-General', in A. Roberts and B. Kingsbury (eds.), *United Nations, Divided World* (2nd edn., Oxford, 1993), 143–82.

FRANKLIN, B., *The Rights of Children* (Oxford, 1986).

FREEMAN, M., *The Rights and Wrongs of Children* (London. 1983).

—— 'Taking Children's Rights More Seriously', in P. Alston. S. Parker. and J. Seymour (eds.), *Children, Rights and the Law* (Oxford. 1992). 52–71.

—— 'The Limits of Children's Rights', in M. Freeman and P. Veerman (eds.), *The Ideologies of Children's Rights* (Dordrecht, 1992), 29–46.

—— 'Introduction: Rights, Ideology and Children', in M. Freeman and P. Veerman (eds.), *The Ideologies of Children's Rights* (Dordrecht, 1992), 3–6.

—— and VEERMAN, P. (eds.), *The Ideologies of Children's Rights* (Dordrecht, 1992).

GALBRAITH, P., and VAN HOLLEN, C., *Chemical Weapons Use in Kurdistan: Iraq's Final Offensive: A Staff Report to the Senate Committee on Foreign Relations* (Washington, DC, 21 Sept. 1988).

GARDAM, J. G., 'Noncombatant Immunity and the Gulf Conflict', 32 *Virginia Journal of International Law* 813 (1992).

——*Non-combatant Immunity as a Norm of International Humanitarian Law* (Dordrecht, 1993).

—— 'The Law of Armed Conflict: A Feminist Perspective', in K. Mahoney and P. Mahoney (eds.), *Human Rights in the Twenty-first Century* (Dordrecht, 1993), 419–36.

GARDNER, J. P. (ed.), *Human Rights as General Norms and a State's Right to Opt Out: Reservations and Objections to Human Rights Conventions* (To be published London, 1997).

GARRAT, D., 'The Role of Legal Advisers in the Armed Forces', in P. Rowe (ed.), *The Gulf War 1990–1991 in International and English Law* (London, 1993), 55–62.

GASSER, H., 'A Measure of Humanity in Internal Disturbances and Tensions: Proposal for a Code of Conduct' 28 *Int'l Rev. of the Red Cross* 38 (1988).

—— 'Ensuring Respect for the Geneva Conventions and Protocols: The Role of Third States and the UN', in H. Fox and M. Meyer (eds.), *Armed Conflict and the New Law: Vol. II—Effecting Compliance* (London, 1993), 15–82.

GHAREEB, E., *The Kurdish Question in Iraq* (Syracuse, NY, 1981).

GLUCKMAN, M. (ed.), *Ideas and Procedures in African Customary Law* (London, 1969).

GOMIEN, D., *Duties of Private Parties Under the Convention on the Rights of the Child: 'An Obstacle to Implementation?'*, Paper from DCI Congress 'Working for Children's Rights' (Finland, 1989).

——(ed.), *Broadening the Frontiers of Human Rights: Essays in Honour of Asbjørn Eide* (Oxford, 1993).

GOODWIN-GILL, G. S., and COHN, I., *Child Soldiers* (Oxford, 1994).

'Graça Machel Joins DCI's Concern', 11.4 *International Children's Rights Monitor* 33 (1994/5).

GRANT, S., 'Protection Mechanisms and the Yugoslav Crisis' 8.1 *Interights Bulletin* 3 (1994).

—— 'Dispensing International Justice: The Yugoslav and Rwandan Criminal Tribunals', 9.2 *Interights Bulletin* 39 (Summer, 1995).

GREEN, L. C., *The Contemporary Law of Armed Conflict* (Manchester, 1993).

GREENWOOD, C., 'The Concept of War in Modern International Law' 36 *ICLQ* 283 (1987).

—— 'Customary Law Status of the 1977 Geneva Protocols', in A. J. M. Delissen and G. J. Tanja (eds.), *Humanitarian Law of Armed Conflict* (Dordrecht, 1991), 93–114.

—— 'Customary International Law and the First Geneva Protocol of 1977 in the Gulf Conflict', in P. Rowe (ed.), *The Gulf War 1990–1991 in International and English Law* (London, 1993), 63–88.

—— 'The International Tribunal for Former Yugoslavia' 69 *International Affairs* 641 (1993).

GROSS, B., and GROSS, R. (eds.), *The Children's Rights Movement* (New York, 1977).

GROTIUS, 'De Jure Belli ac Pacis Libri Tres' (1625), English trans. by F. Kelsey, in J. Scott (ed.), *The Classics of International Law* (New York, 1964).

HADDEN, D., 'The Death Penalty: When the State Kills Young People', 59 *Childright* 7 (Sept. 1989).

HALL, C. K., *Challenges Ahead for the United Nations Preparatory Committee Drafting a Statute for a Permanent International Criminal Court: Reprint of an article in AI UK Lawyers' Network Newsletter, No 21 (Supplement, 1996)* (London, 1996).

HAMALENGWA, G., FLINTERMAN, C., and DANKWA, E. V. O., *The International Law of Human Rights in Africa: Basic Documents and Annotated Bibliography* (Dordrecht, 1988).

HAMILTON, C., 'Children in Armed Conflict—New Moves for an Old Problem' 7 *Tolley's Journal of Child Law* 38 (1995).

HAMMARBERG, T., 'Keynote Speech: Children as a Zone of Peace: What Needs to be Done', in G. H. Aldrich and Th. A. van Baarda, *Conference on the Rights of Children in Armed Conflict* (The Hague, 1994), 10–14.

HAMPSON, F., 'Human Rights and Humanitarian Law in Internal Conflicts', in M. Meyer (ed.), *Armed Conflict and the New Law* (London, 1989), 55–80.

——'Using International Human Rights Machinery to Enforce the International Law of Armed Conflicts' XXXI *Rev. de Droit Militaire et de Droit de la Guerre* 117 (1992).

——'Liability for War Crimes', in P. Rowe (ed.), *The Gulf War 1990–1991 in International and English Law* (London, 1993), 241–60.

——'Means and Methods of Warfare in the Conflict in the Gulf', in P. Rowe (ed.), *The Gulf War 1990–1991 in International and English Law* (London, 1993), 89–110.

——*Violation of Fundamental Human Rights in the Former Yugoslavia: II. The Case for a War Crimes Tribunal* (London, 1993).

——'Fact-Finding and the International Fact-Finding Commission', in H. Fox and M. Meyer (eds.), *Armed Conflict and the New Law: Vol. II—Effecting Compliance* (London, 1993), 53–82.

HANNIKAINEN, L., *Peremptory Norms (Jus Cogens) in International Law: Historical Development, Criteria, Present Status* (Helsinki, 1988).

HAY, A., 'The ICRC and International Humanitarian Issues' 238 *Int'l Rev. of the Red Cross* 3 (1984).

HEINTZ, H. J., 'The UN Convention and the Network of the International Human Rights Protection by the UN', in M. Freeman and P. Veerman (eds.), *The Ideologies of Children's Rights* (Dordrecht, 1992), 71–8.

HENKIN, L. (ed.), *The International Bill of Rights: The Covenant on Civil and Political Rights* (New York, 1981).

HERCZEGH, G., *Developments of International Humanitarian Law* (Budapest, 1984).

HIGGINS, R., *The Development of International Law Through the Political Organs of the United Nations* (London, 1963).

——'Derogations Under Human Rights Treaties' 48 *BYIL*, 281 (1976–7).

——*Human Rights—Proposals and Problems* (Leeds. 1979).

——'Encouraging Human Rights' 2 *London School of Economics Quarterly* 249 (1988).

—— 'Some Thoughts on the Implementation of Human Rights' 89/1 *Bulletin of Human Rights* 60 (1990).

—— *Problems and Process: International Law and How We Use It* (Oxford, 1994).

—— 'The New United Nations and Former Yugoslavia' 8.1 *Interights Bulletin* 19 (1994).

HIMES, J., *The UN Convention on the Rights of the Child* (Florence, 1993).

HINGORANI, R. C., 'Protection of Children During Armed Conflicts', in F. Kalshoven (ed.), *Assisting the Victims of Armed Conflict and Other Disasters* (Dordrecht, 1989), 133–8.

HODGSON, D., 'The Child's Right to Life, Survival and Development' 2.4 *The International Journal of Children's Rights* 369 (1994).

HOHFELD, W., *Fundamental Legal Conceptions as Applied in Judicial Reasoning* (New Haven, Conn., 1919).

HOLT, J., *Escape From Childhood* (New York, 1974).

—— 'Why not a Bill of Rights for Children?', in B. Gross and R. Gross (eds.), *The Children's Rights Movement* (New York, 1977), 319–25.

HOWARD, R. E., 'Dignity, Community and Human Rights', in A. A. An-Na'im (ed.), *Human Rights in Cross-Cultural Perspectives* (Philadelphia, Penn., 1992), 81–102.

'Human Rights Committee Adopts Country Specific Reports', 7.2 *Interights Bulletin* 22 (1992/3).

INTERNATIONAL COMMITTEE OF THE RED CROSS, *Red Cross and Red Crescent: Portrait of an International Movement* (Geneva, n.d.).

—— *The International Committee of the Red Cross: What it is, What it Does* (Geneva, n.d.).

—— *The International Committee of the Red Cross (ICRC)* (Geneva, n.d.).

—— 'The ICRC and Disarmament', 18 *Int'l Rev. of the Red Cross* 91 (Mar.–Apr. 1978).

—— 'Action by the International Committee of the Red Cross in the Event of Breaches of International Humanitarian Law', 21 *Int'l. Rev. of the Red Cross* 76 (Mar.–Apr. 1981).

—— *Presenting the ICRC* (Geneva, 1986).

—— *Commentary on the Additional Protocols of 8 June 1977 to the Geneva Conventions of 12 August 1949* (Geneva, 1987).

—— *ICRC and Children in Situation of Armed Conflict* (Geneva, 1987).

—— 'ICRC Protection and Assistance Activities in Situations Not Covered by International Humanitarian Law', 28 *Int'l. Rev. of the Red Cross* 9 (Jan./Feb. 1988).

—— 'International Humanitarian Law and the Middle East Conflict', 184 *ICRC Bulletin* 2 (May 1991).

—— 'New Draft Declaration of Minimum Humanitarian Standards', 282 *Int'l. Rev. of the Red Cross* 328 (May–June 1991).

—— *The Annual Report of the International Committee of the Red Cross 1990* (Geneva, Mar. 1991).

—— *A Perverse Use of Technology* (Geneva, 1992).

—— *International Conference for the Protection of War Victims* (Geneva, 1993).

—— 'Follow-Up to the International Conference for the Protection of War Victims', 304 *Int'l. Rev. of the Red Cross* 4 (Jan.–Feb. 1995).

—— 'Resolutions of the 26th International Conference', 310 *Int'l. Rev. of the Red Cross* 55 (Jan.–Feb. 1996).

—— and LEAGUE OF RED CROSS SOCIETIES, *Fundamental Rules of International Humanitarian Law Applicable in Armed Conflicts* (Geneva, 1979).

INSTITUT HENRY-DUNANT, *Quatre Études du Droit International Humanitaire* (Geneva, 1985).

INSTITUT DE DROIT INTERNATIONAL (Session de Lisbonne), *First Commission: Problems Arising From a Succession of Codification Conventions on a Particular Subject. Rev. 1.* (N.p., Aug. 1995).

INSTITUTE FOR HUMAN RIGHTS, Åbo Akademi University, *Declaration of Minimum Humanitarian Standards* (Turku/Åbo, Finland 1991).

'International Alert Objectives', 4 *International Alert Update* 2 (Nov. 1994).

'International Criminal Tribunals', 9.2 *Interights Bulletin* 37 (Summer 1995).

INTERNATIONAL INSTITUTE OF HIGHER STUDIES IN CRIMINAL SCIENCES, *The Draft Charter on Human and People's Rights in the Arab World* (Syracuse, NY, 1987).

INTERNATIONAL LAW ASSOCIATION, *Report of the Fortieth Conference: Amsterdam* (Suffolk, 1939).

JOHNSON, D., 'Cultural and Regional Pluralism in the Drafting of the UN Convention on the Rights of the Child', in M. Freeman and P. Veerman (eds.), *The Ideologies of Children's Rights* (Dordrecht, 1992), 95–114.

KAHNERT, M., PITT, D., and TAIPALE, I. (eds.), *Children and War: Proceedings of Symposium at Siuntio Baths, Finland* (Helsinki, 1983).

KALSHOVEN, F., 'Reaffirmation and Development of International Humanitarian Law Applicable in Armed Conflicts: The Diplomatic Conference, Geneva 1974–·77. Part I: Combatants and Civilians' 8 *Netherlands Yearbook of International Law* 107 (1977).

—— *Constraints on the Waging of War* (Geneva, 1987).

—— (ed.), *Assisting the Victims of Armed Conflict and Other Disasters* (Dordrecht, 1989).

KAMMINGA, M., *Inter-State Accountability for Violations of Human Rights* (N.p., 1990).

KARSH, E., and RAUTSI, I., *Saddam Hussein: A Political Biography* (London, 1991).

KENT, G., *War and Children's Survival: Occasional Paper No. 2* (Hawaii, 1990).

—— *Implementing the Rights of Children in Armed Conflict* (Draft) (Hawaii, 21 May 1991).

—— *Rights to International Humane Assistance* (Hawaii, 1993).

—— *Strategy for Implementing Nutrition Rights* (Hawaii, 1994).

—— *Children in the International Political Economy* (Basingstoke, 1995).

KHADDURI, M., *War and Peace in the Law of Islam* (New York, 1979).

KHUSHALANI, Y., *The Dignity and Honour of Women as Basic and Fundamental Human Rights* (The Hague, 1982).

KIRGIS, F., *International Organizations in Their Legal Setting: Documents, Comments and Questions* (St Paul, Minn., 1977 and 1981 (Supp.)).

KODJO, E., 'The African Charter on Human and People's Rights' 11 *Human Rights Law Journal* 271 (1990).

KOOJMANS, P. H., 'In the Shadowland Between Civil War and Civil Strife: Some

Reflections on the Standard-Setting Process', in A. J. M. Delissen and G. J. Tanja (eds.), *Humanitarian Law of Armed Conflict* (Dordrecht, 1991), 225–47.

KORN, D., *Human Rights in Iraq* (New York, 1990).

KOSKENIEMI, M., 'The Pull of the Mainstream', 88 *Michigan Law Review* 1946 (May 1990).

KRILL, F., 'The UN Convention on the Rights of the Child and His Protection in Armed Conflicts' 3 *Mennesker og Rettigheter* 39 (1986).

——'The Protection of Children in Armed Conflicts', in M. Freeman and P. Veerman (eds.), *The Ideologies of Children's Rights* (Dordrecht, 1992), 347–56.

KRUTSCH, W., and TRAPP, R., *A Commentary on the Chemical Weapons Convention* (Dordrecht, 1994).

KUBOTA, Y., 'The Protection of Children's Rights and the United Nations' 58 *Nordic Journal of International Law* 7 (1989).

KUPER, J., 'Briefing: International Law and Children in Armed Conflict' 92 *Childright* 9 (1992).

——'Reservations, Declarations and Objections to the 1989 Convention on the Rights of the Child', in J. P. Gardner (ed.), *Human Rights as General Norms and a State's Right to Opt Out: Reservations and Objections to Human Rights Conventions* (To be published London, 1997).

LARSEN, E., *A Flame in Barbed Wire* (New York, 1978).

LAUTERPACHT, E., GREENWOOD, C., WELLER, M., and BETHLEHEM, D., *The Kuwait Crisis. Basic Documents* (Cambridge, 1991).

LAUTERPACHT, H., 'The Problem of the Revision of the Law of War' 29 *BYIL* 360 (1952).

LAW ASSOCIATION FOR ASIA AND THE PACIFIC, *The Draft Pacific Charter of Human Rights* (Kensington, NSW, 1989).

LEVIE, H. S. (ed.), *Protection of War Victims: Protocol I to the 1949 Geneva Conventions* (New York, 1979–1981).

——(ed.), *The Law of Non-International Armed Conflict: Protocol II to the 1949 Geneva Conventions* (Dordrecht, 1987).

LILLICH, R., *International Human Rights. Problems of Law, Policy and Practice* (Boston, 1991).

LOPATKA, A., 'The Rights of the Child are Universal', in M. Freeman and P. Veerman, *The Ideologies of Children's Rights* (Dordrecht, 1992), 47–52.

——'Importance of the Convention on the Rights of the Child' 91/2 *Bulletin of Human Rights: The Rights of the Child* 56 (1992).

LÜCKER BABEL, M. F., 'Rights of the Child: Ideologies and Realities', 10.1/2 *International Children's Rights Monitor* 18 (1993).

LUTZ, E., HANNUM, H., and BURKE, K. (eds.), *New Directions in Human Rights* (Philadelphia, Penn., 1989).

MAHONEY, K., and MAHONEY, P. (eds.), *Human Rights in the Twenty-first Century* (Dordrecht, 1993).

MANN, H., 'International Law and the Child Soldier' 36 *ICLQ* 32 (1987).

MARTENSON, J., 'Introduction' 89/1 *Bulletin of Human Rights* 1 (1990).

——'Preface', in S. Detrick (ed.), *The United Nations Convention on the Rights of the Child: A Guide to the Travaux Préparatoires* (Dordrecht, 1992), ix–x.

McCoubrey, H., 'Jurisprudential Aspects of the Modern Law of Armed Conflicts', in M. Meyer (ed.), *Armed Conflict and the New Law* (London, 1989), 23–54.

——*International Humanitarian Law* (Aldershot, 1990).

——'Warcrimes: The Criminal Jurisprudence of Armed Conflict' XXI-1-2-3-4 *Revue de Droit Militaire et de Droit de la Guerre* 169 (1992).

——'The Regulation of Biological and Chemical Weapons', in H. Fox and M. Meyer (eds.), *Armed Conflict and the New Law: Vol. II—Effecting Compliance* (London, 1993), 123–39.

McDowall, D., *The Kurds: The Minority Rights Group Report No. 23* (London, 1991).

Meron, T., 'On the Inadequate Reach of Human Rights Law and the Need for A New Instrument', 77 *AJIL* 589 (1983).

——'Towards a Humanitarian Declaration on Internal Strife', 78 *AJIL* 859 (1984).

——(ed.), *Human Rights in International Law: Legal and Policy Issues* (Oxford, 1984).

——*Human Rights Law-making in the United Nations* (Oxford, 1986).

——*Human Rights in Internal Strife: Their International Protection* (Cambridge, 1987).

——'The Geneva Conventions as Customary Law', 81 *AJIL*, 348 (1987).

——*Human Rights and Humanitarian Norms as Customary Law* (Oxford, 1989).

——'The Case for War Crimes Trials in Yugoslavia', 72.3 *Foreign Affairs* 122 (1993).

——'War Crimes in Yugoslavia and the Development of International Law', 88 *AJIL* 78 (1994).

Meyer, M. (ed.), *Armed Conflict and the New Law* (London, 1989).

——'The Role of the International Red Cross and Red Crescent Movement: Problems Encountered', in P. Rowe (ed.), *The Gulf War 1990–1991 in International and English Law* (London, 1993), 224–40.

Middle East Watch, *The Conduct of Iraqi Troops in Kuwait* (New York, 1990).

——*The Bombing of Iraqi Cities* (New York, 6 Mar. 1991).

——*Needless Deaths in the Gulf War* (New York, 1991).

——*Hidden Death: Land Mines and Civilian Casualties in Iraqi Kurdistan* (New York, 1992).

——*Endless Torment: The 1991 Uprising in Iraq and its Aftermath* (New York, June 1992).

——*The Anfal Campaign in Iraqi Kurdistan: the Destruction of Koreme* (New York, 1993).

——*Genocide in Iraq: The Anfal Campaign Against the Kurds* (New York, 1993).

——and Physicians for Human Rights, *Unquiet Graves: The Search for the Disappeared in Iraqi Kurdistan* (N.p., USA, Feb. 1992).

Miller, J., and Mylroie, L., *Saddam Hussein and the Crisis in the Gulf* (New York, 1990).

Minear, L., *Humanitarianism Under Siege: A Critical Review of Operation Lifeline Sudan* (Trenton, NJ, 1991).

——Chelliah, U., Crisp, J., Mackinley, J., and Weiss, T., *United Nations Coordination of the International Humanitarian Response to the Gulf Crisis* (Providence, RI, 1992).

——and WEISS, T., *Humanitarian Politics* (Pennsylvania, 1995).

——, ——and CAMPBELL, K., *Humanitarianism and War: Learning the Lessons From Recent Armed Conflicts* (Providence, RI, 1991).

MOWLANA, H., GERBNER, G., and SCHILLER, H., *Triumph of the Image: The Media's War in the Persian Gulf—A Global Perspective* (Boulder, Colo., 1992).

MUNTARBHORN, V., 'The Convention on the Rights of the Child: Reaching the Unreached?' 91/2 *Bulletin of Human Rights: The Rights of the Child* 66 (1992).

MURSAL, H., 'Report on the Situation in Somalia', in G. H. Aldrich and Th. A. van Baarda, *Conference on the Rights of Children in Armed Conflict* (The Hague, 1994), 26–9.

MUTHOGA, L., 'Violations Committed Against Children', in OMCT/SOS-Torture, *Africa: A New Lease on Life* (Geneva, 1993), 105–12.

NAHLIK, S., *A Brief Outline of International Humanitarian Law: Extract from the International Review of the Red Cross* (Geneva, July–Aug. 1984).

NASIR, J., *The Islamic Law of Personal Status* (2nd edn., London, 1990).

NEWMARK, I., 'The Child Rights Caucus: A New Kid On The Block', UNICEF, *First Call for Children* 10 (January–March 1995).

NGANDJUI, J., 'Do Traditions Clash With Children's Rights?' 10.4 *International Children's Rights Monitor* 6 (1993).

NGO GROUP FOR THE CONVENTION ON THE RIGHTS OF THE CHILD, *A Guide for Non-Governmental Organisations Reporting to the Committee on the Rights of the Child* (Geneva, 1994).

NORRIS, R., 'Observations *In Loco*: Practice and Procedure of the Inter-American Commission of Human Rights', 15 *Texas International Law Journal* 46 (1980).

NSEREKO, D. D., 'Arbitrary Deprivations of Life: Controls on Permissible Deprivations', in B. G. Ramcharan (ed.), *The Right to Life in International Law* (Dordrecht, 1985), 245–83.

ORGANISATION OF AMERICAN STATES, *Basic Documents Pertaining to Human Rights in the Inter-American System* (Washington DC, 1988).

O'BRIEN, W., 'Biological/Chemical Warfare and the International Law of War', 51 *The Georgetown Law Journal* 1 (1962).

O'DONNELL, D., 'Two Steps Forward . . . One Step Backward?' 8 *International Children's Rights Monitor* 5 (1991).

——'The Reservation Generation' 9.1 *International Children's Rights Monitor* 13 (1992).

O'NEILL, O., 'Children's Rights and Children's Lives', in P. Alston, S. Parker, and J. Seymour (eds.), *Children, Rights and the Law* (Oxford, 1992), 24–42.

OJO, O., and SESAY, A., 'The OAU and Human Rights: Prospects for the 1980s and Beyond', 8 *Human Rights Quarterly* 89 (Feb. 1986).

OLSEN, F., 'Children's Rights: Some Feminist Approaches to the United Nations Convention on the Rights of the Child', in P. Alston, S. Parker, and J. Seymour (eds.), *Children, Rights and the Law* (Oxford, 1992), 192–220.

OMCT/SOS TORTURE (World Organisation against Torture), *Manila 91: International Symposium: Democracy, Development, Human Rights* (Geneva, 1992).

——*Africa: A New Lease on Life* (Geneva, 1993).

OPPENHEIM, L. (H. Lauterpacht (ed.)), *International Law: A Treatise. Vol. II: Disputes, War and Neutrality* (7th edn., London, 1952).

OPSAHL, T., 'The Human Rights Committee', in P. Alston (ed.), *The United Nations and Human Rights: A Critical Appraisal* (Oxford, 1992), 369–443.

ORAA, J., *Human Rights in States of Emergency in International Law* (Oxford, 1992).

PALME, L., *Nations Touch at their Summits: 1990 UNICEF Lecture* (London, 20 Nov. 1990).

PAPPAS, A. M., 'Introduction', in A. M. Pappas (ed.), *Law and the Status of the Child* (New York, 1983), xxvii–lv.

——(ed.), *Law and the Status of the Child* (New York, 1983).

PEARL, D., *A Textbook on Muslim Personal Law* (2nd edn., London, 1987).

PENNA, L. R., 'Traditional Asian Approaches: An Indian View' 9 *Australian Year Book of International Law* 168 (1985).

PHYSICIANS FOR HUMAN RIGHTS, *Winds of Death: Iraq's Use of Poison Gas Against Its Kurdish Population* (New Haven, Conn., Feb. 1989).

PICTET, J. (ed.), *Commentary on Geneva Convention IV Relative to the Protection of Civilian Persons in Time of War* (Geneva, 1958).

——*Humanitarian Law and the Protection of War Victims* (Leiden, 1973).

——*Development and Principles of International Humanitarian Law* (Dordrecht, 1985).

PLATTNER, D., 'Protection of Children in International Humanitarian Law', in M. Kahnert, D. Pitt, and I. Taipale (eds.), *Children and War: Proceedings of Symposium at Siuntio Baths, Finland* (Helsinki, 1983), 198–213.

——*Protection of Children in International Humanitarian Law: Extract of the International Review of the Red Cross* (Geneva, May–June 1984).

——'The Penal Repression of Violations of International Humanitarian Law Applicable in Non-International Armed Conflicts', 278 *Int'l. Rev. of the Red Cross* 409 (Sept.–Oct. 1990).

PLAYFAIR, E. (ed.), *International Law and the Administration of the Occupied Territories: Two Decades of Israeli Occupation of the West Bank and Gaza Strip* (Oxford, 1992).

——'Introduction', in E. Playfair (ed.), *International Law and the Administration of the Occupied Territories: Two Decades of Israeli Occupation of the West Bank and Gaza Strip* (Oxford, 1992), 1–22.

'POC Week—For Children', 58 *Amnesty Journal (British Section)* 1 (Oct.–Nov. 1992).

POCAR, F., 'The International Covenant on Civil and Political Rights', in UN, *Manual on Human Rights Reporting* (New York, 1991), 79–125.

QUAKER UN OFFICE, *The Rights of the Child* (Geneva, 1988).

QUENTIN-BAXTER, R., 'Human Rights and Humanitarian Law—Confluence or Conflict' 9 *Australian Year Book of International Law* 94 (1985).

RÄDDA BARNEN, *Report on Child Victims of Armed Conflicts: NGO Forum* (Stockholm, 1984).

——*No Child Soldiers* (Stockholm, Sept. 1989).

——*United Nations Draft Convention on the Rights of the Child: Commission on Human Rights, Debate of 8 March 1989* (Stockholm, 1989).

——*United Nations Draft Convention on the Rights of the Child: Debate on Children in Armed Conflicts. Geneva, December 8, 1988* (Stockholm, 1989).

——*The Rights of the Child* (Stockholm, 1990).

——*Position Paper on Children in War* (Stockholm, June 1990).

——1 *Children of War: A Newsletter on Child Soldiers from Rädda Barnen* (Oct. 1995).

RAMCHARAN, B. G. (ed.), *International Law and Fact-finding in the Field of Human Rights* (London, 1982).

——'The Concept and Dimensions of the Right to Life', in B. G. Ramcharan (ed.), *International Law and Fact-finding in the Field of Human Rights* (London, 1982), 1–32.

——(ed.), *The Right to Life in International Law* (Dordrecht, 1985).

——*The International Law and Practice of Early-warning and Preventive Diplomacy: The Emerging Global Watch* (Dordrecht, 1991).

——'Strategies for the International Protection of Human Rights in the 1990s' 13 *Human Rights Quarterly* 155 (1991).

——'A Reporting System for International Humanitarian Law?', in E. Bello and B. Ajibola (eds.), *Essays in Honour of Judge Taslim Olawale Elias* (Dordrecht, 1992), Vol. ii, 125–33.

RAMOLEFE, A. N. R., 'Sestho Marriage, Guardianship and the Customary-Law Heir', in M. Gluckman (ed.), *Ideas and Procedures in African Customary Law* (London, 1969), 196–207.

RAOUL WALLENBERG INSTITUTE OF HUMAN RIGHTS AND HUMANITARIAN LAW, *Children of War: Report from the Conference on Children of War* (Lund, 1991).

RESOOL, S. M., *Forever Kurdish* (N.p. (USA), 1990).

RESSLER, E. M., *Evacuation of Children from Conflict Areas* (Geneva, 1992).

——BOOTHBY, N., and STEINBOCK, D., *Unaccompanied Children* (New York, 1988).

——TORTORICI, J. M., and MARCELINO, A., *Children in War: A Guide to the Provision of Services* (New York, 1993).

ROBERTS, A., 'The Protection of Civilians in War', 5.4 *Interights Bulletin* 58 (1990).

——'Prolonged Military Occupation: The Israeli–Occupied Territories 1967–1988', in E. Playfair (ed.), *International Law and the Administration of the Occupied Territories: Two Decades of Israeli Occupation of the West Bank and Gaza Strip* (Oxford, 1992), 25–85.

——and GUELFF, R. (eds.), *Documents on the Laws of War* (Oxford, 1989).

——and KINGSBURY, B. (eds.), *United Nations, Divided World* (2nd edn., Oxford, 1993).

RODLEY, N., 'Human Rights and Humanitarian Intervention: The Case Law of the World Court' 38 *ICLQ* 321 (1989).

——'The Work of Non-Governmental Organisations on the World-Wide Promotion and Protection of Human Rights', 90 *Bulletin of Human Rights* 84 (1992).

——'Can Armed Oppostion Groups Violate Human Rights?', in K. Mahoney and P. Mahoney (eds.), *Human Rights in the Twenty-first Century* (Dordrecht, 1993), 297–318.

——'Soft Law, Tough Standards', 7.3 *Interights Bulletin* 43 (1993).

ROSENBLATT, R., *Children of War* (New York, 1983).

ROTBERG, R., and WEISS, T., *The Media, Humanitarian Crises, and Policy-Making* (Cambridge, Mass., 1995).

ROWE, P. (ed.), *The Gulf War 1990–1991 in International and English Law* (London, 1993).

SANDOZ, Y., 'Localitiés et Zones Sous Protection Spéciale', in Institut Henry-Dunant, *Quatre Études du Droit International Humanitaire* (Geneva, 1985), 35–47.

SANTOS PAIS, M., 'The United Nations Convention on the Rights of the Child' 91/2 *Bulletin of Human Rights: The Rights of the Child* 75 (1992).

SCHACHTER, O., 'The Twilight Existence of Nonbinding International Agreements', 71 *AJIL*, 296 (1977).

——'The Right of States to Use Armed Force', 82 *Michigan Law Review* 1620 (1984).

——'United Nations Law in the Gulf Conflict', 85 *AJIL*, 452 (1991).

SCHEFFER, D., 'Towards a Modern Doctrine of Humanitarian Intervention', 23 *University of Toledo Law Review* 267 (1993).

SCHINDLER, D., 'The International Committee of the Red Cross and Human Rights', 19 *Int'l. Rev. of the Red Cross* 3 (Jan.–Feb. 1979).

——and TOMAN, J., *The Laws of Armed Conflict* (3rd edn., Dordrecht, 1988).

SCHMIDT, M., 'The Optional Protocol to the International Covenant on Civil and Political Rights: Procedure and Practice', 4.2 *Interights Bulletin* 27 (1989).

SCHWELB, A., and ALSTON, P., 'The Principal Institutions and Other Bodies Founded Under the Charter', in K. Vasak (ed.), *The International Dimensions of Human Rights* (Westport, Conn., 1982), 231–301.

SCOTT, J. (ed.), *The Classics of International Law* (New York, 1964).

'Sexual Exploitation of Children by UN Blue Helmets: a Case in Liberia', 11.4 *International Children's Rights Monitor* 46 (1994/5).

SHAW, M., *International Law* (Cambridge, 1986).

SHESTACK, J., 'Sisyphus Endures: The International Human Rights NGO', 24 *New York Law School Law Review* 89 (1978).

——'The Jurisprudence of Human Rights', in T. Meron (ed.), *Human Rights in International Law: Legal and Policy Issues* (Oxford, 1984), 69–113.

SIDDIQUI, A. A., 'Children's Rights Within the Moslem Family', 11.2/3 *International Children's Rights Monitor* 4 (1994).

SIEGHART, P., *The International Law of Human Rights* (Oxford, 1984).

SIMMA, B. (ed.), *The Charter of the United Nations: A Commentary* (Oxford, 1995).

SIMPSON, J., *From the House of War* (London, 1991).

SINCLAIR, I., *The Vienna Convention on the Law of Treaties* (2nd edn., Manchester, 1984).

SINGER, S., *The Protection of Children During Armed Conflict Situations: Extract of the International Review of the Red Cross* (Geneva, May–June 1986).

SKOLNIK, A., 'Children in Their Own Right: The View From Developmental Psychology', in E. Verhellen and F. Spiesschaert (eds.), *Ombudswork for Children* (Leuven, 1989), 87–105.

SLUGLETT, M. F., and SLUGLETT, P., *Iraq Since 1958: From Revolution to Dictatorship* (London, 1990).

SOHN, L., 'Human Rights: Their Implementation and Supervision by the United Nations', in T. Meron (ed.), *Human Rights in International Law: Legal and Policy Issues* (Oxford, 1984), 369–401.

——and BUERGENTHAL, T., *International Protection of Human Rights* (Indianapolis, Indiana, 1973).

SORNARAJAH, M., 'An Overview of the Asian Approaches to International Humanitarian Law' 9 *Australian Year Book of International Law* 238 (1985).

STUDY ON THE IMPACT OF ARMED CONFLICT ON CHILDREN, *Scope of the Study of the Impact of Armed Conflict on Children* (Johannesburg, 1994).

SUNGA, L., *Individual Responsibility in International Law for Serious Human Rights Violations* (Dordrecht, 1992).

SUY, E., 'International Humanitarian Law and the Security Council Resolutions on the 1990–1991 Gulf War', in A. J. M. Delissen and G. J. Tanja (eds.), *Humanitarian Law of Armed Conflict* (Dordrecht, 1991), 515–26.

SWINARSKI, C. (ed.), *Studies and Essays on International Humanitarian Law and Red Cross Principles in Honour of Jean Pictet* (Geneva, 1984).

TAVERS, D., 'A Chronology of Events', in P. Rowe (ed.), *The Gulf War 1990–1991 in International and English Law* (London, 1993), 3–28.

TCHIBINDA, J. F., and MAYETELA, N., 'The Rights of the Child in the People's Republic of the Congo', in A. M. Pappas (ed.), *Law and the Status of the Child* (New York, 1983), 183–220.

TERLINGEN, Y., 'Principles for the Effective Prevention and Investigation of Extra-Legal, Arbitrary and Summary Executions', 5.1 *Interights Bulletin* 15 (1990).

——THE AMERICAN LAW INSTITUTE. *Restatement of the Law Third, the Foreign Relations Law of the United States.* (St. Paul, Minnesota, 1987).

—— *The Law of War on Land, Part III of the Manual of Military Law* (London, 1958).

THEYTAZ-BERGMAN, L., 'Out of Time' 11.1 *International Children's Rights Monitor* 10 (1994).

THIRLWAY, H. W. A., *International Customary Law and Codification* (Leiden, 1972).

THOMPSON, B., 'Africa's Charter on Children's Rights. A Normative Break with Cultural Traditionalism' 41 *ICLQ* 432 (1992).

TOMASEVSKI, K., *Children in Adult Prisons* (London, 1986).

UK COMMITTEE FOR UNICEF, *Gulf Crisis Update 3* (London, 13 May 1991).

—— 'Former Yugoslavia', *News In Brief* 3 (Dec. 1993).

—— 'Landmines to Top Agenda at Conference on Inhumane Weapons', *News in Brief* 1 (Sept. 1995).

UK WORKING GROUP ON LANDMINES, *Report on the Review Conference of the 1980 UN Inhumane Weapons Convention—final session held in Geneva from 22 April to 3 May 1996* (London, 1996).

UNITED NATIONS, *Selected Decisions of the Human Rights Committee Under the Optional Protocol* (New York, Vol. i, 1985, and Vol. ii, 1990).

—— *Manual on Human Rights Reporting* (New York, 1991).

—— *United Nations Action in the Field of Human Rights* (New York, 1994).

UNITED NATIONS HIGH COMMISSION FOR REFUGEES, *The State of the World's Refugees* (New York, 1993).

—— *Refugee Children: Guidelines on Protection and Care* (Geneva, 1994).

UNICEF, *Convention on the Rights of the Child: Information Kit* (Geneva, 1990).

—— *Children and Development in the 1990s: A UNICEF Sourcebook* (New York, 1990).

—— *The State of the World's Children 1992* (Oxford, 1991).

—— *The State of the World's Children 1995* (Oxford, 1994).

——*Anti-Personnel Land Mines: A Scourge on Children* (New York, 1994).

—— *The State of the World's Children 1996* (Oxford, 1995).

UNICEF/UK, 'Landmines—A Scourge on Children', *Children First!* 9 (Winter 1994).

United States Department of Defence Report to Congress on the Conduct of the Persian Gulf War—Appendix on the Role of the Law of War: (April 10, 1992) 31 ILM 612 (1992).

URQUHART, B., and CHILDERS, E., *A World in Need of Leadership: Tomorrow's United Nations* (Uppsala, 1990).

VAN BOVEN, T., 'United Nations and Human Rights: A Critical Appraisal', in A. Cassese (ed.), *UN Law/Fundamental Rights: Two Topics in International Law* (Alphen van der Rijn, 1979), 119–35.

——'Reliance on Norms of Humanitarian Law by United Nations Organs', in A. J. M. Delissen and G. J. Tanja (eds.), *Humanitarian Law of Armed Conflict* (Dordrecht, 1991), 495–513.

——'The International System of Human Rights: An Overview', in UN, *Manual on Human Rights Reporting* (New York, 1991), 3–16.

——'Prevention of Human Rights Violations', in OMCT/SOS Torture, *Manila 91: International Symposium: Democracy, Development, Human Rights* (Geneva, 1992), 184–92.

VAN BRUINESSEN, M., *Agha, Sheikh and State* (Utrecht, 1978).

VAN BUEREN, G., 'Special Features of the Assistance and Protection of Children as Victims of Armed Conflict', in F. Kalshoven (ed.), *Assisting the Victims of Armed Conflict and Other Disasters* (Dordrecht, 1989), 127–31.

——*International Documents on Children* (Dordrecht, 1993).

——'The International Legal Protection of Children in Armed Conflicts' 43 *ICLQ* 809 (1994).

—— *The International Law on the Rights of the Child* (Dordrecht, 1995).

VAN DONGEN, Y., *The Protection of Civilian Populations in Time of Armed Conflict* (Amsterdam, 1991).

VAN DIJK, P., and VAN HOOF, G. J. H., *Theory and Practice of the European Convention on Human Rights* (Deventer, 1984).

VASAK, K., 'The Distinguishing Criteria of Institutions', in K. Vasak (ed.), *The International Dimensions of Human Rights* (Westport, Conn., 1982), 215–28.

——(ed.), *The International Dimensions of Human Rights* (Westport, Conn., 1982).

VEERMAN, P., *The Rights of the Child and the Changing Image of Childhood* (Dordrecht, 1992).

——'Proposals From Strasbourg and Brussels' II.1 *International Children's Rights Monitor* 19 (1994).

VERHAEGEN, J., 'Legal Obstacles to Prosecution of Breaches of Humanitarian Law', 27 *Int'l. Rev. of the Red Cross* 607–20 (Nov./Dec. 1987).

VERHELLEN, E., 'Changes in the Images of the Child', in M. Freeman and P. Veerman (eds.), *The Ideologies of Children's Rights* (Dordrecht, 1992), 79–94.

——'Children's Rights in Europe' 1.3/4 *International Journal of Children's Rights* 357 (1993).

——and SPIESSCHAERT, F. (eds.), *Ombudswork for Children* (Leuven, 1989).

VITTACHI, V., *Between the Guns: Children as a Zone of Peace* (London, 1993).

VOLIO, F., 'Legal Personality, Privacy and the Family', in L. Henkin (ed.), *The International Bill of Rights: The Covenant on Civil and Political Rights* (New York, 1981), 105–208.

VOYAME, J., 'United Nations Convention Against Torture and Other Cruel, Inhuman and Degrading Treatment or Punishment' 89/1 *Human Rights Bulletin* 79 (1990).

WALD, M., 'Children's Rights: A Framework for Analysis', 12 *University of California Davis Law Review* 255 (1979).

WALLENSTEEN, P., 'The United Nations in Armed Conflicts: An Overview', in R. Dupuy (ed.), *The Development of the Role of the Security Council* (Dordrecht, 1992), 303–16.

WEISBERG, D. K., 'Evolution of the Concept of the Rights of the Child in the Western World', 21 *Review of the International Commission of Jurists* 43 (Dec. 1978).

WEISS, T., 'The United Nations and Civil Wars', 17 *The Washington Quarterly* 139 (1994).

——FORSYTHE, D., and COATE, R., *The United Nations and Changing World Politics* (Boulder, Colo., 1994).

WEISSBRODT, D., 'The Contribution of International Nongovernmental Organisations to the Protection of Human Rights', in T. Meron (ed.), *Human Rights in International Law: Legal and Policy Issues* (Oxford, 1984), 403–38.

——'Protecting the Right to Life: International Measures Against Arbitrary or Summary Killings by Governments', in B. G. Ramcharan (ed.), *The Right to Life in International Law* (Dordrecht, 1985), 297–307.

——'Ways International Organisations Can Improve Their Implementation of Human Rights and Humanitarian Law in Situations of Armed Conflict', in E. Lutz, H. Hannum, and K. Burke (eds.), *New Directions in Human Rights* (Philadelphia, Penn., 1989), 63–96.

——and McCARTHY, J., 'Fact-Finding by Non-Governmental Organisations', in B. G. Ramcharan (ed.), *International Law and Fact-finding in the Field of Human Rights* (London, 1982), 106–230.

WELLER, M. (ed.), *Iraq and Kuwait: the Hostilities and their Aftermath* (Cambridge, 1993).

WHITEMAN, M., 'Jus Cogens in International Law, With a Projected List', 7 *Georgia Journal of International and Comparative Law* 609 (1977).

WILSON, H. A., *International Law and the Use of Force by National Liberation Movements* (Oxford, 1988).

WOODS, D., *Children Bearing Military Arms* (Quaker UN Office, Geneva, Dec. 1993).

——*Child Soldiers* (Quaker UN Office, Geneva, 1993).

WRINGE, C., *Children's Rights: A Philosophical Study* (London, 1985).

Index